OVER LINCOLN'S SHOULDER

MODERN WAR STUDIES

OVER LINCOLN'S SHOULDER

The Committee on the Conduct of the War

Bruce Tap

University Press of Kansas

© 1998 by the University Press of Kansas

Published by the University Press of Kansas (Lawrence, Kansas 66049), which was organized by the Kansas Board of Regents and is operated and funded by Emporia State University, Fort Hays State University, Kansas State University, Pittsburg State University, the University of Kansas, and Wichita State University

Library of Congress Cataloging-in-Publication Data

Tap, Bruce.
Over Lincoln's shoulder : the Committee on the Conduct of the War / Bruce Tap.
p. cm. — (Modern war studies)
Includes bibliographical references and index.
ISBN 0-7006-0871-0 (alk. paper)
1. United States. Congress. Joint Committee on the Conduct of the War. 2. Governmental investigations—United States—History—19th century. 3. Lincoln, Abraham, 1809–1865. 4. United States—History—Civil War, 1861–1865—Campaigns. 5. United States—Military policy. I. Title. II. Series.
E470.T2 1998
973.7'3—dc21 97-36525

British Library Cataloguing in Publication Data is available.

Printed in the United States of America

10 9 8 7 6 5 4 3 2 1

For Brenda, Bethany, and Kathleen
with much love

CONTENTS

PREFACE

Almost every historian of the American Civil War who has dealt with northern politics has had something to say about the Committee on the Conduct of the War. Indeed, with the exception of the House Committee on Un-American Activities (HUAC) and the Select Committee on Campaign Practices (the Ervin Committee), which investigated Watergate, few congressional committees have gained as much public attention.

Despite its popularity, however, the Committee on the Conduct of the War has attracted few book-length studies. With the exception of T. Harry Williams's *Lincoln and the Radicals* (1941), Hans Trefousse's *The Radical Republicans* (1969), and occasional articles in academic journals, little scholarly attention has been paid to the committee. After reading Williams and Trefousse, I became convinced that each book was inadequate for different reasons. Williams concluded correctly that the committee's overall impact on the northern war effort was negative; however, he drew this conclusion for the wrong reasons, in my opinion. Writing in the late thirties and early forties, Williams was still under the prevailing influence of the bias against radical Republicans. Popularized by William Dunning and carried on in the writings of the so-called revisionist historians such as Avery O. Craven and James G. Randall, this school of thought branded Republican radicals as fanatical, unrealistic, and hypocritical abolitionists who helped cause the Civil War through their incessant agitation on the slavery issue. Williams saw the Committee on the Conduct of the War as dominated by these radical Republicans. Under the guise of antislavery sentiments but motivated by a desire for revenge against the South and hoping to seize power for the Republican party, the committee, in Williams's view, constantly interfered with the Union war effort and hampered Pres. Abraham Lincoln's attempt to direct military affairs.

In the 1960s, when the negative interpretation of the Republican radicals came crashing down, so too did Williams's unfavorable view of the committee. After writing biographies of Benjamin Butler and Benjamin F. Wade, Prof. Hans L. Trefousse considered the joint committee first in an article and then in his masterpiece, *The Radical Republicans*. Unlike earlier twentieth-century scholars, Trefousse emphasized the sincerity of the radical Republicans on the committee and their fundamental ideological agreement with Abraham Lincoln. Although the committee tried to direct military affairs, it was largely unsuccessful, primarily because of Lincoln's superior political skills. Lincoln was able to use and maneuver the committee to achieve his ends—not the other way around. Unlike Williams, Trefousse concluded that the committee's effect on northern military affairs was positive at best and irrelevant at worst.

I attempt to steer a course between Williams's and Trefousse's positions. For the most part, I have agreed with Trefousse in his assessment of the committee members' motivations. They were principled reformers, opponents of slavery, and genuine patriots. Most of their actions probably did not have a direct impact on the war's outcome. Yet I agree with Williams in that there were several instances where the committee's activities did have a substantial negative impact on the northern war effort. The work of congressional committees is more than irrelevant partisan posturing: it has an impact on and gives meaning to decisions and the formulation of policy. The committee's negative impact on military affairs did not stem from the members' devotion to fanatical principles, as Williams has suggested, but from a lack of a firm understanding of military science. The committee was composed of military amateurs who attempted to influence military policy with simplistic, outmoded ideas on the art of warfare. The results of their attempt, as I will demonstrate, speak for themselves.

Though I can modestly boast that *Over Lincoln's Shoulder* is the most thorough study of the committee to date, I hope it will not be the last one. There are still several investigations that receive scant attention in these pages, for reasons of both space and time. And just as I have criticized the motivations and methods of previous historians, I hope that future Civil War historians will examine my work with the same critical approach.

An abbreviated version of chapter 3 first appeared in *Gateway Heritage* and is reprinted here with permission from the Spring 1994 issue of *Gateway Heritage,* Missouri Historical Society, © 1994 by the Missouri Historical Society. Chapter 7 appeared in a slightly altered form in *Civil War History* 42 (June 1996):116–32 and is reprinted here with permission of the Kent State University Press.

ACKNOWLEDGMENTS

Many persons had a hand in this work—too many, in fact, to name individually. Countless librarians and archivists rendered invaluable service on the numerous research trips that I made while working on this project. The staff of the University of Illinois interlibrary loan office provided unflagging assistance in locating and procuring microfilm collections so that several research trips were unnecessary. John M. Hoffmann of the Illinois Historical Survey was generous in the use of his facilities and offered a wealth of information on sources and research tools. Bob Sampson was not only a valued friend but also provided numerous insights and useful suggestions in countless conversations over coffee. My dissertation readers, Walter L. Arnstein and Winton U. Solberg, offered detailed criticism of the manuscript and several helpful suggestions. My dissertation director, Robert W. Johannsen, spent considerable time in critiquing the manuscript and offered penetrating criticism and numerous stylistic comments as well as encouragement. His impact on this project was substantial. My former professor and present friend, Albert Castel, helped see the work through after the dissertation stage. In addition to offering a wealth of helpful advice, he read the entire manuscript twice and provided invaluable comments, especially on the military dimension—not one of my particular strengths. Fred Woodward of the University Press of Kansas believed in the project from the start and offered encouragement throughout the often painful revision process. A number of fellow graduate students provided insights at one time or another during the writing, including Dan Monroe, John Moser, Brian Kenny, Bryon Andreason, Mike Conlin, Colin McCoy, Luann Matthews, and Ji-Hyung Cho. Moreover, readers for the University Press of Kansas offered detailed critical comments. I did not always follow their suggestions and in some cases disagreed adamantly with their conclusions, but the book was considerably strengthened as a result of their criticism. Although many persons had a hand in the construction of this book, I take full responsibility for all errors of fact or interpretation.

I am grateful to several persons for reasons other than scholarly assistance. My parents, Arvin and Pearl Tap, and my parents-in-law, Edward and

Ilagene McCammon, provided emotional strength, understanding, and a host of intangible supports. My two daughters, Bethany and Kathleen, endured patiently a father who was often at the library or, when at home, was constantly tinkering with the manuscript. Finally, the lion's share of emotional support was provided by my wife, Brenda. Her work, sacrifice, and love are as responsible for my completing this project as anything else. To her I will always be grateful.

INTRODUCTION

In early 1973 when the Senate formed the Select Committee on Campaign Practices, popularly known as the Ervin Committee, to investigate the Watergate burglary, no one was more wary of it than Pres. Richard M. Nixon. As his biographer Stephen Ambrose notes, "Nixon knew full well how powerful the subpoena was, how far afield an investigating committee could roam in the pursuit of its inquiries, how easily an ambitious congressman could play to the press in public hearings, and how ineffective White House attempts to cover up would be." Since Nixon initially had become a national figure largely through his involvement on the House Committee on Un-American Activities (HUAC), he could well appreciate the power of select committees of investigation.[1]

In the twentieth century, the record of select committees of investigation has been mixed. The most notorious example of congressional abuse and irresponsible partisan posturing was provided by the House Committee on Un-American Activities. Originally appointed as a temporary committee in 1938 to investigate Communist and Fascist activities in the United States, HUAC was made a standing committee in 1944. The ambiguous phrase Un-American Activities was used to justify a wide scope of investigative activities, some useful, but many undertaken for reasons of personal and partisan advancement. Many congressmen, such as Nixon, used the committee to spotlight themselves and to gain political clout. Critics rightly charged that many of the committee's investigations were partisan witch hunts. By the late 1950s, the committee was falling out of public favor. "There is no congressional power to expose for the sake of exposure," Chief Justice Earl Warren said of HUAC in 1957. In 1959, former president Harry Truman denounced HUAC as "the most Un-American thing in the country today."[2]

Other investigative committees have had a more positive image. During World War II, Sen. Harry Truman headed a special Senate committee to investigate financial irregularities in defense contracts. Although the Roosevelt administration was initially skeptical of the investigations, the so-called Truman Committee compiled an exemplary record primarily because of Truman's determination to keep the committee above the partisan fray:

"There would be no whitewash or witch-hunt . . . no grandstanding for head-lines or any attempt ever to forestall the defense effort." Similarly, the Ervin Committee, in investigating the Watergate affair, performed a useful, per-haps necessary role, given the numerous illegal and unconstitutional activi-ties of the Nixon administration.[3]

The role of other investigative committees is less clear. The Iran-Contra congressional hearings of the mid-1980s generated considerable fervor; how-ever, judgment about the usefulness of this inquiry was split along partisan lines. Democrats argued for its probity and utility; Republicans charged that many congressional inquisitors were motivated by partisan concerns and that the investigation constituted an unwarranted interference in executive mat-ters. Congressional investigations of the current Whitewater imbroglio have produced similar partisan assessments.

One of the most controversial investigative committees, however, belongs to the Civil War era, the Joint Select Committee on the Conduct of the War. Dominated by Republican congressmen and equipped with broad author-ity, it gained notoriety for its wide-ranging investigations. The committee investigated military disasters and subjected defeated generals to rigorous examinations, prompting some observers to draw a comparison with the famous Committee on Public Safety of the French Revolution. The Commit-tee on the Conduct of the War examined military supply contracts and at-tempted to assist the War Department in ferreting out corruption. It engaged in wartime propaganda when it investigated rebel atrocities after the first battle of Bull Run and the Fort Pillow massacre. Moreover, it gave the Lin-coln administration advice—almost constantly. The committee's Republican majority believed that the Union war effort would benefit if directed by offi-cers with staunch antislavery credentials. Regarding military science as superfluous, committee members believed that military skill largely was de-rived from common sense. Further, they attempted persistently to use politi-cal ideology as the measure to evaluate the army's principal leaders, believ-ing that battlefield success inevitably followed from correct political beliefs.

Contemporaries often viewed the committee in partisan terms. Most Republicans claimed that it helped invigorate the war effort, renewed army morale, and eliminated corruption and inefficiency. Democratic critics claimed that it hampered the war effort, conducting partisan investigations to discredit political opponents and flagrantly violating civil liberties. Secre-tary of the Navy Gideon Welles saw the committee as the tool of the War Department, revealing only what the department wanted exposed and bury-ing what it wanted covered up. Emory Upton, a young officer who served with the Army of the Potomac and who later wrote a history of the U.S.

military, characterized the committee members as military amateurs whose constant interference in military policy damaged army morale and gave the Confederacy valuable information. Reporter Ben Perley Poore described the committee as "a mischievous organization, which assumed dictatorial powers." Lincoln's secretaries, John Nicolay and John Hay, who had frequent contact with committee members, gave it mixed marks: "It was often hasty and unjust in its judgements, but always earnest, patriotic, and honest."[4]

Later assessments of the committee's work have varied, reflecting the current dominant historical trends. Around the turn of the century, some historians regarded the committee's work as often misguided but well intentioned and sometimes productive. James Schouler, for instance, claimed that the volumes of testimony were of historical value but that the committee's "proceedings had somewhat of a partisan character." William Whately Pierson, the first historian to study the committee in depth, acknowledged its mistakes but believed its investigations brought about accountability and efficiency in army operations. Other scholars, however, saw the committee as an unnecessary nuisance that extended the war and thereby caused additional loss of life. Carl Sandburg's 1939 assessment in his four-volume biography of Abraham Lincoln combined these views. The committee, Sandburg wrote, "helped Lincoln, and more often interfered with him, for a long time. They sniffed out waste and corruption; they cleared away stenches; they muddled, accused men wrongly and bominated; they played with the glory and despair of democracy."[5]

In the late 1930s, the committee was severely criticized in the numerous works of T. Harry Williams. Reflecting many of the then negative views about the radical Republicans, Williams saw the committee as "the unnatural child of lustful radicalism." According to him, committee members were motivated by fanatical antislavery convictions. They fervently hated the South and hoped to use emancipated blacks as a means to fasten Republican rule on conquered southerners. Ignorant of military affairs, the committee was dedicated to eliminating army leaders who did not subscribe to emancipation, confiscation, and other stringent measures. In Williams's interpretation, the committee held considerable power, the key to which was the ability both to disclose embarrassing testimony about military personnel and to withhold promotions from generals deemed unsympathetic to Republican war goals. According to Williams, the committee forced Lincoln on numerous occasions to make changes in war policy based on its preferences.[6]

For the next twenty years, Williams's interpretation predominated. "This committee supposedly established to aid the war effort," wrote Harry W. Pfanz, "seems to have sought mainly to control the political thinking of the army's commanders." James G. Randall wrote that the problems the committee caused Lincoln and the military were "one of the most vexing phases of Civil War history," and Lincoln biographer Benjamin Thomas contended that the committee "became the spearhead of the radical Republican drive, an agency through which the vindictive group tried to control the war effort."[7]

Historiographic trends, however, began to change in the late 1950s and early 1960s. As African-American activism inaugurated the Civil Rights movement and the Second Reconstruction, Civil War historians began reevaluating the radical Republicans. No longer labeled as unprincipled fanatics, they were viewed as humanitarian reformers. Nor were they seen as ideologically opposed to Lincoln. The differences between the radicals and Lincoln were only superficial; the president and the committee members were united on fundamentals. Along with this reevaluation came a reassessment of the work of the committee. In 1959 Allan Nevins praised it for conducting a much-needed scrutiny of the military while leaving the president and the cabinet alone. Other scholars, such as Eric McKitrick, argued that the radicals, including the committee, energized the war effort through their constant prodding of the president. Hans L. Trefousse directly challenged Williams's thesis, arguing that Republican committee members shared the same goals as the president. According to Trefousse, Lincoln used the threat of committee investigations to achieve his own goals, forcing George McClellan to move in spring 1862, for instance. Trefousse also doubted whether the committee was as powerful as Williams claimed. Lincoln, he noted, rarely changed policy as a result of committee recommendations. Indeed, in Trefousse's view, Lincoln towers above the committee, unleashing it on generals unwilling to fight but protecting military leaders whom he deemed valuable to the Union war effort. With Lincoln firmly in control, the committee, for Trefousse, became a useful tool for the sixteenth president. Howard C. Westwood carried the revised view of the committee to new lengths, arguing that there was no evidence for the charge of executive harassment and praising the committee's investigations: "The Committee was a hard-working, bipartisan group, addressing questions of perfectly legitimate concern to the Legislature during an internecine war."[8]

Yet such revisionist views have not been accepted in every quarter. In 1974 Elisabeth Joan Doyle wrote that the committee "accomplished nothing either of immediate good or lasting significance." E. B. Long noted that the committee's fame was primarily the result of its "high-handed methods." James McPherson's verdict is mixed: "Damned by its critics as a 'Jacobin' conspiracy to guillotine Democratic generals and praised by its defenders as a foe of inefficiency and corruption in the army, the committee was a bit of both." So, too, do recent Lincoln biographers give the committee mixed reviews. In his 1994 account of the Lincoln presidency, Phillip S. Paludan notes that the committee provided useful information to the War Department, yet at the same time it created problems for Lincoln because of its tendency "to push to extreme measures." David Donald, in his masterful biography of Lincoln, evaluates the committee in ambivalent terms, noting that "Lincoln viewed the creation of the Committee on the Conduct of the War with some anxiety, fearing that it might turn into an engine of agitation against the administration."[9]

Despite this background, I find several reasons to examine the Committee on the Conduct of the War. First, many of the committee's major investigations have not been systematically studied by scholars. The investigations of the first battle of Bull Run and the Red River campaign, for instance, have scarcely been examined; others have been studied only superficially. Second, although individual congressmen achieved fame and recognition from their work on the committee, it also must be seen within the larger context of party goals and the institution of Congress itself. Was the committee's work viewed as a legitimate extension of congressional power? Was it consistent with historical precedent? How closely were committee investigations correlated with the work of the Republican caucus and the Republican majority in Congress? If the committee did not act on specific instructions from the caucus, many of its maneuvers were certainly calculated to advance the party's ideological causes and to enhance its electoral prospects. Intriguing in this respect is the Republican committee members' continued reliance on the Slave Power conspiracy as a partisan tool, which Republicans had used in the 1850s to discredit Democratic opponents. During the war, committee members continued to invoke the image to discredit political opponents and the men it deemed incompetent militarily. Generals with Democratic affiliations such as George McClellan or Charles Pomeroy Stone were routinely denounced by committee members because of their alleged tenderness for the South and slavery. Conversely, committee members shielded such favorites as John C. Frémont by linking his opponents to the Slave Power.[10]

A third reason that prompts this study is that previous historians of the committee have not attempted seriously to account for its Democratic members. If congressional committees function as partisan tools of the majority party, how would Democrats be expected to behave on the Committee on the Conduct of the War? How did members of the minority party function in an environment fraught with charges of proslavery plots and the infidelity of West Point generals? Were Democratic members simply forced into

the background by dominant Republican members? If they did play active
roles, how did that square with partisan differences? Did they remain ortho-
dox Democrats, or did constant interaction with a Republican majority corrupt them? Did the dynamics of small-group interaction influence the attitude of minority members? Brooklyn Democrat Moses Odell, for instance,
was an active and involved member of the committee. T. Harry Williams
accounts for his activism by arguing that Odell was a war Democrat who
spurned such Democratic generals as George McClellan because he was
allied with peace Democrats. But Williams overlooks or was unaware of
relevant evidence. First, Odell supported McClellan in 1864. Second,
McClellan certainly was no peace Democrat and was rigorously opposed
by the Vallandigham wing of the Democratic party for the 1864 nomination. Third, Odell's voting record, save for one or two exceptions, was that
of a committed, partisan Democrat even though he was on intimate terms
with the committee's leading Republican members. Thus far, no account
of the committee's activities explains adequately the participation of its
minority members.[11]

A fourth reason stems from my belief that the most important scholarly
works on the committee suffer from questionable assumptions. For instance,
T. Harry Williams is probably correct in his negative assessment of the
committee's overall effect on the Union war effort. Yet Williams does not
account for the nature of the committee's power or provide concrete proof
that its investigations markedly changed Union military policy. Further,
Williams's later military scholarship does not incorporate his negative assessment of the committee's activities. Thus, in *Lincoln and His Generals*
(1952), Williams maintains that George McClellan's lack of success resulted
only from his own personal and psychological shortcomings, not from any
interference by the committee's work. Indeed, the committee, which occupied Williams's scholarly attention for several years, is not even listed in the
book's index. I believe that the committee's role as a political and a military
force needs to be integrated.[12]

Williams and other historians of the period often assumed that the committee was the stalking horse for the radical Republicans, the underlying
assumption being that the radicals were a small, cohesive faction of Republicans distinct from conservatives. Indeed, some historians believed divisions
were so extreme that conservative Republicans probably had more in common with members of the Democratic party. To be sure, there were some
issues, such as Frémont's emancipation proclamation, that seemed to split
the Republican party along these lines; however, as Allan Bogue has demonstrated, interparty, not intraparty, conflict was much more important

throughout the Civil War period. Indeed, Republicans shared a common commitment to what Eric Foner has termed the free labor ideology, a viewpoint that stressed the dignity of labor and the ability of the average person to rise in society through hard work and frugality. Viewing the South as aristocratic and static, the Civil War Republicans had the goal of reconstructing it according to the image of a dynamic, fluid northern society. Though many northern Democrats shared several of the assumptions of the free labor ideology, unlike their Republican colleagues they did not view southern society as fundamentally flawed. The committee therefore should be seen as advancing not the radical viewpoint but the dominant interests of the majority of Republicans. There certainly was conflict and controversy surrounding the committee; however, it was often more the result of jealousy between the legislative and executive branches of government. Most committee Republicans came from Whig antecedents accustomed to legislative dominance. Hence, it was less an issue of radical versus conservative and more an issue of the president versus Congress.[13]

Nor does the historical revisionism of the 1960s clarify matters. Although committee Republicans and the president might have been united on fundamentals, the question of the committee's impact on the war effort remains. If, as Hans Trefousse maintains, no substantial differences existed between the president and committee members on the major issues of the day, Williams's negative assessment of the committee still need not be rejected. Much of Trefousse's argument is based on a romanticized interpretation of the sixteenth president. For Trefousse, Lincoln towers above the petty and often misguided members of the committee; however, unlike less capable leaders, Lincoln was able to manipulate and control these feisty and combative committee members. He allowed them to attack and prod timid and cautious generals, such as McClellan, while shielding others from committee investigation. In Trefousse's view every situation turns out for the best because of Lincoln's wisdom and expertise in human relations. Trefousse sees the committee as an attack dog, but Lincoln, the kindly and benevolent master, held the leash. When appropriate, he might allow the committee members to snap at someone, but he would tighten the leash when aggressive behavior might endanger the Union cause.

Unfortunately, Trefousse's argument, like Williams's position, is based on an unproven premise: the assumption that Lincoln somehow was the unmoved mover of the Committee on the Conduct of the War. Just as Williams fails to address precisely the nature of the committee's power over military policy, so is Trefousse guilty of the same oversight with respect to the relationship between the sixteenth president and the committee. Lincoln resisted the committee's suggestions in some instances, but that does not prove the committee was powerless and lacked influence. The assertion that Lincoln was the invisible puppeteer, coordinating and directing the committee's work to achieve his ends, is based only on a partial reading of the evidence. If Williams has erred in believing that the committee was all-powerful, surely Trefousse has erred in the other direction.

A reevaluation of the committee's work that reexamines the nature of its power and influence on military policy is needed. How influential were congressional committees in determining policy? What weapons could they employ to achieve their goals? What were their limitations? What sort of ideas on military strategy did committee members entertain? Were they qualified to pass judgment on military matters? What was the ultimate impact of committee investigations on the Union war effort?

Members of the Joint Committee on the Conduct of the War worked long and hard on their assignments. No one could accuse them of shirking their duty. They were patriotic; they wanted to win the war. Republican members believed harsh measures were in order and that their constant prodding of the Lincoln administration produced beneficial results. Yet in this book I will demonstrate a disparity between committee goals and reality.

Throughout almost four years of investigation, the Joint Committee on the Conduct of the War had an uneven effect on the Union war effort. Some of its investigations did marked harm. In particular, committee members, largely ignorant of military science, attempted constantly to direct and influence military decisions. The result of their interference spawned distrust and jealousies among the top Union military commanders, helped undermine bipartisan support for the war, increased popular misconceptions about the nature of warfare, and contributed to the politicization of military appointments.

Conversely, some of the committee's activities contributed positively to the war effort. Certain investigations uncovered financial mismanagement among military contractors; others may have reinvigorated northern morale at important junctures during the war. The examinations of the Fort Pillow massacre and the treatment of northern prisoners by Confederates exemplify committee activities that aided the Union cause.

A large portion of the committee's work had little direct impact on the war effort. Its inquiry into the first battle of Bull Run and the disaster at Ball's Bluff during the Thirty-seventh Congress and the examination of the Army of the Potomac and the Red River expedition during the Thirty-eighth Congress required hundreds of hours of testimony and resulted in thousands of pages of it. Yet despite the time and effort, little significant information was uncovered. In most cases, the cause of military disaster was already common knowledge before committee investigations occurred. Although I contend that many of these investigations did not materially harm the Union war effort, they were a waste of time, energy, and resources.

Should Congress have created the Joint Committee on the Conduct of the War? In one sense, this is a superfluous question, but I will amply demonstrate the constitutional legitimacy of such a committee in chapter 1. Despite my own generally negative assessment of its work, I still think that such a committee might have made a significant contribution to the Union war effort if it had been structured somewhat differently. The problem with the Committee on the Conduct of the War was twofold: its members were woefully ignorant of military affairs, and it was given far too much investigative latitude since it was authorized to examine all aspects of military affairs. Thus a committee composed of members of Congress with some military experience and whose scope of inquiry was narrowly defined might have had a positive impact on military affairs. Unfortunately, partisan jealousies often complicate the operations of Congress, and the Civil War era was scarcely different from our contemporary setting.

CHAPTER ONE

To Invigorate a
Timid Administration

When Confederate guns fired on Fort Sumter on the morning of April 12, 1861, a long-festering crisis reached a climax. Convinced that the newly elected Republican administration of Abraham Lincoln sounded the death knell to the institution of slavery, the seven states of the Deep South had claimed the right of secession in the aftermath of the election, and they intended to make that right a reality. In the North, the firing on Sumter created a wave of patriotism. Despite the attack, many northerners believed secession was still only a temporary aberration, the work of wealthy slaveholders that would quickly collapse once the average southerner realized that the Lincoln administration would respond with military force. Immediately following the attack on Sumter, Lincoln called for 75,000 ninety-day state militia troops to suppress the rebellion. In the South, Lincoln's action prompted the secession of the border states of Virginia, North Carolina, Tennessee, and Arkansas; in the North, it produced a flood of volunteers. Indeed the response was overwhelming as individual states quickly met their quotas with many men to spare. "Everything is in an uproar here," wrote William Dean Howells from Columbus, Ohio, "and the war feeling is on the increase, if possible." The attitude of the volunteers was instructive: "The volunteers seemed to be in very good spirits," Howells noted, "and to look on campaigning as something of a frolic."[1]

Northerners regarded secession as a breach of faith, an attack on the nation's laws, and an assault on the institutions of self-government. Living generally in small communities throughout the East and Middle West, northerners participated in local government. The actions of southerners, therefore, were not abstract and impersonal but real and personal. The attack on Sumter temporarily suspended partisan divisions in the North. Before Sumter most northern Democrats had been conciliatory in their attitude toward the South, supporting, for instance, the Crittenden Compromise provisions in winter 1860–1861, but after the attack these same Democrats adopted the more stiff-backed approach of their Republican colleagues. "Party is forgotten," wrote one Democrat. "All feel that our very nationality is at stake." Although regarding secession as a serious breach of national faith, most northerners nevertheless were confident that the South could be quickly subdued and the Union restored. They saw secession as the work of a small minority of fire-eating fanatics such as William Lowndes Yancey and Robert Barnwell Rhett. When the North flexed its military muscle, backed by superior numbers and resources, support for the rebellion would quickly evaporate. Major northern newspapers endorsed this optimistic assessment as did many cabinet members in the Lincoln administration. A less optimistic New Yorker, George Templeton Strong, reported in his diary that in late May 1861 Secretary of State William H. Seward told New York senator Preston King that "he thought there would be no serious fighting at all; the South would collapse and everything would be adjusted." Strong added, "Seward pushes consistency to fanaticism."[2]

The decade that preceded the outbreak of war had been characterized by conflict and change. The 1830s and 1840s had been marked by optimism and perfectionism, culminating in the notion of America as a redeemer nation whose manifest destiny was to lead the world to virtuous republicanism, but the 1850s saw a distinct departure from such optimism. Many of the changes at work in the United States in the 1830s and 1840s generated anxiety and uncertainty. Waves of immigration fueled divisive ethnocultural conflict in the cities of the North, signified in the struggles over temperance, control of public education, and observance of the sabbath. Economic changes in the North resulted in the expansion of cities, promoted industrial growth, and threatened to create a permanent class of dependent wage earners. Northern economic development seemed to drive a wedge between the North and the South. As the North was industrializing and becoming an increasingly market-based economy, the South continued to cling to the old ways of a slower paced, rural economy that did not use free labor but continued its dependence on the institution of slavery. As the decade progressed, this reliance on slavery became the focal point of sectional controversy, particularly the conflict over the expansion of slavery. The controversies arising over events in Kansas and the *Dred Scott* Supreme Court decision threatened to split the nation into two hostile sections. With the election of Lincoln, the secession of southern states, and the firing on Fort Sumter, the great experiment in republican government seemed doomed to end in humiliating failure.[3]

Despite the turbulence of the 1850s and the threat to republican government posed by secession, a basic optimism still permeated the attitudes of many northerners in the aftermath of Sumter. Throughout spring and early summer 1861, most northerners, whether Democrats or Republicans, believed that war was necessary to vindicate republican institutions and to preserve the domain of freedom. "A strong sense of moral purpose underlay the

Northern war effort," writes Earl Hess. "Northerners believed that the conflict was a grand struggle to preserve free government in North America, a struggle that had implications for the preservation of political freedom in the world at large." Although maintaining different viewpoints about the institution of slavery, both Democrats and Republicans believed the viability of democratic institutions was threatened by southern secession.[4]

The leader who directed the northern war effort seemed scarcely qualified for the task. Although a successful lawyer and legislator, Abraham Lincoln was not an experienced executive. The extent of his governmental service consisted of several terms as an Illinois state legislator and a single term as a U.S. congressman. Lacking in significant military experience, the new president had been a bitter critic of war against Mexico, believing that fighting was a barbaric way of resolving differences that could be solved through logic and rationality. As president, perhaps Lincoln's opposition to war caused him seriously to underestimate the strength and depth of secession sentiments in the South.[5]

The outbreak of rebellion did place the president in an unprecedented position. Historically, the national government was rarely involved in the lives of ordinary Americans; the focal point of governmental authority was at the state and local level. Within the federal government, Congress seemed to have the lion's share of responsibilities. The powers of Congress are spelled out in great detail in the Constitution, yet those of the president are much more vague and ambiguous. Spring 1861 was no ordinary time, however, and Lincoln did not waste time worrying over constitutional niceties in taking the steps he believed were necessary in dealing with the rebellion. Instead of calling Congress into session, Lincoln acted in his capacity as commander in chief. In addition to his call for 75,000 three-month volunteers, he implemented quickly a series of measures designed to prosecute the war, including a naval blockade of the Confederacy, an appeal for 42,000 three-year volunteers, and provisions to expand the size of the regular army and navy.

Perhaps most controversial was Lincoln's decision to suspend the writ of habeas corpus. After imprisoning a number of suspected Maryland secessionists in late April, Lincoln ignored the opinions of Chief Justice Roger B. Taney, who argued that the president's suspension of the writ was illegal. Such power, Taney maintained, belonged only to Congress. Lincoln, however, believed that his actions were necessary to prevent Maryland from joining the Confederacy and to preserve the government. As Phillip S. Paludan comments: "For almost the first three months the Civil War was the president's war."[6]

When Congress met in a special session beginning on July 4, 1861, Lincoln asked for approval of the measures he had implemented. Congress endorsed the president's actions, pondering only Lincoln's claim that the power to suspend the writ of habeas corpus belonged to the executive. Congress also enlarged the War Department, granted Treasury Secretary Salmon P. Chase broad authority to borrow money, voted new taxes to finance the war, and passed the first confiscation act on August 6, allowing the seizure of property—including slaves—used to aid the rebellion. Underneath the facade of cooperation, however, was an undercurrent of distrust. Clearly Lincoln had taken most of the initiative, demonstrating his belief that the prosecution of the war was an executive function and revealing a rather Jacksonian conception of presidential power that may have surprised contemporaries. Although uniting behind the president, Congress also was suspicious of his activism. If Lincoln were to take the initiative, then he had better deliver— and deliver quickly. Congressional leaders wanted and expected quick results, an attitude that tended to increase the popular misconceptions about the nature and course of the war.[7]

Many northerners believed that a single battle would force the South to capitulate. The popular view of warfare stressed the ideas of courage and manliness over drilling and professional training. Moreover, many northerners were convinced that their cause was supported by God and therefore could not fail; hence, the South would easily be defeated. "It was supposed," Bruce Catton notes, "that secession would collapse once a blue battle line came over the hills with the sunlight glinting on polished musket barrels." Michigan's Republican senator Zachariah Chandler confidently predicted to his wife that once attacked, the Confederate army would "run like cowards" and that northern soldiers would soon be in Richmond. According to Ohio congressman Albert Gallatin Riddle, many of the nation's leaders as well as the common people "supposed that war meant to march upon the enemy by the shortest route, assail, hang to him, and *lick* him in the most direct way and in the least possible time." London *Times* correspondent, William Howard Russell, attested to the overconfidence as well as to the ignorance of military affairs of American journalists: "I could not help observing the arrogant tone with which writers of stupendous ignorance of military matters write of the operations which they think generals should undertake." Russell also could attest to the optimistic confidence of Secretary of State Seward, who boasted to him that the United States could handle Britain as well as the Confederacy. For many northerners, ending the rebellion seemed a simple matter. "On to Richmond" became the rallying cry. "It was time," wrote Bruce Catton, "to end matters. Specifically, it was time for General McDowell [commander of Union forces in the East] to take his army down to Manassas Plain, crush the rebellion, and march triumphantly on to Richmond. . . . One battle and then it would be over."[8]

Such optimistic illusions, however, were among the first casualties of the war. Under pressure from congressional leaders and public opinion, Brig. Gen. Irvin McDowell drew up a plan of battle and in mid-July marched his inexperienced army toward the Confederate army, encamped at Manassas Junction approximately thirty-five miles southwest of Washington and commanded by Gen. P. G. T. Beauregard. Pivotal to McDowell's plan was preventing Confederate troops under Gen. Joseph E. Johnston at Winchester, some fifty miles to the northwest, from reinforcing Beauregard. The task of holding Johnston in check was given to Maj. Gen. Robert Patterson, a sixty-nine-year-old veteran of the War of 1812 and the Mexican War. Johnston eluded Patterson, however, reinforcing Beauregard and depriving McDowell of a significant numerical advantage. Still, the Union attack on July 21, although launched three hours behind schedule, was initially successful. But late in the afternoon the rebels launched a vigorous counterattack, forcing Union troops to retreat, a rout that quickly sent McDowell's army in disarray back to Washington. To the numerous congressmen who had traveled to the battleground to observe the defeat of the rebel army, the experience was sobering.[9]

The public was outraged when the facts about the battle of Bull Run emerged. "Oh senility, imbecility, ignominy," wrote Count Adam Gurowski, a Polish exile employed as a translator in the State Department. "Today will be known as *Black Monday*," commented George Templeton Strong. "Only one great fact stands out unmistakably," he continued, "total defeat and national disaster on the largest scale." Horace Greeley's *New York Daily Tribune* blamed the cabinet, commenting that "a decimated and indignant people will demand the immediate retirement of the present Cabinet from the higher places of power." *Frank Leslie's Illustrated Newspaper* explained that "'Forward to Richmond' did not mean forward and fail"; instead, it meant forward as quickly as possible with enough forces to defeat the rebels and to occupy Richmond. A constituent of Pennsylvania congressman John Covode wrote that Bull Run had brought forth sentiments "almost beyond belief." The people trusted Gen. Winfield Scott and Lincoln, he explained, but not the cabinet. One of Senator Chandler's correspondents was incredulous at the news of defeat, asking "What in the name of our country's salvation is the matter?" Although a small group of northern intellectuals saw the defeat at Bull Run in positive terms, as an event that would stimulate harsh war measures such as confiscation and emancipation, for the majority of northerners Bull Run had been a shock, a stark contradiction to their belief that the Confederacy would collapse when confronted by northern arms. "The South is not composed of cowards or fools," wrote Ohio attorney and future Union general Thomas Kilby Smith, "and the North will find before they get through that they are not so easily conquered as they had supposed."[10]

Although the defeat at Bull Run did not cause the public or congressional leaders immediately to lose confidence in Lincoln, a series of additional setbacks in summer and fall 1861 created doubts about the president's ability to direct military matters. Shortly after Bull Run, on August 10, 1861, Union forces suffered another defeat at Wilson's Creek, approximately ten miles southwest of Springfield, Missouri. Here, a small force led by Gen. Nathaniel Lyon, a hot-tempered Connecticut native of antislavery convictions, attacked superior forces under Confederate generals Ben McCulloch and Sterling Price. After initial success, Union forces were routed and retreated to Rolla, Missouri, abandoning the entire southwestern corner of Missouri to the Confederacy. Lyon, immensely popular in the North for his role in keeping Missouri in the Union, was killed. Again, there was an outcry against the administration. "If these be victories," wrote George Templeton Strong, "may we soon enjoy a few defeats." The leading Republican organ of the West, the *Chicago Tribune,* reserved special condemnation for Secretary of War Simon Cameron, whom it held responsible for the Wilson's Creek defeat. The people, it asserted, "know that he [Cameron] is mainly, if not wholly, responsible for the disaster in Missouri, and they check the accusation by citing his culpable neglect to send the reinforcements that the gallant Lyon begged." The president, the *Tribune* continued, should listen to the people, who demand "that a Man be Secretary of War." In the aftermath of these defeats, Count Gurowski quoted Sen. Benjamin Wade as remarking, "I do not wonder that the people desert to Jeff. Davis, as he shows brains; I may desert myself."[11]

As summer turned into fall, the Union's war fortunes did not improve, a fact that tended further to discredit the administration. Many Republicans were distressed when Lincoln modified the August 30, 1861, proclamation of Gen. John C. Frémont, commander of the Western Department. Not only did the proclamation place Missouri under martial law, but it also allowed the confiscation of rebel property and proclaimed freedom for all slaves belonging to people loyal to the Confederacy. The proclamation immediately captured the imagination of a public eager for any sign of vigor in waging war. Even the Democratic *New York Herald* and Orville H. Browning, the conservative Republican senator from Illinois and friend of the president, cautiously supported Frémont's course. "I was on the stump in my own State," commented Indiana congressman George Julian, "and I found the masses everywhere so wild with joy, that I could scarcely be heard for their shouts." Despite the proclamation's popularity in Republican circles, Lincoln overruled Frémont, fearing that the proclamation might drive neutral Kentucky into the Confederacy. "What do you think of 'old Abe's' overruling Frémont's proclamation?" Benjamin Wade asked Zachariah Chandler. "So far as I can see, it is universally condemned . . . and I have no doubt that by it, he has done more injury to the cause of the Union, by receding from the ground taken by Frémont, than McDowell did by retreating from Bull Run."[12]

As if matters were not bad enough, the disaster at Ball's Bluff on October 21, 1861, brought northern dissatisfaction to a climax. While Union troops under Brig. Gen. George McCall made a reconnaissance at Drainesville, Virginia, near Leesburg, on October 20, Major General McClellan ordered Brig. Gen. Charles Pomeroy Stone, stationed at Poolesville, Maryland, to make a "slight demonstration" against Leesburg, hoping that Confederates under Brig. Gen. Nathan "Shank" Evans would abandon that important strategic junction. Stone, perhaps taking McClellan's orders too far, sent several companies of the Fifteenth Massachusetts under Col. Charles Devens across the Potomac from Harrison Island at Ball's Bluff, a steep ridge overlooking the river. Proceeding toward Leesburg, these troops were discovered by the Confederates, who drove them back to Ball's Bluff. Informed of Devens's predicament, Stone sent reinforcements under Col. Edward D. Baker, a senator from Oregon and an old Illinois friend of President Lincoln. Faced with the option of crossing the river to help Devens or withdrawing the entire force, Baker chose to cross. Forming an irregular battle line on a plain at the top of the bluff, Union forces presented easy targets for Confederates, who occupied an elevated wooded ridge surrounding the plain. When a Confederate bullet took Baker's life, Union commanders decided that retreat was their only viable option. In order to reach the river, soldiers had to march down a steep, narrow slope. Transportation to cross the river was woefully inadequate. As a result, confusion reigned as Union soldiers attempted to cross while Confederate soldiers peppered them with fire from the surrounding heights. Soldiers crammed into available boats; some threw down their weapons and swam to nearby Harrison Island; others hiked on the Virginia side to a safer place to cross. With 49 dead, 158 wounded, and 714 captured or missing, the battle of Ball's Bluff, although of little real military significance, was a tremendous setback to northern pride and morale.[13]

"The massacre at Ball's Bluff," wrote Adam Gurowski, "is the work of either treason, or of stupidity, or of cowardice, or most probably of all three united." A writer for *Frank Leslie's Illustrated Newspaper* argued that Ball's Bluff was a bigger disaster than Bull Run, and in this case, there were no civilians or an "on to Richmond" crowd to blame. Who was responsible for sending Baker into the "jaws of death," the journalist wondered. "History furnishes no parallel to such insanity, and as we have said already, the ignorance or incompetence which directed the attempt is without excuse." Ben Wade wrote to his son, "In view of the late defeat on the Potomac all is gloomy & despairing here," adding that Lincoln was a fool who was much too influenced by cowardly advisers such as William H. Seward.[14]

The disaster also put a strain on an already deteriorating relationship between Army of the Potomac commander Gen. George B. McClellan and many congressional leaders. Though almost everyone, even the individuals who would later prove to be the general's greatest antagonists, applauded Lincoln's appointment of McClellan to replace Irvin McDowell after the battle of Bull Run, by early October many congressmen were growing impatient with him. Two of McClellan's more vocal critics were Benjamin Wade and Zachariah Chandler. Writing to Chandler in early October, Wade complained that the 200,000-man army stayed behind entrenchments, "occasionally sending forth a *bulletin* announcing that 'the *Capital* is *safe*.'" Wade continued, "I begin to fear that General McClellan himself has more faith in fasting and prayers to chase these d——s out, than he has in the strength of his own regiments." An outraged people, Wade warned, will not tolerate this indefinitely. Ball's Bluff simply added to the suspicions of Wade, Chandler, and other congressmen, about McClellan.[15]

Nevertheless, suspicious as they were of McClellan and sharing an intense distrust of West Point professionalism, Wade, Chandler, and other congressional leaders, encouraged by McClellan himself, initially focused on General-in-Chief Winfield Scott as the real culprit behind the inactivity of the Army of the Potomac. On the evening of October 25, Wade, Chandler, McClellan, and Sen. Lyman Trumbull of Illinois met at the home of Postmaster General Montgomery Blair. The three senators tried to impress upon McClellan the necessity of forward movement, arguing that even a defeat would be better than doing nothing, for a defeat would at least stimulate recruitment. McClellan, however, shifted most of the blame to Scott, telling the senators that he was powerless as long as he remained subordinate to Scott. "[Chandler, Wade, and Trumbull] will make a desperate effort tomorrow," McClellan wrote his wife, "to have General Scott retired at once. Until that is accomplished I can effect but little good—he is ever in my way & I am sure he does not desire effective action."[16]

The next night, Wade, Chandler, and Trumbull, referred to as the Jacobin club by John Hay, Lincoln's secretary, met with the president and, in Hay's words, attempted "to worry the administration into battle." Apparently Lincoln was unimpressed with their arguments. Chandler later complained to his wife that the administration was timid and ineffective. Undoubtedly, the senators also lobbied for Scott's retirement; here they found the president in agreement, for on October 18 Lincoln and the entire cabinet had decided to accept Scott's resignation, tendered earlier that month, and to promote McClellan to general in chief. McClellan had his way; Scott retired on November 1. Still, Chandler was not entirely confident about McClellan. Immediately after their October 26 meeting, Chandler wrote to a Michigan political ally: "The d——l is to pay. There is no plan for a fight here. We can win a victory in 24 hours . . . if only our generals will fight, but the administration & Genl McClelland [*sic*] are equally timid & weak." Unfettered by Scott, McClellan had run out of excuses; his senatorial conspirators expected results, yet they were not forthcoming.[17]

Indeed for many congressmen, the situation seemed to be rapidly deteriorating. In early November, the administration removed Gen. John C. Frémont from his position as commander of the Department of the West, angering many Republican radicals who supported Frémont for his willingness to wage war on the institution of slavery. Making matters worse, Frémont's replacement, Gen. Henry W. Halleck, initiated policies on slavery that were completely opposed to Frémont's. On November 20 he issued General Order no. 3, forbidding fugitive slaves from coming within Union lines, a policy that incensed many Republican congressmen. A little later in the month, Secretary of War Simon Cameron, formerly the bête noire of many Republican radicals, published his department's annual report in which he endorsed arming the former slaves of rebels. When Lincoln forced him to modify the report, there was a storm of protest. By forcing Cameron to change the report, as one St. Louis man wrote the secretary, Lincoln "has given another evidence of that weak vacillation which has characterized all his actions in this war." *Chicago Tribune* editor Joseph Medill, formerly a bitter critic of Cameron, told the secretary that Lincoln had blundered: "You were right and he was wrong."[18]

Most infuriating was the continued inactivity of the Army of the Potomac, training and drilling but never quite ready to go into battle. To a public and congressional leaders unwilling to accept the need for extensive military training, such delays were maddening. With winter approaching, the question on many minds was whether McClellan would engage the enemy or lie idle in quarters. Zachariah Chandler had earlier warned the president that failure to strike a blow at the Confederate army in Virginia "was infinitely worse than another Bull Run." Caroline Wade wrote her husband that "there is getting to be a very uneasy feeling here at the inactivity of the grand army." Many Republican congressmen began to suspect partisan motives, for McClellan was a Democrat and a conservative on the slavery issue. The peculiar institution was increasingly on the minds of many Republicans as Union military failures multiplied in fall 1861. In the immediate aftermath of Fort Sumter and even after the battle of Bull Run, many Republican radicals disavowed any desire to wage war for the abolition of slavery. The stated purpose of the North's war effort was preservation of the Union. Congressional radicals demonstrated this hands-off approach to slavery when, immediately following the battle of Bull Run, they voted overwhelmingly for the Crittenden-Johnson resolution, which stated that the government would not interfere with the domestic institutions of any state as a result of the war. With the military situation growing gloomier by the day, many observers wondered whether the North could afford to keep this hands-off policy toward slavery. Indeed, perhaps this very position on slavery was the explanation for Union military setbacks.[19]

Republican leaders offered various reasons to justify a more forthright position on slavery. Some believed, perhaps naively, that a war for the abolition of slavery was necessary to enliven and motivate northern soldiers. Others argued that since slavery was at the root of the rebellion, failing to attack the peculiar institution might be the cause of Union military reverses. Since the Almighty despised slavery, abolitionists reasoned, how could he bless a cause that ignored this moral blight? "God in his providence is now afflicting us for the crimes committed through slavery," one Illinois resident wrote Sen. Lyman Trumbull. Carl Schurz, a popular German-American leader from Wisconsin and the ambassador to Spain, provided additional reasons. He told Secretary of State Seward that Europe regarded the war as proof that democratic institutions could not work. Most Europeans, Schurz continued, believed that slavery had caused the war and understandably thought "that the destruction of slavery was to be the avowed object of the policy of our government, and that the war would be nothing else than a grand uprising of the popular conscience in favor of a great humanitarian principle." Since the administration spurned such an interpretation, Schurz observed, the cause of the North perplexed Europeans and generated little sympathy. Writing later to Massachusetts antislavery senator Charles Sumner, Schurz argued that only a war against slavery could improve the cause of the Union; otherwise, any victories would be "useless butcheries."[20]

Even more distressing, however, was the nagging sense of doubt that many Republicans felt about the army's leadership. George McClellan, after all, was a Democrat. Ever since that party's emergence as a force in national politics in the 1850s, Republican politicians had castigated the Democratic party as supporters of the South and willing accomplices in expanding the institution of slavery. Linking Union defeats to the presence of Democrats in positions of military leadership, many Republican congressmen easily believed that the army's leadership was sympathetic to the South. "Some contemporaries," writes James L. Morrison, "believed that the nationalism in which West Point took such pride was actually larded heavily with pro-Southern sentiment." In the Senate Chandler told his colleagues that army officers routinely referred to the war as a "'damned black Republican war,' and actually express[ed] their sympathy with the enemy." Even John Sherman, the brother of William Tecumseh Sherman, voiced grave doubts about the quality of a West Point education, arguing that it did not produce the fighting spirit.

Uncertainties about the fidelity of Democratic generals were fed by rumors of party members' participation in disloyal secret societies such as the Knights of the Golden Circle. Established by George W. L. Bickley, a ne'er-do-well Cincinnati physician, the society was allegedly created to extend slavery into Mexico and Central America. Once the war erupted, the Knights supposedly turned their attention to aiding and abetting the Confederacy. Already in fall 1861 there were rumors that linked the Democratic party in the North to the Knights. Hence, in a capital already suffering from impatience and frustration, talk of disloyalty and suspicion of treason increasingly permeated the atmosphere. "Radical congressmen," notes Phillip Paludan, "began to speak of 'dictator,' 'treason,' and 'cowardice.'"[21]

The Birth of the Committee

Suspicions about disloyalty, discontent on the slavery issue, and frustration with the state of military affairs came to a head when the Thirty-seventh Congress convened in early December 1861. Many Republican constituents and newspapers urged Congress to adopt a more vigorous war policy. Much of the criticism was directed at Abraham Lincoln. The *Chicago Tribune* complained that antislavery generals were all too rare in the nation's armies, despite their better track record in battle. One Ohioan complained to Benjamin Wade of Lincoln's inaction and claimed that McClellan was the "laughing stock of the people," and Wade warned another Ohio constituent that Lincoln's policies were prolonging the war and would lead to "a disgraceful compromise." One of Lyman Trumbull's correspondents recommended that Congress be firm and force Lincoln to make war "in earnest." "War costs money," he reminded Trumbull; "it is for you to grant it and impose conditions." Those people who opposed a policy of emancipation, one Massachusetts man wrote Charles Sumner, are dragging out the war; he looked to the opening session of the new Congress to initiate more vigorous policies. A Michigan resident advised Zachariah Chandler to "let the watchword be 'Liberty & Union.' It is astonishing how the Government has managed to be so far behind the people." Another constituent wrote, "The people will sustain their representatives in the most radical steps they may take. Remember this." As subsequent events proved, Chandler not only remembered but followed this advice.[22]

Congress met in early December eager for action. Out of session since the summer, Republican congressmen, in particular, had observed helplessly one military disaster after another. They had in the special summer session agreed to the president's actions retroactively; they had accepted his leadership as commander in chief; they had patiently awaited the movement of the Army of the Potomac, only to be frustrated time after time. They were running out of patience, and for many congressional leaders, the sad state of military affairs reflected negatively on Abraham Lincoln. As Allan Bogue notes, Lincoln's relatively short and lackluster political career did not especially inspire confidence from the party faithful, and several congressmen were prepared to set a course allowing Congress to shape the direction of military policy. Given the Whig antecedents in the Republican party, there was nothing particularly unique about the legislative branch attempting to influence the executive. And despite the president's role as commander in chief, it was commonly thought that Congress ought to play an important part in shaping and directing the armed forces because "in military matters Presidents served as Congress's steward."[23]

The inspiration for congressional maneuvering was the numerous military disasters that had plagued the Union effort that fall. On December 2, 1861, New York Republican congressman Roscoe Conkling introduced a resolution in the House demanding that the secretary of war provide Congress with information about the recent disaster at Ball's Bluff. In the Senate a few days later Chandler followed suit, offering a resolution to create a committee "to inquire into the disasters of Bull Run and Edward's Ferry [Ball's

Bluff], with the power to send for persons and papers." Senator James Lane of Kansas suggested an amendment that would have added the battle of Wilson's Creek to the resolution, but Sen. James Grimes of Iowa introduced a more sweeping amendment by proposing the creation of a joint congressional committee to examine every military disaster. Chandler initially opposed Grimes's proposal, arguing that it would entail an arduous duty, requiring travel across the country; to investigate Bull Run and Ball's Bluff, virtually in the Senate's backyard, would be far less difficult. Lane entered the debate by asserting that the people were much more interested in the fate of Gen. Nathaniel Lyon at Wilson's Creek than they were about Bull Run or Ball's Bluff. Lane demanded to know why Lyon was sacrificed when there was ample time to reinforce him. "The people desire to know whether it was the fault of the President of the United States or of some subordinate officer." He also asked why Cairo, Illinois, was reinforced but not Lyon. Clearly intended as an indictment of John C. Frémont for failing to reinforce Lyon, Lane's amendment was rejected by the Senate. Grimes then proposed his amendment. Consideration of this substitute was postponed when William Pitt Fessenden of Maine requested time to study the resolution more carefully.[24]

Senate debate resumed on December 9 when Chandler renewed the appeal for his own resolution, promising support for resolutions to create separate investigative committees in other military theaters in exchange for adopting his proposal. Grimes argued that a committee with broader powers was more appropriate. Some simpletons in the country, he claimed, blamed the defeat at Bull Run on the presence of a few congressmen on the field of battle, others on the fact that the battle was fought on Sunday. Responding to Lane's earlier remarks, Grimes pointed out that some people blamed Frémont for the disaster at Wilson's Creek, and others claimed that Lyon had had ample time to fall back from danger. "Let the country know what are the facts," argued Grimes. "If they condemn General Frémont, let him be condemned; if they justify him, then in God's name let him be justified." Only Congress, he concluded, was in a position to investigate such matters, and it had a duty to do so.[25]

When Sen. Lafayette Foster of Connecticut, seconding early objections to such a committee raised by Samuel Pomeroy of Kansas and James McDougall of California, argued that military disasters ought to be investigated by military authorities, he was challenged by Fessenden on constitutional grounds. Congress, argued Fessenden, declared war and raised the money necessary to carry it on. When problems arose, Congress could not sit back and do nothing. That would be a dereliction of duty. "We must satisfy the people of this country that things go on well." As representatives of the people, Congress alone had the right to conduct such investigations.[26]

John Sherman, Republican senator from Ohio, next proposed an amendment to Grimes's resolution, broadening it to allow the proposed committee to investigate every aspect of the war including military disasters, the conduct of military personnel, and the actions of every branch of government. Although Sherman is not usually classified among the Republican radicals, he spoke as an ardent critic of the administration. He was especially incensed over the way the government had treated John C. Frémont, and in particular over the actions of Adj. Gen. Lorenzo Thomas, whom Sherman blamed for leaking a confidential report on Frémont that helped bring about the latter's recall. Sherman asked why Thomas was allowed to travel around the country gathering what amounted to gossip, "*stuff* that would not be introduced before any justice of the peace," and then collect it in a report and publish it. With reputations and careers at stake, Sherman wondered how any officer in the U.S. Army could be allowed to act in such fashion. "If Senators overlook this act of a high officer of the Government they fail to do their duty," asserted Sherman, who concluded with a vigorous appeal for unity and patriotism so that the republican institutions of the country might be preserved.[27]

After Sherman's robust speech, Grimes amended his resolution to authorize a joint committee consisting of three senators and four congressmen. Such a committee would examine all aspects of the war and have "the power to send for person and papers." When Sen. Milton Latham of California moved to put the resolution to a vote, it was adopted, 33 to 3. When the House concurred with the resolution without debate on December 10, the Joint Committee on the Conduct of the War (CCW) was created. Although the absence of southerners from Congress gave the Republicans enough votes to pass the resolution without the support of Democratic members, the minority party nonetheless overwhelmingly supported the creation of the committee. Undoubtedly unhappy with the state of the war, many Democrats were equally impatient with the president's handling of military affairs. A few days after the resolution was passed, Vice Pres. Hannibal Hamlin chose the Senate members, selecting Republicans Benjamin F. Wade and Zachariah Chandler and Tennessee Democrat Andrew Johnson. Speaker of the House Galusha Grow of Pennsylvania chose Republicans George W. Julian of Indiana, John Covode of Pennsylvania, and Daniel W. Gooch of Massachusetts. New York's Moses Fowler Odell was the sole Democratic member from the House. Hamlin chose Wade to chair the committee.[28]

Members of the Committee

Born on October 27, 1800, Benjamin F. Wade was a Massachusetts native who could trace his lineage to Puritan roots. Wade followed his three older brothers to Andover, Ohio, and eventually became a lawyer. In 1828 he moved to Jefferson, Ohio, where he formed a partnership with Joshua R. Giddings. Although he rejected the religion of his parents and showed little interest throughout his life in institutional religion, Wade was a vigorous advocate of many of the reforms associated with evangelical Christianity, including abolition, women's rights, and workers' rights. He carried his reformist agenda into politics, joining the Whig party and winning a seat in the Ohio legislature in 1837. Wade was elected state senator and became judge of Ohio's Third Circuit Court before being elected to the U.S. Senate in 1851. He left the Whig party in the aftermath of the Kansas-Nebraska Act and joined the Republican party, serving three successive terms in the Senate before his retirement from politics in 1869.

Perhaps Wade's most notable characteristics were his stubborn combativeness on political issues and his devotion to principle. "His honest and intrepid advocacy of principle has won him an enviable position in his party," the *Continental Monthly* noted in the middle of the war, "and no one possesses the entire confidence of the country to a greater degree than he." In the later 1830s he was a fierce opponent of Ohio's black laws, which discriminated against the state's free black population, despite the great unpopularity of his position. When he began his first term in the Senate, Wade belonged to a small coterie of antislavery senators including Salmon P. Chase, John Hale, Charles Sumner, and William H. Seward. Wade's enthusiasm, moreover, never diminished, despite the unpopularity of the cause. Throughout the secession crisis, he adamantly opposed concessions to the South. After the firing on Fort Sumter, he endorsed a vigorous war, believing that northern superiority in men and material gave the Union great advantages as long as it acted quickly and decisively. Wade's recipe for victory included such radical measures as emancipation and the confiscation of rebel property. Throughout the war, the Ohio senator was skeptical of generals educated at West Point, linking the detached attitude of military professionalism with southern sympathies. Wade also had a stormy relationship with Lincoln, criticizing him for relying on such suspect advisers as William H. Seward and violently disagreeing with his reconstruction policy. Nevertheless, he eventually campaigned for Lincoln's reelection in 1864.[29]

Zachariah Chandler was an ideal partner for Wade. Born in 1813 in Bedford, New Hampshire, Chandler was also from a long line of Puritans.

In the early 1830s, like many New Englanders, he migrated to Michigan, where he became involved in the wholesale dry goods business. Honesty and hard work had transformed Chandler's business into a stunning success by the early 1850s. Like his father's, Chandler's political orientation was Whig, and he entered Michigan's political arena when he was elected mayor of Detroit in 1851. After an unsuccessful run for governor in 1852, Chandler gravitated toward the Fusionist coalition of Free-Soilers, antislavery Whigs, and angry northern Democrats who came together in the aftermath of the Kansas-Nebraska Act. When John C. Frémont carried Michigan for the Republican party in 1856, Chandler was nominated for the U.S. Senate and defeated Lewis Cass for the seat.

Sharing Wade's antislavery convictions, Chandler was equally uncompromising and combative. Opposing any compromise with the South on slavery, he was quoted in the campaign of 1860: "Without a little bloodletting, this Union would not be worth a rush." In February 1861 he opposed sending a Michigan delegation to the Washington Peace Conference. When political pressure forced Michigan's governor Austin Blair to do so, Chandler advised him to send only stiff-backed men. From the beginning of the war, Chandler endorsed such radical measures as emancipation, confiscation, and the arming of black troops. "I consider a loyal Negro," Chandler once remarked, "better than a secessionist traitor, either in the North or the South."

Routinely denouncing northern Democrats as disloyal Copperheads and believing many of the rumors about secret societies, Chandler's frank and bitter rhetoric often placed him at the center of the controversy. In May 1864, while dining at the National Hotel in Washington, he was assaulted by Daniel Voorhees, a Democratic congressman from Indiana, for disparaging comments Chandler had made about members of the Democratic party. Like Wade, Chandler was impatient with the caution of West Point generals. After one interview with McClellan in which the general had explained the necessity of providing a line of retreat before the army could advance, Wade asked Chandler what he thought of military science. "I don't know much about war," Chandler responded, "but this is infernal, unmitigated cowardice." Although Chandler supported Lincoln's reelection in 1864, he too was often impatient with the president's handling of war matters.[30]

Born in North Carolina in 1808, Andrew Johnson came from an impoverished background, the son of tavern servants. Apprenticed as a tailor, Johnson eventually made his way to Tennessee, settling first at Rutledge and then moving on to Greeneville. After he had built a successful business as a tailor, Johnson turned to politics, holding a number of local government positions and entering the Tennessee state legislature in 1835. In 1842 Johnson was elected to the U.S. House of Representatives, where he served ten years. In 1853 he was elected governor of Tennessee, and in 1857 he re-entered national politics when he was elected to the Senate. When Tennessee seceded from the Union after the surrender of Fort Sumter and Lincoln's call for troops, Johnson, whose eastern Tennessee constituents were overwhelmingly opposed to secession, stayed in the Senate, the only senator from a seceding state to do so.

Imbued with the ideology of Jacksonian strict constructionism and harboring no doubts about the morality of slavery, Johnson seemed a natural antagonist to such radical Republicans as Wade and Chandler, especially with their penchant for using harsh, antisouthern rhetoric. Yet many Republicans, and undoubtedly his committee colleagues, were impressed by his strong statements against secession. "I am a Southern man, sharing the prejudice of my region, and I am no abolitionist," Johnson told a crowd at Newport, Kentucky, in fall 1861, "but I tell you, my fellow countrymen, that secession has done more harm today than all the abolitionists in the country put together since we were a nation." Although a southerner and committed to states' rights, Johnson did not accept John C. Calhoun's concept of nullification. Johnson "believed in states' right and defended the right of slavery," writes his biographer Albert Castel, "but his concept of the Constitution derived from Andrew Jackson and not John C. Calhoun. Johnson argued that slavery could best be protected inside rather than outside the Union and that the preservation of the Union must come above all else." Johnson also gloried in his plebeian origins, bitterly denouncing the aristocratic, planter class as patricians. The patricians had engineered secession, and Johnson was willing to adopt harsh measures to punish them, using language that undoubtedly impressed his colleagues on the committee. When Johnson resigned his Senate seat to become military governor of Tennessee in March 1862, he was replaced on the committee by Indiana's Joseph A. Wright; nevertheless, throughout the war, Johnson remained interested in the affairs of the Committee on the Conduct of the War.[31]

John Covode was born in Westmoreland County, Pennsylvania, in 1808. Lacking formal education, he worked as a blacksmith and farm laborer and eventually became involved in the establishment of the Westmoreland Coal Company in 1847. Covode also invested heavily in railroads and was a close friend of J. Edgar Thompson, president of the Pennsylvania Railroad. He entered local politics in 1832 as a Whig. In 1854 he was a Fusion candidate for the House of Representatives. Securing election, he served successive terms until he retired from Congress in March 1863, making an unsuccessful attempt to capture the Republican nomination for governor of Pennsylvania from incumbent Andrew G. Curtin. After serving as an investigator for the War Department, Covode was reelected to Congress in 1866.

Covode endorsed many of the harsh measures advocated by Wade and Chandler. He had gained national headlines in 1860 when he chaired a House Committee that investigated alleged frauds committed by the Buchanan administration. "Covode is shrewd but illiterate," noted Secretary of the Navy Gideon Welles, "a match and more than a match for men of high culture, reputation, and acquirements." As a veteran member of the House of Representatives who had had experience with previous congressional investigations, Covode was an ideal candidate for membership on the Committee on the Conduct of the War.[32]

George Washington Julian was born in Wayne County, Indiana, in 1817. Strongly influenced by his mother's Quaker beliefs and the writings of Unitarian minister William Ellery Channing, Julian became a full-blown abolitionist in the mid-1840s and endorsed numerous other reforms, including women's rights and homestead legislation. A lawyer by profession, Julian initially joined the Whig party but left it for the Free-Soil party in 1848. In that same year, he was elected to Congress as a Free-Soil candidate but was defeated for reelection when Oliver P. Morton, the future governor of Indiana and Julian's persistent political opponent, supported the Whig candidate.

Julian eventually joined the Republican party and was reelected to Congress in 1860. Perhaps the most radical of the Republicans on the committee, Julian was fiercely combative, and his congressional speeches were bitterly partisan, denouncing Democrats in the most vituperative terms as well as castigating fellow Republicans insufficiently radical. His father-in-law, noted abolitionist Joshua R. Giddings, admired his devotion to principle but told his daughter that Julian was too grim, lacking "hope and *charity*." He not only endorsed emancipation but also favored full political and civil rights for blacks. Nor was Julian afraid to interact with blacks socially, despite the unpopularity of such actions. When war broke out, Julian quickly endorsed the confiscation of rebel property; he also favored breaking up southern plantations and redistributing the land to white and black veterans. Like many of his committee colleagues, Julian had his differences with Lincoln. In fact, Julian had not initially supported Lincoln's nomination in 1860 because he regarded him as too conservative. Even though he was skeptical of Lincoln's reelection he supported the president for a second term because he saw it as critical to winning the war.[33]

Daniel W. Gooch of Massachusetts was the legal expert of the committee. Born in Wells, Maine, in 1820, Gooch studied law at Dartmouth and

Indiana Republican George Julian delivered some of the most forceful speeches in the House to advance the committee's causes. (Courtesy of the Indiana Historical Society)

graduated in 1843. Entering the Massachusetts House in 1852, Gooch was elected to the U.S. House of Representatives in 1858, where he served consecutive terms until his retirement from Congress in 1865. Although a Republican, Gooch was not a consistent radical and in several committee investigations differed from his Republican colleagues. Notable in this regard was his refusal to endorse a committee report vindicating John C. Frémont's tenure as commander of the Department of the West and his authorship of a minority report defending conservative Republican Nathaniel Banks for his role in the ill-fated Red River expedition in spring 1864. On other occasions, however, Gooch vigorously defended the work of the CCW against the objections of its congressional critics. His legal expertise was demonstrated repeatedly in committee hearings by his systematic and penetrating examination of witnesses.[34]

The only Democratic House member of the committee, New York's Moses Fowler Odell, was also its most obscure member. Born in Tarrytown,

New York, in 1818, Odell obtained a position in the New York Customs House in 1845 and was elected to Congress in 1860, representing Brooklyn. A prominent member of the Methodist church, Odell had a well-established reputation for integrity and honesty. A staunch Douglas Democrat, Odell bitterly denounced secession in spring 1861. "I had but one feeling and one purpose in my heart," Odell later reflected. "One country and the Old Flag was my watchword, and I thank God that ignoring party ties, and personal interest, I was enabled, unswervingly, to bend the best energy of my mind and body to aid in the accomplishment of this object."

Described incorrectly by Elisabeth Joan Doyle as a political hack, Odell played an active and important role on the committee, despite significant ideological differences with its Republican majority. He attended most committee meetings and was given numerous tasks on various subcommittees. Like Gooch, Odell refused to sign the report on Frémont, earning harsh criticism from Frémont's wife, Jessie Benton Frémont; on the other hand, he signed a report highly critical of George McClellan, a move that earned him contempt in many Democratic circles. T. Harry Williams describes Odell as a war Democrat, and his support for the abolition of slavery in the District of Columbia and for the Thirteenth Amendment suggests that his political philosophy changed as a result of the war. In most respects, however, Odell maintained traditional Democratic beliefs of strict constructionism, white supremacy, and states' rights. Accordingly, he often voted against confiscation measures, opposed the use of black troops, and supported a mild reconstruction policy. Still, Republicans on the committee trusted Odell and even supported his campaign for reelection in 1862.[35]

Why were these members chosen to serve on the Joint Committee on the Conduct of the War? Hamlin's choice of Wade and Chandler was logical. Not only was Hamlin well acquainted with the two men, but he also shared their skepticism about Lincoln's abilities. The choice of Andrew Johnson was probably made through consultation among Wade, Chandler, and Hamlin. With his tough rhetoric against southern aristocrats, Johnson might possibly cooperate with his republican cohorts on the committee. It is not known if Hamlin consulted with Lincoln in making his choices; many Republican veterans were skeptical of Lincoln's abilities at this stage of the war, and it is conceivable that Hamlin did not consult the president, instead relying on his Senate colleagues for advice.[36]

Wade's biographer, Albert Gallatin Riddle, has contended that "nobody but Wade was thought of for chairman." Yet since Chandler had introduced the resolution that created the committee, he was entitled not only to mem-

Although he did not always side with his Republican colleagues, Daniel W. Gooch provided valuable service with his penetrating examination of witnesses. (Courtesy of the National Archives)

bership but also to the chairmanship. According to the *Detroit Post and Tribune*, however, Chandler suggested to Hamlin that Wade be chosen chairman because he had extensive legal experience, which Chandler lacked. Given Wade's legal credentials and his long experience in the Senate, Hamlin's decision was sensible.[37]

There is little information about Galusha Grow's choices for membership on the committee. By the era of the Civil War, the Speaker's office had evolved into a fairly powerful one. Since most members served for short periods of time, no automatic seniority system existed for committee assignments, leaving the Speaker considerable latitude in making his selections. Indeed, the Civil War House of Representatives was hardly the professional group of elite lawmakers that exists today; it was much more amateurish.

Although the Speaker weighed seniority and experience in making his choices, he was not absolutely bound by such considerations.

Certainly the Speaker, in exercising his discretionary judgment, wanted to advance the interest of the party and specifically that faction within the party that had brought him to power. At the same time, other considerations, such as sectional balance or the placation of a rival, also figured into the equation. Galusha Grow had defeated Frank Blair and Schuyler Colfax to become Speaker and was considered the most radical of the three. Undoubtedly Grow's selections for the CCW were made in accordance with the wishes of that faction of the Republican party, which had put him in his office. Elisabeth Joan Doyle has argued that Grow followed Chandler's wishes in making his House selections. Although there is no hard evidence for such an assertion, Grow conceivably could have consulted with Chandler and perhaps Wade as well.

It seems equally certain that Grow's choices were made in relation to the actions of the House Committee on Government Contracts. This committee, appointed in July 1861, had turned against congressional radicals by attacking their darling, John C. Frémont, and Grow clearly wanted to avoid such a fiasco. If, as Allan Bogue maintains, nineteenth-century congressional committees were partisan tools, then the choice of Julian and Covode, when combined with Wade and Chandler, gave radical Republicans a working majority of four to three, thereby ensuring their dominance without a repeat of the Contracts Committee's conduct. Moreover, Covode's previous experience on a congressional investigating committee boosted his qualifications. Gooch, initially thought to be a conservative Republican, might have been a concession to the Blair faction.[38]

The appointment of Odell as the sole Democratic member from the House seems straightforward enough. Since the committee was expected to be an important one, Grow most likely chose Odell because of his relative obscurity. Whatever the committee's Republican majority decided to do, Odell would either have to comply or refuse to participate in its deliberations. The biggest mistake Grow could have made would have been to name a prominent Democrat such as Clement Vallandigham or Samuel S. Cox to the committee, who might be outvoted by the majority but who would surely challenge the Republican majority in Congress or in Democratic newspapers when its actions appeared too partisan. Odell, however, a freshman member and relatively unknown, did not pose a threat. To bury prominent Democrats on obscure committees and to appoint obscure Democrats to prominent committees was undoubtedly a sound political axiom, one that Grow followed in making his selections.[39]

Although there is no specific constitutional provision for congressional committees of investigation, Congress assumed such powers early in the history of the Republic, relying on past precedents of parliamentary investigations. Indeed, many legal commentators argue that investigative powers are a logical deduction from powers granted to Congress under the Constitution. Since the powers of Congress are elaborated in much more detail than are those of the president, both houses were much more active in the mechanics of lawmaking than were nineteenth-century executives. Without investigative committees, the work of Congress would be almost impossible to carry out.

Most commentators agree that Congress has the right to investigate its own members and to make inquiries with respect to legislation. More controversial, however, are legislative attempts to investigate the executive branch of government, an undertaking implied in the resolution empowering the Committee on the Conduct of the War. Although one could argue that the separation of powers prohibits congressional interference with the executive, as indeed opponents of the committee did argue periodically, such a complete separation of powers was not generally accepted by Civil War contemporaries. Congress appropriates funds, passes laws, even creates various executive departments, practices that imply a degree of oversight. As early as 1854, Attorney General Caleb Cushing admitted that Congress had the right to ask cabinet heads for information at any time. As Sen. William Pitt Fessenden argued during the debate over the CCW, since it was Congress that supplied the appropriations for the war, that body had an obligation to investigate military operations, despite lacking executive control over them. Indeed, with a few notable exceptions, such as Andrew Jackson, many Americans undoubtedly feared a strong executive, perhaps a cultural aversion that reflected the revolutionary generation's association of strong executive power with monarchical tyranny. Most politically active Americans in 1860 expected some congressional oversight of the executive's war policies.[40]

Precedent also justified the creation of the Joint Committee on the Conduct of the War. As early as 1792 Congress had assumed the power to investigate the executive and military affairs, inquiring into the disastrous expedition of Gen. Arthur St. Clair to drive Indian tribes from the Northwest Territory. In this case, the specific rationale was that public monies had been wasted and had to be accounted for. The Washington administration complied with congressional demands for information while reserving the right to withhold any considered damaging to the public good. In 1818 a Senate committee investigated the activities of Andrew Jackson in Florida. It criticized Jackson's conduct as a violation of his instructions; however, it made no recommendations for a future course of action. And of course there was the investigative committee that John Covode had chaired, charged with examining how patronage and printing contracts had been handled by the Buchanan administration. This committee had examined some eighty witnesses and uncovered evidence that President Buchanan had used printing patronage to create favorable press for the passage of the Lecompton constitution.

Hence, the creation of the Committee on the Conduct of the War was justified by previous examples and by constitutional prerogatives. This committee, however, was different because of the vagueness of the resolution that had created it. Previous investigative bodies were aimed at a specific disaster or event and were therefore limited by the scope of the resolution that created them. The CCW, on the other hand, was created by an elastic resolution that, if used aggressively, gave it the potential for exercising great influence.[41]

"Your committee proceeded to discharge of the duty devolved upon them," an 1863 CCW report declared, "and have labored zealously and, they trust, faithfully for that purpose." By its own acknowledgment, the committee did not envision its true purpose as legislative; indeed, only two pieces of legislation were introduced into Congress that originated in the CCW. Instead the committee considered its role as one of investigation and recommendation. "Your committee therefore concluded," the report continued, "that they would best perform their duty by endeavoring to obtain such information in respect to the conduct of the war as would best enable them to advise what mistakes had been made in the past and the proper course to be pursued in the future."[42]

Investigate is what the committee would do. Equipped with a stenographer, William Blair Lord, meeting almost every day while Congress was in session, and continuing to operate after the legislative sessions, the committee did labor zealously. It gathered information from investigators, from witnesses it examined, and from trips by its own members. It investigated almost every major Union defeat during the course of the war, among them the first Bull Run, Ball's Bluff, Fredericksburg, and Chancellorsville. It looked into lesser military disasters such as the Red River campaign, the Crater disaster at Petersburg, and the attack on Fort Fisher. The investigation of whole military departments, such as John C. Frémont's administration of the Department of the West in 1861, fell within its scope. Further, a variety of other war-related areas were subject to committee investigations, including alleged rebel atrocities after the battle of Bull Run, the treatment of Union prisoners in Confederate prisons, the Fort Pillow massacre, the government's negotiation of ice contracts, the design and construction of light-draught monitors, trade in military districts, the protection of enemy property, and irregularities in the Quartermaster's Department in New York. The result of these extensive investigations was the publication of eight volumes of reports and testimony.[43]

The committee met in the basement of the capitol in the Committee on Territories room, and its proceedings were secret. Although witnesses were warned of this prior to giving testimony, some, notably John C. Frémont, violated this provision. On other occasions, committee members themselves, for specific reasons, leaked information to the press. For example, in fall 1862 John Covode, campaigning for the Republican party, used secret committee testimony in a public speech in Philadelphia. To gain flexibility, the committee scrapped any quorum provisions, allowing testimony to be taken even when only a single member was present. Although critics contend that the provision allowed Wade and Chandler to dominate committee proceedings, the rule was also a matter of practicality. It allowed one or two members to take testimony at the scene of an investigation or to travel to a witness, as when Moses Odell traveled to New York to take the statement of Winfield Scott during the investigation of Bull Run.[44]

During the course of its tenure, the CCW was subjected to violent criticism, but there was little hostility from the press when the committee was formed. The Democratic *Chicago Times,* for instance, ridiculed Chandler for introducing his resolution demanding an investigation of Ball's Bluff and Bull Run, but it said nothing about the committee's subsequent formation. Undoubtedly, the relative lack of comment stemmed from the expectation of many northerners that Congress ought to play a significant role in the direction of military affairs. Observers who did note the birth of the committee were usually its most partisan advocates. "The Congress appointed a War Investigating Committee, Senator Wade at its head," wrote Adam Gurowski. "There is hope that the committee will quickly find out what a terrible mistake this McClellan is, and warn the nation of him." A sympathetic New York Republican wrote approvingly to Chandler about his resolution for an inquiry into Ball's Bluff and Bull Run: "It seems that regular army officers & doughfaces can make any amount of blunders & all will be right." The *Chicago Tribune* noted that members of the committee "represent the progressive elements of the two houses, and they will rake things fore and aft in their search to place responsibility for our army's inaction in the proper quarter."[45]

In other periods of national crisis, expressions of national unity and great cooperation between the executive and legislative branches of government were apparent, but Abraham Lincoln experienced only a brief period of cooperation. The creation of the Committee on the Conduct of the War provided the means for impatient and patriotic congressmen to keep tabs on the administration and to ensure that Congress was kept well informed on the implementation of military policy. These Republican congressmen believed that through the CCW they could exercise considerable power. Except for the power to call witnesses, gather testimony, and conduct hearings, however, little constitutional basis existed for influencing executive decisions. Yet one relevant factor that Republican leaders might have had in mind was the influence that the House Committee on Government Contracts had recently achieved.

Charged with investigating fraud in the negotiation of military contracts, the Contracts Committee had already gained a degree of notoriety with its disclosures of fraud under John C. Frémont's tenure as commander in the West—a discovery that contributed to his removal from command. Although the committee did not publish its first official report until mid-December, Republican congressmen were aware of the potential power and influence wielded by an investigative body, either through its reports or simply from information leaked to the press. Indeed, in the case of the Contracts Committee, Lincoln actually used its members to achieve his ends since it consisted of several moderate Republican congressmen, such as Elihu Washburne, who were the president's supporters. In creating the Committee on the Conduct of the War, congressional leaders hoped to use the investigative committee as an independent weapon both to check and influence the executive branch if necessary. In the hands of such prominent Republicans as Wade and Chandler, armed with the power of exposure, an investigative committee might prove to be a powerful influence on government policy.[46]

In January 1862 Caroline R. Wade, the wife of Benjamin Wade, wrote gloomily about the inactivity of the Army of the Potomac. In her opinion, the only hope for the country was the newly formed Committee on the Conduct of the War. "If the nation *is* to be saved," she predicted, "that committee will be the efficient instrument." Given the temptation to use the committee as a vehicle to advance partisan objectives, its role in strengthening the Union war effort was questionable; it could become simply a nuisance to military authorities and administration officials. Granting that Congress had the right to investigate, it was still a matter of debate whether such investigations produced good or evil. As Brian Holden Reid remarks, "Clearly, the Joint Committee had a legal warrant to investigate the matters in which it chose to interest itself. A more equivocal conclusion may be delivered on the prudence, skill, judgement, and justice with which it exercised that power."

Could a congressional committee composed of civilians largely ignorant of military affairs contribute to the Union war effort? How would their investigations be regarded by the military or by the administration? What did the committee hope to uncover? Could it make army offices more conscientious in the discharge of their duty, or would it simply demoralize them? Would it gather information for legislation? Was it performing an oversight function? The committee members had wide latitude to inquire into any matters conceivably connected with military affairs. Was the ambiguous resolution that had created it a wise decision? Many of the answers depended on how the committee attempted to discharge its duties. It could subpoena witnesses, recommend legislation, and publish reports. If used properly and skillfully, this last function could become a tremendous power in shaping public opinion. Because the military was ultimately in the hands of a civilian leader, a president who presumably wanted to be reelected and therefore needed the support of important congressional leaders, the power of public disclosure could become a significant tool in shaping military policy. Clearly, the extent of the committee's potential influence depended on the president's response to its actions.[47]

Although the formation of the committee generated little publicity, by war's end it was the subject of bitter partisan controversy. Radical newspapers argued that its investigations had aided the war effort by bringing more accountability among the nation's military leaders and the individuals supplying war materials. Its critics saw the committee members as rank amateurs, interfering in military matters, motivated by purely partisan motives and having a demoralizing impact on the army. A thorough examination of the committee's activities should reveal its effect on the Union's military effort.

CHAPTER TWO

Investigating Bull Run and Ball's Bluff

Patterson and Bull Run

Reflecting on the responsibility of his party after the firing on Fort Sumter, Stephen A. Douglas offered some advice to a fellow Illinois Democrat:

> There was but one path of duty left to patriotic men[;] it was not a party question nor a question involving partizan policy it was a question of Government or no Government—Country or no country and hence it became the imperative duty of every Union man—Evry [*sic*] friend of Constitutional liberty to rally to the support of our common country, its government and Flag as the only means of checking the progress of revolution and preserving the Union of the States.

The outbreak of hostilities ushered in a novel political situation. For Republicans, the exercise of political power within the context of the Civil War was both new and perplexing. For Democrats, accustomed to majority status, playing the role of a loyal opposition in an uncertain political environment was equally difficult. Appeals for the suspension of partisan politics, as Douglas endorsed, abounded in the early stages of the conflict, with Union party coalitions springing up in many states in summer and fall 1861. Indeed, some political insiders believed that the war would end traditional partisan politics. Lincoln's friend and later Supreme Court justice David Davis told Secretary of War Simon Cameron that political parties were dead and that Republicans could no longer exist as a party organization. The administration bolstered this idea in the distribution of its military patronage, appointing a number of Democrats to high-ranking positions in the army. But the path that Douglas and others were advocating was antithetical to the traditions of American political life. By mid-1862 explicit partisan politics returned as the majority of Democrats rejected the Union party alternative and actively reestablished their independent Democratic organizations for the fall elections.[1]

In assessing the revival of partisanship, historians have emphasized a number of issues. Republican legislation on slavery, including the abolition of slavery in the District of Columbia in April 1862 and the Second Confiscation Act of July 1862, convinced many Democrats by mid-1862 that a war for emancipation had replaced the war for the Union and the Constitution. Economic depression, particularly in the Northwest where the closing of the Mississippi River was acutely felt, convinced many small farmers with Democratic leanings that their economic interests were being sacrificed to New England fanaticism. Moreover, arbitrary arrests, particularly of vocal Democratic critics of Republican policies, persuaded many members of the opposition party that they were being persecuted for political reasons.[2]

Although rarely mentioned in this context, the investigations of the Joint Committee on the Conduct of the War into the Union army's defeats at Bull Run and Ball's Bluff may have contributed to the reemergence of partisanship. In examining Bull Run and Ball's Bluff, the committee took deliberate aim at the philosophy of conciliation, the dominant thought on how war should be waged in the early stages of the conflict. Proponents of conciliation assumed that secession was the work of a few wealthy slaveholders who had seduced the bulk of the southern population into endorsing their cause. Widely supported by many prominent West Point–educated Union military officers and by Democratic political figures, this viewpoint sought to minimize the war's impact on southern civilians. Advocates of conciliation argued that if property rights (slaves included) were scrupulously protected, most average southerners would come to their senses and secession would eventually collapse.

Shortly after the war's beginning, however, Republican members of the CCW had become vociferous critics of conciliation, arguing that harsh measures should be enacted, regardless of their impact on southern civilians. Conciliation was widely accepted among the nation's regular army officers, which increased committee members' skepticism of it since they distrusted profoundly the majority of the nation's professionally educated soldiers. In its two initial investigations, the committee targeted a Democratic general who endorsed conciliation and who was conservative on the issues of slavery and property confiscation. Convinced that the war provided the opportunity for the triumph of free labor values, the committee's Republican majority believed that an army dominated by conservative Democrats jeopardized their goals. Employing typical Republican partisan strategies of the 1850s, when northern Democrats were routinely portrayed as dupes of Slave Power, the committee cast such generals as Robert Patterson and Charles Stone, well-known advocates of conciliation, in similar roles. Generals who fought for the Constitution or the Union without attacking the peculiar institution could not achieve military success or implement the war aims of the Republican party. Through its attacks on conservative advocates of conciliation, the committee formed the vanguard of Republican policy on slavery and on the vigorous prosecution of the war, but in so doing it helped destroy cooperation with the Democrats and thus complicated the waging of the war.[3]

Democrats had enthusiastically rallied around the flag in the aftermath of Fort Sumter; however, despite such patriotic displays, there remained a persistent skepticism about the consequences of civil war. Schooled in the eighteenth-century political philosophy of the English Whig party, nineteenth-century Democrats were wary of the excesses of power that were possible during a civil war and thus qualified narrowly their support for it. They would not endorse a war that sought to impose radical social and economic changes on the South; rather, they wanted simply to restore the Union and preserve the Constitution. Nor would most Democrats support a war that imposed harsh measures on southern civilians. Suspicious of military power, Democrats were distrustful of its excesses, whether it was directed toward innocent southern civilians or toward the restriction of the civil liberties of northerners. In the Bull Run and Ball's Bluff investigations, the CCW demonstrated that Republicans cared little about Democratic sensibilities in waging war. In the first, a Democratic general was made a scapegoat because he practiced conciliation; in the second, the despotic behavior that many Democrats associated with civil war was demonstrated in the arrest and imprisonment of Charles Stone.[4]

When Congress convened in December 1861, there were many indications that Republicans were no longer willing to wage the limited war that appealed to Democrats. The previous summer, in the aftermath of Bull Run, Congress had passed the Crittenden-Johnson resolution, an assurance to northern Democrats and the border states that the war had nothing to do with the abolition of slavery in the seceded states. In December the same Congress refused to readopt the resolution. "So stands the record of republican adherence to their vociferous 'Union' expressions of last summer and fall," remarked the Democratic Illinois *State Register*. A few days later, radical Republicans in Congress launched a bitter attack on Maj. Gen. Henry Wager Halleck for his General Order no. 3, which forbade fugitive slaves from coming into Union lines in his Department of the West. Republican congressman Owen Lovejoy of Illinois spearheaded the attack; Halleck was defended by Missouri's Frank Blair and Phillip Fouke of Illinois. During the course of the debate, radical Republican George Julian of Indiana attacked the administration, accusing it of endorsing the return of fugitive slaves to rebel owners. Lovejoy concluded the debate with a warning to supporters of Halleck's policy: "I am opposed to the Army of the United States being turned into slave catchers." If the army contained men who would fight only if slaves were returned, the nation was better off without them.[5]

In such an environment, the Joint Committee on the Conduct of the War began its investigation of the battle of Bull Run. Various explanations for the defeat had circulated for months. One popular reason, particularly among Democrats, held that radical Republicans were responsible for the catastrophe. Not only had these fanatics goaded the administration into battle much sooner than was reasonable, but the presence of a number of these same congressmen on the battlefield (including committee members Wade and Chandler) had added to the confusion. James Gordon Bennett's *New York Herald* championed this viewpoint, arguing that a small coterie of Republican congressmen, including Wade, Chandler, and Grimes, were the principal culprits. "The darkness of the caucus meeting cannot hide such doings from the public eye," the *Herald* commented. And if he were wise, Lincoln would "cut his administration from this abolition Jacobin club."[6]

Perhaps the most common interpretation for the Bull Run disaster focused on Maj. Gen. Robert Patterson, whose mission had been to prevent Johnston's forces at Winchester from reinforcing Beauregard at Manassas. In early July, Patterson's force of 15,000 men crossed the Potomac at Williamsport, Maryland, and advanced south to Martinsburg, Virginia. After remaining there for a number of days, Patterson marched further south to Bunker Hill, forcing Johnston to retreat to Winchester. At Bunker Hill, however, Patterson grew cautious. Scott had ordered him to attack Johnston but only if he felt certain of success; otherwise, he was to make a demonstration to hold Confederate forces there. Believing that Johnston had 40,000 men, and with his own force on the verge of disintegration because of the expiration of the three-month enlistee's terms, Patterson ruled out any offensive operations.

On July 16 Scott told Patterson that McDowell was ready to move; the next day Patterson sent out a small force that advanced toward Winchester until it came to a roadblock of felled trees and other obstructions that the Confederates had set up. Believing that McDowell would engage Beauregard on July 17 or 18, Patterson assumed his demonstration of the previous day had fulfilled his orders, and he retreated to Charlestown, Virginia. But McDowell had delayed in formulating a plan of attack. Meanwhile, on July 18, Johnston had been ordered to leave for Manassas, and most of his forces arrived on July 20 and 21, just in time for the battle. That Johnston had eluded Patterson was not a complete surprise, for Patterson had telegraphed the War Department as soon as he detected Johnston's absence on July 20, a full day before the battle. For many observers, however, Patterson had failed to fulfill his orders and was solely responsible for the Union defeat. "The only person everyone seemed to blame without qualification was Patterson," William C. Davis writes, "and he certainly deserved much of it."[7]

Robert Patterson was born in Ireland in 1792 and emigrated to Pennsylvania in 1798. On the eve of the Civil War, with the exception of Winfield Scott, he was the most experienced officer in the U.S. army, having served in the War of 1812 and the Mexican War. To many Republicans, however, Patterson was an ideal scapegoat. Not only was he a lifelong Democrat with business connections in the South, but he also was known for his support of southern rights, conservatism on slavery, and advocacy of conciliation. Just after the firing on Fort Sumter, angry Philadelphia residents, suspecting Patterson of southern sympathies, demonstrated at his home, jeering and pelting his house with rocks. Only when Patterson promised to lead them into battle did the crowd disperse. On June 3, 1861, Patterson aroused more suspicions when he told his troops, "It is your duty to punish sedition, you must protect the loyal, and, should the occasion offer, at once suppress servile insurrection."

After the Bull Run campaign, Republican newspapers routinely denounced him for questionable loyalty and his endorsement of conciliation. The *New York Daily Tribune* recommended that Patterson be court-martialed for "slackness of movement," but the *Chicago Tribune* was more vindictive, insinuating that Patterson was a friend of the South and slavery: "The miserable old man, is sipping his mint julips [sic] in elegant leisure, near the Pennsylvania border, diversifying his labors by returning escaped niggers to their rebel masters and imprisoning newspaper correspondents for reporting his inaction." Another Republican newspaper called for a formal investigation of his role in Bull Run, reasoning that his actions "give sufficient consistency to the previous suspicions of Patterson's fidelity."[8]

Understandably, Patterson believed he was being persecuted because his political sympathies were "not of the same party as the Administration." London *Times* correspondent, William Howard Russell, claimed that Patterson was being blamed because "his men would insist on going home in the face of the enemy as soon as their three month terms were up." Although Patterson was honorably discharged from the service shortly after Bull Run, the rumors continued. "Intimations against my loyalty have been insidiously circulated," Patterson complained to Cameron in fall 1861. "From the silence of my immediate commander [Scott], I can infer [that] he does not design to relieve me from the odium attached to these reports and rumors." A New York chaplain who accompanied Patterson's troops during the Bull Run campaign reported that Patterson would not attack because "he did not wish to shed blood" and that he waged war "on peace principles."

Another story suggested that Patterson was the brother-in-law of his Confederate counterpart in the valley, Joseph Johnston. One Philadelphia man, just prior to the committee's investigation, told Benjamin Wade that he had met a black man recently who had been impressed into Confederate service at Winchester. While there, he claimed to overhear Johnston say that he had received a letter from Patterson and that the two were relatives.[9]

That such a clamor should be raised against Patterson was not completely surprising, but his supporters believed it was unwarranted. Patterson's assistant adjutant general, Brig. Gen. Fitz-John Porter, complained to Ohio senator John Sherman, a volunteer aide to Patterson, about the unfairness of such attacks. "An *attack* by us upon Winchester would have been folly & ruin," claimed Porter; "the General has done his whole duty and he should have the credit, not opprobrium." The facts, Porter continued, showed that Patterson did far more than could be expected, given his resources; had McDowell won a victory Patterson would have been glorified. Eventually he would be vindicated, Porter predicted, and "that reaction will be made use of politically against the government."[10]

Nor was Patterson inactive in his own defense. On July 26, 1861, the *New York Times* printed a letter he had written dated the day before, claiming that Johnston was entrenched at Winchester and had received substantial reinforcements. With the terms of his own troops about to expire, he thought it prudent to fall back to Charlestown. In early August, he complained to John Sherman that he did not want to incriminate anyone, "but I will not permit others to relieve themselves from their error at my expense." Later in the month, he wrote Sherman asking for his help in securing his official correspondence. Although both Lincoln and Cameron, according to Patterson, had talked to a number of field officers who found "no fault whatever" in his actions, he was considering asking for a court of inquiry to clear up the matter.[11]

In November 1861, still concerned that he was a public scapegoat for Bull Run, Patterson began lobbying officials in Washington for a court of inquiry. He wrote to Secretary of War Cameron "that further silence on my part would confirm the impression that I plead guilty to the charges against my honor, my loyalty, and my military capacity." While waiting for the War Department to respond, Patterson delivered a public speech in Philadelphia defending his action and using his official correspondence, which had never been made public. The gist of his speech shifted the blame to then General-in-Chief Winfield Scott. According to Patterson, he had obeyed faithfully the intent of Scott's orders and had scrupulously kept him informed of his movements. Not only was Scott aware of Patterson's decision to move to

Charlestown, but he also had notified Scott when Johnston left Winchester the day before Bull Run.[12]

When the War Department finally responded to Patterson's request, it was refused on the grounds that Scott was in Europe. Failing to persuade Cameron, Patterson approached the president, who assured Patterson that he had obeyed his orders and done his duty. When asked about an investigation, Lincoln wavered, according to Patterson, telling him that public figures could never fully "escape abuse." As a last resort, Patterson asked Sherman to bring up his case in the Senate, and on December 17 Sherman introduced a resolution asking the War Department to publish the relevant correspondence on Bull Run. The request was denied on McClellan's advice that such a disclosure would not be in the public interest.[13]

Denied vindication through normal military channels, Patterson was pleasantly surprised to learn that the newly formed Joint Committee on the Conduct of the War would investigate Bull Run, beginning in late December. "At the time," Patterson wrote, "I was much gratified, supposing, of course, that the investigation would be full, fair, and candid." His elation, however, was short-lived, for Patterson soon became convinced that the committee was a "Star Chamber proceeding" whose object was "to prepare a report setting all fair play and truth at defiance."[14]

Thus the committee began its first examination of military affairs. Not only would the investigation of Bull Run set the tone for committee activities throughout the war, but it also would reveal basic attitudes toward military men and matters. If the committee were to inquire into all aspects of military affairs, then presumably some familiarity with strategic ideas, weaponry, the logistics of supply, and the training of an army might be appropriate. As a group, however, committee members were woefully ignorant of military matters and seemed particularly unqualified to pass judgment on military issues. In many respects, they resembled President Lincoln, the person constitutionally charged with prosecuting the war. Yet, unlike Lincoln, whose military ignorance was also tempered by a marked capacity to learn and understand the complexities of military strategy, members of the committee did not mature in their views on the conduct of war primarily because they did not deem it necessary; they already knew all that was essential.

In many respects, the committee's view on military affairs reflected popular prejudices against an educated, professional soldiery. The idea that high morale or "determination itself" would be sufficient to produce military victory prevailed. The popular view that courage and moral purity would suffice for training and discipline was much to the committee's liking. Throughout the war, the CCW showed a preference for the generals who endorsed

forward movement and frontal assaults and who spoke the rhetoric of vigorous action; it expressed disdain for generals who emphasized planning,
logistics, strategy, and a hands-off policy toward southern civilians. The
observation of Albert Castel that due to lack of alternatives frontal assaults
were the most prevalent type of battlefield tactic might appear to vindicate
the committee's viewpoint. Yet its preference for these methods was not the
outcome of any rational, scientific process but was based on a crude, intui-
tive sense that head-on combat was manly and brave while reliance on tactics and maneuver was cowardly.[15]

Not all committee members spoke extensively on military topics; however, Wade, Chandler, and Julian did frequently express opinions that revealed simplistic, amateurish, and unrealistic views on warfare. Echoing
popular misconceptions, they believed that the South could be defeated in a
single battle. Of course, this view was directly at odds with the opinions of
many professionally trained soldiers. As William T. Sherman would later
write, the North must understand "that the entire South, man, woman and
child are against us, armed and determined. It will call for a million men and
several years to put them down." Since the South would be fighting defen-
sively, it would have numerous advantages, advantages further strengthened
by one particularly significant technological innovation. The advent of the
minié ball and the use of rifled weapons revolutionized tactics.

Previously, it was possible to carry out frontal assaults successfully, but
the increased range of the rifle and the rapidity of fire meant that tactical
defense had gained an overwhelming advantage. "Bullets worked their greatest execution against the bodies of men advancing to the assault," writes John
K. Mahon. It was therefore not only possible but probable that the Confederacy, despite fewer soldiers, could survive for an extended period of time
by remaining on the defensive, which signaled the utter impossibility of defeating the South in a single dramatic confrontation, a fact lost on most
civilians. "Many civilians," writes Jones, "failed to understand the virtual
impossibility of fighting a single battle that destroyed an enemy or to grasp
the primacy of the defense and retreat." The reality of a prolonged defensive
war had little impact on the members of the CCW, who, like many civilians
and inexperienced volunteer soldiers, continued to hold uninformed views
on warfare.[16]

Throughout the Civil War, CCW chairman Benjamin Wade persisted in
the belief that the essence of military strategy was to confront the enemy and
slug it out until one of the combatants was annihilated. Hence, it is not surprising that early in the war Wade accused Gen. George McClellan of personal cowardice when the latter explained why a forward advance was not

in order for the Army of the Potomac in January 1862. Wade displayed similar ignorance in February 1862 when he confronted McClellan and asserted, "These 150,000 men . . . could whip the whole Confederacy if they were given a chance, . . . if I were their commander I would lead them across the Potomac, and they should not come back until they had won a victory and the war was ended, or they came in their coffins."[17]

A failure to grasp reality characterized the committee's assessment of a number of other tactical innovations adapted during the war, including the value of entrenchment. Had some generals adopted this practice earlier, it would have paid tremendous dividends. No doubt Albert Sidney Johnston's surprise attack on Grant's army at Shiloh would have been far less effective had Grant's army entrenched. And as military historians point out, by early 1863 entrenchment was universally adopted by the commanders on both sides—whether acting on the offensive or the defensive. Indeed, toward the end of the war, the common soldiers on both sides would entrench without waiting for orders; their outlook on warfare and on the definition of courage and manhood changed markedly as a result of combat experience. The viewpoint of committee members, however, remained static throughout the conflict. They seemed oblivious of the implication of technological developments, viewing them with scorn and ridicule, as if they were an indication of personal cowardice. For Wade and Chandler, entrenchment was a mark of a defective West Point education that stressed defense over offense. "You can set your West Point graduates to digging," Wade contemptuously remarked in one Senate debate in early 1863 although the value of such a practice should have been self-evident.[18]

Committee members were persistent critics of West Point and its graduates and believers in the intrinsic superiority of volunteer troops over regular army troops. When Massachusetts senator Henry Wilson proposed a bill in early 1862 to increase the size of the regular army, Zachariah Chandler was enthusiastic in his praise of volunteer soldiers while disparaging professionals. The fighting in the war, he argued, had been done by volunteers, "and I have quite as much faith in their continuing to do the fighting as I have in the Regular Army." Referring to West Point officers as do-nothing soldiers, Chandler characterized McClellan's reliance on military science as infernal cowardice. Indeed, Chandler was so confident in the ability of volunteer troops that he envisioned going to war with Great Britain if it recognized the Confederacy. "If England wants war we are ready and anxious," he blustered in fall 1861, just after Confederate envoys James Mason and John Slidell had been seized.

One of Wade's persistent themes was that military training was overrated. In January 1863 he spoke out against West Point, urging its abolishment. No national military academy need be established, he reasoned; state schools would include military science among their subjects, and individuals with a natural aptitude for warfare would emerge from the multitudes. As late as June 1864 Wade still spoke disparagingly of military training as a necessary component to facilitate fighting efficiency:

> You need not tell me that it adds courage to a man to go about drilling him until he is a worn out or a war-worn soldier. Give me the man with all the spirit and dash that a young man has about him when he goes fresh from home in all the vigor of life. He will never fight better than he does then, and the old idea that a soldier must be in training for several years before he is fit for the field is not at all applicable to our soldiery.

That a person who held such naive views on warfare chaired a major committee with broad discretion to investigate military matters certainly raises questions as to the utility of committee investigations.[19]

Distrusting regular army officers and military science, the committee clung to a simplistic psychopolitical concept of military strategy. To ensure military victory, northern troops had to be properly motivated. In order to achieve high morale, the Republican political program and war ideals had to be implemented. Once these goals were achieved, the Union soldiers, led by right-thinking generals, would overwhelm southern armies. Committee members assumed, without proof, that harsh war measures—the emancipation of slaves, the confiscation of rebel property, severe treatment of Confederate prisoners of war—would motivate Union soldiers and turn them into superior warriors without the benefit of adequate drilling and training. Furthermore, the committee's Republican majority in a cavalier manner dismissed the conciliatory viewpoint of most military men as not only flawed but also as fundamentally disloyal. "Why, sir, I am informed that a very large number of your generals in command to-day have more sympathy with the enemy than they have with the loyal cause," Chandler declared in the Senate in December 1861.[20]

Committee members gave numerous speeches throughout the war that expressed their ideas of warfare and military strategy. George Julian made clear his viewpoint most bluntly in a speech before the House of Representatives in early 1863. In reconstructing military history to that year, Julian, who endorsed emancipation as a war goal early on, applied a crude formula for evaluating military performance. "Democratic policy not only gave birth to the rebellion," he told the House, "but Democrats, and only Democrats, are in arms against their country." For Julian, every battlefield setback was the result of military leaders who were imbued with Democratic war goals— supporting a war for the Constitution and the Union but not attacking the institution of slavery: "Democratic policy, by thus perpetually deferring to slavery as a sacred thing, and to slaveholders as a superior order of men, has smothered that feeling of resentment in our armies which else would have been evoked, and the lack of which . . . [is] one of the serious obstacles to our success." Explanations were simple: victory resulted from high morale, equated with antislavery ideas; defeat was the consequence of Democratic war goals—restoring the Union and maintaining the Constitution without explicit reference to abolishing slavery. Julian and other committee members believed that too many Democrats were in high positions in the army, motivated by the wrong ideals. As he took great pains to demonstrate in his speech, these Democrats were responsible for the principal Union defeats.[21]

When the CCW began taking testimony on Bull Run in late December, many witnesses offered a variety of reasons for the disaster. A few, such as Gen. Charles Sanford, a commander of New York volunteers under Patterson, and Gen. Irvin McDowell, were extremely critical of Patterson's role. Many witnesses, however, talked only briefly of Patterson's failure, citing a variety of other reasons for the defeat that included the inexperience of the soldiers, the confusion that hampered the movement of the troops on the morning of July 21, delays in receiving supplies from Washington that forced McDowell to delay his attack by a couple of days, and the capture of two Union artillery batteries at a pivotal moment during the afternoon of the battle. Committee members focused on Patterson from the beginning, however, often asking leading questions designed to produce the desired response. In their zeal to discredit Patterson, they even suppressed documents that, while not exonerating his conduct, did add plausibility to his claims.[22]

On January 2, 1862, the *New York Daily Tribune* reported that Patterson would testify and that "the Committee will probably develop some curious facts." The journalist for the *New York Herald* predicted that if the correspondence between Scott and Patterson were published, the latter would be vindicated. Patterson's session before the committee was tense. When he asked to have unfavorable testimony read to him, Wade angrily responded, "We are not impeaching the conduct of any man. We are merely endeavoring to get all the light we can upon the conduct of the war." Wade did not want to allow Patterson to make his statement because, according to Patterson, he planned to introduce his official correspondence. Only when Andrew Johnson intervened was Patterson allowed to continue.[23]

There were many errors committed in Patterson's campaign in the valley, in particular, his chronic overestimation of Johnston's forces, which prompted his excessive caution and ultimately allowed Johnston to elude him. On this evidence Patterson could be rightly blamed for contributing to the defeat at Bull Run. Yet a number of points were in his favor, and Patterson developed them in his statement before the committee. First, his command, composed largely of three-month volunteers, was on the verge of disintegration, and he had communicated this fact to Scott in numerous dispatches. Second, Patterson had outlined his proposed movements, including his march to Charlestown, in a July 9 dispatch, specifically asking Scott if these proposed movements were sanctioned. When he received an affirmative response on July 12, Patterson believed the movement to Charlestown had been approved. Third, Scott had assured him that McDowell would attack Manassas on July 17; when Patterson retreated to Charlestown on the same day, he believed he had fulfilled the essence of Scott's orders. Finally, when he received positive information that rebel forces at Winchester had moved, he notified the War Department on July 20, a full day before Bull Run. He understood why the War Department had denied a court of inquiry, but as a consequence he had been subjected to "all manner of misrepresentations. . . . I am confident," Patterson concluded, that "this committee will see fair play."[24]

If Patterson expected fair play and the allegations of disloyalty and incompetence to be set aside, he was in for a rude shock. On January 8, 1862, Patterson was cross-examined by the committee. Daniel W. Gooch, the CCW's ablest lawyer, conducted the bulk of the examination and attempted to show that in moving from Bunker Hill to Charlestown on July 17, Patterson had violated the spirit of Scott's orders. Even though Scott had approved Patterson's July 9 proposal to move to Charlestown, Scott's consent presupposed that Patterson had fulfilled his obligation to keep Johnston at Winchester, Gooch maintained. If Patterson failed to do so, had not Scott ordered him to follow Johnston to Manassas? Patterson agreed, but his orders were contingent on his ability to hold and then to pursue Johnston. With the terms of his troops expiring, he could do neither. Referring to the dispatches of July 20 and 21, he claimed he had informed Scott not only of Johnston's movements but also of the disintegration of his force and his subsequent inability to pursue. Why had Patterson left Bunker Hill for Charlestown in the first place, asked Gooch, when he knew that Johnston would then be free to leave. His force was rapidly deteriorating, Patterson replied. "Why did you not communicate that fact to General Scott?" Gooch continued. Patterson quickly pointed out that he had sent telegrams to the War Department on July 16, 17, and 18, each warning Scott that his command was rapidly breaking up: "Active operations towards Winchester cannot be thought of until [the three-month enlistees] are replaced by three year men."[25]

Committee members, however, failed to accept Patterson's interpretation of these documents. "My question is," Gooch repeated, "why did you not inform General Scott that you were not then in a condition to offer any obstacle to Johnston's joining Beauregard?" Scott should have known this from the messages, Patterson maintained. As late as July 18, in response to a message from Scott, Patterson specifically asked whether he was ordered to attack but had received no reply. Further, Patterson assumed that his obligation ended on July 17, when McDowell would move. Why had Patterson assumed, Gooch continued, that the battle had taken place on that day when Scott had said on July 18 to be on guard lest Johnston elude him. Patterson argued that he had never supposed McDowell would delay four days and that Scott should have said as much in his messages. Still, if he had been ordered to attack, he would have complied. Since Patterson had been unable to hold Johnston, Wade asked if it was not important to let Scott know that Johnston had started for Manassas. "Undoubtedly it was," replied Patterson, "and the instant I got the information it was communicated to him." "As soon as he started you communicated the information?" asked Wade. "Not as soon as he started," Patterson countered, "but as soon as I knew it [July 20], without a moment's delay." Here was the most fundamental impasse. Clearly Patterson's behavior was far from distinguished, yet the committee refused to accept any of his explanations. This rigidity characterized the committee's treatment of the witnesses who defended Patterson's military record.[26]

Patterson's appearance before the committee did not generate much comment in the press, certainly not the kind of coverage produced by John C. Frémont's later appearance before the same body. Still, some newspapers noted the event. The *Boston Herald* remarked that the committee had positively established that Scott had never ordered Patterson to attack; the Washington correspondent of the *New York Herald* wrote that an important dispatch from Scott to Patterson had been tampered with so that Patterson never knew Scott's intentions (although the newspaper did not indicate who had altered the correspondence). Even Simon Cameron, whom Patterson had previously regarded as uncooperative, told Patterson that he had done his duty. Patterson, however, was unhappy with the way the committee had handled the investigation and believed his reputation was still tarnished by charges of secessionist sympathies. In late January he complained to John Sherman that his son Francis's nomination for brigadier general was being opposed "because his father is charged and most falsely with disloyalty." *Vanity Fair* gave substance to Patterson's charges that he was widely regarded as an incompetent general of questionable loyalty, publishing a satirical poem about the nomination, "Pater and Pater's Son."

> Most folk believe that we lost Bull Run
> By fault of General Patterson.
> And now his eldest hope, how queer!
> As a reward's made Brigadier!
> This way of paying for defeat
> The cause thereof, is rather neat.
> But let us trust—excuse the pun—
> the youth won't turn out *Pater's son.*

Undoubtedly angered by such attacks, Patterson asked Sherman to consult with Minnesota senator Henry Rice and then to defend him on the floor of the Senate.[27]

Patterson achieved a measure of restitution, but it was not through John Sherman or Henry Rice; it came from Francis P. Blair Jr. in the House of Representatives. Blair was no friend of the Committee on the Conduct of the War and was particularly annoyed with the committee's attempts to rehabilitate the reputation of his archenemy John C. Frémont, with whom Blair had quarreled bitterly over affairs in Missouri. Debate in the House on February 15 began harmlessly enough when an appropriation for the committee's stenographer was up for consideration. Charles Wickliffe of Kentucky used this as an opportunity to assail the committee for usurping executive authority and violating the separation of powers. Bull Run was raised when Wickliffe attacked those members of Congress who had been on the field of battle on July 21, implying that they had contributed to the Union defeat. Responding, Owen Lovejoy claimed that it was common knowledge that Patterson's failure to hold Johnston at Winchester was the real reason for defeat and that both Scott and McDowell agreed on this particular. When Frank Blair asserted that Patterson had informed Scott that Johnston had left for Manassas at least one day before the battle, committee members John Covode and Daniel Gooch lashed out. "I say that General Patterson never telegraphed any such thing to General Scott," Covode declared. Gooch agreed, asking Blair for the authority for such a statement. "I know the fact," Blair insisted, and both Lincoln and Scott were aware of it. Lincoln wanted to call off the attack, Blair continued, but Scott "disregarded the wish and advice of the President on the subject." Though Blair believed Patterson's overall conduct in the campaign was deplorable, he had at least aired a new perspective. When Covode insisted that Blair reveal the source of his information, Blair retorted, "The gentleman had better call me before his secret committee." Covode replied, "The gentleman substituted his belief and introduced it here as a matter of fact."[28]

On February 17, 1862, debate on the appropriation for the committee's stenographer continued. Armed with a dispatch from Patterson's aide, Col. Craig Biddle, Blair once again asserted that Scott had known of Johnston's presence at Bull Run at least one day before the battle. The point here was not whether Patterson personally sent the dispatch, argued Blair, but that it was sent. Covode did not reply to Blair, and Gooch admitted that his only real argument with Blair was whether Patterson had personally sent the dispatch. The issue of Patterson's loyalty was brought up when Cong. Horace Maynard of Tennessee claimed that secessionists in his state, where Patterson had relatives, had spread rumors questioning his loyalty. Charles Biddle of Pennsylvania then defended Patterson's loyalty, citing his Mexican War record and claiming that anyone who knew Patterson would never make such a charge.[29]

Patterson thanked Biddle for his remarks before the House, but he was extremely vexed with Blair for what he deemed to be "uncalled for and improper remarks." Angry because Blair did not regard his overall campaign as successfully executed, Patterson said he was surprised that Blair had drawn these conclusions with the information available to him, especially since the "course I pursued and the handling of my column had the decided approval of every officer in the Regular army." One Philadelphia resident, writing under the pen name "Vindex," also castigated Blair for his remarks. Patterson was being unfairly persecuted for his actions by "political enemies," the writer claimed. When the facts emerge, he predicted, Patterson's enemies will be covered "with shame and ignominy."[30]

Even in spring 1862, many Republican newspapers still claimed that Patterson had given Scott no warning of Johnston's movements on July 20. The *New York Daily Tribune* reported in late March that Moses Odell was traveling to New York to interview Winfield Scott, recently returned from Europe. The reason for the trip, the *Tribune* argued, was "some discrepancy in the testimony of Gen. Patterson and other officers in regard to the operation of the formers division." Scott's testimony was an extremely brief statement that did little to clear up the controversy. Scott admitted he had not read much of the relevant correspondence. Still, on April 1 the *Tribune* reported that the committee had conclusive evidence that Scott's orders to Patterson were clear and that the latter had not kept Scott informed of his movements. The *Tribune* also claimed that Scott had not received a message from Patterson informing him that Johnston had left Winchester. In a similar vein, the first issue of a new Republican journal, the *Continental Monthly,* featured an unflattering article about Patterson's conduct in the Shenandoah Valley. Claiming that Patterson's loyalty was not at issue, the article nonetheless contained a number of suggestions to the contrary, arguing that "rebel Thugs" idolized him.[31]

When Patterson published a defense of his Shenandoah campaign a few years later, he revealed that he had sent this message to Scott on July 20: "With a portion of his force Johnston left Winchester by the road to Millwood the afternoon of the 18th. His whole force was about thirty-five thousand two hundred." Patterson also maintained he had presented a copy of this dispatch to the committee. When John Covode saw the dispatch, according to Patterson, he acknowledged it to be true and claimed he had heard the same message from different sources.[32]

There can be little doubt that such a message was sent. First, it was generally common knowledge in Washington among journalists. London *Times* reporter William Howard Russell observed on July 20 that it was well known that Johnston had evaded Patterson. General Samuel P. Heintzelmen testified to the committee that Simon Cameron had given this information to McDowell a full day before the battle. Second, a copy of this dispatch appears in the *Official Records.* Patterson clearly would have presented the committee with a copy because it strengthened his case; however, when the committee published its report on Bull Run in April 1863, the dispatch did not appear among the documents submitted with Patterson's testimony. Since this was one of the most pivotal documents in his case, such an oversight was damaging and raises the question of why it was omitted.

Perhaps the critical dispatch was omitted by an oversight. Indeed, without concrete evidence, it is impossible to claim with absolute certainty that such an oversight was deliberate. At the same time, when the report on Bull Run appeared in April 1863, all pretense of bipartisan cooperation with the Democratic party had vanished. To place the Democrat Patterson, an advocate of conciliation, in the worst possible light by putting a disproportionate amount of the blame for Bull Run upon him certainly fit the beliefs and the motives of the committee's Republican majority. Democratic members of the committee surely had no interest in allowing such an omission. Throughout the investigation Moses Odell did not seem sympathetic toward Patterson, probably believing him to be old and incompetent. Perhaps Odell was not aware that the document had been left out of the published testimony, or if he was, he might not have thought it made much difference, given Patterson's overall conduct in the campaign. Andrew Johnson had spoken up for Patterson at his hearing before the committee, but when the report was published Johnson was long departed, replaced by Sen. Joseph A. Wright of Indiana. Wright had not participated in the hearings on Bull Run and at the time that the reports were being compiled was already back in Indiana, having been defeated for reelection in January 1863. Since he knew little about the investigation, Wright was not in a position to defend Patterson, even if he believed he had been wronged.

Throughout its investigation of Bull Run, the actions of the Committee on the Conduct of the War revealed that they had prejudged the matter, intending to make Patterson the scapegoat. First, a critical piece of evidence was overlooked—evidence that strengthened Patterson's case. Second, in view of the rumors that had circulated with respect to Patterson's disloyalty, the committee could have addressed that issue in a clear statement, yet it did not, thereby encouraging hearsay and innuendo.

Since Patterson was no longer an active general, the Bull Run investigation did not attract the sort of attention that other committee investigations generated. Still, to Democrats familiar with the facts of the case, a certain uneasiness must have prevailed, for there was a clear partisan aspect to the committee's proceedings. Undoubtedly, Patterson's conservatism on the slavery issue played a role in the treatment he received. At the same time, however, a larger bone of contention for committee members was the style of warfare, conciliation, that Patterson stood for, a limited war in which southern civilians would not suffer unduly. This conciliation style of warfare was most distinctly identified with the Democratic party, which wanted a war for the restoration of the Union and the preservation of the Constitution. Most Democrats believed that these goals could not be achieved if slavery was attacked or if the property rights of southern civilians were disregarded. Suspicious that the Civil War might provide a convenient excuse for the assumption of unwarranted powers, Democrats thought that the only legitimate method of waging war against the South entailed scrupulous regard for the rights of southern civilians. Republicans on the committee disagreed, and Patterson was a convenient scapegoat for the CCW's frustration with other prominent Democratic generals such as George McClellan. With the attack on Patterson in the Bull Run investigation, the committee communicated to the army's leadership that it regarded conciliation as a flawed military perspective that suggested lukewarm patriotism and a questionable commitment to suppressing the rebellion.

The committee's investigation raised the question of whether bipartisan cooperation, based on restoring the Union, could last for the duration of the war. For Democrats who accepted the conservative or conciliation point of view, the committee's work engendered a number of concerns. The fate of Charles Stone and the tactics employed in the investigation of the Union defeat at Ball's Bluff helped convince many Democrats that bipartisan cooperation with the Republican party was no longer practical or even desirable.

Ball's Bluff and Charles Stone

While at McClellan's headquarters on October 21, 1861, President Lincoln received news of the disaster at Ball's Bluff and of the death in that battle of his close friend, Oregon senator Edward D. Baker. Some forty miles northwest of Washington, Ball's Bluff was near the town of Leesburg, Virginia, an important link in Confederate communications between Centreville, Virginia, and the Shenandoah Valley. Hoping to dislodge rebel forces from Leesburg, McClellan ordered Union troops under Gen. Charles Pomeroy Stone stationed near Poolesville, Maryland, to "make a slight demonstration" against Leesburg from the Maryland side of the river. Stone immediately sent scouts across the Potomac who reported an unguarded rebel campsite. Hoping to take advantage of this piece of intelligence, Stone quickly dispatched several companies of the Fifteenth and Twentieth Massachusetts under Col. Charles Devens to investigate the report.

Devens, however, found no rebel camp, and after moving toward Leesburg, was quickly hard-pressed by rebel forces under Gen. Nathan Evans. Once Stone was apprised of Devens's situation, he ordered Baker to the scene with one battery of artillery and several companies of troops from the First California and Forty-second New York. A popular Republican politician but lacking military experience, Baker was reckless in his subsequent actions. Stone had not ordered him to cross the river regardless of all hazards. Instead, Baker was to examine the situation and then cross to support Devens or order him to retreat across the Potomac. Without bothering to inquire into the condition of Devens's command, Baker sent his entire force across the Potomac and deployed them in a clumsy military formation at the top of Ball's Bluff. It was not an easily defended spot, and Union troops were quickly in danger of being annihilated by Confederate forces. When Baker was killed in the melee, Union commanders decided to beat a hasty retreat down the bluff and recross the Potomac. Attempting to cross the river under heavy rebel fire and with limited means of transportation, Union forces quickly became disorganized. In the resulting confusion, almost one-half of Baker's command of 1,700 were killed, wounded, or captured.[33]

Shocked and mortified at the news, the president returned to the White House, where telegrams were received from General Stone, Baker's immediate superior, and Francis G. Young, an aide to Baker. Each spoke of confusion and disaster. On October 22, McClellan wired the president that the affair was far more serious than he had initially thought. When the facts about Ball's Bluff became public, a predictable outcry arose. "A disaster infinitely more serious in proportion to numbers engaged than that of Bull Run was suffered by the national forces at Edward's Ferry," declared *Frank Leslie's Illustrated Magazine,* the writer asking who had sent Baker into the "jaws of death."

The attempt to assign blame for Ball's Bluff not only created a controversy that lasted for months, but it also caused partisan strife in Congress. Many members of the Democratic party believed that blame for Ball's Bluff was assigned on the basis of political beliefs. The behavior of the Republican-dominated Committee on the Conduct of the War caused many Democrats to question the notion of bipartisan cooperation on the basis of the Union and the Constitution. Through the agency of the CCW, the investigation of Ball's Bluff became a referendum on war goals, and Democrats who were conservative on slavery and who endorsed conciliation viewed as fundamentally disloyal to the cause of the Union.[34]

The target in the Ball's Bluff investigation was Charles Pomeroy Stone. Born in Greenfield, Massachusetts, in 1824 and an 1845 graduate of West Point, Stone saw action in the Mexican War. He continued his military service until 1855, when he resigned to enter private business in California. Stone was in Washington, DC, prior to Lincoln's inauguration, and at the suggestion of Winfield Scott, he organized a force of volunteers to support the scanty number of regular troops in the city, thus ensuring that the inaugural went smoothly. Stone's conservatism and devotion to Democratic principles was well known. When Lincoln's friend Leonard Swett, a Bloomington, Illinois, lawyer, thanked Stone for his efforts on behalf of the president, Stone told him "that Lincoln should not be grateful to him, that he opposed his election, and that his efforts were 'for saving the Government.'" Stone was subsequently reappointed to the regular army as a colonel and received a brigadier general's commission in the volunteer army.[35]

Finger pointing began before the tragedy of Ball's Bluff was even a day old. Thurlow Weed, the Albany newspaper editor and an influential New York Republican, was at the White House shortly after news of the disaster reached Washington. While he was there, Baker's brother and son arrived and presented blood-stained papers alleged to be Stone's orders to Baker. According to Weed, the papers proved that Baker had followed Stone's orders. When Weed left to visit Secretary of State Seward, he happened to meet Assistant Secretary of War Thomas A. Scott, who was on his way to the Associated Press office with an account of the battle mildly unfavorable to Baker. After talking to Weed, however, Scott immediately went to the White House, confirmed Weed's story, and altered the press release to absolve Baker of any responsibility for the disaster. Other people were not so charitable to Baker. General McClellan told his divisional commanders that "the disaster at Leesburg was caused by the errors committed by the immediate Commander [Baker]—*not* General Stone." He later told his wife, "The man *directly* to blame for the affairs was Col. Baker who was killed—he was in command, disregarded entirely the instructions he received from Stone & violated all military rules & precautions."[36]

Supporters of Stone and of Baker soon were involved in a bitter dispute prompted by the publication in Washington newspapers of purported real copies of Stone's orders to Baker. According to these orders, Stone had given Baker a peremptory order to cross the Potomac and "make a dash on Leesburg." "I will obey General Stone's order but it will be my death-warrant," Baker reportedly had said. Republican newspapers quickly attacked Stone. "Is it generally deemed the part of a reconnaissance," asked the *Chicago Tribune*, "to make a dash in the center of the enemy's camp?" Another newspaper complained that Ball's Bluff was just another blunder by a regular army officer. It contrasted the situation of Stone with that of John C. Frémont, who, while performing his duties in the West, was constantly under attack by the administration; Stone, a regular army officer, would not even be investigated. The *Ashtabula Sentinel,* a radical newspaper in Benjamin Wade's hometown, continued this theme, arguing that it was absurd for the administration to talk about removing Frémont from his command when regular army officers survived such disasters as Ball's Bluff: "The people will want to know the standard by which competency is measured, when McClellan manages the movement on Leesburg, so as to lose a whole regiment in a mere demonstration."[37]

According to Stone, however, the orders published in the press were a "shameless forgery." Shortly thereafter, the *Washington Daily Intelligencer* published true copies of the orders, which had directed Baker to cross the river or to withdraw at his own discretion and to push the enemy if possible, but not to advance too far so as to avoid a trap. In Stone's official report on the matter, he claimed that the allegations of Baker's friends forced him to reveal "distinct violations of my orders and instructions" by Baker. Baker knew, Stone claimed, that the means of transportation to cross the Potomac were limited, and Stone assumed that Baker, once he had decided to cross, must have believed he had sufficient transportation. "That Colonel Baker was determined at all hazards to fight a battle is clear from the fact that he never crossed to examine the field," Stone told Assistant Adj. Gen. Seth Williams, nor did he even inquire about the position of troops already on the Virginia side until his entire force was over the river: "The plain truth is that this brave and impetuous soldier was determined at all hazards to bring on an action, and made use of the discretion allowed him to do so." When Francis G. Young, Baker's aide, filed an unsolicited report stating that the transportation between Harrison Island and Ball's Bluff was irregular and unorganized, Stone argued that his report was the product of a "fertile imagination." Young, claimed Stone, was acting as Baker's quartermaster and thus transportation was his own responsibility.[38]

When Congress met in December, Ball's Bluff was still a sore spot. New York congressman Roscoe Conkling introduced a resolution into the House demanding an explanation of the disaster from the War Department, and the battle played a prominent role in the debate establishing the Joint Committee on the Conduct of the War, which was expected to investigate the matter. As the committee prepared to investigate, the controversy accelerated. Newspapers reported that Stone was returning fugitive slaves and engaging in questionable communications with rebel commanders in the area. "Nigger catching," argued the *Chicago Tribune,* was Stone's "chief distinction." On December 18 Massachusetts senator Charles Sumner denounced Stone on the floor of the Senate. Stone, claimed Sumner, "is now adding to his achievements . . . by engaging in . . . the work of surrendering fugitive slaves." Even worse, continued Sumner, was his use of Massachusetts troops to do so, thereby discouraging enlistments. Sumner's comments drew an angry response from Stone, who denounced the speech as "a slander and a falsehood." "There can hardly be better proof that a soldier in the field is faithfully performing his duty," Stone told Sumner, "than the fact that while he is receiving the shot of the public enemy in front he is at the same time receiving viterpuration [*sic*] of a well-known coward [a clear reference to Sumner's beating at the hands of Preston Brooks] from a safe distance in the rear."[39]

It would be an exaggeration to claim that Democratic newspapers rushed to Stone's defense, but a number of them were uneasy about the attack on him, particularly because he was being persecuted for his conservatism on slavery and his determination, like so many regular army officers, to engage in warfare that would have minimal impact on southern civilians. Besides, the specific charge that Sumner raised, though politically popular in antislavery quarters, was certainly no violation of law. If Stone returned fugitive slaves to loyal owners, he was well within U.S. law and official government policy. Hence it is understandable that Democratic newspapers believed that a vindictive, partisan attack was being launched, one that violated the no-party calls of the previous summer and fall. The *Chicago Times* denounced Chandler, "the abolition Senator," when he introduced a Senate resolution to investigate Ball's Bluff. Claiming that Republicans made excuses for generals such as Frémont who agreed with them on the slavery issue, it asserted, "It is true that no general on the Potomac has made an abolition proclamation or is the god of any political party, and therefore has no friends to screen him from investigations." The Illinois *State Register* denounced Chandler for introducing another resolution instructing the Senate's Committee on Military Affairs to retire generals unwilling to attack slavery; it saw a test on the slavery issue being administered, and it spoke of a plot being fomented by Republican radicals "to array an opposition to the administration's policy in regard to the slaves." James Gordon Bennett's *New York Herald* denounced congressional radicals for endorsing war measures that were unconstitutional: "If the abolitionists in Congress will pass an act which abolishes the Constitution and dissolves the bonds of Union, then, we ask, for what is it that the nation is shedding its blood and treasure?" Similarly, Delaware's Sen. James F. Bayard spoke of a Republican plan to oust members of the Senate who would not endorse Republican war goals: "It would make my heart lighten to tell these Jacobins and fanatics exactly what I think of them."[40]

The leading Republicans on the committee, however, cared little about offending Democrats and destroying coalitions. Wade, Chandler, Julian, and Covode dismissed bipartisanship if they thought it compromised the war goals of the Republican party. Julian later reflected on early efforts to suspend partisan differences, declaring, "Very nearly allied to the policy of conciliating our opponents and thus building up their power, was the project of the Union party, encouraged by Republican politicians simultaneously with the beginning of this Administration." Committee Republicans had fervently assaulted the South, the Slave Power, and its northern Democratic allies throughout the 1850s, and they had enjoyed success by denouncing these opponents in vituperative terms. They saw no particular reason to abandon such a strategy, particularly when their constituents demanded rigorous measures against the South and severe punishment for northern Democrats who were tender toward the rebels. They viewed the war in terms of the struggle of free labor as opposed to the slaveocracy. Southern society would have to be completely remade, and on this point, there could be no compromise. Hans Trefousse remarks that "Wade's determination to remake the South after the conflict also corresponded to his deep-seated conviction that without social revolution the war would have been fought in vain."

Special venom was reserved for West Point, whose conservative Democratic graduates were viewed as having southern sympathies. The conciliationist tendencies among the regular army officers was, in and of itself, enough to cause doubts about the fidelity of army leadership in the minds of Republican committee members, and they were well aware that General Stone was a stickler when it came to protecting the rights of southern civilians and preventing plundering. Such attitudes toward war convinced many committee members that West Pointers were not serious about waging war. Chandler believed many regular army officers openly sympathized with the rebellion, and he and his colleagues' opinions on these matters were reinforced by the views of constituents. One of Chandler's correspondents spoke of the sorry state of the Army of Potomac and of the necessity of "purging the rottenness of this truly Democratic institution." Another complained that the whole problem with Ball's Bluff was that McClellan was trying to shield Stone "on the ground that West Point graduates must stand by each other." We could never hope for victory, he continued, with officers only "half loyal to the cause." As for Stone, he wondered, how "such small materials" could be made a brigadier general. Yet another correspondent praised Chandler for his resolution to investigate Ball's Bluff, saying, "It seems that regular army officers & doughfaces can make any amount of mistakes and all will be all right." These regular army officers, he continued, "are so accustomed to bow down to slavery they don't know any better." An Indianapolis man wrote Julian that his son had perished in the rebellion, "his beautiful face marred by traitors; himself a victim of Slavery. The administration did not notice the fact." Our leaders, he concluded, are more concerned with the escape of a slave than with one who is butchered by these southern aristocrats.[41]

The tenor of the committee's investigation was foreshadowed in the Senate in mid-December when a bill for increasing the number of West Point cadets was under consideration. Both Wade and Chandler raised vigorous objections to it, although it was sponsored by fellow radical Henry Wilson of Massachusetts. "I do not believe there can be found an institution on the face of the earth, or in the history of the world," argued Wade, "that has turned out so many false, ungrateful men as have emanated from this institution," an assertion that could not be supported statistically. Linking West Point with the oligarchic, closed society of the South, the antithesis of the Republican vision of a free labor society, Wade continued, "It is aristocratical;

Ohio Republican senator Benjamin F. Wade was chairman of the Committee on the Conduct of the War and a fierce critic of West Point. (Courtesy of the Cincinnati Historical Society)

it is exclusive . . . and it stands in the way of merit being advanced." Chandler then joined the attack. West Point had played false with the nation, he argued, and now provided the South with so many officers that the North's ability to wage war was hampered. Military education was fine, he thought, "but in God's name put no more West Point officers upon us at this time." The message was clear. Conservative West Point generals could not be trusted because they had much in common with the enemy; their intransigence on slavery and their determination to wage a limited war would hamper the Union effort and the triumph of Republican free labor principles.[42]

On January 5, 1862, Stone made his first appearance before the committee, but even earlier his opponents were actively attempting to prejudge the investigation. *New York Daily Tribune* editor Horace Greeley had already received communications that suggested that one of Stone's subordinates, Col. Charles A. Gorman, would deliberately distort matters to protect Stone. And Greeley had other information. He wrote Wade about a case in which Stone allegedly had refused a request from a northern woman to recover the body of her husband who had fallen at Ball's Bluff, a response that suggested rebel sympathies. The testimony of Confederate general Evans, according to Greeley, clinched the case: Evans stated that Stone had shown the warmest affections for southerners when he had been a student at West Point. The committee was also busy behind the scenes, gathering information that was damaging to Stone. It had at its disposal, one witness later testified, "a large corps of informers . . . whose business led them into all sorts of examinations of men and things at [the committee's] suggestion." The negative portrait of Stone that emerged as a result of the committee's investigation was probably due in part to the work of these informants.[43]

Stone was testy in his appearance before the committee. After refusing to answer questions about McClellan's plans, Stone gave a brief synopsis of his version of the battle. Critical to his testimony was his insistence that he had not given Baker a firm order to cross the Potomac. "You did not give Colonel Baker an order to cross?" inquired Wade. "No, sir; I did not," Stone replied. "Fortunately, there was a written order found in his hat, in which I gave him discretionary orders." Julian asked if there had been sufficient transportation to cross the river. Stone had his doubts but claimed that that problem was Baker's immediate responsibility, adding that Baker had not detailed any crews to manage the boats. Chandler asked why the troops that were crossed at Edward's Ferry, further down the Potomac, had not been sent to Ball's Bluff. Stone replied that the presence of rebel batteries made such a move hazardous.[44]

"It is said of you that you take slaves and return them to secessionists," Wade told Stone. "That is a slander that has been circulated very freely," responded Stone, "and, I am sorry to say, by men in official position. . . . It has been uttered on the floor of the Senate." According to Stone, he followed every directive of the War Department with respect to fugitive slaves. He did not allow slaves to be harbored in his camp, and on occasion, he had turned slaves out for selling whiskey to his troops. If slaves came into his lines from the enemy, he put them to work in the Quartermaster's Department. Julian

asked about a slave who might come into Stone's camp who was being pursued by a rebel slaveowner. Hesitating slightly, Stone claimed he had known
only one such case, and he had refused to surrender the slave because he was
known to have worked on rebel fortifications. When the session finally came
to an end, Stone's impression was that he had satisfied the committee members with the exception of Chandler, who he claimed asked foolish questions
and seemed not to understand the answers Stone gave.[45]

If members of the committee had been skeptical of Stone, his testimony
did little to allay their suspicions. Undoubtedly, these suspicions were further aroused a few days later when Roscoe Conkling raised the issue of Ball's
Bluff on the floor of the House. Angry that the War Department had ignored
his resolution asking for information about the disaster, Conkling, fresh from
his own examination of the battle site, was determined to force the issue in
Congress. Some radicals were privy to Conkling's intentions. Charles Sumner
wrote to Massachusetts governor John Andrew that Conkling would make
a speech in the House against Stone, "exposing [him] as responsible for the
disaster at Ball's Bluff. I think this will be well." Conkling was particularly distressed at the response of the War Department to the resolution; on
McClellan's advice, the department claimed that any response to it was not
in the national interest. "The resolution relates to a great national concern,"
Conkling argued, "it relates to an event which I believe to be the most atro-
cious military murder ever committed in our history as a people." Conkling
wanted to know why Ball's Bluff was chosen for the crossing, and why
adequate transportation was not provided. Stone had the means, yet only
1,700 out of an available 7,500 men were able to cross. This battle was over
before it began, Conkling asserted: "Their movements had been watched from
the start; and the rebels had prepared for them a feast of death, and had
calculated the number of guests who should partake of it." Conkling then
moved to resubmit his original resolution to the War Department.[46]

Democrats and border state Unionists were quick to respond to Conkling.
Military matters, argued William A. Richardson of Illinois, ought to be left
to army officials. "What are you going to do next?" he asked, "discuss it
before a town meeting?" John J. Crittenden of Kentucky concurred with
Richardson, arguing that Congress had no business investigating matters that
belonged to the executive. The only guaranteed effect of such prying, he
claimed, would be the demoralization of the army and a diminution of credibility for its leaders. "Let the army do its own business and we do ours,"
Crittenden recommended. Owen Lovejoy accused Crittenden of denying
civilian control of the military; we can and must investigate the military,
Lovejoy insisted. Shifting the debate to a referendum on slavery, he asserted,

"The generals who conduct our armies have no soul or earnestness in the cause," a lack that he linked to their refusal to attack slavery and that thus diminished the military's chances for success. "We have been ruled, tyrannized over, by this slave power long enough," argued Lovejoy, and must no longer let this institution stand in the way. When the resubmitted resolution, which simply asked for information about Ball's Bluff, came to a vote, it passed 79 to 54. Each Republican member of the committee voted for it; Moses Odell did not vote.[47]

The Committee on the Conduct of the War continued to take testimony on Ball's Bluff for the rest of January and February 1862 in a rumor-charged atmosphere, increasingly hostile to Stone for his alleged affections for the South. In an article intended to paint him as resembling the slave oligarchs of the South, the *Chicago Tribune* described Stone as "fussy, pompous, and vain." Not only did he admire slavery, the newspaper charged, but Stone also would much rather return fugitive slaves to their masters than care for his own wounded. "The public will be willing to hear how fully Gen. Stone is responsible for the Ball's Bluff disaster, and even to hear that he has resigned." The *New York Times* reported that rumors were spreading so rapidly about Stone that it doubted that he could ever be effective as a commander.

Adding to the mood of distrust were persistent rumors of disloyalty in the Army of the Potomac. Newspaper reports claimed that an army surgeon appeared before the committee and told of the treasonous attitudes of many regular army officers. He quoted one officer as saying that "he would like to turn his artillery on Congress before inflicting any harm on Jeff. Davis." The surgeon would not reveal the name of the officer because it would have been unfair to single him out when "the same feeling [is] common among regular West Point officers." The hostility of West Point officers toward any attack on slavery, according to one newspaper, convinced Wade that the Knights of the Golden Circle had hundreds of lodges in the army, "instituted and patronized by West Point officers, most of whom were Breckinridge Democrats, as bitterly proslavery now as either Breckinridge or Jeff Davis." In such an overheated environment, Stone could hardly expect a fair hearing.[48]

"It is a sort of standing joke among us," testified Maj. J. J. Dimmick of the Second Regiment of the New York State militia, "that this is a very civil war." Indeed the testimony of many witnesses who appeared before the committee painted Stone as an ally of the South. Lieutenant Phillip J. Downey, also of the Second New York, claimed Stone allowed one woman to pass over the Potomac into rebel territory with a huge trunk and other materials, which Union soldiers were not allowed to examine. The same woman, Downey contended, was known to have a husband in the rebel army. Further, Stone regularly allowed letters to pass from the Maryland side to the Virginia side to residents who were known to be "strongly secesh." Major Dimmick also testified to the exchange of packages and letters between both sides as well as numerous flags of truce. "The impression seems to be that General Stone is altogether too civil to the rebels," stated Dimmick, who also claimed that Confederate officers had the highest regard for Stone, referring to him as "a gentleman." Many of the soldiers, however, regarded Stone as a traitor and secessionist. Colonel George W. B. Tompkins questioned Stone's loyalty because he did not allow troops at Edward's Ferry to flank Confederate forces attacking Baker at Ball's Bluff. "Did you see any batteries, or anything of that kind that would have prevented your going up to Ball's Bluff?" asked Chandler. "No, sir, I did not," answered Tompkins. "We did not receive any fire from any batteries." Few men in his regiment wanted to serve under Stone, he added. Wade asked if they doubted his military skill or his loyalty. "Both," replied Tompkins. "I heard one officer in my own camp say distinctly that General Stone was a secessionist, and he would stake his existence on it."[49]

The testimony most devastating to Stone's military abilities was presented by Baker's aide, Francis G. Young. Young's motives were not only to clear Baker's name but also to punish Stone for court-martialing Young shortly after Ball's Bluff for absence from his regiment without leave. After Young was dismissed from the service in early January, he wrote President Lincoln, complaining that "overzeal for my Regiment and in defending the memory of Col. Baker are the real cause of my trouble."[50]

Young appeared before the committee on the morning of January 16. He portrayed Stone as a harsh, aristocratic officer who was responsible for Baker's death. According to Young, on October 20, Stone sent Baker and his California Regiment to Conrad's Ferry and then issued a peremptory order to cross the river when gunfire was heard. When Young asked for additional orders, Stone "spoke very imperiously and curt, as he always does, and said: you have your orders sir." When Baker was told this, he exclaimed, "That can't be." There was not enough transportation, Baker insisted: "Young, you are sure you understood Stone?" Once Baker crossed his troops at Ball's Bluff, he expected Stone to send up troops from Edward's Ferry. When Young later asked Stone about this, he replied, "No one knew better than Colonel Baker that it was impossible to reinforce you on the left . . . because there is a fortification half-way between the two places."

CHANDLER: If there was a fortification there, do you suppose it had any guns in it then?

YOUNG: I never heard that there were. I have been riding up and down there on the Maryland side, as I would up and down Pennsylvania Avenue here, and I never heard of it.

WADE: And the first mention you ever heard of it was the excuse of General Stone for not sending reinforcements up to you?

YOUNG: Yes, sir.[51]

Perhaps the most controversial feature of Young's testimony was his claim to possess true copies of Stone's peremptory orders directing Baker to cross the Potomac as soon as he heard firing on the Virginia side. Young told the committee that he had preserved these orders, covered with Baker's blood and brains, and had had them published to demonstrate that Baker was not responsible for the disaster. He passed these copies on to Assistant Secretary of War E. D. Townsend, who, at the time, had promised to return them at Young's request but who now refused to do so.

For a number of reasons, however, Young's story seems preposterous. If Thurlow Weed is to be believed, the White House had already seen copies of the so-called orders. If they demonstrated conclusively that Stone had given Baker a peremptory order, then surely Lincoln would have done all in his power to exonerate Baker and cashier Stone, especially since Baker was his friend. There was no reason for him to allow the War Department to suppress evidence in this case. Second, even by Young's admission, Lincoln was skeptical of his account of the battle, finding it riddled with contradictions. So worried was he about his lack of credibility with the president, Young persuaded Wade to talk to Lincoln on his behalf. Third, surely the committee would have asked the War Department for copies of such orders if they did exist. Young probably was confused about the exact meaning of the orders, being a novice in military matters, and he had an obvious motive for advancing his interpretation. Since Stone held him responsible for the bungled transportation, such a reading of the orders shifted the blame back to Stone. And Young could throw additional suspicion on Stone by attacking his loyalty, which he did with impunity, remarking that "General Stone is pretty unanimously regarded as not a true, loyal man."[52]

Stone was not without defenders before the committee. Captain Clinton Berry, stationed at Edward's Ferry, supported Stone's claim that rebel batteries prevented forces there from coming to Baker's assistance. Moreover, he discounted testimony that suspect communications were being exchanged with the enemy. "I was always under the impression that if such communications were sent over," he told the committee, "General Stone had his reliable, good Union men over there to give him information." Church Howe, a quartermaster in the Fifteenth Massachusetts, testified that there was frequent communication with the rebel side but that all letters and packages that passed back and forth were entirely regular; there was nothing sinister about them. Although Howe believed Stone had ordered Baker across the river, Howe was critical of Baker's battlefield tactics, claiming he never examined the field of battle or consulted anyone about it. Finally, Howe claimed that rebel batteries prevented forces at Edward's Ferry from helping Baker. "Are you sure there were guns in that work at the time of that battle?" asked Wade. "We always had reason to believe so," replied Howe. "I am particular about that," Wade countered, "because you are the first man who had ever seen any guns there that we have come across." Apparently Wade's memory was failing him because just four days earlier, Clinton Berry had claimed that Union troops at Edward's Ferry were prevented from moving to Ball's Bluff because of rebel batteries.[53]

From the moment it received negative testimony about Stone, the committee passed the information to the War Department. On January 11, 1862, a subcommittee consisting of Chandler, Gooch, and Odell was appointed to present Simon Cameron with testimony on Stone. On January 27 a new subcommittee composed of Gooch, Chandler, and Julian met at the home of the new secretary of war, Edwin M. Stanton. Stanton was a political enigma. A Democrat who had been attorney general in the Buchanan administration, Stanton nevertheless had strong antislavery connections, including a law partnership with Benjamin Tappan. Given Stanton's service in the Buchanan administration, many Democrats saw his appointment as a concession to them; others, however, complained that Stanton lacked firm convictions, and apparently he was adept at maneuvering between different political factions. One Pittsburgh resident told John Covode that Stanton was a bully boy and that no one in the city was quite sure about his political convictions.

Still, from the beginning of his tenure as war secretary, Stanton got along well with the committee, and it performed a number of investigative services that the War Department was unable to do itself. Although it is unknown what transpired at the January 27 meeting between Stanton and the committee, surely it was more than coincidence that Stanton issued orders for Stone's arrest the next day, despite Wade's later contention that the committee had nothing to do with it. McClellan convinced the secretary to delay the orders, insisting that Stone should have an opportunity to answer such testimony before the committee. On January 31 Stone once again appeared before the CCW.[54]

When Stone appeared, he told the congressmen he did so at Stanton's direction and that he knew nothing about the character of the evidence against him except that it impugned his loyalty. Without allowing Stone to examine the testimony against him, Wade summarized it: he was negligent in providing transportation, he allowed communications to take place and permitted flags of truce of questionable character, and he allowed the rebels to build fortifications right under his guns. Stone responded to each charge but particularly bristled at the second one, stating that it was a "humiliation I had hoped I never should be subjected to." Referring to his service in Washington during the early days of the Lincoln administration, Stone asserted, "I could have surrendered Washington. And now I will swear that this government has not a more faithful soldier." None of his communications with the enemy at Leesburg was improper, Stone argued, and each had the sanction of the War Department. Every package received from the rebels was thoroughly examined, and most of the items sent to the rebels were provisions for Union prisoners who were inadequately supplied in Confederate prisons; the enemy never received any military information from these exchanges. As to the first charge, Stone claimed there was sufficient transportation at Ball's Bluff, but Baker, who had discretionary power, had mismanaged it. The last charge was equally false, and Stone wondered where the committee had secured its information since neither of his artillery experts had testified before it. "I believe I have stated to you all that we deemed of importance," Wade told Stone near the conclusion of his interview, "and, of course we are very glad to hear your explanation."[55]

In early February the *New York Daily Tribune* wrote that previous reports of Stone's arrest were untrue but that Stanton and the committee were in consultation on the matter. It is doubtful that the committee was convinced that Stone had adequately refuted testimony against him. Had they been, Stanton would have modified his order to arrest Stone and relieve him from command. Indeed, throughout the latter part of January and early February, many Republicans were convinced that disloyalty existed in the Army of the Potomac and that it accounted for delays and lack of military success. *Chicago Tribune* editor Joseph Medill complained to Stanton about lukewarm officers in the army who were virtually secessionists and would not strike at the rebels or their slaves. We are a "*betrayed people,*" Medill told Stanton. One of Wade's constituents complained that "there is treachery to the Republic at work." Wade's own son, James, wrote his mother, "I am discouraged with the progress of the war and do not see any prospect—the traitors are still in the majority at Washington and in the army."

These negative opinions surely increased the pressure for Stone's arrest, tainted as he was with charges of disloyalty. Attorney General Edward Bates described a meeting between Col. James Van Allen and McClellan in early February, during which McClellan had said that the committee wanted a victim, and Van Allen had replied, "Yes—and when they have once tasted blood, got one victim, no one can tell who will be the next victim!" On hearing this, McClellan supposedly "colored up, and the conversation ceased." Although Bates claimed to know little about Stone's case, he believed that if Stanton succumbed to committee pressures it would create a "precedent for congressional interference with the command of the army." "I wrote a *confidential* note to Mr. Stanton," Bates observed, "to put him on his guard against hastily complying with the demand."[56]

Nevertheless, the order stood; and McClellan, on February 8, 1862, ordered Stone's arrest and imprisonment in Fort Lafayette. Allen Pinkerton (who also used the name E. J. Allen) had presented McClellan with the evidence of a Leesburg refugee that corroborated many of the allegations made in committee testimony. McClellan's motivation is unclear, although if he failed to follow Stanton's directive, he could have been removed from command. Perhaps he thought that an arrest followed by a court-martial would be the only way for Stone to redeem his tarnished reputation.[57]

The actions and motives of Democratic members on the committee during the Ball's Bluff investigation are puzzling. If Stone was being cast in the role of a southern-sympathizing tool of the Slave Power, then Andrew Johnson and Moses Odell should have defended him, arguing that Stone was being assailed by Republicans on the committee because his reasons for fighting the war had nothing to do with slavery. A number of factors could have influenced Johnson and Odell. First, personal reasons might have prevented them from speaking out forcefully for Stone. Both members surely were aware that Republicans were using Stone indirectly to attack George McClellan, the rising political hopeful of the Democratic party. Johnson possibly regarded McClellan as a powerful political rival for the 1864 Democratic presidential nomination. Second, neither Odell nor Johnson was a military expert; therefore, when presented with evidence that impugned Stone's loyalty and military judgment, they could have believed it. Further, each had made a number of public statements denouncing secession and disloyalty. "I am for the Constitution of the country and the enforcement of the laws—for the Stars and Stripes—for the flag which has protected us all," Odell had told a New York City audience. "That flag has been trailed in the dust by those whom it protected. I have no apology to make for those who did this, and I have no quarter to give until that insult has been avenged." Ironically, on the day Stone made his second appearance before the committee, Johnson addressed the Senate, delivering a scathing speech in support of expelling Indiana senator Jesse D. Bright for treasonous activities and denouncing any talk of peace or compromise. "Talk not of compromise now," Johnson told Democratic advocates of peace. "What, sir, compromise with traitors with arms in their hands? Talk about our 'southern brethren' when they lay their swords at your throats and their bayonets at your bosoms!" Neither Odell nor Johnson had any sympathy for alleged secession sympathizers.[58]

Moreover, as some social psychologists suggest, the dynamics of the small group often suppress dissent and ideological differences. Both Johnson and Odell were more than token members of the committee; each was active in its affairs and therefore an integral member. In such a situation, members of small groups tend to gloss over differences and place a premium on consensus. As Irving L. Janis writes, "Members consider loyalty to the group the highest form of morality." Hence, while maintaining their ideological differences with Republican members, Johnson and Odell at the same time had compelling reasons not to question the direction of the committee's investigation of Ball's Bluff.[59]

Many Republicans were exuberant at the news of Stone's arrest. "General Stone, the slave catcher, has been broken in his command, and sent to Fort Lafayette under arrest," rejoiced the *Chicago Tribune.* Count Adam Gurowski wrote "bravo" in his diary when he received the news. "At the best," he continued, "Stone was one of those conceited regulars who admired slavery, and who would have wished to save the Union in their own peculiar way." After Bright's expulsion from the Senate, wrote the Indiana *True Republican,* Stone's imprisonment was the next best thing for the country. "The trumpet has sounded for the advance of our armies," the *New York Daily Tribune* wrote, "and the knell of traitors within already tolls." Similarly the *New York Times* believed his arrest was a good thing, claiming that the conclusion reached by the committee mirrored public opinion on the matter. Even more significantly, the *Times*'s Washington correspondent assumed that the committee's work had "doubtless led to this action against Gen. Stone."[60]

Opposition newspapers were skeptical of Stone's arrest, sensing partisan motivation. The *New York Herald,* for instance, characterized the arrest as a tragedy and suggested that the committee's entire investigation was really aimed at smearing McClellan. The *New York World* was not surprised at the arrest of Stone, yet it wondered why, if suspected of treason, he was kept in command for three months following Ball's Bluff. A few weeks later, the *National Intelligencer* complained that Stone had been imprisoned for three weeks but not charged with any crime. Indeed for many Democrats, Stone's arrest must have symbolized an increasing Republican intolerance on the issue of civil liberties. Though not referring to Stone specifically, Delaware senator James F. Bayard was extremely worried about excesses in that regard and could not have been pleased with the arrest. Complaining that his own speeches in the Senate were being confiscated by lowly officials in the Post Office, he complained, "'Like master like man'—and if the necessity of the times permits such invasions of civil rights by those high in power, what must we expect from their underlings." Even though many Democrats did not regard the arrest as a partisan act, some still must have viewed it with suspicion. It typified the excesses of power that many observers feared would stem from civil war.[61]

Stone's arrest caused a good deal of mortification within the Army of the Potomac. Some officers believed that he was responsible for the Ball's Bluff disaster, but few thought him guilty of deception and treason. "I must believe [Stone] is the victim of political malice," Gen. George Gordon Meade wrote his wife, "and that he will be vindicated from the charge of treachery and collusion with the enemy." Similarly, Gen. Samuel P. Heintzelman simply denied that Stone was capable of the disloyalty with which he was charged. Perhaps most disturbing to regular army officers was the increasing hostility toward West Point officers that the committee and radical newspapers expressed. Meade described the *New York Tribune* as downright violent in its hostility toward West Pointers. Indeed, one associate of Gen. Benjamin F. Butler, who acted as an unpaid investigator for the committee in early 1862, remarked that committee members were obsessed with the issue of loyalty: "The fidelity of the officers in the army," he recalled, "was a constant topic of discussion." Clearly, mistakes and irresponsibility should not be covered up; however, if the committee was predisposed to play the treason card as the explanation for every Union military setback, that strategy was bound to be counterproductive in the long run. It might cause army officers to become less forthcoming and more inclined instinctively to band together to ward off the politicians. In attacking Stone, the committee undoubtedly thought it was helping the Union war effort by discrediting and helping to remove a general who endorsed the conciliation style of warfare. Instead, it may have created additional concern among regular army officers and triggered the military's defense mechanism against these overly zealous civilian overseers.[62]

Meanwhile, Stone and his lawyers, Henry Parker and Joseph Bradley, attempted in vain to ascertain the reasons for his imprisonment and the nature of the charges against him. "I know there are men vile enough to fabricate proof to condemn you," Bradley warned Stone, shortly after he had approached Stanton unsuccessfully. Thwarted by War Department red tape, Bradley and Parker made little progress on the case. At the end of March, Bradley complained to Stanton that even as Stone's attorney, he was still completely ignorant of the charges against his client. Since he had recently seen newspaper reports of an impending court-martial for Stone, he wondered if charges had been preferred: "And I beg leave to ask if as his friend and counsel I may be permitted to see [the charges]." Failing to elicit a response from Stanton, Bradley and Parker finally enlisted the aid of Democratic senator James McDougall from California.[63]

McDougall, a Douglas Democrat, introduced a resolution in the Senate on April 15, 1862, requesting information about the exact circumstances of Stone's arrest, the charges against him, and the precise reason he had not been tried for any offense. Stone was no traitor, asserted McDougall, but the victim of rumor and innuendo. On three separate occasions, he had asked for a court of inquiry relative to Ball's Bluff; each time he was assured that he had nothing to worry about. Yet Stone was then arrested and imprisoned, without knowing who ordered his arrest or the charges against him. When his attorneys attempted to get information, McDougall continued, they received only cries of ignorance from the War Department. Taking direct aim at the Committee on the Conduct of the War, McDougall continued, "Has this form of Government been changed, and have we, instead of a President, a Senate, and a House of Representatives, a council of seven, not of ten, who wield absolute power and dominion?" Stanton refused to answer inquiries on the matter, charged McDougall. Stone had rights under the articles of war, but they were ignored. Unfortunately, he concluded, similar acts of oppression were happening throughout the North, a situation completely at odds with Americans' constitutional heritage and British traditions.[64]

I have listened for two hours to a "string of platitudes," responded Ben Wade. Bristling at McDougall's attack on the committee, he asserted that the CCW had had nothing to do with Stone's arrest. The committee had simply followed the instructions of Congress; it had investigated this matter and turned over the testimony to the proper authorities, although Wade did acknowledge that "probable cause" existed for Stone's arrest. Wade was disgusted with Stone's defenders who would use the Constitution to shield him: "Sir, I am tired of hearing these arguments in favor of traitors." He wondered why men like McDougall never mentioned the outrages being inflicted on loyal Union men in the South by traitors.[65]

McDougall answered Wade in the Senate on April 21. Assailing the committee for its secrecy, McDougall charged that it had never shown Stone any of the testimony against him. When Wade claimed that this accusation was false, McDougall asked why Stone's own attorneys had never seen the testimony or any charges against him. "Is there any law to punish traitors which contravenes the Constitution?" asked McDougall, "I take it not. The Constitution is the supreme law of the land, and the humblest man may invoke it." Wade spoke of prosecuting known traitors, yet the committee was not the judge. Shifting his attack to Stanton, McDougall argued that his actions were tyrannical and arbitrary: "Sir, who is this Secretary of War?" First he was a Breckinridge man, then a loyal Union supporter; "Sir, he belongs to the party in power."[66]

Wade asked why McDougall was assailing the committee; its members had simply carried out their constitutional duty by reporting its testimony on Ball's Bluff to the proper authorities. McDougall's charges were typical of a senator who was trying to reconstruct the old Democratic party, the rotten party of Buchanan and Breckinridge. "Just think of it," Wade asserted, "the southern Buchanan traitors reconstructing with the Breckinridge traitors of the North." McDougall's idea of the Constitution would hamper loyal men trying to uphold the nation. "We are yet told on this floor," Wade charged, "that we should be tender-footed, that we cannot tie the hands of a miserable traitor from giving information to the enemy. . . . Is that the logic of the Senator?"

When the Senate moved to a discussion of where to send his resolution, McDougall bristled at the suggestion that it be referred to the Committee on the Conduct of the War. When Chandler entered the debate, claiming that McDougall did not understand the committee's methods, an angry exchange followed. "Does the Senator from Michigan undertake to say that I have said anything . . . false?" asked McDougall. "I say that any man who says this is an inquisitorial committee says what is false," Chandler replied. When McDougall tried to follow up, he was denied the floor. "I will not answer your question," Chandler asserted. "You cannot afford to answer it," McDougall retorted. Chandler once again replied that any such accusation was false. Amid cries for order, McDougall shouted, "Do not shake your finger at me." The committee had done its duty, Chandler shot back, and had not acted irresponsibly. When Henry Wilson suggested that the resolution be adopted and sent directly to the president, the Senate agreed and the debate came to a halt.[67]

The Wade-McDougall debate took place in a context of increasing political suspicion. Democrats were skeptical of Republican commitment to the
professed war goals of preserving the Constitution and the Union, especially
in view of a number of Republican proposals on slavery and violations of
civil liberties. James Bayard, for instance, denounced the abolition of slavery
in the capital as a short-sighted measure that would destroy "any lingering
Union sentiments in the South." He wrote, "God help a country governed
by such men as now hold power—no one else can."

Wade's performance in the Senate particularly reinforced Democratic
suspicions. The *New York Herald* claimed that even Wade's friends thought
his remarks to McDougall were unwise. The reporter for the *Chicago Times*
attacked Wade for claiming that anyone who argued for constitutional liberties was a traitor: "Thank God, it requires something more than the *ipse dixit*
of such a man to convert the most sacred constitutional rights into treason."
Although there might have been some cause for Stone's imprisonment, holding him so long without trial was unacceptable. Still, "The impression pre-
vails in the best informed circles that his alleged offense is political and not
military, and that is far below the grade of treason." The *Indianapolis State
Sentinel* claimed that the men in control of the country, many serving on "the
notorious War Committee," assailed the principles upon which the country
was founded: freedom of the press, freedom of speech, and the writ of habeas corpus. The Illinois *State Register* attacked Wade for introducing a bill
shortly after the McDougall debate imposing a fine on anyone who falsely
claimed to have been arbitrarily imprisoned. Comparing such legislation to
the Alien and Sedition Acts, editor Charles Lanphier asserted, "Thus government officials are to have license to ride unmolested over the rights of
citizens, arresting and imprisoning whom they please."[68]

Republican supporters of Wade and the committee had a far different
reaction to his exchange with McDougall; most appreciated his no-holds-
barred approach and begged for more. Many clearly understood that the
attack on Stone was fundamentally a struggle against the conservative, conciliatory style of warfare practiced by West Point professionals. One soldier
in the Fourth Ohio Regiment told Wade that his remarks were admired by
"every man who is *earnest* in this war." A Massachusetts man wrote, "I love
to see these half and half traitors—cut up piecemeal," and a Chicago resident claimed that men like McDougall had been treated with far too much
tenderness in the past. "By the by," he wrote, "can't you wing that fellow
Vallandigham in some way[,] it would afford me much pleasure." A Dayton
man wrote Wade that McDougall had shown his "traitorous heart" during
the debate: "These are scathing truths, which when proclaimed in the pres-

ence of our Golden Circle traitors make them hang their heads like condemned criminals."[69]

After Lincoln received the Senate's resolution, he responded by stating that Stone had been arrested on his "general authority" but that he had not been tried because of difficulties in procuring witnesses for a military trial. He promised that charges and a trial would "be furnished him in due season." How much Lincoln knew of the particulars of the case is open to question. By his own admission a few years later, he knew little of the circumstances surrounding Stone's arrest since those events occurred when his son Willie had fallen ill and died. Stone's attorney, Joseph Bradley, was granted an audience with the president in late April. According to him, Lincoln insisted that Stanton had assured him that Stone was aware of the charges against him. When Bradley bluntly informed the president that this was not so, "he was a good deal surprized I thought at the directness and perhaps a little at the promptitude and vein of the reply." Lincoln told Bradley to see Stanton on the matter, but Bradley was skeptical that any good would come from a meeting with the secretary, especially since Stanton would probably connect Bradley with McDougall's attack on him.[70]

If Stone and his friends thought that Lincoln's response to the Senate would ensure a speedy disposition of the general's case, they were sadly mistaken. As the summer wore on, Stone remained in jail, finally making a personal appeal to the president on July 4, 1862. His effort eventually paid off; Stone was released from Fort Hamilton on August 16, 1862, some six months after his initial arrest and imprisonment. After sparring with War Department bureaucrats for several months, he was finally allowed to return to the army, taking a position as chief of staff for Gen. Nathaniel Banks in the Department of the Gulf in May 1863. When Banks's forces were defeated during the Red River expedition in April 1864, many Republican newspapers immediately blamed Stone for the disaster, despite little evidence to support such charges. Undoubtedly viewing him as a liability, the administration dismissed Stone from his position shortly thereafter. He finally resigned his regular army commission in September 1864 and went to work as a mining engineer. In 1869 he was recruited by the Khedive of Egypt to serve in the Egyptian army as a lieutenant and then as chief of staff; he remained there until 1883. Stone died in New York City in 1887, spending the last years of his life working as an engineer.[71]

Before Stone reported to Banks, however, the Committee on the Conduct of the War was extremely interested in once again interviewing him. Its members' motivations had changed significantly, for now their chief purpose was to discredit McClellan and damage his political prospects as the Democratic nominee for president in 1864, prospects already considered favorable in early 1863. Stone made his final appearance before the committee on February 27, 1863. What a difference a year had made. Instead of the mutual sparring, Stone was treated most courteously. He made a clear refutation of the charges against him, providing much more detailed explanations of his behavior. Previously, Stone had given incomplete answers to certain strategic questions because he had been so instructed by McClellan. This time he was more forthright, telling the committee that the entire Ball's Bluff maneuver had gone forward on the understanding that troops under Gen. George McCall were performing reconnaissance at Drainesville, Virginia, about a dozen miles from Ball's Bluff, and would thus be available to render assistance to Stone's forces under Baker. The point of the whole maneuver was to force rebel troops to abandon Leesburg, Virginia. McClellan, he claimed, had never given him a clear indication that these troops were being withdrawn on the day of the battle. Further, Stone gave exact accounts of the nature of questionable communications with rebel forces, indicating that in most circumstances he was acting in accordance with orders from General Scott and the War Department. "Why did you not give us these explanations when you were here before?" Wade inquired. "Because, if the chairman will remember," Stone responded, "the committee did not state to me the particular cases."

When Wade asked him who was responsible for his arrest, Stone was uncertain, although he told Wade that he no longer believed the committee had "solicited" his arrest. Stanton suggested the arrest was made at McClellan's insistence, but McClellan maintained it was Stanton's doing, prompted by the committee. Stone did tell the committee that only McClellan had the power to bring him before a court-martial. Undoubtedly Stone's change of tone in this round of testimony was colored by his sense that he had been abandoned by McClellan during the crisis.[72]

According to the *Detroit Post and Tribune,* the committee believed that Stone was merely the scapegoat, protecting a much higher army official. The likely suspect appeared before the committee just after Stone in early March 1863, Gen. George B. McClellan. Although removed from command in November 1862, McClellan was still popular in the country and particularly admired by the rank and file of the Army of the Potomac. The committee's Republican majority was locked in a deadly political struggle with the general for the very principles it believed were at stake in the rebellion. With the electoral gains Democrats had made in the fall 1862 elections, McClellan, a probable presidential nominee, represented a particular threat. The committee was already in the middle of constructing a report on the operations of the Army of the Potomac, which they hoped would crush McClellan; but saddling him with responsibility for the Ball's Bluff disaster would similarly serve to damage the general's reputation, a fact that he was well aware of and determined to contest at all costs.[73]

In an undoubtedly tense and hostile atmosphere, McClellan gave the committee a brief synopsis of his own actions during the Ball's Bluff affair. Daniel Gooch asked him whether he had informed Stone of the movements of General McCall. McClellan replied that he believed he had told Stone about McCall's movements; however, he never suggested that Stone cross the river, only that he make a demonstration. "I did not contemplate any crossing of the river by that order," McClellan told Wade, but wanted "merely to show a force in the vicinity of the river." When Wade replied that he did not understand how a demonstration on the Maryland side could possibly force the rebels to evacuate Leesburg, McClellan responded that he had informed Stone that McCall was at Drainesville and that "heavy reconnaissances were to move out in all directions." The problem was that by the time Stone's troops made their demonstration, McCall had already left Drainesville.

When McClellan returned for questioning on March 2, 1863, Gooch focused on Stone's arrest and who had ordered it. McClellan responded that he had followed an order given to him by the secretary of war, based on testimony taken by the committee. When this evidence was more or less corroborated by Allan Pinkerton, McClellan carried out the order. When asked why Stone had not been tried, McClellan said that although he had reminded Stanton several times, each time he was told that the committee was not through taking its testimony. "Was it understood that the committee were to prepare the case, or charges, against General Stone?" asked Gooch, adding that "the committee never had any such understanding." "My recollection is very clear that the Secretary gave me that understanding," McClellan responded.

Strictly speaking, Gooch was surely correct. The committee was not preparing a case against Stone, in any legal sense, because congressional committees did not engage in such activities. On the other hand, the suggestion that Stanton would not use its testimony and that it had nothing at all to do with Stone's arrest was both inaccurate and misleading. Stone's lack of a trial clearly had more to do with the secretary of war than with McClellan. Stephen Sears writes that McClellan did make several attempts to provide Stone a court of inquiry but without success. And it is only fair to point out that

McClellan was away from Washington, preoccupied with the Peninsula campaign during most of Stone's imprisonment.[74]

When the committee published its report on Ball's Bluff in April 1863, its criticism of Stone was considerably muted. Although the report stated that the transportation was inadequate for crossing large number of troops, the committee did not hold Stone completely accountable and seemed to believe his claim that he never received a call for reinforcements until it was too late. Neither did it make a judgment as to the possibility of sending forces from Edward's Ferry but merely indicated that testimony on this point was conflicting. Moreover, the committee took great pains to persuade the public that it had had nothing to do with Stone's arrest, that it had simply presented testimony against him to the proper authorities. As to why Stone was never made aware of the charges against him, the committee "have never been informed."[75]

Although the final report contained little of the venom and hostility that the committee had previously directed at Stone, the more subdued tone was not an indication that the committee's partisan spirit had diminished. Indeed, political partisanship often took its cues from the committee's activities. By the time the report was published, Stone was simply of little use to the CCW. His career ruined, his loyalty questioned, he presented no threat to Republican electoral chances or to the war goals envisioned by Republican committee members. He had been a useful symbol to parade before the country as an example of half-hearted Democratic prosecution of the war, but the real enemy was the man who had a legitimate chance to capture political power, George B. McClellan. By spring 1863 committee efforts were almost exclusively focused on discrediting him.

The methods employed by the committee in the investigations of Bull Run and Ball's Bluff are instructive. Its strategies and tactics not only contributed to the politicization of the army, but they also may have helped sharpen partisan divisions. Republican committee members no doubt felt justified in such activities in terms of the ideological goals of their party: to support generals who were conservative on such issues as confiscation and slavery meant the possibility of reunion with slavery still intact and southern society preserved.

The committee's position on a bipartisan approach to the war could best be summarized by George Julian's remarks in the House in February 1863. He claimed that the Republican party stood for freedom and that the Democrats, both devotees of Douglas and Breckinridge, stood for slavery. To allow them to direct the war would only entail shameful compromise, argued Julian, who asserted that the war's disasters stemmed from the administration's lack of firmness in advocating Republican principles. Instead it had adopted Democratic ideas, and disaster had been the result:

> Democratic policy, through General Patterson as its representative, detained a large army in the valley of Winchester which should have marched against General Johnston and his inferior force, thus securing the defeat and route of our army, instead of decisive victory . . . which would have crowned our arm. Democratic policy, personified by General McClellan and General Stone, sent Colonel Baker and his gallant men across the Potomac against a superior force, with one scow and two small boats as the only means of transportation.[76]

Indeed, in the eyes of Julian and committee Republicans, all military shortcomings could be traced to the actions and beliefs of Democratic generals.

Julian clearly felt justified in making such accusations; however, the performance of the committee in these two investigations had to raise doubts as to the utility of its activity. If the CCW had no qualms about attacking members of the opposition party, then bipartisan support for the war could not continue. Moreover, in the Ball's Bluff investigation, an active general had been attacked, creating a precedent for further investigations of any unsuccessful general. To Samuel P. Heintzelman, a corps commander in the Army of the Potomac, Stone's arrest and imprisonment was "as high-handed an outrage against personal liberty as could have been enacted during the Middle Ages." Yet an even greater danger lurked, for surely the real lesson to be learned from these investigations was that political beliefs influenced the judgments of the congressional inquisitors. If a military leader repudiated a politically conservative view of the war, he might, in the event of a military failure, avoid an embarrassing investigation. More important, a shrewd officer might acquire some potentially powerful allies when the time came for future advancement in the army.[77]

Critics of the committee would have been justified in questioning the point of the investigations. Little had been proved; little useful information had been discovered that previously had been unknown. In fastening the blame for Bull Run on Patterson, the committee was simply parroting the conclusions that many observers had drawn immediately after the battle. To avoid appointing an incompetent general to an important post was hardly a striking discovery. In the case of Ball's Bluff, the evidence established that someone in the army had erred although it was uncertain who that someone was. The committee refused to believe that Baker was at fault; it ultimately did not believe that Stone was directly culpable and largely for ideological reasons blamed McClellan. Hence, the only definite result of the Ball's Bluff investigation was that someone in the army's high command had erred, which was certainly apparent in the immediate aftermath of the battle without the aid of a congressional investigation.

The committee's work was problematic because it offered no practical solutions to the problems it uncovered, but then again, it could not. Given its members' lack of military background, the CCW was not capable of formulating precise solutions; it could fall back only on its rather elementary views of hard fighting and on the effect that rigorous political measures might have on raising army morale. Perhaps the investigations did not materially detract from the Union war effort, but it is unlikely that they aided it. At worst, they were an annoying side show; at best, a superfluous waste of time, energy, and resources.

CHAPTER THREE

Reconstructing
Emancipation's Martyr

At the same time that the Committee on the Conduct of the War was investigating the Union defeats at Bull Run and Ball's Bluff, it also inquired into the reasons for John C. Frémont's removal from the Department of the West. In Frémont's case, the committee attempted to return to command a general who had early on repudiated conciliation and who, in the view of the CCW's Republican members, agreed with their ideas about warfare.

At the outbreak of the Civil War, John C. Frémont was already a popular, even romantic, figure among the American public. Widely known for his expeditions exploring the western United States, the Pathfinder, as he was dubbed, was also the first presidential nominee of the newly formed Republican party in 1856. Because of Frémont's strong antislavery beliefs and his willingness to adopt harsh measures against the Confederacy, many Republicans rejoiced when in summer 1861 Lincoln appointed him to the top position in the West, comprising Illinois and all U.S. land from the Mississippi to the Rocky Mountains. To a party that had risen to power in the 1850s by employing harsh antisouthern rhetoric, Frémont seemed ideally suited to wage the type of war that many congressional Republicans envisioned, punishing the traitorous rebels by freeing their slaves and confiscating their property. Frémont, they believed, would repudiate conciliation and put the Slave Power in its place. Yet he quickly fell out of favor with an administration less willing to pursue vigorous measures early in the conflict. Shadowed by persistent charges of military incompetence and financial corruption, Frémont was relieved of command in early November 1861.[1]

Supporters of the general, however, would not let the issue rest. Convinced that charges of corruption and extravagance were fabrications, they accused the administration of dismissing Frémont for his antislavery beliefs, in particular, his August 30, 1861, proclamation that had authorized the seizure of rebel property and the freeing of slaves. The proclamation, however, had been quickly overruled by the president for a number of reasons, the most important being Lincoln's conviction that Frémont's policy would have a negative effect on the border states, particularly Kentucky. Believing that Kentucky's support for the Union was pivotal to the success of the northern military effort, Lincoln thought that Frémont's policy violated the official northern war goal, embodied in the Crittenden-Johnson resolution, to restore the Union without interference with slavery. Since the proclamation took direct aim at the institution of slavery, the president reasoned that it might alienate Kentucky residents (many of whom were slaveholders) and drive them into the Confederate camp. When Frémont was later removed from command, his supporters claimed that his proclamation was the sole reason for his dismissal. Frémont, they asserted, was a victim of proslavery politicians who thought that the Union could be reconstructed with slavery intact and who believed in benevolent treatment of the southern populace. Frémont's plight was one motivation behind the formation of the Joint Committee on the Conduct of the War. Not only would it attempt to invigorate a lackadaisical administration, but it would also rehabilitate Frémont and restore an advocate of vigorous war measures to an active command.[2]

From the moment he took command of the Department of the West, Frémont was controversial, and not solely because of his proclamation of emancipation. He was blamed for military disasters in his department. Just after he assumed command, Union forces under Gen. Nathaniel Lyon attacked a superior Confederate force at Wilson's Creek, southwest of Springfield, Missouri; Lyon was killed in the battle and Union troops were forced to fall back to Rolla, Missouri. Frémont was quickly criticized for failing to support Lyon adequately, despite receiving several urgent pleas from him for assistance. A few weeks later, Confederate forces under Gen. Sterling Price moved north and surrounded Union troops at Lexington, Missouri, approximately 200 miles west of St. Louis. Although Frémont ordered troops under Jefferson C. Davis at Jefferson City, Samuel Sturgis in western Missouri, and John Pope in northern Missouri to reinforce the troops in Lexington, none arrived on time and the Union force, under Col. James Mulligan, surrendered to Price on September 20, 1861. Opponents of Frémont pointed to this disaster as proof of his incompetence in military matters and lobbied the administration for his removal.[3]

Even more damaging to Frémont's position was a bitter feud that developed with the Blair family. Influential in national as well as in Missouri politics, Frank Blair Jr. and his brother, Postmaster General Montgomery Blair, had initially pressured Lincoln for Frémont's appointment to the top command in the West. But when Frank Blair and Frémont quarreled over contracts and military strategy, the Blairs became convinced that he was an incompetent bumbler and worked for his removal. Moreover, unflattering reports circulated throughout the country about the state of Frémont's department. He was accused of being inaccessible to people with important military information, and it was widely rumored that unscrupulous contractors in his department were defrauding the government, routinely over-charging on such items as rifles, horses, clothing, and construction materials.[4]

President Lincoln was caught in the middle. Frémont's opponents argued for his removal, but his supporters claimed that the charges against him were grossly exaggerated. Angry that Lincoln had modified his proclamation, they charged that opposition to Frémont resulted from his antislavery convictions. In order to make an informed decision, Lincoln sent several observers to his department to examine operations. In mid-September, Montgomery Blair and Quartermaster General Montgomery Meigs visited Missouri, and Secretary of War Simon Cameron traveled there in mid-October, accompanied by Sen. Zachariah Chandler and Adj. Gen. Lorenzo Thomas. None of these observers had anything good to say about Frémont, and Thomas, at Cameron's request, compiled a particularly unflattering report of his operations. When this same report was leaked to the press, Frémont's supporters were outraged. Adding weight to these negative assessments was the investigation of the House Committee on Government Contracts, whose members went to St. Louis in late October to examine allegations of corruption in the Department of the West. Created in July 1861, the Contracts Committee was formed to uncover fraud in military supply contracts. Although chaired by New York Republican Charles Van Wyck, the committee was dominated by two Republican congressmen, Henry Dawes of Massachusetts and Elihu Washburne of Illinois. Washburne, a close friend of the president, was amazed at the extent of corruption uncovered in Frémont's department. He wrote Lincoln that "the disclosure of corruption[,] extravagance and peculation are utterly astounding. We think the evidence will satisfy the public that a most formidable conspiracy has existed here to plunder the Government and that high officials have been prominently engaged in it."[5]

Throughout fall 1861, rumors of Frémont's impending removal circulated periodically. Whenever they did, bitter protests arose against the administration along with charges that Lincoln was betraying the antislavery principles of the Republican party. "My soul is full of bitterness," wrote one Indiana Republican after reading a report of Frémont's imminent removal. He was being sacrificed for his principles, the man continued, and the talk of waste and extravagance had been invented "simply to blind the people. . . . I hope for nothing from this administration," he concluded, "may the devil do well by them." A western newspaper complained that the administration ignored such disasters as Bull Run and Ball's Bluff while spending too much time on petty financial matters in Frémont's department: "After all these criminal blunders and in the midst of them, cabinet meeting after cabinet meeting is held, to see if Frémont has not, in the perilous condition of Missouri, had to pay a little too much for some of the munitions of war!"

Nevertheless, given Cameron's negative report and the revelations of the Contracts Committee, Lincoln decided that Frémont had to go. On October 24 the president sent the necessary orders to Maj. Gen. Samuel Curtis in St. Louis but attached a number of conditions to protect himself from charges that he had been unfair to Frémont. For weeks, the general had pursued Sterling Price and his Confederate army in southwestern Missouri. Since Frémont was apparently always on the verge of a great battle, Lincoln's orders stipulated that he was not to be relieved if he was either in the midst of battle or about to fight one. In such fashion, the president guarded against charges that he had deprived Frémont of a great victory and a chance to rebuild his military reputation. Correctly judging that neither of Lincoln's conditions applied, Curtis arranged for the orders to be executed. On November 4, 1861, Frémont was relieved and replaced by Maj. Gen. David Hunter.[6]

Frémont's removal created a sensation. Gustave Koerner, a prominent German-American political leader and an aide to the general, reported that "the conduct of the German troops at Springfield [Missouri] almost amounted to mutiny when Frémont was removed." Richard Smith of the *Cincinnati Gazette* asked Treasury Secretary Salmon Chase, "What meaneth these boisterous outbursts of indignation and these low mutterings favorable to a Western Confederacy that we hear?" Recruiting had fallen off, claimed Smith, and the people were no longer buying bonds to fund the war. He cautioned, "We are threatened with a revolution in the North." William Coggeshell, a secretary of Ohio governor William Dennison, reported, "Indignation at the removal of Frémont very decided. He may have been indiscreet . . . but he struck one Key Note [the proclamation], which has widespread vibrations." Many of Frémont's supporters contended that he had been denied the opportunity to prove himself in battle; the *New York Daily Tribune,* for instance, erroneously believed that he was on the eve of an important battle. The president, it claimed, had the right to remove any general, but the timing of this order was troubling in Frémont's case, since, the paper believed, his removal was intended to deny him an important victory.[7]

Lincoln and the country, however, had not heard the last of Frémont. The Blairs and their allies, though relieved with his removal, fretted that his supporters would attempt to rehabilitate the general by portraying him as a martyr for his antislavery beliefs. A correspondent of George McClellan complained that leading New York abolitionists would give Frémont a "grand triumphant entry" when he visited New York City in late November. "It is part of the program of the abolitionists," he warned, "to create opposition to the administration, and I would . . . suggest that the opportunity not be given them."

Many Republican congressmen, however, were clearly annoyed with Frémont's removal. "The Cabinet will find," wrote Indiana's Schuyler Colfax, that "there are a good many Frémont men left, despite the thousand charges against him." One constituent of Sen. Benjamin Wade recommended that he "stand up again for Frémont[,] for the people are for him whether he was right or wrong." A correspondent of Zachariah Chandler decried the attack on Frémont as shameful, describing it as one of the most infamous acts of the war. Frémont had been somewhat extravagant, the writer allowed, but how many millions had such defeats as Ball's Bluff and Bull Run cost the nation? According to Iowa's senator James W. Grimes, Frémont had been removed because of his proclamation. After he had issued it, Grimes told Sen. William Pitt Fessenden, a "regular conspiracy was entered into to destroy his influence in the country and with the army." Members of the Contracts Committee, Grimes claimed, were old enemies of Frémont and "were easily and speedily induced to let Cameron go, and begin on [Frémont]." One of the members of the Contracts Committee indeed admitted that none of the frauds could be linked to Frémont personally. No doubt many radicals in Congress shared the attitude of Colfax and Grimes.[8]

When the Joint Committee on the Conduct of the War was created in early December 1861, a primary reason for its formation was the administration's treatment of Frémont. Throughout the congressional debates, Grimes had championed the general's cause, and John Sherman, Republican senator from Ohio, had given the administration a savage tongue-lashing for publishing Adj. Gen. Lorenzo Thomas's report on Frémont's department. When the committee began taking testimony on his administration of the West in early January 1862, its actions were unsurprising.[9]

Before the investigation, however, Jessie Benton Frémont, Schuyler Colfax, and Horace Greeley actively campaigned to gain support for the general. Writing to Boston minister Thomas Starr King, Jessie Benton Frémont stated that her husband "was not willing or reconciled to see the cause [emancipation] muddled away or betrayed by those elected to uphold and promote it." The president, she continued, "would be in Springfield today & Mr. Seward in Albany if the voters of last November could have seen the record of this November." To Colfax she wrote, "Its about time for honesty to assert itself & send the shams to their original level."[10]

Colfax took up Frémont's cause by publicly responding to the attacks of hostile journalists. When the Washington correspondent for the *Chicago Tribune* wrote that he could not identify a single Frémont supporter in Con-

*Committee Republicans remained devoted to John C.
Frémont, despite his lackluster military performance.
(Courtesy of the Carl Sandburg Collection, University
of Illinois at Urbana-Champaign)*

gress, Colfax responded with a public letter to the paper. There were scores
of Frémont supporters, claimed Colfax, including Congressmen Thaddeus
Stevens, John F. Potter, C. B. Sedgwick, and John Covode. It was true, he
reasoned, that money was wasted in the West; however, much of this abuse
was the result of Frémont's subordinates, many of whom he neither had
appointed nor had the power to remove.[11]

Horace Greeley's *New York Tribune* tried to gain support for Frémont
by answering such hostile newspapers as the *New York Herald* with the
argument that he was no worse than anyone else. The *Tribune* claimed
Frémont's critics ignored that an investigation of any department in the army
would have uncovered waste and fraud. When he had arrived in St. Louis,
Frémont had faced crisis upon crisis, and it simply would not have been prac-

tical or wise to have worried too much about costs under such circumstances. The public should focus on Frémont's accomplishments. He put an army of 50,000 men in the field and constructed fortifications around St. Louis, which saved the city. Although he was assailed for the purchase of Hall carbines after the War Department had sold them for scrap, these same weapons were still being used in the field. Greeley concluded, "Thank God that we may never have Generals who will spend anything more precious than dollars and cents."[12]

In early January 1862, Vice President Hamlin wrote to his wife that Frémont was reported to be in line for another command, "but I do not know how it is." The people closer to Frémont, however, were confident, expecting a complete vindication before the CCW. "The Sergeant at arms of the Senate has just been in to give the subpoena of the Joint Committee for the Genl. to attend," wrote Jessie Benton Frémont; "this is the end of our silence & now will come justice & retribution." The (Richmond) Indiana *True Republican,* the organ of radical committee member George Julian, predicted that Frémont would silence the charges of his critics "and at one fell swoop he will drive *his enemies* and their accusations so deep into the pool of infamy, that neither *Tempus* nor *Eternum* can extricate them."[13]

On January 10, 1862, Frémont appeared before the committee. The *New York Daily Tribune* reported that the general gave an "elaborate" defense of his work in Missouri. In reality, the result of this first interview was anticlimactic; Chairman Wade asked Frémont only to prepare a written statement and appear before the committee at a later date. In the meantime, Frémont's supporters in Congress took the offensive. On January 14, 1862, Julian delivered a scathing speech in the House defending Frémont and castigating the administration for its caution on the slavery issue: those who believed that this rebellion had nothing to do with slavery were sadly mistaken. The rebellion had everything to do with slavery; why else had only slaveholding states revolted? "It is slavery which to-day has the government by the throat, and thus thrusts upon the issue of its life and death." Julian regretted that the administration handled slavery with "careful and studious tenderness." The administration's conduct toward Frémont was proof of its tenderness toward the rebels. Frémont had issued a proclamation of emancipation that was welcomed by the people, but the president had overruled him. If the administration was serious about winning the war, such caution toward slavery must vanish. For reasons of military necessity and morality, Julian concluded, the destruction of slavery must be the central objective of the war.[14]

Just a few days after Julian's speech, on January 17 Frémont appeared a second time before the committee. He read a carefully constructed document calculated to refute every charge brought against him as commander in the West. Not only had he assumed a command that was in total disarray, but he also had had no specific instructions from either the president or the War Department. Lacking supplies, weapons, and men, Frémont stated that he wrote Lincoln that he "would hazard everything for the defense of the Department you have confided in me, and trust to you for support." Since Lincoln never replied, Frémont assumed that he had been given carte blanche, a fact, he continued, that was confirmed by earlier instructions from Montgomery Blair. Blair had telegrammed Frémont: "You will have to do the best you can, and take all needful responsibility to defend and protect the people over whom you are especially set." In Frémont's view, Lincoln's silence and Blair's words justified his decision to take bold measures.[15]

Frémont next moved to specifics. He did his best to reinforce Lyon at Wilson's Creek and indeed was making arrangements to do so when Lyon attacked the enemy instead of waiting for reinforcements. He had also taken care of a number of ordnance matters without the necessary paperwork. In Washington Quartermaster General Meigs approved his actions because of the urgency of affairs in Missouri. Despite the problems and the chaos he had encountered, the Contracts Committee descended upon him in St. Louis, "encouraging insubordination, discrediting and weakening the authority of the commanding general then absent in the field," and generally attempting to make a case to the public for Frémont's removal. In regard to his proclamation of August 30, 1861, Frémont argued that it was necessitated by turbulent conditions in Missouri. Immediately after this, he claimed, he began to lose favor with Lincoln. Despite the obstacles, he had still managed to put an army in the field and was in pursuit of Price when he was removed from command.[16]

When Frémont returned for questioning on January 30, he found an extremely friendly group, with the exception of Moses Odell. Daniel W. Gooch conducted the bulk of the examination, asking questions designed to corroborate the main points of his previous testimony, for instance, inquiring why Frémont had built fortifications around St. Louis. Frémont replied that St. Louis was the center of his department, and the rebels wished to conquer the city. Frémont initially had instructed a Major Kappner to build five forts, but he then had switched to a more expensive contractor, Californian E. L. Beard, who charged considerably more because of the speed with which he was expected to construct additional fortifications. Gooch asked if Frémont had ever been asked to stop construction of these fortifications.

FREMONT: I was.
GOOCH: From whom did that order issue?
FREMONT: From the Secretary of War, through General Thomas.
GOOCH: Was the order complied with?
FREMONT: By me, no sir.

Frémont explained that he had told his adjutant general to protest to Cameron but never complied with the order because he thought the safety of St. Louis would be jeopardized: "I acted in my right as commanding general of that department, carrying on military operations. I considered the stoppage of these fortifications as inexpedient, and possibly dangerous for the army in the field."[17]

A few moments later, it was revealed that in late October Lincoln's close friend, Ward Hill Lamon, had gone West to recruit troops to complete a Virginia Union brigade. Illinois governor Richard Yates wanted the regiment, known as the Yates Phalanx (the Thirty-ninth Illinois), to be sent East with Lamon. Frémont obliged, in part, as a favor to Yates because of the number of troops he had already provided Missouri. "Was there not a military necessity," inquired Moses Odell, "why you should not have let that regiment go?" Frémont's reply was amazing. "Not strictly, I think. If there was not a military necessity for continuing the fortifications at St. Louis, there was not certainly a military necessity to keep one regiment, more or less, there." Frémont of course had just told the committee that he had protested and ultimately had not stopped work on the fortifications because they were a military necessity. For months, the generals and his supporters had been building the myth of Frémont, the wronged martyr of emancipation who was deprived of supplies and troops as his army relentlessly chased Price out of Missouri. That he would so casually allow this transfer of troops without protest seems remarkable. When Odell asked whether the transfer of the troops was costly, Frémont's response was equally remarkable: "That was not for me to consider at all. If it is agreeable to the President, and pleased him, that was all that concerned me."[18]

Had the majority on the committee not been in such a hurry to reconstruct Frémont's military reputation, they might have pursued this incident. It was hardly a military issue for Frémont, but, as with most controversies in his department, it was political. Ward Hill Lamon had indeed gone West to complete his Virginia brigade, although the precise authority he had from

Lincoln was hazy. Lamon's initial impression of affairs in the West was un-favorable, and he sent Lincoln a letter highly critical of Frémont and his military talents. Yet just a week later, Lamon recanted, telling Lincoln that a change in command at that juncture would be dangerous.

Lamon had received a number of letters during that week from Frémont, dictated by Jessie Benton Frémont, explaining the difficulties plaguing him and urging Lamon to exert his influence with the administration on Frémont's behalf. Yet it was probably the transfer of the Thirty-ninth Illinois from Missouri at this critical time that served as the quid pro quo. In exchange for the troops, Lamon would use his influence with Lincoln to keep Frémont in command. Thus Lamon and Frémont made common cause against Elihu Washburne of the Contracts Committee, who had not only attacked Frémont but had also complained to Lincoln of Lamon's activities in the West and of the bills generated by the transfer of the troops. For the conservative Lamon to ally himself with Frémont is puzzling, especially when one considers his well-known hatred for radical Republicans. Yet more significant is the fact that Frémont would weaken himself militarily for political leverage, a deci-sion that the majority of committee members would have preferred to ignore.[19]

Predictably, the committee took up the issue of Frémont's emancipation proclamation, taking great pains to allow the general to reiterate the point that his troubles with the Lincoln administration had begun with it. Julian asked, "You never heard of any dissatisfaction until the publication of that proclamation?" "No, sir," Frémont responded, "and I think the papers I have submitted to the committee will show that up to that time no dissatisfaction on the part of the administration had been shown." The committee mem-bers conveniently chose to forget, however, how controversial Frémont's proclamation was at the time. The pivotal border state of Kentucky was not firmly in the Union fold, and President Lincoln rightly believed that Frémont's actions were too provocative. As he reminded Illinois senator Orville Brown-ing, a conservative Republican who ironically supported Frémont's procla-mation, "You must understand that I took my course on the proclamation *because* of Kentucky." Frémont's policy, at the time, contradicted the senti-ments expressed by Congress in the Crittenden-Johnson resolution, and it represented a repudiation of conciliation. By using Frémont's testimony, the committee created the image of the general as the martyr of emancipation, assailed by the administration and by greedy politicians such as Frank Blair and removed from command on the eve of a great victory to satisfy proslavery interests and political hacks, thus frustrating the will of the people.[20]

Montgomery and Frank Blair appeared before the committee on Febru-ary 5 and 7. The former read a short, prepared statement during his session, but the latter was questioned in detail by a number of committee members, and he offered a vastly different interpretation of events in Missouri in fall 1861. Yet the testimony of both brothers was largely a pro forma exercise since the majority of committee members already believed that Frémont had been fully vindicated. As for the rest of the witnesses called before the committee during the latter part of February, the vast majority were pro-Frémont, including a number of persons who had served on his staff. Charles Zagonyi was head of Frémont's bodyguard; Maj. James Savage, Col. Isaac Wood, and Col. Anselm Albert were members of his staff. E. L. Beard, though not a staff member, had a vested interest in presenting pro-Frémont testimony since he had made a big profit on the construction of the St. Louis fortifications. A few of the witnesses were critical of Frémont, including Gen. David Hunter, who had succeeded him as commander of the department, but there were no witnesses from the Blairs' side. When Samuel Glover, a prominent St. Louis political figure and Blair ally, approached the committee with information on Frémont's affairs, he was ignored. There could scarcely have been a better group of witnesses for a whitewash.[21]

For all practical purposes, the investigation might as well have ended with Frémont's initial testimony. According to Jessie Benton Frémont, after he read his testimony, some of the committee members wanted to determine "the case then & there on its reading. The Chairman, Mr. Wade, said no witnesses were needed, that it was all proved up & every charge against Mr. Frémont exploded." She repeated this to Ralph Waldo Emerson, who was visiting Washington and called on her just after Frémont testified, telling him that Wade "had expressed himself, in terms more than elegant, to her on the outrage done to Frémont." She wrote Frederick Billings, an attorney and associate of the Frémonts, of their plans to give the testimony "immediate publicity," an act supposedly illegal under the committee's secrecy provisions. Once it was publicized, she reasoned, "the administration has only two courses open. One, to give Mr. Frémont such a command as his position entitles him & as the public will demand for him," or else, she concluded, "to recognize that he is so much identified with the principle of emancipation that they dare not endorse him & for that rule him out of the war." Just a few days later, Greeley's *Tribune* demanded publication of Frémont's testimony, claiming the people had a right to know his response to the numerous charges put forth in the Thomas report and by the Contracts Committee.[22]

At the January 25 meeting of the CCW, Gooch and Johnson were instructed by the other members to meet with the president to discuss Frémont's military administration of the West. On January 30 Gooch reported to the committee the results of the interview; no written record was kept. Nevertheless, it is not improbable that the subject of a new military command for Frémont was broached. A number of committee members were receiving pro-Frémont letters from their constituents confirming the course of action pursued by the committee's majority.[23]

Early in February, the *New York Times* reported that many congressmen, including members of the committee, were making urgent requests to Lincoln for Frémont's restoration to active duty. From Missouri, Gen. Henry Halleck, then commanding the Department of the West, wrote George McClellan that a movement was under way, through congressional maneuvers and mass meetings, to force the president to reappoint Frémont. Early in the month Benjamin Wade wrote Charles Dana of the *New York Tribune* "that the investigation has proceeded far enough to convince me beyond a doubt that no man since Admiral Byng was sacrificed by a weak and wicked administration to appease the wrath of an indignant people." Wade vowed to use his influence with Secretary of War Stanton to restore Frémont to an active command. Although he might have acted earlier, Wade continued, the committee had "only just reached a point in the investigation, enabling me to know with *certainty* that I am right." While no doubt sincere, Wade's statement was extraordinary considering that when he wrote Dana only one witness besides Frémont had been before the committee, and the Blairs had not yet testified.

On February 7 Jessie Benton Frémont wrote Frederick Billings that committee members had just met with Stanton, telling the secretary that Frémont had been completely exonerated "and that they came to ask for him a command." Stanton, she claimed, agreed to meet with Frémont that very evening to discuss his preferences. The secretary was already favorably disposed toward him, having told Dana on February 1, 1862, that "if Frémont has any fight in him he shall (so far as I am concerned) have a chance to show it, and I have told him so." As if to symbolize Frémont's vindication, the couple attended Mrs. Lincoln's ball on February 7, where the president introduced them to the McClellans. "The significance of so marked an occurrence," wrote the *New York Times*, "did not fail to impress the hundreds lookers-on, always ready to take and act upon an official cue." A few days later, a confident James Savage, an aide to Frémont, told John Fiala, Frémont's chief engineer in St. Louis "of the certainty of his receiving a command again and of his desire that you shall share his fortunes." Greeley's *New York Daily Tribune* reported that those in well-informed circles claimed Frémont would get a new command because he had been cleared of the charges against him by the Joint Committee on the Conduct of the War.[24]

Somewhat puzzling in the committee's zeal to vindicate Frémont is Zachariah Chandler's role. Unlike the other members, Chandler had had the opportunity to observe affairs in Missouri firsthand with Cameron and Thomas in mid-October 1861. He was not impressed and promptly wrote his wife that "Frémont is a failure." Yet Chandler apparently chose to overlook this. Undoubtedly, as a strong supporter of emancipation and other rigorous measures, he was ideologically sympathetic to Frémont. Here was a man who wanted to punish the rebels and crush the Slave Power. More important was Chandler's deteriorating assessment of the abilities of Army of the Potomac commander, George McClellan. As early as October 27, 1861, Chandler wrote his wife that Frémont, though disorganized, had at least attempted to act, but McClellan "has accomplished *nothing*." As fall turned into winter and the Army of the Potomac sat idle, Chandler grew angrier with McClellan. Adam Gurowski expressed Chandler's sentiments when he remarked that although Frémont had numerous problems in the West as well as personal shortcomings, he "had started a great initiative at a time when McClellan and three-fourths of the generals of his creation considered it a greater crime to strike at a *gentleman* slaveholder than to strike at the Union." Even with his faults, Frémont had struck a blow against slavery; McClellan had done nothing.[25]

By March 1 Frémont still had no appointment, and his supporters launched a two-pronged offensive to discredit the general's detractors and to force Lincoln's hand. First, Horace Greeley published Frémont's written statement before the CCW, complete with supporting documents and letters, including an August 26, 1861, letter from Montgomery Blair to Frémont critical of both Lincoln and Chase. Despite the secrecy provisions of committee proceedings, the *New York Daily Tribune* claimed the publication of this statement had met "with the approval of the committee, who will not withhold the balance of the testimony when the case shall be completed." Gooch, however, in the House on March 7 claimed to have had no knowledge of Frémont's intention to publish his statement, telling House members that Frémont had been informed of the secrecy provision of committee proceedings just as the other witnesses had been. Yet it is clear from Jessie Benton Frémont's January 21, 1862, letter to Frederick Billings that the Frémonts had always planned to publish the testimony. Undoubtedly they had the tacit consent of Wade, Chandler, Julian, and Covode. Indeed, given Wade's prior communication with Charles Dana, *Tribune* editor Horace Greeley must have known that the chairman wanted Frémont restored to an active command. In publishing Frémont's statement, Greeley clearly advanced the committee's objectives. Moreover, as official committee testimony, the publication carried more weight than any personal statement Frémont could have published. Further, the publication of Frémont's testimony might counteract the unflattering revelations in the recent report of the Contracts Committee, demonstrating the power of disclosure that congressional committees wielded.[26]

The counterpart to Greeley's publication was a speech in the House by Republican John P. C. Shanks from Indiana who had served as an aide to Frémont in Missouri. Shanks took particular aim at the Contracts Committee and at a resolution censuring Frémont for the purchase of 5,000 Hall carbines from contractor Simon Stevens, a young lawyer who had studied under Thaddeus Stevens but was no relation. The weapons had been scrapped for $3.50 apiece by the Ordnance Department and bought by Stevens from another contractor for $12.50. Stevens had had them machined for $1.00 and then had resold them to Frémont for $22.00, realizing a substantial profit from the transaction. According to Shanks, there was nothing wrong with Frémont's purchase of these weapons since at the time he was desperately short of rifles. If there was a guilty party, it was General Ripley of the Ordnance Department who had sold the weapons for $3.50 when they were still valued at $17.00, according to published government guidelines of August 1861.[27]

Shanks believed that Frémont was the victim of proslavery forces, "wily politicians," he claimed, who saw Frémont's emancipation proclamation as an opportunity to assail the general. Since they knew that the masses supported the proclamation, however, these enemies smeared Frémont with charges of corruption and fraud in an attempt to influence the people. "And yet we are told that he is inefficient. By whom?" thundered Shanks, "why sir, by that cabal which has pursued him because of his proclamation." Thus justifying Frémont's most controversial action in the course of his speech, Shanks concluded:

> Sir, the life, the labor, the plan, and the success of this great western campaign, is General John C. Frémont's. History and the honest judgment of mankind will give it to him, and he will yet have the reward of his labor, combinations to the contrary notwithstanding.[28]

After Shanks's speech and the publication of Frémont's testimony, Frank Blair could no longer contain himself. Accused by Thaddeus Stevens of "deserting the Republican Party" and ignored by the CCW, Blair undoubtedly sensed that Frémont's supporters were close to attaining another command for their idol. It was time for Blair to strike back. Late in February 1862 he began to plot his course. He asked Gen. John Schofield in Missouri to send him materials on affairs in the West, explaining that he had the opportunity "to get the matter fairly before the public." If Schofield could add anything that would "cause the matter to arrest public attention," added Blair, "it would be well to do so." On March 7, 1862, Elizabeth Blair Lee reported that Frank Blair would speak out against Frémont in Congress on that day and that his father "has counselled him to be moderate in tone & let facts *proved* facts do the work."[29]

Responding to Shanks's speech and the publication of Frémont's testimony in the *Tribune,* Blair addressed the House on March 7, 1862. Citing a recent article in the *Atlantic Monthly,* "Frémont's One Hundred Days," Blair ridiculed the intended comparison of Frémont to Napoleon Bonaparte: "Can imagination conceive of Bonaparte returning to Paris, and announcing that he had lost two armies, liberated two negroes, and published a bombastic proclamation?" According to Blair, Frémont was responsible for the disasters at both Wilson's Creek and Lexington because in each case he had had adequate troops to respond but had failed to use them. Blair thought it ironic that Frémont was always ready to take credit for any military success, accepting the praise for raising and equipping a sizable fighting force in the West; however, when disasters occurred, then Frémont was nowhere to be found, and his huge army "a mere imagination of men, and a thing unreal." The real army Frémont recruited "was that army of contractors who settled down upon us like obscene birds of prey upon a carcass." As for Shanks's contention that Frémont's opponents were part of a proslavery faction, Blair hoped he was not included in such a characterization, for his opposition to slavery was well documented. Far from being on the verge of a great victory when he was relieved, Frémont had instigated mutiny among the troops and had even entertained notions of defying the president and setting up for himself.[30]

When Blair finished, Schuyler Colfax rose to respond. Although the Indiana Republican was a friend of both Blair and Frémont, his political sympathies were more in tune with the latter. Frémont was far from perfect, Colfax maintained, and he should not have published his committee testimony. "But I think that something ought to be pardoned to a man who had poisoned arrows hurled against him from every side." Frémont had made mistakes, but so had many other generals, Colfax asserted; they were not attacked with the same intensity as Frémont.[31]

Colfax dismissed Blair's assertion that Frémont had had ample troops to rescue Lyon and Mulligan. Lyon had appealed directly to the War Department on a number of occasions and was ignored. When Frémont assumed command, Cairo, Illinois, an important strategic point at the junction of the Ohio and Mississippi Rivers, was also threatened. There was neither time nor troops to help both, and since strategically Cairo was more important, Frémont's decision to reinforce it was correct. So, too, had Blair exaggerated the number of troops available to Frémont to relieve Lexington. Colfax was in St. Louis on September 14 when Frémont received the news of that attack. He had fewer than 8,000 troops in the St. Louis vicinity, and then "the tears stood in his eyes as he handed me two telegram dispatches," each of which required him to send 5,000 troops east. Frémont refused to protest because he had already been unjustly charged with insubordination. To make matters worse, the Contracts Committee arrived in St. Louis to assail him with *ex parte* testimony while refusing to allow him to see the charges against him. Surely Frémont was entitled to a trial; even common criminals were. Although he was not perfect, he was pursuing the enemy in the field, and he did infuse energy and spirit into the troops. Colfax concluded that he certainly deserved better than he received.[32]

As the radical press predicted, Frémont was given a command; at a cabinet meeting on March 11, Lincoln appointed him to the Mountain Department in Virginia. No doubt Frémont's supporters, including the majority of the CCW members, felt vindicated. Predictably, Democrats were irritated with Lincoln's maneuver, seeing it as a concession to Republican radicals and questioning the Republican party's commitment to a war waged for the Constitution and the Union. One correspondent of Ohio congressman Samuel Cox, characterizing Frémont as a "crazy adventurer" and an "unscrupulous agitator," described the appointment as very discouraging.

A few weeks later the chaos and mismanagement of Frémont's department was outlined in the report of the Holt Commission, a three-member group appointed by Lincoln to settle claims in Frémont's department, and many Democrats wondered how the president could have given him another command. Illinois congressman Anthony Knapp sent a copy of the report to Charles Lanphier, editor of the Illinois *State Register*, and commented, "examine & see how then the President can give such a man a command after such an exposure." Also disappointed were many members of Lincoln's own party, including his close political adviser David Davis, who, as a member of the Holt special claims Commission, had viewed firsthand the results of Frémont's chaotic administration. "I observe with profound regret," Davis told Judge Advocate Joseph Holt, "that General Frémont has been appointed to a command." Whether this was an important or unimportant command was irrelevant, argued Davis; "It is nevertheless an endorsement of him by the Administration & will be viewed in this light by the country." Abolitionists in Illinois were jubilant, Davis complained, and even the *Chicago Tribune,* one of Frémont's earliest critics, had become a warm supporter.

The Blairs gave a slightly different interpretation to the appointment. Elizabeth Blair Lee reported that Frank Blair took the news of Frémont's appointment poorly. Montgomery Blair, however, took it "blandly," believing that with this maneuver Lincoln had "annihilated the abolition junto— & that we now present the South a United front." Though Frank obviously felt a sense of personal defeat with Frémont's reappointment, Montgomery, who had not been consulted on the decision, believed Lincoln had outmaneuvered party radicals. He had given in to their demands for a command, but once he had yielded to them, they could expect little else in the near future. Besides, the Mountain Department, consisting of West Virginia and parts of Tennessee and Kentucky, was hardly a prestigious command. Thus did one of Greeley's correspondents interpret Frémont's reappointment, arguing that McClellan's "intimate friends" were not upset because they realized that Frémont would have little influence.[33]

Lincoln clearly had little faith in Frémont's military abilities, and his high-handed actions in the Department of the West most likely convinced the president that he was not to be trusted. Yet in any given situation, Lincoln had a variety of different interests to satisfy. The typical congressman's approach to such problems was vastly different from the president's because of the difference in constituencies. Republicans and Democrats from safe districts could afford to make blatantly partisan demands without fear of electoral repercussions; hence, a Democrat from southern Indiana, for instance, could afford to criticize the Frémont appointment and demand that the president exclude such radicals from the military. On the other hand, a radical such as George Julian, with an equally radical constituency, could fearlessly make the opposite demand. Only the president, whose national constituency contained these competing elements, had to weigh every decision, hoping to achieve a balance. As Montgomery Blair reasoned, perhaps appointing Frémont to a minor post was the best way to meet radical demands while not risking a complete break with Democrats and border state Unionists.[34]

The final word on Frémont, however, was yet to be heard, since the Contracts Committee's resolution was still before the House. It instructed the secretary of the treasury to adjust the claim of Simon Stevens for the sale of 5,000 Hall carbines from $22.00 each to $12.50 each. Frémont's supporters in the House, principally Colfax, Shanks, Stevens, and Conkling, harshly attacked the Contracts Committee on several occasions, accusing it of being driven by intense hatred of Frémont. Throughout the country, leading radical organs continued their assault on the Contracts Committee, charging it with damaging the unity of the Republican party. Elihu Washburne and Henry Dawes defended its actions, arguing that they would not whitewash corruption and that the resolution implied no personal censure of the general. The resolution finally passed by a substantial majority, 103 to 28.[35]

Neither Gooch nor Covode voted on the resolution. Julian voted against it, and Odell voted with the majority, a vote that would earn the censure of Jessie Benton Frémont. Distressed with Odell's tough questioning during Frémont's appearance before the committee and by comments he had made to the House about her husband, she wrote Julian that Odell was "more true to his pro-slavery demands than to the truth." She urged Julian to aid Frémont by publicizing all he knew about her husband's tenure in the West. As for Odell, she threatened, "I can take care of Mr. Odell & will attend to his defeat next week," a threat she could not ultimately carry out.[36]

Although ardent Frémont supporters might have been angered by passage of the Hall carbine resolution in the House, they still must have been pleased with the efforts of the CCW to rehabilitate the general. Frémont had been given a military command, and although he resigned it in late June rather than serve under a former subordinate, John Pope, that was his choice. Even more pleasing was the publication of the committee's official report in April 1863. Gooch, Odell, and Joseph A. Wright (who had replaced Johnson in March 1862) did not sign the report, choosing instead to submit the testimony without comment, but the committee's majority vindicated Frémont's military administration of the West. According to them, he had rightly judged that emancipation was a critical weapon in fighting the war. Ultimately, they described his command as "eminently characterized by earnestness, ability, and the most unquestionable loyalty."[37]

T. Harry Williams has argued that the Joint Committee on the Conduct of the War was dominated by reckless fanatics determined to force the issue of emancipation regardless of the consequences. The reappointment of Frémont to a military command demonstrated the power that congressional radicals had over Lincoln. Hans L. Trefousse, however, has contended that the power of the radicals has been overstated and that the president was rarely forced to carry out measures he disagreed with. The Frémont imbroglio illustrates that the truth lies somewhere between these two arguments. That Lincoln bowed to radical pressure seems indisputable. Given Frémont's military incompetence, the only reason for Lincoln to give Frémont any command was to appease elements in his own party. Yet certain members of the committee and of Congress would have welcomed Frémont as a suitable replacement for George McClellan as commander of the Army of the Potomac.

As Montgomery Blair observed, Lincoln's placement of Frémont in the Mountain Department revealed that the president could not be completely cowed by party radicals.[38]

When the Republican party emerged from the political realignments of the 1850s, it gained popularity through the use of antisouthern rhetoric and the image of the Slave Power, conceived of as an oligarchic group of southern slaveholders who allegedly dominated the nation's political machinery. An effective political weapon, this rhetoric continued to serve Republicans during the Civil War. For the Republican majority on the Joint Committee on the Conduct of the War, the Slave Power became a standard explanation for military disasters. Defeats were brought on by conservative Democratic generals who sympathized with slavery and were in reality the tools of southern slaveholders. The committee saw a proslavery plot behind John C. Frémont's removal from the Department of the West. Critics who opposed Frémont and his policies of emancipation and confiscation were in league with the enemy, whether they were Democrats, border state Unionists, or even conservative members of the Republican party. There could be no compromise on slavery. As George Julian stated, "If the Lord be God, serve him; but if Baal, serve *him*. There can be no middle ground. This . . . is a war between the government and slavery, and no man can really serve two masters at the same time." In reconstructing their martyr for emancipation, the majority of Republicans on the committee believed that they had served the Lord.[39]

One wonders, however, how well the committee served the public interest in lobbying for Frémont and helping him secure a command. As Archer Jones has written, "Frémont had 'all the qualities of genius except ability,'" and his subsequent poor performance in the Shenandoah Valley indirectly contributed to the failure of the Peninsula campaign in spring and summer 1862. Even more disturbing was the committee's tendency to reinforce some unhealthy practices in military appointments. Numerous northern military professionals complained bitterly that politics influenced such decisions. General-in-Chief Henry Halleck learned this firsthand, later complaining, "I have done everything in my power here to separate military appointments and commands from politics . . . but the task is hopeless." Even some volunteer officers recognized the damage wrought by political appointments in the military. "Pope, Sigel, Frémont, and the whole batch of political Generals are objects of honest terror to every soldier in the Union army," wrote one captain. Certainly the committee did not create this situation. Even if it had never been formed, several Washington politicians would have been active in trying to influence military appointments. Still, committee activities tended to reinforce unfortunate practices. In the case of Frémont, the committee was not his only supporter, but its sponsorship was clearly an important factor in his receiving a new command. His appearance before the committee, the publication of his testimony, and the committee's close connections with Edwin Stanton were instrumental in convincing Lincoln to reassign him to the Mountain Department. By pressuring the president to make a military appointment based on political beliefs, not on military ability, the committee harmed the Union war effort.[40]

CHAPTER FOUR

"McClellan Is an Imbecile If Not a Traitor": The Investigation of the Army of the Potomac

The most important activity that the Committee on the Conduct of the War undertook during the Thirty-seventh session of Congress was its investigation of the operations of the Army of the Potomac and its commander Gen. George Brinton McClellan. A conservative Democrat who believed in restoration of the Union but not in the abolition of slavery, McClellan held war goals that were antithetical to those of the Republican party. He favored limited war, directed by military professionals and fought by armies but exempting as much as possible innocent enemy civilians from the harsher aspects of war and restricting such measures as the confiscation of property to an absolute minimum. He was probably the most prominent advocate of conciliation among the nation's military officers. Assuming that secession had been engineered by a small group of slaveholders and that the majority of southern whites were loyal, McClellan believed that by scrupulously avoiding harsh measures, the majority of southerners could be convinced to reenter the Union. McClellan's style of warfare was consistent with the goals set forth by the Crittenden-Johnson resolution. He would wage a limited war that would simply restore the Union and keep bitter passions in check. "While [the South's] armies were defeated, their prisoners of war should be handled humanely and their civilians' property scrupulously protected." Conciliation, McClellan believed, could restore the Union.[1]

Although many Republicans agreed that secession had been the work of a minority of powerful slaveholders, they disagreed with McClellan's approach to war. The power of the slaveholders was immense, many Republicans argued, and their influence on the majority of southerners was great; thus were they able to engineer secession in the first place. George Julian characterized the Slave Power in 1852: "The powers of government are in their keeping, and they determine all things according to the counsels of their will." Therefore, the only hope for breaking the rebellion was to enact rigorous measures that would crush the Slave Power and allow a reorganization of southern society according to the dynamic model of northern free labor. Radicals such as Benjamin Wade, Zachariah Chandler, and Julian had no real strategic conception of hard war; however, they felt instinctively that only harsh measures such as confiscation, the arming of black troops, and emancipation would crush southern society. Conciliatory policies of Democratic generals had to be resisted, for if they were allowed to dictate war strategy and goals, the basic underlying conflict between the hierarchical slave society and the fluid free labor society of the North would remain unresolved. "To argue that we were fighting for a political abstraction called the Union and not the destruction of slavery," Julian declared, "was an affront to common sense, since nothing but slavery had brought the Union into peril, and nothing could make sure the fruits of war but the removal of its cause." During the course of its investigation, the committee strove not only to remove McClellan from his command and to discredit his conservative approach to war but also to strike him down as a political alternative to the Republican administration.[2]

More than any other of its activities, the investigation of McClellan strained the relationship between President Lincoln and the CCW. Lincoln, striving to keep coalitions of Republicans, Democrats, and border state Unionists intact, hesitated to wage a harsh war for fear that this fragile fabric would unravel. He also supported McClellan far longer than many Republican congressmen, partially because of political considerations. Wade, Chandler, Julian, and John Covode worried much less about alienating Democrats, believing that their constituents wanted rigorous measures implemented to punish the South for the war. Indeed, in their view, Lincoln's caution often diminished his reputation, already made suspect by his Kentucky birth and by his conservative Whig antecedents. Although the committee and the president ultimately remained united, its members often pursued the investigation of McClellan with complete disregard for Lincoln's political calculations.[3]

Born on December 3, 1826, George B. McClellan was the son of a prominent Philadelphia physician. Entering West Point in 1842, McClellan got along well with southerners and graduated second in his class in 1845. Upon graduation, he was assigned to the Army Corps of Engineers and served with distinction in Mexico, where a number of characteristics surfaced that would emerge again during the Civil War. Like many West Point graduates, he had a "thorough contempt for the civilian management of the conflict." Following the teachings of the French strategist Henri de Jomini, McClellan believed that war should be planned and fought by professionals, without the undue interference of civilian advisers. He despised the volunteers, for they conducted war in a nonprofessional manner and if not strictly controlled would loot, pillage, and steal from civilians—behavior acutely offensive to

McClellan's military professionalism. Indeed, as Stephen Sears observes, McClellan's caution on the battlefield may be attributed partly to his lack of confidence in volunteer soldiers. He left the army in the mid-1850s, to work for the Illinois Central Railroad as an engineer and was soon made a vice president in the company.[4]

During the secession crisis, McClellan rallied to the Union, accepting a commission from the Ohio legislature as a major general in charge of the state's volunteers. Early on, McClellan made it clear that he fought for the restoration of the Union and not for the abolition of slavery. When campaigning in western Virginia in summer 1861, he promised to protect the property of southern civilians and to put down servile insurrection. "Help me dodge the nigger," McClellan wrote Samuel Barlow in fall 1861, "*I* am fighting to preserve the integrity of the Union & the power of the Govt.—on no other issue." Although McClellan sympathized with blacks brutalized by slavery, he could not abide abolitionism. "I will not fight for abolitionists," he wrote his wife.[5]

After the Union defeat at Bull Run, Lincoln chose McClellan to replace Irvin McDowell as commander of the forces that became the Army of the Potomac. It was a popular choice, yet McClellan's position on protecting slave property caused Wade and Chandler to view him with distrust. They quickly grew impatient with him in fall 1861 because the army did not go forward. Convincing Wade, Chandler, and Lyman Trumbull in late October that the delays were caused by General-in-Chief Winfield Scott, McClellan enlisted the help of these senators in securing Scott's removal. Of course, these same men expected quick and vigorous action once Scott was removed. They did not appreciate the organizational and logistical problems McClellan faced in order to put an army of 100,000 in the field—a far greater army than any American general had ever sent into battle. According to the committee and to popular opinion, the only real attribute needed for military success was common sense. Popular opinion, as Herman Hattaway and Archer Jones write, stressed "courage and enthusiasm and overlooked logistics and strategy."[6]

Shortly after the committee was formed, Chandler summoned Gen. Samuel Heintzelman, a divisional commander in the Army of the Potomac, to his room at the National Hotel. In an army dominated by conservative Democratic officers, Heintzelman was one general who would not return fugitive slaves to their masters, possibly the reason that Chandler singled him out. When Heintzelman arrived late in the afternoon on December 16, Chandler locked the door and talked for two hours on military affairs. The senator asked if Heintzelman knew anything about McClellan's plans or if he

ever called councils of war. Heintzelman replied that he had never been consulted by McClellan on any military matter. Although he had made several
recommendations to McClellan, his suggestions were routinely ignored. When
the committee began taking testimony in late December, it made similar findings among other officers in the Army of the Potomac. Indeed, the CCW discovered McClellan and anti-McClellan factions, based not so much on politics, as some historians have asserted, but on personal loyalty to McClellan.
Young officers such as Fitz-John Porter and William Buel Franklin, both West
Point classmates of McClellan, were privy to his plans, but senior officers such
as Heintzelman and McDowell were completely ignorant of them. After two
weeks of investigation, the committee echoed the sentiments of Attorney
General Edward Bates: "Nobody knows [McClellan's] plans. The Secretary
of War and the President himself are kept in ignorance of the actual condition of the army and the intended movements of the General."[7]

When the committee began taking testimony on December 24, the division between the officers quickly became apparent. Both Heintzelman and
McDowell testified that they were virtually ignorant of McClellan's plans
and did not know whether the Army of the Potomac would advance in the
near future. Wade asked Heintzelman if it were not unusual for a commander
like McClellan to conceal his plans. Very much so, replied Heintzelman.
Echoing much of Heintzelman's testimony, McDowell also believed a forward advance was in order. It was time to move, he advised; the men were
in fine spirits, but the roads would prevent movement if the army waited much
longer.[8]

A strikingly different note was struck by the testimony of two of
McClellan's favorite divisional commanders, William Franklin and Fitz-John
Porter. Franklin admitted that McClellan did not have councils of war. Although he knew something of McClellan's plans, he refused to reveal them
to the committee until he had consulted with McClellan. Franklin then dodged
every question with the plea of ignorance, or if he did answer a question, he
qualified his answer with the claim that his knowledge was limited. To this
an impatient Wade replied, "This nation is making an extraordinary effort.
Next March we shall be 600,000,000 in debt for what we have already done."
But, Wade continued, "nothing has yet been done, . . . everybody knows that
our finances are not in a condition to keep this up eternally. All this is hanging upon one man who keeps his counsels entirely to himself." Wade concluded by saying that McClellan lacked the reputation of a Wellington or a
Bonaparte and asked how the nation could trust him.

Like Franklin, Porter evaded many of the committee's inquiries. Wade
asked if the Army of the Potomac would attack or go into winter quarters.

"That is a question I cannot answer," Porter responded. "I merely ask your military opinion," Wade countered. "I am in possession of information in regard to intended movements . . . and I decline giving any information whatever in relation to future movements, or what they ought to be," Porter responded, adding that perhaps the committee should ask McClellan himself about some of these matters. The committee ended its session none the wiser for its efforts.[9]

Shortly after the committee's investigation began, the *New York Daily Tribune* reported that its progress was frustrated because no officer would reveal McClellan's plan without consulting with him first. When McClellan became ill with typhoid fever in late December, the situation seemed more serious. Alarmed at the secrecy, even the hostility, of some of McClellan's generals and increasingly impatient with the lack of movement by the army, the committee sought and received an appointment to meet with Lincoln on the evening of December 31. "You are murdering your country by inches in consequence of the inactivity of the military and want of a distinct policy in regards to slavery," Wade told Lincoln. Although the president was beginning to have his own doubts about McClellan, he tried to deflect the congressional critics. The next day he wrote to McClellan, assuring him that the committee members meant no harm. He had met with them the previous evening for one-half hour, "and I found them in a perfectly good mood," a bit of a distortion considering Wade's language. "As their investigation brings them acquainted with facts," Lincoln concluded, "they are rapidly coming to think of the whole case as all sensible men would."[10]

According to McClellan, the committee, representing radical Republicans in Congress, used his illness to assail Lincoln and to lobby for his replacement. Their object "was not the restoration of the Union," argued McClellan, "but the permanent ascendancy of their party, and to this they were ready to sacrifice the Union, if necessary." Yet it was not only the so-called radicals who were anxious about McClellan. Before the committee's meeting with Lincoln, Attorney General Bates, hardly a radical, told the president that it was Lincoln's duty to act, that action could not stop simply because McClellan was ill. Bates, however, was afraid that he "spoke in vain. . . . I greatly fear that [Lincoln] has not *the power to command*."[11]

Nor did McClellan's comments accurately reflect the motives of the Republican party and the members of the committee. It was not just the radicals who complained about McClellan, desiring to discredit and replace him. Republicans from all parts of the country, representing radical and conservative elements, were upset about the military stalemate and the lack of an effective policy on slavery. Indeed, much of the impatience with McClellan's inactivity stemmed from the common view of military matters that tended to discount organization and training. One constituent wrote Pennsylvania congressman Edward McPherson that half the men in the army probably would not volunteer again if given the opportunity because the army would not strike at slavery. "The virus of slavery, the Black Pox," he complained, "is so strongly infused into so many of our leading men." It was ironic that the Slave Power yet controls "the powers that be, from striking the root of the evil."

Chairman Wade received a host of letters in early January complaining about Lincoln's lack of ability and military policy. A Gallipolis, Ohio, man warned Wade that the people would rebel if the army did not move soon, that they were not taking Lincoln seriously because he did not have a policy. Another constituent wrote that Lincoln was completely unequal to the present task; yet another urged radical measures including emancipation and confiscation of property. The people, he informed Wade, were sick and tired of conservative principles and asked if Americans were for freedom or slavery. In demanding action and rigorous measures, the committee was not advancing the interests of a small radical faction within Congress but the wishes of many Republicans throughout the country.[12]

Dissatisfied with their December 31, 1861, interview with Lincoln, the committee sought and received another meeting, this time with the entire cabinet, on the evening of January 6. Before the meeting, Chandler began testing the waters on behalf of General McDowell as a replacement for the ailing McClellan. Basing their views on McDowell's testimony, committee members found him more competent than McClellan. On January 5, 1862, Chandler visited Secretary of the Treasury Salmon P. Chase, who had played a major role in securing the top command for McClellan, and argued for his removal. Then on January 6 at 7:30 P.M. the committee met with Lincoln and the cabinet in what proved to be a stormy session. "The members of the Committee, especially Messrs. Chandler, Wade, Johnson, Odell, and Covode," wrote Chase, "were very earnest in urging vigorous prosecution of the war, and in recommending the appointment of Major-General McDowell to command the Army of the Potomac."

One newspaper reported that Wade made a two-hour speech castigating the administration for its lack of action. The speech, the newspaper claimed, greatly upset the president. According to Julian, committee members were angered most over Lincoln's absolute ignorance of McClellan's intentions. "We were greatly surprised to learn that Mr. Lincoln himself did not think he had the *right* to know" McClellan's plans and that he must simply trust his judgment. Secretary of State William Seward defended McClellan, stating that he had unbounded confidence in him, but Chase, according to Julian, was sympathetic to the committee's viewpoint. Julian, however, misrepresented Chase's enthusiasm for the committee's position. In Chase's own account, he defended McClellan, arguing that he had too many responsibilities and needed help from other generals. As an early supporter of McClellan and an eager advocate of his promotion to the top military command, Chase was unlikely to give up on him quickly. Besides, McClellan had outlined his military plans to the secretary in early December when Chase informed him of an impending crisis in financial markets as a result of the army's inactivity. Assured that the army would move by mid-February, Chase had not yet lost confidence. When the meeting ended, the only concrete accomplishment the committee could claim was Lincoln's promise to meet with McClellan to discuss how some of his many responsibilities could be delegated.[13]

Adam Gurowski claimed that the committee had completely exposed McClellan but that Seward and Montgomery Blair had protected him. "And Lincoln is in their clutches," he complained. Chase wrote his daughter that everyone was growling at Lincoln to put some life into military affairs, but with McClellan ill, no one (except himself presumably) knew what his plans were. Still, the committee meeting must have made some impression on the president. These were, after all, prominent men within his party and he could not simply ignore them.

Moreover, as Benjamin Thomas points out, Lincoln was himself growing impatient with the West Point clique, and he made two significant moves shortly after the meeting. First, he directed McClellan to go before the committee at "the earliest moment your health will permit." Perhaps he believed that the committee's prodding would do the general some good. Second, urged by Attorney General Bates to become commander in chief in fact and to compel his generals to report to him regularly and also encouraged by Quartermaster General Montgomery Meigs to question McClellan's divisional commanders, Lincoln scheduled a January 10 meeting with McDowell, Heintzelman, and Franklin. McDowell endorsed a forward movement on Manassas, but Franklin objected, proposing instead a flanking maneuver up the James or York River. On the night of January 11, the strategy sessions continued, with the majority of cabinet officers attending in favor of McDowell's plan. Informed by his colleague Franklin that another meeting was scheduled for the night of January 13, the recovering McClellan was able to attend the meeting. Here he further alienated Lincoln by refusing to reveal his plan in front of the cabinet, whispering to Meigs that Lincoln could not keep a secret. After McClellan told Lincoln, without revealing his plan, that he did have a definite date for movement, the meeting ended. Even Chase, heretofore his supporter, was shocked and angered by McClellan's behavior. Undoubtedly, he would have been angrier had he known that the next day McClellan leaked details of his plan to the *New York Herald* reporter Malcolm Ives.[14]

A few days later, McClellan confronted his antagonists on the Committee on the Conduct of the War. Impatient with the lack of information about military progress and irritated by the recalcitrance of McClellan's pet generals to reveal the army's intentions, committee members asked McClellan why he did not attack. McClellan replied that there were not enough bridges across the Potomac and that his communication with Washington was not yet perfected. Good commanders, he continued, always secure their retreat. Chandler replied, "Before you strike at the rebels you want to make sure of plenty of room so that you can run in case they strike back?" "Or in case you get scared," Wade allegedly chimed in. Undoubtedly McClellan was vexed at these responses, correctly assuming that he was in the presence of military novices. It was also unlikely that he could completely disguise his contempt for these civilians attempting to influence military affairs. When Wade later asked Chandler what he thought about military science, the latter replied, "I don't know much about war but this seems to me to be infernal, unmitigated cowardice."[15]

Committee members must have been incredulous a few days later when they read a report of their private interview with McClellan. Not only had he leaked a report to the *New York Herald* about the session, but it was also a substantially different account from what committee members remembered. On January 12 the *Herald* had reported that the committee was using McClellan's illness as an occasion to assail him "for the purpose of overthrowing his hard-earned and well-deserved popularity. The plan is to supersede him in favor of either Frémont or Senator Ben Wade, who represents the radical sentiment." In a later article, however, the *Herald* claimed that McClellan had patiently answered the committee's questions, showing them how ignorant they were about military matters. "The committee now admit," James Gordon Bennett editorialized, "that till illuminated by General McClellan, they were beginning at the wrong end, and putting the head where the tail belonged." According to the *Herald*, McClellan convinced the committee of the folly of a direct assault on Manassas.[16]

Not only was the *Herald*'s report inaccurate, but more important, it also added to the committee's mistrust of McClellan. Even before their conference with him, Wade, Chandler, and Julian were already skeptical of McClellan's loyalty. Completely oblivious of the huge organizational task before McClellan, the committee regarded his caution as a sign of cowardice—or worse, disloyalty. Reports circulated throughout Washington in January about southern sympathizers among the army's leaders, and the alleged treasonable communications of Charles Stone reflected poorly on McClellan. Combined, the rumors suggested questionable patriotism to Republicans on the committee. Ironically, neither of the committee's two Democrats seemed particularly eager to defend McClellan. They, too, were affected by the widespread rumors of disloyalty. As members of Congress, they probably sensed McClellan's hostility to any civilian meddling, whether by Democrats or Republicans. They might have regarded McClellan's planting of the story in the *Herald* as a show of bad faith, reinforcing the opinions of their Republican colleagues. And their close contact with Republican members no doubt worked to stifle any objections they might have had about the committee's methods of investigation.[17]

If members of the committee were of one mind, such was not the case in the country as partisan lines began to emerge in regard to McClellan and the advance of the army. Although some Democrats were critical of McClellan's generalship and some Republicans wary of attacking him, the major divisions were between parties, not, as some historians have contended, between conservative and radicals within the Republican party. Not only were Republicans from every background increasingly disconcerted with McClellan, but they also placed much of the blame for the slackness of military affairs on the president. "From the character of the men appointed to control our army and the *inaction* of the army," one Peoria man warned Lyman Trumbull, "it is too plainly to be seen that a strong party will soon grow up here even in Illinois in opposition to the prosecution of the war." One of Chase's correspondents from Boston wrote, "I greatly fear that the President is not up to the task and to the demands of the time, and that we shall not achieve this object until we have a President more fully alive to the claims of truth and justice." Another Illinoisan wrote to Elihu Washburne, complaining that McClellan had forced Lincoln to fire Simon Cameron because he advocated arming blacks. "Why did he not like Jackson tell [McClellan] to resign and go to H——l?" Another man warned, "They curse Lincoln & call him a *Damed* [sic] old *traitor* & they curse our Cabinet & all Congress for not passing some laws that will strike the root of the evil." One of Chandler's constituents complained that the army was afraid to move "for fear that they might hurt somebody's negro." The writer also expressed displeasure that Lincoln would trust the top position in the army to a Democrat. Wade's wife, Caroline, wrote a lengthy letter that no doubt echoed some of her husband's concerns. No one has confidence in McClellan, she claimed, and Lincoln, the only person who could make him move, was "too much afraid that slavery would be hurt by a forward movement, or too weak to take an independent stand." Meanwhile, the people grew more and more impatient. We have a large army, she continued, well supplied, "eager for a fight and wanting nothing but a leader who had the loyalty and courage to bid them on."[18]

Democrats increasingly saw Republicans retreating from the war goals of the Union and the Constitution in favor of emancipation. Illinois congressman Anthony Knapp told Illinois *State Register* editor Charles Lanphier that "the ultras are quietly gathering their force & I look for an open rupture between them & [the] administration." He continued, "Many [Republicans] will not vote funds for the war unless it [is] given an abolition slant." One of Samuel S. Cox's correspondents asked how, as a Democrat, Cox could support an "abolition crusade." The *Boston Herald* argued that the Committee on the Conduct of the War was creating "a fire in the rear hotter than ever before assailed against men in such positions [army commands]." Wade was the special target of abuse from Democrats in Ohio. Up for reelection, many people saw him as hostile to the Union coalition that they had entered into with Republicans. One of Cox's constituents wondered if Cox could manage to get "Gen Ben Wade tied to the tale of a jackass and then let him kick him to death. . . . I mean *Wade* not the jackass." And Cox himself, responding to a savage attack on McClellan in the House by radical Ohio Republican John Gurley in early February, counterattacked with equal venom. According to Cox, McClellan was abused because he was not an abolitionist: "Ah, there is the trouble! Can you wonder that Wendell Phillips, whose speeches are hailed so rapturously by this class, declared that he should deplore a victory by McClellan because the sore [slavery] would be salved over, and it would only be the victory of a slave Union."[19]

Finally, Lincoln lost patience with McClellan and issued General War Order no. 1, calling for a forward movement of all Union armies by Washington's birthday and directing McClellan to move on the rebel army at Manassas. Lincoln's action at least forced McClellan to reveal the details of his Urbanna plan, a turning movement that would transport the Army of the Potomac, via water, to Urbanna, Virginia, located on the Rappahannock River approximately sixty miles northeast of Richmond. Such a maneuver would place him in the rear of the main Confederate army at Manassas Junction. With secure communications and supply, McClellan then hoped to move against Richmond and force the Confederate army to attack him, thereby gaining the advantage of tactical defense. Members of the committee took heart at Lincoln's action. Secretary of War Edwin Stanton, who was quickly gaining the confidence of committee members as he lost the confidence of McClellan, wrote Wade, informing him of Lincoln's order when it became official. Julian claimed that McClellan "had opposed all forward movement of the Army of the Potomac." And Chandler told Julian, "Old Abe is mad, and the war will now go on."[20]

Temporarily satisfied that Lincoln's general order might prod the intractable McClellan into action, the committee spent the majority of its time in the first weeks of February on the Stone and Frémont cases. Throughout the nation, however, it was quickly evident that Lincoln's general order had not appeased many Republicans. While McClellan tried to convince Lincoln to change his order and instead adopt his Urbanna plan, he continued to lose support. One of his strongest Republican supporters had been *New York Times* editor Henry Raymond, who began losing faith in McClellan—although he withheld negative comment in his newspaper in deference to Lincoln. He expressed a number of concerns to Brig. Gen. James Wadsworth, however. Raymond claimed that McClellan had deliberately deluded the public into believing that an early advance would take place but that the weather conveniently prevented it. Stanton, Raymond asserted, was losing faith in McClellan and would shortly deprive him of control of all armies, limiting his command to the Army of the Potomac. He doubted that McClellan had any plan, save what he might have inherited from Scott. Significant in this context was Raymond's prediction that the Union party coalitions would not survive. "We shall have the old party division between Democrats & Republicans," Raymond told Wadsworth. Joseph Medill, the fiery editor of the radical *Chicago Tribune,* also complained about McClellan. Urging Lincoln to attack slavery to forestall European recognition of the Confederacy, Medill argued that "Gen. McClellan has ruined your administration and the country. . . . He is a do-nothing," whose real problem was his devotion to the Union with slavery.[21]

McClellan certainly was not unaware of growing Republican discontent. Department of the West commander Henry Halleck told McClellan of a recent conversation with a Missouri member of Congress and warned him that the abolitionists were maneuvering to replace him either with Wade or Nathaniel Banks. The only difficulty, claimed Halleck, "was in deciding between the two." Although McClellan had powerful friends, including Bennett's *New York Herald,* he was becoming increasingly skeptical of his one-time ally Edwin Stanton. Rumors circulated around Washington about Stanton's duplicity toward McClellan. He had initially viewed Stanton's appointment as being to his advantage, regarding the secretary as a buffer against hostile congressmen and the president, whom Stanton uncharitably referred to as the "Illinois ape" and the "original gorilla." Marsena Patrick, the provost marshal of the Army of the Potomac, reported "that [Stanton] is running a jealous opposition to McClellan—sold out to the [NY] Tribune & thwarting McClellan in every possible way." Another man wrote McClellan that rumors persistently placed him in opposition to the president and the secretary of war.[22]

The committee began to pursue McClellan again in the middle of February and worked to accomplish two objectives: the reorganization of the army into corps, a move that would take power away from McClellan's pet generals; and lifting the blockade of the lower Potomac River, which the Confederates had closed since the previous fall by mounting batteries at strategic points on the Virginia shore. On February 18 Moses Odell brought up the latter issue at the committee's daily meeting, moving that "the proper authorities" be informed of the "necessity of immediate steps being taken to break the blockade." The significance of the blockade was more symbolic than practical, since Washington was not jeopardized by it. Still, many congressmen regarded it as a national disgrace, an obstacle that lessened the Union's status in the eyes of European nations. On February 19 a subcommittee consisting of Wade and Andrew Johnson was appointed to meet with Stanton to discuss the subject, and the committee adjourned early so that Wade and Johnson could meet the secretary at the War Department. Wade explained Odell's points to Stanton and included a letter submitted on the subject from Covode's concerned constituents. Stanton sympathized with Wade but contended that he was powerless on the matter; McClellan, however, was in the building and, at Stanton's request, he agreed to meet with the congressmen.[23]

Here was a classic confrontation. On one side stood the West Point professional, refined, aloof, and contemptuous of civilian meddlers. And on the other stood two self-made men, the Republican radical who despised West Point and mistrusted McClellan's political conservatism and the Tennessee tailor who, despite sharing similar political convictions, was jealous of the general as a political rival and who shared Wade's mistrust of his polished, aristocratic manners. Wade asked if McClellan was aware of the necessity of lifting the blockade. McClellan replied that he would investigate and report back to the committee; in any event, it would be only a matter of days, not weeks, he assured them. Still, there were certain measures, such as securing a line of retreat, that had to be accomplished before the army could land troops. Hearing this, Wade erupted; he was tired of caution. The Army of the Potomac had 150,000 of the best men in the country and could "whip the whole Confederacy if they were given the chance; if I were commander," Wade declared, excitedly, "I would lead them across the Potomac, and they should not come back until they had won a victory and the war ended, or

they came back in their coffins." At the conclusion of this passionate diatribe, McClellan said nothing, but he noted that Stanton had not said one
word in his defense. Later, Johnson reported the substance of the interview
when the committee reconvened that same day, noting that despite Wade's
frank and emphatic language, Stanton endorsed every word uttered.[24]

Whether the army should retain its divisional structure or reorganize into
corps was a delicate question, one that involved some important considerations, such as whether a commander should be allowed to choose his own
subordinates, regardless of rank. The committee believed that McClellan's
existing divisional command structure was inefficient and allowed him to
rely on his own pet generals while passing over more experienced ones—many
of whom seemed more sympathetic to the committee's ideas on how the war
should be conducted. On February 18 Stanton met with Heintzelman to discuss corps organization. Stanton favored such a reorganization, promising
Heintzelman the command of a corps, but McClellan opposed the change,
arguing that he needed to test the army in the field to determine who the
best corps commanders were. Heintzelman also told Stanton that he had never
discussed military matters with McClellan, which no doubt reinforced
Stanton's determination to convince the president of the necessity of corps
organization.[25]

On February 25 committee members met with the president to urge the
adoption of the *corps d'armee,* arguing it was a much more efficient mode
of operation. Lincoln temporized; he had not thought much about it and
McClellan opposed its adoption. The meeting ended without resolving the
issue, although Wade and Chandler, undoubtedly noting that McClellan had
not advanced according to Lincoln's General Order no. 1, urged immediate
forward movement and threatened to debate McClellan's tardiness before
the entire Senate if he failed to move quickly. On March 3 the committee
sought and received another interview with Lincoln on the same subject. The
meeting, however, degenerated into a heated exchange between Wade and
Lincoln about removing McClellan. If McClellan were to be removed, who
should replace him, asked Lincoln. "Well, anybody!" Wade exclaimed.
"Wade," the president replied, "anybody will do for you but I must have
somebody."[26]

Events in March rapidly added to the committee's skepticism about
McClellan. Feeling threatened, Confederate general Joseph Johnston evacuated his troops from Manassas and Centreville and fell back behind the
Rappahannock to Culpeper, removing any strategic advantage to McClellan's
proposed Urbanna plan. When McClellan advanced his army the next day
to investigate, the fortifications [were] proved to be much less formidable

than he had supposed. The discovery that part of the rebel artillery was in reality painted logs, popularly dubbed Quaker guns, created a public sensation, even though McClellan knew about them. According to Julian, these revelations caused the committee to question McClellan's loyalty and intensified their efforts to secure his removal. "No tyrant or despot could dare to maintain such a man [as McClellan] in the service," Gurowski complained to Wade. Nor were only the so-called radicals upset with McClellan. "Upon the whole," commented Edward Bates, "it seems as if our genl. went with his finger in his mouth on a fool's errand, and that he has won a fool's reward." McClellan quickly felt the heat. "I regret that the rascals are after me again," he complained to his wife shortly after his advance on Manassas. "I had been foolish enough to hope that when I went into the field they would give me some rest, but it seems otherwise."[27]

In the Republican press, attacks on McClellan accelerated. After seeing the wooden guns at Manassas, our soldiers "fairly cried for shame," wrote the *Chicago Tribune*. While proslavery newspapers claimed a great victory for McClellan, the *Tribune* insisted that it, too, wanted to congratulate the general: "He is fully entitled to the glory of having out-camped Beauregard." The committee's negative impressions were reinforced when several of its members visited the Manassas fortifications on March 14 and interviewed witnesses. Each one claimed that the revels had far fewer troops than was reported and that the strength of the works had been grossly overstated. Chandler asked Bayard Taylor, a correspondent of the *New York Daily Tribune* who had accompanied McClellan's staff to the battlefield, if there were any doubt that a force of 100,000 would have destroyed rebel forces at Manassas. "Not the slightest," replied Taylor.[28]

As the committee fumed about Manassas, McClellan was putting the finishing touches on a different strategy. Previously, in a council of war called by the president on March 8, McClellan's generals had approved the Urbanna plan by a vote of 8 to 4. Although skeptical, Lincoln complied but placed a number of conditions on the plan. First, he implemented corps organization, giving Heintzelman, Sumner, Keyes, and McDowell commands—the very generals, with the exception of Keyes, who had voted against McClellan's plan. Second, he specified that the capital must remain entirely secure. Third, he stipulated that only two corps would be allowed to leave via the Chesapeake Bay until the blockade on the Potomac had been lifted.

On March 13, 1862, in another council of war, McClellan proposed Fortress Monroe, on the James-York Peninsula, as a new base of operations, and his generals agreed. Although corps organization was viewed as a setback for McClellan, Stanton eventually relented on immediate implementation, telling McClellan he could temporarily ignore the order if it would delay his departure. Before leaving for the peninsula, McClellan received another setback when the president relieved him from his position of general in chief, confining his operations to the Army of the Potomac. Although McClellan's enemies understandably regarded this move as a rebuke, Lincoln also had practical considerations in mind. With the massive Peninsula campaign about to begin, it was simply too much to expect McClellan to be in charge of other theaters. Unfortunately, the matter was not handled properly; McClellan found out about the demotion through the newspapers before he had received official notification.[29]

As McClellan departed for Fortress Monroe on March 17, 1862, debate over his generalship intensified. Ethan Allen Hitchcock, a retired regular army officer recently hired as an adviser to Stanton, claimed that when he met the secretary just after arriving in Washington, he was immediately offered McClellan's command. "On reporting to the Secretary," Hitchcock recalled, "almost without a word of preface he asked me if I would take McClellan's place in command of the army of the Potomac." A few days later, Stanton renewed the offer, providing Hitchcock extensive proof of McClellan's incompetence. Anson Stager, head of the U.S. Military Telegraph Corps, argued that much of the commotion over McClellan was the result of his friends promoting him as a presidential candidate. This possibility, according to Stager, "sets all the politicians at work to kill him off."[30]

George Gibbs, a naturalist who had earlier accompanied McClellan on a surveying expedition in the West, told him that Stanton was angry because McClellan was trying to put the Democratic party back together "instead of moving against the rebels." But Gibbs had a suggestion. McClellan could thwart Stanton by reaching out to conservative Republican members in Congress, and he suggested men such as Ira Harris of New York, Jacob Collamer and Solomon Foote of Vermont, and Orville Browning of Illinois. Instead of pursuing this strategy, however, McClellan continued to cultivate leading Democratic newspapers. Writing to Samuel Barlow, McClellan claimed that he was not afraid of the abolitionists' criticisms. "All I ask of the [Democratic] papers is that they should defend me from more malicious attacks." His confidant, Brig. Gen. Fitz-John Porter, communicated with Manton Marble, editor of the *New York World,* a leading Democratic journal, outlining McClellan's plans and asking for his help since the "abolition element" was working against McClellan.[31]

Even though McClellan had finally been prodded into action, the committee distrusted him and was determined to discredit him. In so doing, however, there were dangers. As one Pittsburgh resident warned Covode,

McClellan had a powerful grip on the masses; if he were attacked, it might backfire, especially if his Peninsula campaign was successful. Still, committee members were convinced that with McClellan in charge of the nation's biggest army, the war could not be won. His caution and slow movement suggested questionable loyalty, and his political conservatism dictated a conciliatory approach to waging war, a flawed approach in the eyes of the committee's Republican majority. Rigorous measures were needed to invigorate the northern war effort and to reconstruct southern society in the image of the democratic, free labor North. These issues no doubt weighed heavily on the members when they met Secretary Stanton on March 24. Stanton expressed dismay, conceding that McClellan was surrounded by disloyal subordinates but that Lincoln seemed to have newfound confidence in him. The situation seemed to be at an impasse.[32]

Two significant events did occur shortly after this meeting. First, in response to pressure from Frémont's supporters, Lincoln detached Louis Blenker's division and assigned it to the newly created Mountain Department. Then on April 2, James S. Wadsworth, a brigadier general in charge of Washington defenses, reported to Stanton that he had only 19,022 green troops available with which to defend the capital. Moreover, several commanders were making demands on his troops, which would reduce his force even further. Wadsworth also maintained that his troops were so unfit that they could scarcely operate the heavy artillery defending the city. Stanton reacted immediately, detailing Ethan Hitchcock and Adj. Gen. Lorenzo Thomas to determine whether McClellan had complied with Lincoln's orders to secure the capital. After a quick investigation, they assured Stanton that McClellan had not done so. Shortly thereafter, Wadsworth himself explained the situation to Lincoln. The next day he appeared before the committee, reinforcing its members' intense distrust of McClellan and their suspicions about his loyalty. That same day Lincoln instructed Stanton to hold back McDowell's corps, depriving McClellan of 35,000 men and creating an open rupture between the administration and the nation's top general.[33]

When he heard that McClellan had been deprived of McDowell's corps, Heintzelman remarked, "At what a time to do such a thing. It is a great outrage." McClellan wrote his wife, "The idea of depriving a General of 35,000 troops when actually under fire!" And to Montgomery Blair he complained, "I am deprived of the means I have counted upon." Even McDowell, who McClellan was convinced had been intriguing against him for months, told William Franklin that this detachment was designed to hurt McClellan. "McDowell told me," Franklin told McClellan, "it was intended as a blow to you. That Stanton had said that you intended to work by strategy, and not by fighting, that all the opponents of the administration centered around you." Undoubtedly, this news increased McClellan's hostility toward Stanton. After the war, Gen. William Rosecrans told Fitz-John Porter that when he went to Washington to see Stanton sometime in April 1862, Stanton told him, "I wish you and McDowell could get into Richmond before that d——d little cuss McClellan."[34]

Had McClellan deliberately failed to secure the capital? Not in the least. Spread throughout the Washington vicinity and the Shenandoah Valley were over 70,000 troops. What he had failed to do, as a result of his contempt for civilian leadership, was to inform the Washington authorities about the use of these troops. Ironically, the only exception was General Wadsworth, with whom McClellan had discussed the matter. It appeared to some observers that McClellan's opponents, particularly Stanton and the committee, deliberately contrived to take troops away from him to make him fail. McClellan's supporters charged that Republican radicals were afraid he would end the war before slavery was abolished. Yet members of the committee had lived through the Bull Run disaster, the Ball's Bluff fiasco, the Potomac blockade, and McClellan's seemingly endless delays. When he finally advanced on Manassas in early March, they felt his credibility was shattered and even began to question his loyalty. When Wade published reports in late March that linked McClellan with the Knights of the Golden Circle in the late 1850s, such suspicions were increased. That he might leave the capital vulnerable was completely consistent with suspicions the committee harbored about McClellan; hence they attempted to hold back McDowell, not to guarantee McClellan's failure but, in their eyes, to save the capital.[35]

Not only did the committee members question McClellan's commitment to the war, but they also objected strongly to the manner in which he conducted it. From his campaign in western Virginia, they knew that his concept of war was limited, involving only armies, not civilians. "It is my intention," McClellan had said during that campaign, "to cause the persons & property of private citizens to be respected." Confiscation of civilian property and emancipation of slaves were to McClellan unacceptable as well as unchristian. The problem for the Republican committee members was how this policy of conciliation could be discredited before it muddled and bogged down the entire war effort.[36]

Nor did committee members understand the strategic significance of the turning movement McClellan planned in his Peninsula campaign. Having observed firsthand in the Crimean War the effects of rifled weapons,

McClellan knew the huge advantage afforded defense in any conflict. Like his West Point instructor, Dennis Hart Mahan, he rejected the direct frontal assault recommended by the committee and other civilians as foolhardy and too costly in terms of casualties. McClellan believed that maneuver was superior to fighting. Accordingly, moving on Richmond via the James-York Peninsula offered McClellan a couple of advantages. First, by using water transport, McClellan's supply line and communication would be secure. Second, by positioning his troops behind the Confederate army and threatening Richmond, McClellan would force the Confederates to attack him and thus give him the advantage of tactical defense. As for those individuals concerned about the safety of Washington, McClellan well knew that with a Union army threatening Richmond, the Confederacy could ill afford to make a serious push on Washington. Of course, the plan is different from the execution; however, the important point is that regardless of McClellan's performance, his strategic ideas were not intrinsically flawed, as committee members seemed to think.[37]

Convinced, however, that McClellan's style of warfare was doomed to fail, committee members began to accelerate their attacks on the philosophy of conciliation. In early April the CCW began an investigation of alleged rebel atrocities against Union dead in the aftermath of the battle of Bull Run. The report published in early May painted a picture of southern behavior as ghastly and barbarous. Surely a society as depraved as the South did not merit the type of tender treatment accorded it by the likes of McClellan. At the same time, individual committee members spoke out before Congress for more vigorous war measures. Wade, Julian, and even Joseph Wright from Indiana, the newest Democratic committee member, delivered speeches in favor of a harsh confiscation bill. Julian was particularly effective in denouncing the policy of conciliation, portraying opponents of rigorous measures as conspirators in a proslavery plot against freedom. According to Julian, the argument that the Constitution forbade measures such as confiscation was fallacious, the "sickly higgling of pro-slavery fanatics, or the poorly disguised rebel sympathy of sniveling hypocrites." But the tide was turning against the tender-footed, Julian predicted, as he closed with a particularly stinging passage:

> The defenders of slavery and its despicable apologists will be nailed to the world's pillory, and the holiest shrines in the temple of American liberty will be reserved for those who shall most faithfully do battle against this rebellion, as a gigantic conspiracy against the rights of human nature and the brotherhood of our race.[38]

The Peninsula Campaign

While the committee was busy investigating rebel atrocities, the debate over McClellan's campaign continued even as he was laying siege to Yorktown. As if depriving McClellan of McDowell's corps were not bad enough, the administration then committed another blunder when it informed McClellan that McDowell would approach Richmond, traveling south from Fredericksburg. McClellan had driven Confederate forces from Yorktown and advanced up the peninsula to Seven Pines on the outskirts of Richmond. In order to hook up with McDowell, McClellan positioned his troops on both sides of the Chickahominy River, isolating Fitz-John Porter's corps on the north side. But then the administration changed course. "I have this moment just received a dispatch from the Presdt who is terribly scared about Washington," McClellan wrote his wife. "[He] talks about the necessity of my returning in order to save it! Heaven save a country governed by such counsels!" Worried that Stonewall Jackson's troops in the Shenandoah were aiming for the capital, Lincoln held back McDowell's troops, just as the Confederates wanted. Thus, aided and abetted by two incompetent political generals, Banks and Frémont, Confederate authorities achieved their objectives. With recent rains swelling the Chickahominy, Porter's corps was in a precarious position when Johnston's army attacked it on May 31; only quick action by Gen. E. V. Sumner saved him. McClellan's supporters could plausibly claim that Jackson had hoodwinked the administration and that in the process the Army of the Potomac had been sacrificed.[39]

But there is another side. McClellan was inordinately slow and cautious. Instead of attacking Yorktown, where he outnumbered Confederate forces 70,000 to 17,000, his caution allowed Johnston to reinforce Confederate troops under John Magruder, forcing McClellan to settle for a siege. "Your call for Parrott guns from Washington alarms me," a concerned president wrote McClellan, "chiefly because it argues indefinite procrastination." And early on, McClellan showed a persistent propensity to overestimate the size of enemy forces, promoting a never-ending cry for reinforcements. The snail-like pace with which the Army of the Potomac advanced up the peninsula after Yorktown and McClellan's failure to strike the weak Confederate right and move on Richmond after the battle of Seven Pines convinced his opponents that he never intended to engage the enemy.

Further, there was evidence that McClellan was resisting the corps arrangement specified by Lincoln in March, confiding in Porter and Franklin while ignoring the more experienced Keyes, Heintzelman, and Sumner. "The conduct of Gen. McClellan is giving great dissatisfaction in this army, particularly about Gen Porter," Heintzelman remarked. "No less than three Generals spoke to me about it & one of them this morning was afraid his name would have to be Porter before he would be able to do anything." Commenting on this situation, Lincoln wrote to McClellan, "It is looked upon as merely an effort to pamper one or two pets, and to persecute and degrade their supposed rivals. . . . Are you strong enough, even with my help—to set upon the necks of Sumner, Heintzelman, and Keyes all at once?" As the month of May drew to a close, there were plenty of legitimate reasons for doubting the military capabilities of George B. McClellan.[40]

By the end of May, committee members were frustrated. There was no progress on the military front. In their opinion, McClellan was wasting the Army of the Potomac in the swamps around Richmond. Indeed, in mid-May, Wade received a distressing letter from *New York Daily Tribune* reporter Samuel Wilkeson that revealed McClellan's blundering in the battle of Williamsburg. According to Wilkeson, McClellan was not even present at the encounter. Making matters worse was McClellan's report of the battle, which built up his favorites at the expense of generals such as Heintzelman, who had actually managed it. The news was depressing and frustrating, yet the committee could do nothing. McClellan had the army on the peninsula and his limited style of warfare still seemed to please the president. Although the report on atrocities had created some excitement, there was no noticeable departure from the conservative policy of waging war. Indeed, in some respects there were setbacks, as when the president overruled David Hunter's May 1862 proclamation liberating slaves in the Department of the South, which theoretically included South Carolina, Florida, and Georgia.

The last day of May, Wade received a disturbing letter from a constituent. Every local Republican, the man wrote, believed McClellan to be a traitor. Many men would not enlist because they had no desire to dig trenches under McClellan. Chandler was also clearly frustrated with McClellan's behavior. Early in June, Edward Bates reported that Chandler had shown up in the lobby of Willard's Hotel, drunk, "and abused Gen: McClellan roundly, calling him a liar and a coward!" When Gen. Samuel Sturgis, who happened to be in the lobby, castigated him for the remarks and called him a liar, Chandler went away.[41]

Shortly thereafter, suspicions about McClellan increased as rumors spread throughout the country that wounded soldiers after the battle of Seven Pines had been left outside in the rain while Union troops had guarded the White House, a small house belonging to the wife of Gen. Robert E. Lee. Although McClellan answered a pointed inquiry from Secretary Stanton, telling him the structure was inadequate for a hospital and that no wounded soldiers had suffered unduly, the issue was nonetheless debated on the floor of the House when Wisconsin's John Potter submitted a resolution demanding information on the matter. In a spirited debate several members of Congress denounced McClellan's actions. The rumors surrounding the White House affair probably prompted Wade to visit the Army of the Potomac in mid-June. Shunned by McClellan, Wade visited with a number of disaffected corps commanders, including Heintzelman. Wade, according to him, was bitterly against the rebels and endorsed confiscation. "He is for taking everything from the rebels," Heintzelman stated; "he is also for an onward movement. He did not like the movement of the army to this point, but preferred a march by land."[42]

As June wore on, Republicans and committee members grew more depressed about McClellan's behavior; it seemed as if he would never fight. As Stephen Sears argues, McClellan was quickly losing the will to fight. The carnage and casualties from Seven Pines had a noticeable effect on him. "I am tired of the sickening sight of the battlefield, with its mangled corpses & poor suffering wounded," he wrote his wife; "victory has no charms for me when purchased at such costs." After Robert E. Lee, who had assumed command of the Army of Northern Virginia, attempted to destroy Porter's corps at Mechanicsville on June 26 in the first major battle of the Seven Days, McClellan thought briefly about advancing on Richmond with the other wing of his army but was easily persuaded not to do so by Franklin and Porter. Instead, believing that his communications and supply lines were not secure enough, he changed his base of operations to the James River, in effect, a retreat. During the retreat, McClellan was often distant from the battlefield and gave few orders, leaving his subordinates to fend for themselves. By the end of the Seven Days on July 1, McClellan lacked the will to command. "Never did I see a man more cut down than Genl. McClellan was," remarked Gen. Andrew A. Humphreys. "He was unable to do anything or say anything."[43]

McClellan, however, was still capable of avoiding responsibility. He persistently argued that he was not responsible for the fate of the army because he faced overwhelming numbers and was denied reinforcements. After the battle of Gaines Mill on June 27, McClellan telegraphed Stanton, his one-time friend but now a bitter antagonist: "If I save this army now I tell you plainly that I owe no thanks to you or any other person in Washington— You have done your best to sacrifice this Army." Although a bewildered telegraph operator omitted the last offensive sentence from the telegram, the gist of the message was plain enough; McClellan made the defeat of the army a partisan issue. Events on the peninsula discouraged Republicans throughout the country. "McClellan is certainly a fool," Horace Greeley told Joshua

Giddings, and "probably a traitor." Giddings, in turn, told his son he did not trust McClellan because of his proslavery views and his willingness to protect General Lee's property. Even more distressing was the president's behavior. Despite events on the peninsula, Lincoln still maintained faith in McClellan. Before he returned home to Indiana after the congressional session was over, George Julian visited the president at the White House. Lincoln, according to Julian, looked thin and haggard, but he still had faith in McClellan.[44]

Reaction to the Peninsula Campaign

Most members of the committee were convinced early that summer that McClellan had to be dismissed, despite the president's confidence in him, and they found two windows of opportunity. They could use negative committee testimony to discredit McClellan, and they could push Republican general John Pope on Lincoln as a suitable replacement. Eager to dispose of McClellan, Chandler pursued the first option with enthusiasm. As early as June 23, he tried to persuade the committee to allow him to use its testimony before the Senate. He was prevented from doing so by the vigorous objections of Daniel Gooch, who argued that committee members should be allowed to use testimony only in executive sessions of Congress but not before the public. Yet Chandler was not to be thwarted. Describing McClellan as a traitor who "deserves to be shot," he introduced a resolution in the Senate on July 7 directing the secretary of war to release all army orders pertaining to the advance of the Army of the Potomac from February 22, 1862, to May 1, 1862, as well as figures on troop strength. Everybody knew the army had been sacrificed, he claimed, and many people were blaming the secretary of war. According to Chandler, only the president or General McClellan could be responsible for the fate of the army. "It is one of those two," Chandler contended, "and no third man"; but whoever it was "should suffer the extreme penalty of law, for this nation has been disgraced by the division and loss . . . of the army of the Potomac." After first charging McClellan with leaving the capital unprotected, Chandler ended his speech by castigating him for failing to advance on Richmond after the battle of Seven Pines.[45]

When Chandler attempted to renew the discussion on July 11, he met with stiff resistance from an unlikely source, fellow committee member Joseph Wright. The former governor of Indiana was U.S. minister to Prussia when the Civil War broke out and was skeptical of the Lincoln administration. His promise to refrain from partisan politics and his commitment to Union coalitions, however, made him a good candidate to replace rival Jesse Bright as senator when the latter was expelled from Congress in February 1862. Indiana Republican Calvin Fletcher urged Gov. Oliver Morton to appoint Wright over Republican Richard Thompson of Terre Haute because Wright "would unify the union party more effectively than any other man." And Wright had assured Fletcher, "I will vote for as strong a confiscation Bill as any Administration can carry out." A little later, Morton interviewed Wright, and when the latter assured the former that he supported a vigorous war and would not engage in partisan politics, he was appointed to fill Bright's seat until the legislature could meet to decide on a permanent candidate. Shortly after he arrived in Washington, Wright was appointed to the Committee on the Conduct of the War to replace Andrew Johnson, whom Lincoln had recently named military governor of Tennessee.[46]

Unfortunately for Wright, his position on the war and his appointment by Morton created as many enemies as it did friends. Radicals such as Julian were skeptical of Wright because they believed the Unionist position compromised the principles of the Republican party. Democrats were critical because they believed Morton was trying to use the appointment to destroy their party. They noted bitterly how Wright had repudiated the platform of their state's January convention. Wright, noted the *Chicago Times,* says parties are "dead, dead, dead . . . but we venture to the prediction that in a little while he will turn up a living witness that political parties are not dead. He will turn up a full-blown republican in his own person." Republicans urged Wright to support their position, but Democrats cautioned him to remain conservative on slavery and other radical measures. And so it was that every time Wright cast a vote in the Senate he was assailed. Democrats complained when he supported a rigorous confiscation bill; Republicans blasted him when he failed to support the bill abolishing slavery in the District of Columbia. Schuyler Colfax's comments to Fletcher were typical:

> [Wright] has already cast votes that many regret—agst the President's Emancipation Resl—agst. Abolishing Slavery D.C.—agst. prohibiting slavery in the Territories. . . . And he has gratified many going for Confiscation so earnestly, by recognizing Hayti & Liberia. On the whole however, he has voted oftener against what you & I like than for it.[47]

Wright rose to contest Chandler's attack on McClellan, claiming he did not understand why Chandler would introduce such a resolution since its only point was "to bring contempt and dishonor upon one of the generals in American service." Though disclaiming any desire to defend McClellan's record, Wright objected to Chandler's line of argumentation because it implied that McClellan was a criminal. "I am not pleading for party," Wright asserted, claiming that such an attack would divide the country and delight the rebels. If McClellan were to be charged with treason, Wright asked what the effects would be on the country. Chandler responded that Wright misunderstood his intentions, which were simply to put the people in touch with the facts, not to make criminal charges.

Seconding Chandler's remarks was Lyman Trumbull, who also argued that the people had a right to know the facts and asked if Wright did not trust the people. He never doubted the people, Wright replied; "I want Union," he asserted; "I will support the Administration." After extended debate, Chandler's resolution was adopted 34 to 6; Chandler and Wade supported it, with Wright opposed.[48]

Chandler was far from finished with McClellan. As he told his wife the next day, "McClellan is an imbecile if not a traitor. He has virtually lost the army of the Potomac." Stanton, he claimed, was being unfairly maligned, but "*I will stand by him*. . . . The right must prevail," he predicted; "I *know* I am right." On July 15, with Wright, Gooch, and Wade absent from the committee, Chandler renewed his motion to allow committee members to use testimony before either house of Congress. Without the opposition of Wright and Gooch, the motion passed.[49]

The very next day, Chandler blasted McClellan in the Senate, introducing committee testimony to support his points. When Wright interrupted, challenging the right to use the testimony, Chandler silenced him by referring to the motion the committee had passed. Unaware of the vote, Wright yielded to Chandler, who continued his denunciation of McClellan, claiming that he had ignored General War Order no. 1, left the capital undefended, and wasted an army of 158,000 in the swamps of Virginia. "Human ingenuity could not have devised any other way to defeat that army," he concluded; "divine wisdom could scarcely have devised any other way to defeat it than that which was adopted." When Chandler finished, Wright explained to the Senate that though he was a member of the committee, he knew nothing about the use of secret testimony, adding that he believed Chandler had no right to use it. Benjamin Wade then complemented Chandler's speech by denouncing McClellan in public speeches in late July, claiming that McClellan was for "digging and not for fighting," as if the (eminently practical and sensible) policy of entrenchment were a sign of cowardice.[50]

McClellan took the attack in stride, telling Samuel Barlow, "I do not think it best to reply to the lies of such a fellow as Chandler—he is beneath my notice, & if the people are so foolish as to believe aught he says I am content to lose their favor & to wait for history to do me justice." Democratic newspapers, however, reacted angrily. The *New York Herald* denounced congressional committees for interfering with the war effort. Though Chandler claimed that only traitors would oppose his speech, the *Herald* remarked that "only traitors and fools will support and applaud him." Manton Marble's *New York World* suggested that this "meddlesome committee" stay out of military affairs. *Vanity Fair* ridiculed the senator's speech in "Chandler":

> Who is this Chandler—inquisitive wretch!—
> Who clamors so loud and so long
> For papers and letters,
> And bothers his betters—
> Insisting that somebody's wrong?
>
> Who made him Senator—dignified name!—
> And sent him to Washington,
> Bawling and brawling,
> Disgracing his calling
> In the light of the mid-day sun?
>
> Why should our country—best and beloved!—
> Suffer her secrets of State
> To open so easy
> To Chandler the greasy—
> While the Wheels of Government wait?[51]

Many of Chandler's supporters, however, applauded his efforts. "We feel much obliged to you for your exposure of that windbag & humbug McClellan," wrote a New York man. "Someone must speak truths," wrote another, "unpalatable though they may be to rebel sympathizers." Yet another correspondent congratulated Chandler and urged the enactment of rigorous war measures. "God grant that the people," she said, "may soon see that our only hope is in the most radical measures yet proposed." But Chandler's efforts had missed effects.[52]

Chandler clearly was motivated by patriotic impulses when he attacked McClellan. He wanted to invigorate the nation's army and boost the country's sagging morale. However, publicly to attack the general of the nation's largest army, particularly when that same army was in a vulnerable position, was both unwise and irresponsible. Howard C. Westwood argues that Chandler's action "was no harassment of Lincoln." On the contrary, it was frustration with Lincoln that prompted Chandler's action. Lincoln would not accept the committee's position on McClellan (at least not as quickly as committee members wanted). Chandler was not content simply to offer advice to the president, and his ill-advised speech was a bid to direct and control executive action. With this speech and the use of committee testimony, the CCW had stepped beyond its authorization. It was not a question of drafting future legislation; it was not a question of the executive refusing to enforce laws that Congress had passed. Representing the committee, Chandler was attempting to mobilize public opinion to force the president to act in certain ways. Information, taken in the strictest confidence, was placed before the public for the express purpose of pressuring Lincoln to relieve McClellan of his command. And, as subsequent events demonstrated, the effect on the morale of many of the Army of the Potomac's leading generals was not beneficial as they became increasingly alienated from the Republican administration.[53]

But there was another issue involved. In attacking McClellan, the committee did not distinguish between the strategy of the Peninsula campaign and the way in which that strategy was implemented. As some historians have argued, one must make the distinction. A slightly more aggressive general might have brought the proposed turning movement to a victorious conclusion. Yet in the eyes of many northerners, the entire peninsula strategy had been discredited. According to Archer Jones, "This meant that it became politically impossible for any general to repeat the movement to the Peninsula, even if Lincoln had permitted it. Thus this made one more strategic complexity for the Union high command." For this, the Committee on the Conduct of the War was at least partially to blame.[54]

Meanwhile, Lincoln still had an important decision to make, namely, what to do with McClellan's Army of the Potomac at Harrison Landing. As it languished on the banks of the James River in early July, McClellan persistently lobbied the administration for reinforcements. With Congress on the verge of passing a more radical confiscation act, he feared that a more violent phase of war was coming. With this in mind, he recorded his thoughts on conducting war in the famous Harrison Landing letter. The war "should be conducted upon the highest principles known to Christian Civilization. ... Neither confiscation of property," he argued, "political executions of persons, territorial organizations of states or forcible abolition of slavery should be contemplated for the moment." Private property should be respected, and pillaging considered a high crime. "A system of policy thus constitutional and conservative ... would receive the support of almost all truly loyal men, would deeply impress the rebel masses and foreign governments." Yet, McClellan warned, "A declaration of radical views, especially upon slavery, will rapidly disintegrate our present Armies." When Lincoln visited Harrison Landing on July 7 to discuss the plight of the army, he was given the letter. Although he expressed no opinion on the subject to McClellan, his views could not have been favorable since he was just days away from drafting the Emancipation Proclamation.[55]

Indeed, as Lincoln's biographer David Herbert Donald points out, the president had soured on the style of warfare proposed by McClellan: "That policy had been pursued for over a year and Lincoln was convinced that it had failed." Sharing the Harrison Landing letter with his cabinet, Lincoln's changing point of view encouraged the radical members, including Stanton and Chase, giving them and the committee the opportunity to put forward John Pope. Born in Kaskaskia, Illinois, Pope was the son of Judge Nathaniel Pope. A West Point graduate, he was one of the few regular army officers with Republican sentiments, a distinct advantage in summer 1862. Since he had a successful record in the West, Stanton invited him to Washington to combine the separate commands of McDowell, Frémont, and Banks into the new Army of Virginia, a position Pope assumed on June 26. Pope and his supporters, however, had greater ambitions. Even before Pope arrived in Washington, a New York merchant, A. T. Stewart, was busily touting him as a replacement for McClellan. Accompanied by Illinois senator Orville Browning, Stewart met with Lincoln and expressed his opinion. Meanwhile, Pope's wife Clara wrote her husband that he would definitely get Banks's, Frémont's, and McDowell's commands and he might even replace McClellan. Lincoln, his confidence in McClellan rapidly diminishing, needed little persuasion.[56]

After he arrived in Washington, Pope quickly began to cultivate congressional leaders. On June 25 he delivered an address to the House of Representatives in which he attacked slavery and ridiculed McClellan's estimates of rebel forces opposing him near Richmond. Then, on July 8, he was summoned before the Committee on the Conduct of the War. Although the ostensible reason for his appearance was to discuss the strategy of his new command, Pope criticized McClellan at every opportunity, telling committee members that the strategy behind the Peninsula campaign was flawed. His charismatic and aggressive style impressed the committee. Wright asked if he planned to act on the defensive, merely guarding Washington. "I mean to attack them at all times that I can get the opportunity," Pope replied. By discrediting McClellan's strategy and promising aggressive action, Pope apparently excited most committee members, who seemed unaware that his battle strategy was totally out of step with developments in weaponry, making such reckless offensive operations extremely hazardous.[57]

Shortly after he spoke with the committee, Pope delivered an address to his troops in which he ridiculed McClellan's strategic methods. Pope advised

John Pope's bold, aggressive rhetoric made him a committee favorite. (Courtesy of the National Archives)

his army to discard such terms as lines of retreat. "Success and glory are the advance," he said, "disaster and shame lurk in the rear." The address was followed by a series of general orders, issued on July 18 and July 20, which directly opposed the sentiments expressed in McClellan's Harrison Landing letter. Pope's orders, probably drafted with Stanton's help, authorized the army to live off the land (although supplies would be paid for), permitted army officials to force civilians to work, and allowed the army to send out of its lines any male who failed to swear a loyalty oath to the Union. Pope's orders seemed the perfect complement to the Second Confiscation Act, passed on July 17, which authorized the seizure of property and slaves of known rebels. To many Republicans, it seemed that a new, harsher war had been inaugurated, one that would ultimately destroy the root of the rebellion and allow a reconstruction of southern society. It was simply a matter of placing the army in the hands of men who would implement the new strategy.[58]

Pope claimed to have made his address and orders "to infuse vigor into the army by stirring words," but many observers recognized his actions as a direct attack on McClellan and his policy of conciliation. McClellan and his friends in the Army of the Potomac were determined to resist this change. "Watch my new friend Pope," McClellan wrote to Randolph Marcy; "I fear he is in collusion with Chandler, at least I am so informed." Fitz-John Porter remarked to a friend in the U.S. Census Bureau, "I regret to see that Gen'l Pope has not improved since his youth and has now written himself down (what the military has long known) an ass." According to Marsena Patrick, once Pope's orders were issued, his soldiers acted as though they had the right "to rob, tyrannize, threaten & maltreat any one they please. . . . I do *not* want to serve under Gen. Pope. . . . I have not a particle of confidence in him."[59]

With the session of Congress ended, committee members were in their home states campaigning for the fall election. Congress, during the nineteenth century, was not in session for much of the year, which presented a major problem in continuity since congressional committees normally did not conduct business when Congress was not in session. Just when the committee seemed on the verge of seeing McClellan replaced with Pope, the session ended. Committee members could attack McClellan in speeches as they began the fall campaign; however, they were powerless to effect policy in the capital. Instead, they looked to the two most sympathetic cabinet officers, Stanton and Chase, to continue the war on McClellan and his policy of conciliation.

Stanton had always worked well with the committee and shared many of the Republican majority's beliefs. Although Wade and Chase did not get along personally, they still saw eye to eye on McClellan and the threat his war policy represented to Republican ideals. Making their job a little easier was the fact that Lincoln was rapidly losing confidence in McClellan. When McClellan's chief of staff Randolph Marcy came to Washington on July 4, he told Stanton that, if not reinforced properly, the army might have to capitulate. "This excited Stanton very much," recalled Orville Browning, "and he went directly to the President and reported what had been said." Lincoln, too, was upset at such defeatist language and lectured Marcy: "I understand you have used the word 'capitulate'—that is a word not to be used in connection with the army." On July 13 Marcy told McClellan that Lincoln was becoming impatient and might relieve him if he did not advance soon. Stanton and Chase also knew that Lincoln had rejected the conservatism of McClellan's

Harrison Landing letter since he had drafted an emancipation proclamation and signed the Second Confiscation Act as well as the Militia Act, both of which provided for using blacks in noncombat military roles.[60]

Toward the end of July, Chandler wrote Chase reminding him of the necessity for a change in the administration's war policy. "We are compelled to disclaim the whole policy of the Administration," he complained, or recruits could not be secured for the army. Chase, in frequent consultation with Stanton, had already been working to effect such a change. On July 21 he met with Pope and Valentine B. Horton, a Republican congressman from Ohio. While Horton railed against McClellan's generalship, Pope played the sycophant, claiming that slavery must be destroyed and promising to employ blacks as army laborers. On July 22 Chase conversed with Lincoln, urging him to get rid of McClellan because he was not loyal to the administration. Lincoln, however, could not be persuaded to relieve McClellan for Pope. The reasons were simple. Since the quarrel between McClellan and the administration, particularly with Stanton, had become so politicized, Lincoln undoubtedly believed that to put Pope over McClellan would be more than many Democrats could tolerate. They had already been forced to swallow abolition in the District of Columbia and the Second Confiscation Act. With Lincoln contemplating emancipation, replacing McClellan might ruin all hope of a bipartisan approach to the war. McClellan indeed wrote Barlow at the end of July that the administration would not relieve him because of his support in the army and from the public. So seriously did Lincoln regard the public's perception of the dispute between Stanton and McClellan that in early August he addressed a Union meeting in Washington and attempted to convince the audience that the differences between the two men were not as great as many supposed.[61]

Lincoln did appoint Henry W. Halleck as general in chief on July 11, however, and Stanton and Chase, with Pope's assistance, contrived to use Halleck as a tool to deprive McClellan of his army and to give it to Pope. "Pope is making a little light, and gives promise of a great deal more," Chase wrote, "but everything depends on General Halleck—If he is the right man in the right spot all may, with God's favor, go well." As soon as Halleck arrived in Washington, he was forced to deal with the question of the fate of the Army of the Potomac, whether to reinforce it or withdraw it from Harrison Landing. There was considerable divergence of opinion among the officers in the army; and, ironically, even those supposedly hostile to McClellan, such as Heintzelman, favored remaining on the peninsula. Shortly after Halleck arrived in Washington, he traveled to McClellan's camp to confer with him and his corps commanders. After Halleck returned to Washington, McClellan began pressing his case by letter: "I still feel that our true policy is to reinforce this army by every available means & throw it again at Richmond." He also appealed to Halleck's political conservatism. "If we are permitted to do so, I believe that together we can save this unhappy country and bring this war to an early termination," McClellan wrote. "I fear the results of the *civil* policy inaugurated by the recent Acts of Congress and practically enumerated by General Pope in his series of orders to the Army of Virginia."

Meanwhile, Chase continued his assault on McClellan in cabinet meetings. On August 3 he complained that the nation's leading generals were "hostile to the Administration." Referring specifically to McClellan and Don Carlos Buell, Chase claimed they were incompetent and slow. That same day, Halleck decided to recall the Army of the Potomac and ordered McClellan to transport his troops from the James River to Acquia Creek. According to Secretary of the Navy Gideon Welles, Chase and Stanton conspired to withdraw McClellan's army and have the bulk of it transferred to Pope. The unspoken assumption was that if Pope were to win a victory, it would be politically possible for Lincoln to replace McClellan with him.[62]

Stanton and Chase's scheme would work, however, only if Pope's army was victorious. When McClellan and his men were recalled, Pope's Army of Virginia was advancing southward along the eastern edge of the Shenandoah Valley. He had gone as far as Cedar Mountain, only to have Nathaniel Banks's advance troops driven off by Stonewall Jackson. Then, when Lee was sure that McClellan had left the peninsula permanently, he decided to move north and destroy Pope's army before McClellan could reinforce it. Unfortunately for Pope's supporters, there were already early signs that McClellan would cooperate with Lee more than with Pope. As John J. Hennessy has written, "American military history includes few more disturbing streams of correspondence than this," describing McClellan's August 1862 letters. "I have a strong idea that Pope will be thrashed during the coming week—& very badly whipped," McClellan wrote his wife; "he will be & ought to be—such a villain as he ought to bring defeat upon any cause that employs him." Fitz-John Porter was equally hostile. "Pope is a fool," he wrote; "McDowell is a rascal and Halleck has brains but not the independence[,] trying to satisfy Stanton & President & public in opposition to principle and judgement."[63]

Events quickly came to a head. Dividing his army in two, Lee sent Jackson to march around Pope's army to the northwest, gain possession of his supply depot at Manassas, and cut his communication with Washington. An overconfident Pope believed he would be able to trap Jackson before he could reunite with Confederate troops under Gen. James Longstreet. The problem was finding Jackson. On August 29, with Jackson's divisions located, Pope's army attacked. Bad luck, Pope's ineptitude, and McClellan's and his subordinates' passivity combined to contribute to his defeat. In position to flank Jackson on the left, Porter, lacking positive orders to do so, did nothing. Then when Pope belatedly did order him to attack, he was unable to comply because Longstreet's troops, coming to Jackson's support, were in front of him. On August 30 Pope, still unaware of Longstreet's presence on the battlefield, assailed Jackson and weakened the Union left in an attempt to overwhelm him. When Longstreet launched a vigorous counterattack on the Union left, northern forces quickly fell back. That evening a beaten, demoralized army retreated down the Warrenton Turnpike to Washington.

Pope had not been helped by McClellan, whose stubborn passivity had deprived him of William Franklin's and Edward Sumner's troops; McClellan had invented a myriad of excuses to prevent their moving. Although short of disloyalty, McClellan's attitude during the campaign was hardly that of a disinterested patriot: "I believe I have triumphed!! Just received a telegram from Halleck stating that Pope & Burnside are very hard pressed—urging me to push forward reinforcements & to *come myself as soon as I possibly can!* Now they want the 'Quaker' & the 'procrastinator,' the 'coward.'" McClellan's wife shared his scorn for Pope, writing, "I *try* to look sorry when I hear anything has happened to that brilliant individual [Pope], but it is terribly hard work to feel so." At the height of the crisis, McClellan sounded petty, spiteful, and evasive in his communications with Halleck. On August 29 he suggested two options to Lincoln, to combine forces and link up with Pope or "to leave Pope to get out of his own scrape & at once use all of our means to make the Capital perfectly safe." For a general who claimed to have such affection for the men of the Army of the Potomac, he displayed a particularly callous attitude toward their plight, since some of these same soldiers were fighting under Pope.[64]

With Pope's defeated army heading for Washington, Lincoln's cabinet staged a minirevolt. Angered with what they considered McClellan's perfidy, Chase and Stanton prepared a statement detailing McClellan's misconduct and demanding his dismissal. Chase took the statement to various cabinet members for their signatures and planned to confront Lincoln with it. Besides Chase and Stanton, Bates and Caleb Smith enthusiastically endorsed the document. Seward was conveniently out of town, and Blair, whose sympathies for McClellan were well known, was not consulted. When Chase saw Gideon Welles on August 31, he asked for his support. Although Welles no longer trusted McClellan, he would not sign the statement, declaring it was disrespectful to the president. The next day, Chase attempted to convince Welles to sign a less objectionable report, explaining that the intent was not to embarrass Lincoln but to ensure the administration's survival. According to Welles, Chase "frankly" stated his intention was to "disgrace" McClellan, "that he . . . believed McClellan ought to be shot, and should, were he President, be brought to summary punishment." But Lincoln did not let the cabinet officers control him even though he was disappointed with McClellan's behavior. After Ambrose Burnside refused command, Lincoln and Halleck decided they had no choice but to stick with McClellan and gave him command of the Washington defenses. When Stanton "excitedly" informed the cabinet of this decision on September 2 before Lincoln arrived at the meeting, "general surprise was expressed." "The bitterness of Stanton on the reinstatement of McClellan," Montgomery Blair told Porter years later, "you can scarcely conceive." Lincoln justified his actions, claiming that since the capital was in danger, McClellan was the best man for the job; his defensive expertise was acknowledged by virtually everyone. Thus McClellan was back, and Pope was sent to Minnesota to fight the Sioux.[65]

Lincoln's decision was probably based on two important considerations. First, he knew the army was partial to McClellan. As Secretary Welles acknowledged, "My convictions are with the President that McClellan and his generals are this day stronger than the Administration with a considerable portion of this Army of the Potomac." This state of affairs was disturbing, especially when Lincoln knew and acknowledged that leading officers of the army had allowed victory to slip away because "they were vexed at Pope." Lincoln's second reason was political. With the Democrats already exercised over radical measures enacted by Congress, if Lincoln were to dismiss McClellan, they would claim it was a partisan maneuver, which could seriously hurt the war effort and damage the Republican party in the fall elections.[66]

Despite these reasons, Lincoln's decision to put McClellan in charge remained controversial. John Pope was probably the most angry, believing that he had been deliberately sacrificed by the McClellan element in the Army of the Potomac. "Is it that I am to be deprived of my command because of the treachery of McClellan & tools?" he asked Henry Halleck. He then promptly brought charges against Fitz-John Porter for disobeying orders.

Democratic organs rejoiced over Lincoln's decision, however, claiming the president had demonstrated his independence from the "radical abolition program," which the majority of the cabinet supported. The Republi-

can *New York Times* believed Lincoln's decision was the correct one, given
McClellan's defensive skills, but many other Republicans were incredulous.
A Philadelphia man asked John Covode why Lincoln had reappointed
McClellan, wondering if his blunders before Richmond had not been enough
to convince the president that he was both a fool and a coward and suggest-
ing that Pope had been deliberately beaten down like Frémont. An agitated
Zachariah Chandler asked Assistant Secretary of War Peter Watson, "Is there
any hope for the future?" To Illinois senator Lyman Trumbull he remarked,
"This is *treason* . . . call it what you will." Chandler also suggested to
Trumbull a meeting of northern governors to force Lincoln to make changes
in policy by claiming recruitment would otherwise suffer. When Pope's report made its way into the *New York Times* with its charges that the failure
of Second Bull Run had resulted from lack of any help from McClellan,
Franklin, and Porter, Chandler was outraged: "Are mutinous *traitorous*
Generals *now* controlling our destiny? If so! What are we fighting for? . . .
For God's sake let us save the Government. Treason is raising its hideous
head all over the land." Chandler closed his letter to Chase, asking, "Confi-
dentially tell me what next?" Chase wrote Chandler that Pope's report was
no exaggeration; however, he had been totally unprepared for Lincoln's
decision to put McClellan back in command. Still, he was powerless to act
with respect to war measures. Stanton also wrote Chandler that he appreciated his concerns but was unable to effect change.[67]

For committee members, the second battle of Bull Run and the reappointment of McClellan must have been particularly frustrating. From December
1861 through summer 1862, they had endeavored to force the army into
action and to remove the man whose political conservatism prevented the
war from being waged as they believed it should be. They had witnessed the
president's capitulation to McClellan in the presence of vocal Republican
opposition in the cabinet. The Slave Power was alive and well. After the
Union's Pyrrhic victory at Antietam, where McClellan had foiled Lee's inva-
sion of the North and forced the Army of Northern Virginia to retreat south
of the Potomac River, Lincoln gained enough confidence to issue the preliminary Emancipation Proclamation, which created a temporary revival of
morale among committee members and Republicans in general. "Hurrah for
Old Abe and the Proclamation," Wade wrote to Julian. But affairs quickly
settled into the familiar pattern of the administration trying to make
McClellan move and McClellan never being quite ready. Even a presidential
visit to the Army of the Potomac's headquarters in early October could not
prod him into action. Soon Halleck and McClellan were engaged in a written sparring match, Halleck urging forward movement and McClellan mak-

ing excuses. "He has lain still twenty days since the battle of Antietam," Halleck complained to his wife; "I cannot persuade him to advance an inch. It puts me all out of patience."[68]

Republicans were particularly impatient because they believed McClellan's inactivity would ruin them in the fall elections. Indiana governor Oliver Morton stressed this anxiety in an early October letter to Lincoln, claiming if the armies did not make significant progress in sixty days, the cause would be lost. Abolitionist Lydia Maria Child wrote Charles Sumner that she believed McClellan was playing a political game, "amusing the country with promises, and reconnaissances, but avoiding battle, because his object was to prolong the war until the next presidential election, and then to sell the country to the slaveholders." The army would have pursued Lee into Virginia, she explained, "if General McClellan had not been playing false." Chandler claimed that Michigan would certainly vote Republican that fall, but McClellan's inactivity was still hurting the cause. He called on Trumbull, Wade, and James Harlan of Iowa to stump the state with him. "Old Fossil Whiggery has united with Vallandigham conspiring to overthrow the Radicals *but* it will not be done in this state," he wrote Chase.[69]

With the fall elections behind him, Lincoln removed the recalcitrant McClellan from command on November 7, 1862, replacing him with Ambrose Burnside. Personally, the president was hesitant to give McClellan up. According to David Davis, Lincoln "was the last man to yield to the necessity of McClellan's removal. . . . He wished to give him every chance. Halleck . . . insisted on his removal." As expected, the decision was cheered by Republicans but jeered by Democrats. "God will save us yet!" the *New York Daily Tribune* rejoiced. "It took months of stubborn, criminal, fatal paralysis, in the face of a foe contemptible in every strength save hoodwinking our Commanding General, to cut us from this fond delusion." Schuyler Colfax wrote Lincoln, "Our people send grateful thanks for Burnside's appointment, changing despair into confidence & hope." Democrats throughout the country charged that McClellan had been sacrificed to please abolition fanatics. "Their intrigues," Bennett's *New York Herald* commented, "have pursued him from the day that he was first called to the command of the Army of the Potomac." The *Chicago Times* claimed not to be dismayed with McClellan's dismissal because the radicals never would have allowed him to succeed. When Halleck published his report on the Army of the Potomac's operations since Antietam, it was extremely critical of McClellan. Chandler remarked, "Halleck's report has put the last clod of earth upon McClellan's coffin lid. . . . I am only sorry the game is so small."[70]

The committee's harassment of George McClellan undoubtedly bolstered his prospects as the 1864 Democratic presidential nominee. (Courtesy of the National Archives)

What had the committee accomplished in its extensive investigation of the Army of the Potomac? Certainly it would give them too much credit to say that their influence brought about McClellan's removal. Clearly that was their goal; however, when Lincoln finally removed McClellan from command, he did so on his own terms. Perhaps, as Hans Trefousse points out, the committee acted as a lever for Lincoln, allowing him to prod the cautious McClellan into action. Yet one can argue that such prodding made McClellan more stubborn and recalcitrant. Generally, as with Bull Run and Ball's Bluff, the committee's activities were largely superfluous, a waste of time and resources.

Yet there was one major negative ramification. Lacking military knowledge, the committee members tended to reinforce amateurish and naive opinions about warfare through their actions. In McClellan's case, the investigation, along with Chandler's public attack, helped discredit the general's strategy—the turning movement of the Peninsula campaign—on the grounds that it was cowardly. The committee continued to promote offensive warfare—forward movement and frontal assault—with no regard for the appropriateness of such maneuvers. Aggressiveness by Union officers was not an undesirable characteristic, but committee members failed to comprehend that aggressiveness without a proper understanding of the realities of strategy and weaponry could be a detriment to northern forces. Given their assumptions about military matters, their investigations unfortunately reinforced popular misconceptions about warfare and limited the strategic options of the Union high command. In the process, the CCW helped create ill feelings and distrust among the Union's West Point officers with respect to their civilian overseers.[71]

Chandler described McClellan as small game, but he clearly was wrong. The committee had labored consistently for harsher war measures and vigorous leadership, as necessary components for a Republican victory in the fall elections. Yet the results of the elections hardly demonstrated a Republican triumph. As committee members soon realized, the elections indicated trouble on the horizon. The Democrats captured a number of states and possessed much power in the nation's army, making it quickly apparent that McClellan was far from forgotten. He was being put forth as the next Democratic nominee for president, and there were constant cries and demands for his return to the Army of the Potomac. When Congress met in December 1862, the committee launched a five-month effort to ensure that McClellan and his notion of limited war remained politically and militarily vanquished.

CHAPTER FIVE

The Fall Elections, West Point, and the Crisis of 1862–1863

Although members of the Joint Committee on the Conduct of the War were overjoyed with the removal of McClellan from command on November 7, 1862, the results of the fall elections were far from pleasing. After losing the governorships of New Jersey and New York, the state legislatures of Illinois and Indiana, and twenty-five seats in the House of Representatives, Republicans throughout the country had reason to be uneasy. Democrats capitalized on a variety of issues. Arbitrary arrests and Lincoln's suspension of the writ of habeas corpus allowed them to charge the administration with violating the Constitution. Economic depression, particularly in the Midwest because of the closing of the Mississippi River, created resentment among many small farmers who claimed that their economic interests were being sacrificed while railroads and eastern industry prospered. The preliminary Emancipation Proclamation fueled northerners' fears of free blacks and led to charges that Republicans were no longer fighting for the Union but for black equality. In Illinois, an ill-advised attempt by the War Department to settle newly freed slaves or contrabands there caused a hostile outcry against the administration. Underlying the dissatisfaction, however, was the failure of Union armies to win significant victories, which led to the perception of a weak and indecisive administration. "The New York and other elections are simply a reproof of the inactivity of the Government—and the confused state of finances," wrote Boston attorney John Chipman Ropes. "They have nothing to do with the nigger question. With the administration military success is everything—it is the verdict which cures all errors." Echoing these sentiments, Edwards Pierrepont consoled defeated New York Republican gubernatorial candidate James S. Wadsworth: "The country was tired of inaction—disgusted with the delay and determined that the President should hear & heed a voice which had not been regarded for a long time."[1]

The Context of the Fall Elections

James McPherson has argued that the fall elections were not a rebuke to the administration, however. Although their majorities were reduced in several states, Republicans held the vast majority of governorships. They retained control of the House and realized a slight increase in their majority in the Senate. It was the slightest off-year election loss in twenty years, McPherson argues, noting that despite the so-called electoral setback, Lincoln still felt strong enough to remove McClellan from command and follow through on his Emancipation Proclamation.[2]

McPherson is undoubtedly correct, but his analysis fails to capture contemporary perceptions of the election's significance. Many Democrats were convinced that the election represented a solid repudiation of Republican policy. According to the *New York Herald,* the election results did not mean the war would cease "but that the war shall be prosecuted for the maintenance of the Union, and for nothing else." George Boutwell, a Massachusetts radical elected to Congress that fall, noted that the election encouraged House Democrats to become "confident and aggressive." John Dean Caton, a justice on the Illinois State Supreme Court, interpreted Democratic victories in a public letter to New York governor-elect Horatio Seymour. Although Republicans attributed their losses to the administration's unwillingness to implement harsh measures against the rebels, Caton maintained that the reverse was true. Republican war goals were unconstitutional, particularly the Emancipation Proclamation: "It was the Proclamation," he asserted, "which produced revolution in the North—a peaceful and a constitutional revolution." Democratic victory meant the repudiation of barbaric measures and a return to the policy of conciliation: "Every act of kindness and mercy opens a new avenue to reconciliation and peace," Caton counseled, "every act of brutality and barbarity closes the door leading to these rebels."[3]

Republicans brushed aside this interpretation, claiming the opposite was true. It was a timid, vacillating administration, too subservient to the concerns of conservatives, that had caused defeat. "If Lincoln will only cut loose now from Border state sympathizing and would be northern conservatives," wrote one Michigan Republican, "and drive the war to the utmost power of the government[,] we will carry everything before us in 1864." German-American leader Carl Schurz castigated Lincoln for making bad patronage decisions and elevating leading Democrats to positions of high military authority, a certain recipe for defeat and a sentiment echoed by other Republicans. Some newspapers complained that Republican defeat was due to soldiers absent in the field who were prevented from voting in their states—an objection based on the unprovable assumption that Republicans vastly outnumbered Democrats in the army. Still, regardless of the reasons given for the defeat, few people interpreted the elections as anything but a repudiation—an outcome that not only jeopardized Republican war goals but also the very life of the Republic.[4]

Republican attitudes toward these reverses were aired in a meeting between Lincoln and three party members. Shortly after the election, Lincoln met with Pennsylvania congressmen William Kelley, Edward McPherson, and James K. Moorhead to discuss the election results. Kelley, who had overcome numerous obstacles to recapture his seat, credited his victory to his willingness to support a vigorous war and his persistent calls for McClellan's removal. When Lincoln asked McPherson, who had lost a safe district, the cause of his defeat, McPherson talked around the issue until Kelley told Lincoln, "My colleague is not treating you frankly." When Lincoln assured McPherson he wanted frankness, McPherson said he had lost because the incompetent McClellan had been retained in command. Turning to Moorhead, Lincoln said, "And what word do you bring? . . . You, at any rate, were not defeated." Moorhead indicated that his victory was unrelated to Lincoln's actions and that Pittsburgh Republicans were upset with the president. Moorhead had overheard one say that "he would be glad to hear some morning that you had been found hanging from the post of a lamp at the door of the White House." The losses were serious. Few Republicans cared whether this was the least significant setback in twenty years; it was a rebuke in the midst of Civil War, calling into question whether the war would continue and under what conditions.[5]

Members of the Committee on the Conduct of the War had been active participants in the fall campaign and undoubtedly viewed the elections with mixed emotions. In general, they saw the results as a repudiation of Lincoln's management of the war. Had it not been for their work in securing the removal of McClellan, committee members believed that the Republican party would have suffered even more substantial losses. Hence, they interpreted the election as an incentive to redouble their assault on the conservative elements of the Union military establishment.

The Republican committee members survived their reelection battles except for John Covode, who decided to pursue the Republican nomination for governor of Pennsylvania. House members Daniel W. Gooch and George Julian were reelected, although Julian faced considerable opposition, first battling antiradical factions within his own party and then bucking the Democratic trend in Indiana that fall. Senate Republicans Wade and Chandler also won reelection in their state legislatures, although neither regarded his election as a foregone conclusion. In each state, opponents used Wade and Chandler's committee work in an effort to discredit them, portraying each senator as an opponent of the administration whose actions hampered the Union war effort.[6]

Democratic members of the committee faced even stiffer challenges. Although Joseph Wright had differed with Chandler over his attack on McClellan, he supported the Republican administration that fall. As early as July, Lincoln urged Wright to campaign in Terre Haute, Indiana, the congressional district of bitter Democratic critic Daniel W. Voorhees. Wright was convinced that regular Democratic organizations were fronts for treasonable activities. In early August, he told Salmon Chase that dangerous men were working against the administration in Indiana. Wright made some seventy-five speeches in Indiana and Illinois, where he appeared with Tennessee Unionist William (Parson) Brownlow. Republicans applauded his actions. "Governor Wright," wrote the (Springfield) Illinois *State Journal,* "justly regarded every one a traitor who did not support the Administration unqualifidely [sic]; just as much a traitor as a rebel in arms against the North." Democrats, on the other hand, ridiculed Wright as a turncoat. When the preliminary Emancipation Proclamation was issued, Joseph J. Bingham's (Indianapolis) *Daily State Sentinel* castigated so-called Union Democrats such as Wright: "Is that part of their contract they made in their alliance with the Republicans? Will they sit down to the abolition feast to which they are invited as willing and cheerful guests?" With the election of a Democratic legislature that fall in Indiana, Wright's days in the Senate were numbered. As soon as the legislature met in January 1863, it dispensed with the renegade, choosing David Turpie to complete Bright's term and then Thomas Hendrick to a new six-year term.[7]

The election results raised questions about how both Republicans and Democrats would proceed, if the war effort would be impeded and if Republican antislavery principles would be compromised. New York Republican boss and William Seward's associate Thurlow Weed left immediately for Albany after the election to meet with Horatio Seymour and other Democrats "and prevail upon them, if possible, to take Patriotic grounds." An Indiana man in the army expressed disappointment at the election of Democrats Daniel Voorhees and Thomas Hendrick in his state. "They are desperate in their fortunes," he warned Cong. Schuyler Colfax, "and bitter in their sympathies as was [Jefferson] Davis." *New York Times* editor Henry Raymond warned Lincoln that any attempt to make the war an abolition crusade would alienate the border states, advising that the president should proceed with the Proclamation but should make sure it was published as a military measure. Already suspicious of Democrats, Chandler complained also about Secretary of State Seward, whom he saw as responsible for Lincoln's indecision. "Seward is the evil genius of this administration," he told his wife, "we can crush this rebellion . . . shall we! God hurry."[8]

In the midst of this doubt and uncertainty, Union defeat at Fredericksburg on December 13 accelerated the sense of crisis among Republicans and gave the Committee on the Conduct of the War its opportunity to alter the direction of the Union war effort and to invigorate the nation's sagging morale. McClellan's replacement, Ambrose Burnside, had solid credentials from his successful management of the Roanoke Island expedition off the coast of North Carolina in early 1862. Although Lincoln had offered him the top command on two previous occasions, Burnside had turned him down in deference to his friend McClellan, claiming that he lacked the ability to assume such an important command. In fall 1862, however, McClellan censured him for what he considered tardy movement both at South Mountain and Antietam. When Lincoln offered Burnside the command for the third time, he accepted, partly to prevent the position from going to Joseph Hooker, who had been angling for it for months and whom Burnside regarded as unscrupulous.[9]

Aware of the popular clamor for forward movement, Burnside was determined to strike a blow quickly. Feinting in the direction of the Orange and Alexandria Railroad toward Warrenton, Virginia, Burnside instead moved his army to Falmouth, where he intended to cross the river at Fredericksburg and move on Richmond. Arriving at Falmouth on November 19, he completely surprised Lee but could not cross the Rappahannock River because previously ordered pontoon bridges had not arrived. General-in-Chief Halleck claimed that he thought Burnside intended to cross at the junction of the Rappahannock and Rapidan Rivers west of Fredericksburg, making the arrival of the pontoons less critical. By the time the pontoons did arrive, Lee was apprised of the Union army's movements. He positioned his army on the heights behind Fredericksburg to oppose Burnside's progress.[10]

Burnside stubbornly clung to the idea of crossing at Fredericksburg, drawing up a plan for a two-pronged attack. Edwin V. Sumner's right Grand Division would assault the Confederate position at Marye's heights, and William Buel Franklin's left Grand Division, positioned below Fredericksburg, would assault Lee's right, preventing him from reinforcing his left and thus dividing his army in two. Hooker's Grand Division would operate in the middle and funnel troops to where they were most needed. The battle began on the morning of December 13, and Burnside's plans began to unravel. When Franklin received his orders from Burnside that morning, he thought Burnside had changed his plans. Franklin believed that his Grand Division was to make a diversionary attack, so he sent forward his smallest division, commanded by George Gordon Meade. Although Meade's troops came close to breaking through the Confederate position, they were not supported properly and fell back. Meanwhile, Sumner's Grand Division launched an all-out assault on Marye's heights, only to be subjected to murderous slaughter. Sumner's only hope was for Franklin to relieve the pressure by vigorous assault on the Confederate right. About 3:00 P.M., Burnside ordered Franklin to make such an attack; although promising to do his best, he never made the assault, and the Union attack on Marye's heights ended, an ignominious failure.[11]

Distraught and blaming himself for the numerous casualties (12,000 as it turned out), Burnside wanted to renew the attack the next day, vowing to lead personally his old Ninth Corps. A council of war, however, changed his mind and the Union army recrossed the Rappahannock. Darius Couch, commander of the Second Corps, summed up the futile attack on Marye's heights: "We were asked to achieve an impossibility." Taken together with the fall electoral setbacks, the defeat at Fredericksburg marked the low point of the Union war effort.[12]

Democratic newspapers wasted little time in criticizing the administration. Instead of blaming Burnside, they took particular aim at Lincoln, Halleck, Stanton, and the War Department. Manton Marble's *New York World* declared, "Again have you, Abraham Lincoln, by the hands of Henry Halleck and Edwin M. Stanton sent to death thousands upon thousands of our brothers and friends." According to the *New York Herald,* Burnside did his best, but the War Department hampered him by failing to deliver pontoon bridges on time. The *Chicago Times* called for the reinstatement of McClellan, a sentiment seconded by many in the army. "From the feeling here," wrote Stephen Weld, an aide to former Fifth Corps commander Fitz-John Porter, "I think we shall see General McClellan in command soon." Another private remarked, "I suppose the radicals have got enough of Burnside now and will want another change. . . . I am sick of such useless slaughter, McClellan never made an attack and failed, and never showed such stupidity as Burnside has."[13]

Republicans were similarly outraged but worried more about how the disaster might alter the party's war goals. "Slaughter and infamy," wrote Adam Gurowski, "the Lincoln-Seward-Halleck influence gave Burnside the command because he was to take care of the army. And now Burnside has fulfilled their expectations." Ohio diarist William Coggeshell recorded that Burnside's defeat was encouraging peace Democrats such as Vallandigham who saw opportunity for compromise with the Confederacy and the formation of a new party "to preserve slavery." David Davis, Lincoln's close friend and recent Supreme Court nominee, wrote his friend Leonard Swett, "Many men are in despair and openly say that they fear there can never be a reunited people." One of Chandler's constituents worried that the defeat might force the president to suspend the Emancipation Proclamation: "For *God's* sake, don't let the President back down on his proclamation." Ohio congressman William Cutler observed that McClellan's supporters rejoiced at the defeat and were doing all in their power to destroy the administration. "We are at sea & no pilot or captain," he complained; "it really seems as though the ship of state was going to pieces in the storm. The Democrats cry peace & compromise—clamor for McClellan—blame the *radicals*—in a word do everything in the world to embarrass the govt."[14]

In the Senate, angry Republicans criticized the administration, expressing hostility toward Secretary of State Seward, whom they regarded as responsible for the administration's tepidity. Benjamin Wade, chairman of the CCW, was perhaps the most vociferous in his denunciation of Seward, telling the Senate that another cabinet officer "informed him that there was a back stairs & malign influence which controlled the President, and overruled all decisions of the cabinet, and he understood Mr. Seward to be meant." Vice President Hannibal Hamlin reported that the sentiment was prevalent, writing to his wife Ellie, "[Seward] has been regarded as a millstone around the Administration."[15]

The CCW became a focal point in the crisis when the Senate passed a resolution introduced by Minnesota's Morton S. Wilkinson, authorizing it to investigate the battle and to determine which officers were responsible for the disaster. When the committee met on December 18, it decided to visit the Army of the Potomac at its winter quarters in Falmouth. This was no routine investigation, some committee members believed; it would play a major role in redirecting the Union war effort. "The fact is," Chandler wrote his wife the day before the visit, "the country is gone unless something is done at once. . . . What that something is I think I know & shall try and accomplish. We must have men in command of our armies who are anxious to crush the rebellion." The present military leadership, Chandler complained, did not take heart in the cause. His comments reveal the basic approach that governed the committee's investigation. Military victory resulted from vigorous, perpetual forward movement; defeat from caution, concern over strategy, and defective war goals. Instead of seeing Burnside's defeat for what it was, a foolhardy plan dictated by popular pressure for military action (no doubt helped along by the CCW's incessant clamoring), the committee attempted to paint Burnside as the martyred victim of a West Point–dominated military establishment.[16]

The committee arrived at Falmouth on the morning of December 19 and immediately began to take testimony. Only Joseph Wright failed to make the trip. Democratic papers were skeptical of the visit. The *New York Herald* hoped that the investigation would not be a mere whitewash, for the issues were simply too important. The *Chicago Times* was less optimistic. "We have had nothing but blunders in the War Department from the first," the paper noted, "and abolition committees, without brains enough to comprehend these blunders, and too much blinded by partisan bigotry to report fairly if they did comprehend, have been inquiring into them."

The visit began inauspiciously as the Senate's sergeant-at-arms, George T. Brown, who accompanied the congressmen, arrived so drunk he had to find a tent in order to lie down. Nevertheless, the committee's visit was viewed by the army with a great deal of apprehension, and rumors circulated about an impending reconstruction in the cabinet. Meeting first with General Burnside, committee members were favorably impressed. George Julian later told Ohio congressman William Cutler that Burnside was "true, loyal & earnest." Instead of making excuses, he accepted the bulk of responsibility for the disaster himself. He did, however, make one pertinent observation in a private talk that Julian later reported: "Our soldiers, he said, were not sufficiently fired by resentment, and he exhorted me, if I could, to breathe into our people at home the same spirit toward our enemies which inspired them toward us." No doubt Julian regarded such passivity as the logical outcome of the conciliatory policy practiced by McClellan and his cohorts.[17]

When Burnside was questioned by committee members, he pointed the finger at no one, but it was obvious from his testimony that he regarded the principal reason for defeat the delay in receiving pontoons. As Gooch later told William Cutler, the responsibility for the delay rested with "subordinate officers." When Burnside had met with Halleck at Warrenton on November 12, shortly after taking command, he had outlined his plans to him and received presidential approval for them a few days later. But when Burnside's chief engineer telegraphed Col. Daniel Woodbury, commander of the engineering brigade and responsible for the pontoon movements, Woodbury had not yet heard of the order. Since Burnside had to familiarize himself with a new command, it was not unreasonable for him to assume that Halleck would attend to the details—but Halleck had not. When the pontoons did begin to move toward Falmouth, their arrival was delayed by bad weather, allowing Lee to concentrate his forces at Fredericksburg and removing any element of surprise Burnside might have gained.

As for the battle itself, Burnside assumed full responsibility, telling committee members that it was simply a matter of assaulting a position that was too well defended. Nor was Burnside overly critical of Franklin for failing to carry the left, claiming delay in crossing the river allowed the Confederates to concentrate a big force in his front. "Since you have assumed command of the Army of the Potomac," Gooch asked, having recent newspaper reports in mind, "have all of its movements been made . . . according to your own judgement, or have some of them been directed by the general in chief, the Secretary of War, or the President of the United States?" "They have all been made in accordance with my own judgment," Burnside replied.[18]

When Gen. George Meade visited Burnside's headquarters on December 19, he found him busily engaged with committee members, who insisted that Meade talk with them. Meade no doubt expected rude treatment, particularly from Chandler, with whom he had clashed earlier when Meade was stationed in Detroit. Knowing that Meade's testimony was crucial in exonerating Burnside, committee members were friendly to the conservative West Pointer. John Covode even claimed Meade as a fellow Pennsylvanian. "What the result will be I don't know," Meade wrote his wife the next day, "though it is said that John Covode affirmed that when he got back he was going to raise a howl, and intimated that it would not be against Burnside."

Meade claimed that Burnside had convinced the committee that he had been ordered to cross the Rappahannock—the reverse of Burnside's testimony. "It is understood," Meade wrote, "[that] Halleck says, 'This army shall go to Richmond if it has to go on crutches.'" In subsequent interviews, generals Edwin V. Sumner, William B. Franklin, Herman Haupt, and Joseph Hooker, however, suggested nothing of the sort. Instead, each emphasized the failure of the pontoon train to arrive on time. Hooker, angling as usual for his own advancement, was critical of Burnside for his stubborn insistence on going through with his plan, despite losing the element of surprise, and with Franklin for failing to commit enough men in his attack. Writing to McClellan shortly after the committee's visit, Franklin claimed the real cause of defeat was the delay in the pontoons. He told McClellan, "I think that whoever is responsible for that delay deserves to be hanged for it."[19]

The committee attempted to discover who was responsible for this delay. Montgomery Meigs, interviewed on December 22, claimed Burnside had expressed concern only about supplying his army but had never mentioned pontoons. And Colonel Woodbury acknowledged receiving Burnside's orders on November 12 but cited numerous complications that prevented the train from leaving until November 19. Poor weather delayed its arrival until November 25. Woodbury had anticipated some of these problems and unsuccessfully tried to get the order delayed for five days. Not only was he unaware of Burnside's intentions, but he had no idea that the situation was urgent. "Had the emergency been made known to me," Woodbury testified, "I could have disregarded the forms of service—seized teams, teamsters, and wagon-masters for instant service."[20]

Expecting vindication for Burnside, his private secretary, Daniel Larned, anticipated the publication of the committee's report. Working frantically after their return from Falmouth, the committee interviewed Halleck, Meigs, and Woodbury and submitted their report to Congress on December 23. It quickly appeared in newspapers across the country. The testimony, submitted without the committee's comment, painted a favorable portrait of Burnside; however, an unfavorable image of the Union high command emerged, one in which confusion and bureaucratic red tape thrived. Burnside's plans were clearly thwarted by the delay in the pontoons, but no one seemed willing to assume responsibility for it. Radical Adam Gurowski focused on General-in-Chief Halleck. Characterizing him as a "red-tapist" and a "small petti-fogger," he remarked, "Halleck alone is responsible for the non-arrival of the pontoons." Elizabeth Blair Lee, sister of Montgomery Blair, was more general, writing, "Certain it is that the Congressional report makes out our Generals—the most brainless—inert set that ever the world saw—& Halleck is the chief of Imbeciles—His own evidence is enough to hang him." One of Wade's correspondents remarked, "All the military heads in Washington—Halleck, Meigs, Ripley [Ordnance] & the rest should be sent where they could not trouble the nation again."[21]

Apart from raising an outcry against the army's high command and keeping Burnside in command, the report accomplished little. "[Burnside] made a mistake," Vice President Hamlin wrote his wife, "but we must not discard him for *one* mistake. Let us feel confident of better results next time. He is a true man & will try to do his duty." Yet the sympathy for Burnside generated by the committee was contradicted by his own actions, especially when he wrote and subsequently published a letter acknowledging his own responsibility for the disaster, thereby taking pressure off the administration. "I think that [Burnside] has done himself an injustice by writing it," William Franklin told McClellan, "but you may imagine how Abe and his councillars rejoice to see such a letter." Halleck blamed the nation's problems in the aftermath of Fredericksburg on politicians who would "cut each other's throat for the sake of 'office.'" Although it is unclear whether he specifically referred to the Committee on the Conduct of the War, Halleck would undoubtedly have included them, observing that there was not one capable leader in the entire Congress. Far from restoring confidence, the committee's report, taken in conjunction with Burnside's letter, most likely generated doubt and uncertainty, particularly about what should be done in the future. Lacking spe-

Over Lincoln's Shoulder

cific recommendations for effectively reorganizing the Union high command, the committee's report, instead of reassuring the North, must have increased despair and feelings of war weariness.[22]

Adding to northern disillusionment was the attempt of Republican congressmen to force Lincoln to remove Seward from the cabinet. On the evenings of December 16 and 17, the Republican caucus formed a committee of nine senators—including Wade—to meet with the president and demand Seward's resignation. His conservative lukewarmness was viewed as a principal reason for war disasters. "All the radicals are hostile to him," David Davis reported to Leonard Swett. Yet this was hardly an issue pitting conservatives against radicals; Vermont conservative Jacob Collamer headed the committee. Rather, it was a Republican plea for fervor and energy in conducting the war, a plea to which few party members objected.

Meeting the president on the evening of December 18, the committee of senators presented Lincoln with three hours' worth of objections to war policies. Wade was particularly blunt, telling Lincoln that he had appointed too many men to positions of military leadership who were unsympathetic to Republican war goals. Most prominent among their demands was their desire that Seward be dismissed. Both Seward and his son Frederic had given their resignations to Lincoln when they learned of the caucus. Believing the senators were "in earnest" but confused, Lincoln agreed to meet the committee with the entire cabinet the next evening. When the senators returned, every cabinet officer, Seward excepted, was present. Undoubtedly, the senators were surprised when they were assured that the cabinet was united on major war issues and that policy was conducted upon consultation of all its members. When an embarrassed Salmon Chase, the source of much of the senators' information to the contrary, was forced to acknowledge this practice, Lincoln had triumphed over his congressional critics. Chase offered his resignation, but Lincoln refused to accept his as well as Seward's, thus thwarting the attempt to reconstruct his cabinet. It was a fitting event to end a confusing and chaotic year.[23]

One certainty, however, was that the election of 1862, taken together with the Fredericksburg fiasco, had revitalized the Democrats. In the House, Ohio's Samuel S. Cox delivered a scathing denunciation of Republican policies, claiming that the fall elections vindicated conservatism. He denounced the administration for removing McClellan in order "to appease the ebony fetish." Burnside, too, he claimed, would become "another sacrifice to the mumbo jumbo of abolition." Cox and other conservatives were so confident about the verdict of the fall elections that they believed they could elect their own Speaker to the Thirty-eighth Congress by uniting Democrats with conservative Republicans and border state Unionists. When January 1, 1863, arrived and Lincoln implemented the Emancipation policy, Thurlow Weed reported from Albany that leading Democrats were raising a howl. He informed Seward, "They say that it is now only a war about the 'nigger' and swear that they will make that issue." From Illinois, radical Grant Goodrich reported that Democrats intended to revolutionize the state, "that such is the resolve of the Democrats and that no President, no General shall stop it." Only military victories, he warned, could stem the tide.[24]

The vast majority of Democrats, however, having no treasonous intentions, constituted a loyal opposition. Yet given the context of electoral and military setbacks and the rhetoric of compromise and peace, it is easy to understand the sense of crisis many Republicans experienced. Clearly an irritant for committee members, as they began their work in the new year, was the persistent call for the return of their nemesis, George McClellan. Such sentiments were common enough in the army. Ironically, committee members failed to see how their own activities might have contributed to the resurgence of McClellan's popularity. As Herman Hattaway and Archer Jones observe:

> The conviction of many officers and rank and file that politicians had ordered the army into the suicidal Fredericksburg attack further depressed the morale of the Army of the Potomac. Radical rhetoric and the activities of the Committee on the Conduct of the War convinced them that the strategy of enthusiastic head-on attack had been imposed on the army. Many repined for McClellan.

Indeed, shortly after McClellan's removal from command, one private remarked, "I think the whole army thinks as much of McClellan to-day as they ever did. We ask no better leader." After Fredericksburg, Robert McAllister, a colonel in the Eleventh New Jersey, wrote his daughter, "There is not near the enthusiasm that we had when Genl. McClellan had the lead. There is a feeling of doubt hanging around everyone, officers & men." Another soldier, John Chipman Gray, wrote John Ropes, "I wish [the administration] had been scared a little more and then we might have McClellan."

When the *New York Herald* reported rumors of Burnside's impending resignation in early January, it called for the reinstatement of McClellan: "Everyone would be satisfied except the rebels, the negro-worshippers and the two California lawyers who pretend to control the War Department." But to allow McClellan's return was to lose the entire contest, in the committee's opinion, since its members had labored diligently for almost a year to secure his removal. It meant a return to conciliatory methods and a retreat from the war goals of the Republican party.[25]

Distrust of West Point

Adding to the committee's fears was a nagging insecurity about the loyalty of key officers within the Army of the Potomac, particularly those sympathetic to George McClellan. Although such suspicions can easily be dismissed today, given the apprehension of the time, the number of high-ranking generals hostile to the Republican party gave a certain plausibility to such fears. As Russell F. Weigley observes, sufficient hostility already existed between West Point officers and civilian leaders on the means of conducting war. "Distrusting civilians and politicians in war, and as much as possible turning a deaf ear to them, many of the professional officers closed their minds to the tendencies toward unlimited and revolutionary war." Because of such an attitude, many West Point officers were deemed tender toward the South, lacking the proper attitude to wage war, and therefore of questionable loyalty.[26]

The committee earlier had expressed skepticism about McClellan's loyalty, but their suspicions increased markedly about the fidelity of Porter and other Democratic generals, particularly after the second battle of Bull Run. Although evidence shows their loyalty never wavered, their hostile language and lackadaisical actions on the battlefield gave committee members the opposite impression. Chandler, for instance, was convinced that Porter was a traitor, later claiming to have a witness who quoted him as saying, "I was not true to John Pope and there is no use denying it." Chandler never revealed who had made this statement, but combined with Porter's unflattering comments about Pope's generalship, revealed during the course of his December 1862 court-martial, the charges gain a certain plausibility. During fall 1862, a number of incidents occurred that undoubtedly increased the committee's distrust of many regular army offices. By early 1863, the committee was convinced that disloyalty plagued the Union high command and, in order to be effective, the Army of the Potomac must be purged of conservative generals.[27]

Certain incidents increased the committee's paranoia about the fidelity of regular army officers. General Herman Haupt, an associate of John Covode, provided disturbing evidence of lukewarm patriotism from Second Bull Run. Charged with operating the Orange and Alexandria Railroad,

Michigan's Zachariah Chandler doubted the loyalty of many of the northern army's principal generals. (Courtesy of the State Archives of Michigan)

Haupt had authority from Halleck to arrest anyone who interfered with it. According to Haupt, many officers close to McClellan wasted two or three days trying to arrange railroad transportation when they could have marched to Pope's aid in a day. Shortly before the battle of Bull Run, Haupt was expecting a train of wounded prisoners at Alexandria but found the train had been taken over four miles outside the city by an intoxicated Gen. Samuel D. Sturgis, who was trying to arrange for the transportation of his own troops. When Sturgis was shown an order authorizing Haupt's control of the railroad, thinking it was from Pope, he bellowed, "I don't care for John Pope a pinch of owl dung." This hostile attitude toward Pope, maintained Haupt, was common among regular army officers.

Shortly after the battle, the wife of slain general Philip Kearny wrote to Lincoln claiming that her husband had been sacrificed. "Your high officers failed to do their duty," she claimed, and her husband knew he was being sacrificed by "knaves" and "traitors." *Cincinnati Gazette* correspondent Whitelaw Reid spoke of threats of dictatorship and talk of "provisional government" as common among army officers. "Never heartily in favor of Republican institutions," he commented, "it was not unnatural that [army officers] should look for opportunities of personal aggrandizement in the wreck of the institutions which they believed the convulsions of the war were sure to bring." Massachusetts senator Henry Wilson told Secretary of the Navy Gideon Welles of a conspiracy among Army of the Potomac officers "for a revolution and the establishment of a provisional government." Among the rank and file in the army the hostility toward Pope and any leader connected with the administration was a matter of concern for Republican leaders. "You cannot conceive of the intense feeling against Pope, McDowell, and Stanton," wrote one soldier. Another remarked, "I have not yet heard a favorable opinion expressed of McDowell nor of Pope: the former is frequently called a 'traitor.' . . . These sentiments are recorded as representative of the views of men from all parts of the country with whom I have conversed."[28]

"To tell you the truth," Elizabeth Blair Lee told her husband, "West Point is not making much reputation by this war." She was putting it mildly. Little occurred during fall 1862 to improve the image of regular army officers. When Lincoln issued the preliminary Emancipation Proclamation, Republican newspapers focused on the opposition of regular army officers in the Army of the Potomac. Characterizing West Pointers as the "dregs of the proslavery Democracy," the *Pittsburgh Daily Gazette* asserted that they would receive the Proclamation with disgust. Indeed McClellan did contemplate publicly opposing the president's Proclamation but was convinced by Montgomery Blair, Republican general Jacob D. Cox, and others not to do so.

Nevertheless, the attitude demonstrated by West Point officers and their devotees is instructive. Shortly after Antietam, Cox was attending church services in camp when John W. Garrett, president of the Baltimore and Ohio, approached him. Mistaking him for Fitz-John Porter, Garrett praised him for his devotion to McClellan and spoke of Washington leaders in unflattering terms. He then whispered to Cox, "But you military men have that matter in your own hands, you have but to tell the administration what they must do, and they will not dare disregard it!" When a dumbfounded Cox responded, "What do you mean, Sir?" Garrett realized his mistake and beat a hasty retreat. Porter's own political comments, as reported by his aide Stephen M. Weld, surely would have disturbed committee members. According to Weld, Porter had said that the South would never be defeated "with the present course the Administration is pursuing." Porter was extremely upset with Lincoln for interfering in military affairs. The conservative Weld agreed with these sentiments, asking his father, "Now have we not had enough of civilians like the President undertaking to manage the campaign?"[29]

One of the most disturbing and revealing incidents in the army that fall concerned the dismissal of Maj. John J. Key, a staff officer working in the office of General-in-Chief Halleck and the brother of Thomas Key, a colonel on McClellan's staff. Shortly after Antietam, John Key was overheard expressing his opinion about why the rebel army was not destroyed after the battle: "That is not the game, . . . the object is that neither army shall get much advantage of the other; that both shall be kept in the field till they are exhausted, when we will make a compromise and save slavery." When interviewed by Lincoln, Key apparently made no attempt to deny the statement, and Lincoln promptly dismissed him from service. Republican newspapers claimed the incident proved that such opinions were common in the army, that secret organizations existed, patronized by West Point officers and dedicated to compromise with the South and salvaging slavery. Even the president, though disparaging secret societies in the Army, acknowledged the pervasiveness of this attitude. After Second Bull Run, he had told private secretary John Hay that McClellan and his friends apparently wanted Pope to fail. Later he wrote Key that he had dismissed him to set an example: "I had been brought to fear that there was a certain class of officers in the army, not very inconsiderable in number, who were playing a game to not beat the enemy when they could, on some peculiar notion as to the proper way of saving the Union." Key, according to Lincoln, had made absolutely no attempt to distance himself from that viewpoint, and so "I dismissed you as an example and a warning to that supposed class."[30]

Events at Fredericksburg undoubtedly had convinced committee members that West Point's perfidy was alive and well. Even before the battle, Burnside's private secretary, Daniel Larned, was skeptical of the McClellan devotees in the Army of the Potomac. His supporters were busy inflating his reputation, and "should any mishap take place in the Army of the Potomac Burnside will get it right & left." Immediately after the battle of Fredericksburg, Larned remarked "that *jealousness* & political intrigue *are* greater enemies than our open foe." The full implications of these jealousies did not become wholly apparent to the committee until later.

Meanwhile, reinforcing its suspicions were the revelations emanating from the court-martial of Fitz-John Porter for disobedience to Pope in the Second Bull Run campaign. Early in the new year, Porter complained to McClellan that he was being treated unfairly. "The whole power of the Administration was thrown against me," he complained, "and now the radicals say that the court began to smell your return to power and were influenced by it." Though Porter was tried by a prejudiced court and, as later evidence proved, unfairly convicted, the court-martial proceedings added to the already low image of West Point's reputation. Instead of putting down the rebellion, the army leaders apparently preferred to engage in petty and spiteful bickering. Knowledge of Porter's indiscreet comments about Pope in official correspondence reinforced misgivings about Democratic leadership within the military. With the army inactive after a humiliating defeat and the Democrats seemingly revitalized, individual committee members decided to take the initiative to reinvigorate the war effort.[31]

Although the attitude of some regular army officers toward civilian leaders was cause for concern, committee members and other Republican congressmen seemed to forget that their actions might have contributed to the atmosphere of intense factionalism and hostility among the army's leading officers. The committee had questioned McClellan's loyalty, publicly criticized his generalship, and, along with leading cabinet officers, attempted to replace him with John Pope. In the numerous committee investigations of 1861 and 1862, it was self-evident that its members took a dim view of conservative West Point professionals and that they used what amounted to political tests in evaluating fitness for command. Thus the hostility and factionalism were, in part, the natural consequences of the committee's investigations.

To committee members, however, the principal problem plaguing the Union war effort was the lukewarm attitude of the country's West Point–educated generals. In order to revive the nation's sagging morale, individual committee members delivered key speeches before Congress in early 1863. Benjamin Wade began the offensive with an emotional attack on West Point in the Senate on January 15, exploiting common resentments against military science and professionalism that typified popular opinion. Objecting to an appropriation bill for the institution, Wade instead recommended that West Point be abolished. "That was the hot-bed from which rebellion was hatched, and from thence emanated your principal traitors and conspirators," he told the Senate. The recent courts-martial, he suggested, revealed nothing but "petty jealousies," which proved the institution was "utterly detrimental to public service." According to Wade, West Point was a southern institution based on aristocratic notions and privilege but suppressing talent and merit:

> We select an unsophisticated young man and put him in this institution, and before he is permitted to learn military science, he his taught to despise his own democratic section of the country, and is taught to despise labor, and the simplicity of northern institutions; and he is taught there to admire above all things that two-penny, miserable slave aristocracy of the South.

Despite Wade's best efforts, however, the Senate passed the appropriation bill 29 to 10. Committee members voted against it, but a number of ardent Republican radicals, including Charles Sumner, John P. Hale, and Henry Wilson, supported the measure.[32]

Shortly after Wade's attack on West Point, Joseph Wright made his attempt to reinvigorate northern morale by publicly castigating peace Democrats for detracting from the war effort. Although he had campaigned for the administration in the fall elections, Wright still considered himself a Unionist, arguing that the rebellion meant that partisan differences ought to be suppressed. When Lazarus Powell of Kentucky argued that no one had an obligation to support a war that employed unconstitutional means, Wright ridiculed his position, delivering a forceful rebuttal that would earn him the praise of many Republicans. "Would they then counsel submission to traitors and yield to their domination?" Wright asked, suggesting that the actions of successful Democrats and their denunciations of the Lincoln administration in Illinois, New Jersey, and New York had created division and anxiety in the North. Then in a conclusion that led the gallery to erupt in applause, Wright made an impassioned plea for patriotism:

> I would say, let us bury the past, let us forget party affiliations, all party names and distinctions, and then, upon the altar of our country, swear by eternal God this government shall *be one;* it cannot be *two;* it cannot be *three;* it cannot be *four;* it *must be one,* or it is *nothing.*[33]

Despite the best efforts of Wade and Wright, gloom and despair continued to pervade the capital, fueled by constant rumors of compromise and disloyalty. Republican governor Richard Yates wrote Salmon Chase that his state was on the verge of revolution; the slightest provocation would create violence in southern Illinois. William Orme, a brigadier general serving in Missouri, seconded Yates's observation, writing his friend David Davis: "The peace party [in Illinois] is very much stronger than you have any idea of— And unless we gain some signal & decisive victories, all hope will have fled the country." Chandler complained to his wife that disloyalty was "rearing its hideous head in the Senate again." Committee members continued to receive complaints about the administration's lack of earnestness along with demands that Seward be dismissed from the cabinet. One woman wrote Wade, "I think you will find that all of Mr. Seward's followers are thought to believe the Union is done for." One of Covode's correspondents wrote him that wherever men met in public, they "talk over disappointments and disasters with bitter discontent against the Administration. . . . *Nothing* will satisfy the public mind but a *reconstruction* of the Cabinet, and this demand grows stronger daily and *must* be listened to." Lincoln frustrated the actions of all "earnest men," complained Ohio congressman William Cutler, who recorded in his diary that the feeling in Congress was that God was aiding the Confederacy. Referring to the course of Seward and Lincoln, Chandler told his wife, "God only knows what we are coming to."[34]

Nor were military affairs proceeding with any success. Although briefly cheered by the success of Maj. Gen. William Rosecrans at the battle of Stones River in Tennessee, affairs in the East quickly put a damper on any enthusiasm. Thwarted earlier in an attempt to advance the army immediately after

Fredericksburg, Burnside finally produced a plan that Halleck approved and prepared to move forward on January 19. But the weather turned against him when rain changed the roads into quagmires. The inglorious Mud March was the last action the Army of the Potomac would see until spring, and it ended Burnside's tenure as its head. On January 28, 1863, Lincoln appointed Joseph Hooker to the top command.[35]

Committee reaction to this change was mixed. Julian was enthusiastic about Hooker but wondered if he could handle a command as big as the Army of the Potomac. And several committee members expressed a feeling that Burnside had been sabotaged by McClellan's friends in the Army of the Potomac. Rumors surfaced in mid-January that William Franklin and other generals had interfered with Burnside's plan by going directly to Lincoln and convincing the president to stop the army from moving. Thus, instructed by a Senate resolution, the committee began investigating Franklin's role in interfering with Burnside's plans. As Chandler wrote his wife, Franklin was McClellan's friend and was *"not to be trusted."* Hooker's appointment was a good thing if he would be allowed to fight. McClellan's men controlled the Army of the Potomac, Chandler stated, and they were against Hooker; yet, Chandler predicted, "This we shall soon change."[36]

Slowly emerging in the committee's thinking was the need for a master stroke, a move that would permanently discredit McClellan and his conservative friends in the Army of the Potomac, allowing generals who were in sympathy with Republican ideology to prosecute the war. In December, Michigan senator Jacob Howard introduced a resolution calling on the committee to report on its activities "with all convenient speed" to Congress. Disclosure was, after all, one of the principal means by which congressional committees could advance their agendas and wield influence. Publication of such reports might be the death blow to McClellan and other conservative generals. Chandler wrote his wife that the committee's report would destroy McClellan. It would be a bold counterstroke, preventing his return, ruining his political prospects in 1864, and permanently ridding the Army of the Potomac of conservative influence so that the war could be vigorously waged. Throughout February and March committee members earnestly applied themselves to the task at hand.[37]

Although not every witness who came before the committee was hostile to George McClellan, the majority clearly were. Irritated by his favoritism toward pet officers, they gave an unflattering portrait of his abilities as commander, testimony the committee could use for partisan advantage. Maj. Gen. Samuel Heintzelman, for instance, castigated McClellan for laying siege to Yorktown, making a less than vigorous pursuit of the Confederate army after the battle of Williamsburg, and for failing to counterattack the Confederate right after the battle of Seven Pines on May 31, 1862. An even more shocking revelation, which has been confirmed by Stephen Sears, was McClellan's absence from the field of battle during major engagements and a predisposition to allow subordinates to make crucial decisions on the battlefield. "Was the Seven days' battle fought under the direction and orders of General McClellan," asked Gooch, "or did each corps commander fight his own troops as he thought best?" Heintzelman replied, "The corps commanders fought their troops entirely according to their own ideas." Heintzelman's verdict on the Peninsula campaign was echoed by Generals Erasmus D. Keyes, Edwin V. Sumner, John G. Barnard, Silas Casey, and the commander of the Army of the Potomac, Joseph Hooker, who testified that the failure of the Peninsula campaign was due to "the want of generalship on the part of our commander."[38]

In the effort to discredit McClellan, a number of relevant points were rarely discussed during these sessions, undoubtedly because they were in his favor. Neither Keyes nor Heintzelman bothered to mention that McClellan had been deprived of McDowell's troops, despite their complaints about it at the time; Keyes had even written an angry letter on the matter to New York senator Ira Harris. Although McClellan's absence from many battles was troubling, in some instances he did have an excuse; during the battle of Seven Pines, he was bedridden with malaria. Nevertheless, this fact never emerged in testimony, despite its being common knowledge among the army's top commanders. Moreover, several of the witnesses harbored deep personal grudges against McClellan. Keyes, for example, had written several letters to Secretary Chase complaining of McClellan's treatment; hence, his testimony was hardly unbiased.

The committee's overriding goal, however, was not to provide an objective hearing on the military prowess of George McClellan. Indeed, even if it had been predisposed to hear both sides of the matter, the significance of McClellan's maneuvers would have been lost on committee members. They had already rendered the verdict before the hearings began. As one McClellan admirer in the army observed, "These committees of investigation seldom are really just. They are appointed and start with a foregone conclusion . . . call their witnesses and put their questions accordingly." The hearings were only a matter of how to present the evidence so that McClellan's military ideas and political aspirations could be crushed. Once the report was before the public, committee members surely hoped that conservative generals would be purged from the Army of the Potomac and replaced by leaders who would endorse Republican political goals.[39]

Great pains were also taken to blame Pope's defeat at Second Bull Run on McClellan and to discredit his performance at Antietam by focusing on his failure to pursue Lee after the battle. General-in-Chief Halleck told the committee that part of Pope's defeat was due to the slowness with which Army of the Potomac troops came to him. When Wade asked about the delay, he replied, "It may have resulted from the officers generally not feeling the absolute necessity of great haste in reinforcing General Pope." Wade asked if this would have changed the outcome of the battle. "I thought so at the time," Halleck responded, "and still think so." When Wade asked Joseph Hooker the reasons for the defeat at Second Bull Run, alluding to a conspiracy against Pope, the general responded, "I always felt that he was not supported promptly." John Covode's colleague, Gen. Herman Haupt, testified that troops landed at Alexandria in mid-August easily could have marched to reinforce Pope; instead, they remained at Alexandria, waiting for rail transportation that was already overtaxed. Although Haupt would not directly implicate McClellan, the committee drew its own conclusions.[40]

Edwin V. Sumner criticized McClellan's generalship at Antietam, telling the congressmen that he committed troops in a piecemeal fashion. Ambrose Burnside testified that McClellan refused to give him reinforcements to follow up his attack on the Confederate left even though he knew that Fitz-John Porter had 15,000 to 20,000 troops that had not seen action that day. Gooch asked why the enemy was not pursued after the battle. Burnside claimed the conventional wisdom that the army was too cut up. When asked if his own troops could have fought, he replied, "I have no doubt they could."[41]

When George McClellan was summoned to appear before the committee in late February and early March, he realized the significance of the occasion. "I have many—very many—bitter enemies here—they are making their last grand attack," he wrote his wife; "I *must* & *will* defeat them, for I know that I am right & have tried to do my duty." In two sessions, comprising over twenty pages of printed testimony, Gooch systematically reviewed every detail of McClellan's tenure as commander. The committee's purpose was not so much immediately to challenge McClellan but to gather his written testimony so it could be examined against that of the other generals, for on almost every material detail of the campaign, the testimony of the other witnesses contradicted McClellan's.

Asked if Heintzelman could have taken Yorktown if he had attacked right away, McClellan answered, "No; I do not think he could have done it. When we did advance we found the enemy intrenched [sic] and in strong force wherever we approached." About the possibility of following the enemy into

Richmond after the battle of Seven Pines, he replied, "I do not think it would have been possible at that time to have taken our artillery with us." McClellan explained that such a move would have placed the army at the gates of Richmond without cannons. "It is true, is it not, that the enemy retreated in confusion after the battle of Fair Oaks?" McClellan replied, "I have no means now of telling in what condition the enemy retired; and I do not remember receiving information of any special panic in Richmond." Referring to the battle of Savage Station, Gooch asked, "Did you yourself direct the movements of the troops, or were they directed by the corps commanders?" McClellan said that he gave general orders but corps commanders handled the specifics. And so it went, all the way through the battle of Antietam.[42]

At the end of the first session McClellan confessed that he was worn out by "that confounded Committee." But the committee had what it wanted from him and could contrast his testimony against the contradictory accounts of numerous subordinates. Gooch, for instance, believed the committee had sufficient evidence to prevent McClellan's restoration to command. As one political observer reported, the committee's sessions with McClellan had "favorable results."[43]

The committee was simultaneously developing a powerful case against McClellan's friend, William Franklin. When Ambrose Burnside appeared before the CCW on February 7, 1863, he told a tale of intrigue in which Franklin was a principal player. Shortly after Fredericksburg, Burnside proposed to assume offensive operations by crossing the Rappahannock several miles below the town in an attempt to flank Lee's army. Unknown to Burnside, but most likely known to Franklin, Generals John Cochrane and John Newton, divisional commanders in Franklin's Grand Division, obtained passes and quickly set out for Washington. According to Cochrane, the two attempted to secure interviews with either Henry Wilson, chairman of the Senate Committee on Military Affairs, or Moses Odell. Their intention was to communicate the dispirited condition of the army and the impracticality of Burnside's proposed movements. Since both Wilson and Odell were out of town for the holidays, they went to the White House, where Seward arranged a meeting with the president. So disturbed was Lincoln with these revelations that he immediately wired Burnside, ordering him to suspend operations. When the perplexed commander came to the White House the next day, Lincoln would not reveal the source of his information or comment on his plans, telling Burnside that he must talk to Halleck. After consulting with him, Burnside found that he was of little help and would make only the most general suggestions. When Burnside returned to camp, he discovered that the details of his plans were widely known; that line of operation had to be abandoned. Burnside, however, did not reveal before the committee his attempt to resign in early January, a resignation the president had refused to accept. "I deplore the want of concurrence with you, in opinion of your general officers," he told Burnside, "but I do not see a remedy." Nor did Lincoln see any reason to switch generals at the time. It was a sad commentary on military affairs, an army with a general who was not allowed to implement his plans but who, nevertheless, was kept in command by a president who seemed not to know what to do next.[44]

Burnside then told the committee the details of the infamous Mud March. He had formulated a new plan to cross the Rappahannock above Fredericksburg, but after a delay of two or three days, the weather changed for the worse and halted army operations. Again, prominent officers, he informed the committee, had vocally opposed the movement at the expense of the army's morale. Although he did not mention Franklin specifically, his opposition was well known. "Franklin has talked so much and so loudly to this effect that he has completely demoralized his whole command and so rendered failure doubly secure," remarked Charles Wainwright, an artillery officer in the Army of the Potomac. Burnside tried to bring the issue to a head by issuing an order that provided for the dismissal of a number of these troublesome officers, including Franklin, William F. Smith, and Joseph Hooker. The president had to choose between seeing that the order was carried out or accepting Burnside's resignation. Although he relieved Franklin, Lincoln chose not to enforce the order and instead replaced Burnside with Hooker. How much the committee knew of these intrigues before Burnside's testimony is debatable; in any case, the effect was shocking. As Julian noted, Burnside "gave the most startling testimony as to the demoralization of the Army of the Potomac, the bickerings and jealousies of the commanding generals, and the vexations of the President in dealing with the situation."[45]

In its initial report on Fredericksburg, the committee had published testimony without comment. Then it began a radical revision, one that connected defeat to the actions of William B. Franklin. Since he was a close associate of McClellan and a fellow West Point graduate, many committee members already viewed Franklin as soft on the South and slavery, just the type of general the committee wanted purged from the army. Understandably, Burnside's revelations increased their desire to discredit conservative leadership, and a different account of the battle of Fredericksburg immediately began to take shape.

After interviewing Newton and Cochrane and determining that Franklin had figured prominently in the intrigues against Burnside, the committee began to construct a case to discredit his actions at Fredericksburg, expanding on points uncovered in Burnside's earlier testimony. On March 16, 1863, George Gordon Meade, whose division had attacked the Confederate right under Franklin at Fredericksburg, testified that he would have carried the Confederate entrenchments if properly supported: "There is no doubt that if large re-enforcements had been thrown in immediately after my attack we could have held that plateau."[46]

Armed with this evidence, the committee then summoned Franklin to appear. "I never dreamed that this was considered as a strong attack," he replied when asked why he had not better supported Meade's division. His orders instructed him to attack with only one division, he said, and to prepare to pursue the enemy toward Richmond, ignoring the fact that his orders actually instructed him to attack with "not less than one division." Gooch next asked Franklin whether Burnside had given him an order that afternoon to attack with his entire command. "I remember the message which General Burnside sent. It was not an order; it was more like a request to me to do it, if I thought I could, and I sent back word that I could not." Referring to the report of Brig. Gen. James Hardie, who served on Franklin's staff during Fredericksburg, Gooch countered that Franklin had stated that he would attempt to do so. The attack was already under way, Franklin replied, and he could do nothing to modify it. After Franklin denied that he had directed Newton to talk to the president, the interview ended. However, he knew he was being singled out as the cause of the Fredericksburg disaster. "I find now having been before the War Committee," he told McClellan, "that Burnside gave me a peremptory order to move my whole force." The committee was convinced that he had disobeyed it and would not hear James Hardie or William F. Smith on the matter. "They went over everything unfairly," Franklin complained, "their evident intention was to get up something that would injure 1st you & 2nd me—that is so far as my evidence is concerned."[47]

Committee members were also active in Congress trying to bolster the nation's sagging morale. With pivotal measures such as the Conscription Act under consideration, Julian took the offensive. On February 18 he delivered one of the most blistering philippics of the war, castigating Democratic opposition to Republican war measures as part of a giant proslavery conspiracy. Blaming every military disaster on Democratic generals and principles, Julian dealt at length with the failures of George McClellan: "Democratic policy at this moment clamors for [McClellan's] restoration . . . and every man who loves negro slavery better than he loves his country, and would sooner see the Republic in ruins than the slaves set free, is the zealous advocate and unflinching champion of General McClellan." Proslavery officers in the Army of the Potomac had forced the president to modify Frémont's emancipation proclamation early in the struggle. Even though the policy eventually had been adopted, Democrats, Julian reasoned, who held four-fifths of the positions in the army, prevented Frémont's return to an active command and kept many antislavery generals relegated to insignificant positions. The president must change his policy and dismiss every advocate of slavery who occupied a public position. Encouraging Lincoln to make war in earnest, Julian concluded with an appeal that every weapon necessary to put down the rebellion be used.[48]

Julian followed up his speech with a visit to the White House a few weeks later, where he urged the appointment of Frémont to a military command as a way to invigorate the country and boost morale. Despite Frémont's undistinguished performance in the Shenandoah Valley, Julian and other committee members continued to believe that his presence in the army would increase morale. Instead of admitting to Julian that he doubted Frémont's military abilities, the president deflected the request, telling him he did not know where to put Frémont. He then became more candid: "It would stir the country on one side and stir it the other way on the other. It would please Frémont's friends, and displease the conservatives," just as his Emancipation Proclamation had earlier done. Disappointed, Julian later wrote, "These observations were characteristic, and showed how reluctant he was to turn away from the conservative counsels he had so long heeded."[49]

In early March the committee was working diligently on its reports. In order to assist it, Congress extended its life for thirty days beyond the end of the Thirty-seventh session. Wade and Chandler remained in Washington during the recess to take testimony; joined by the other members a few weeks later, they worked frantically to complete their task. Although Chandler was worried that Odell might object to the finished product, he predicted that the final report would damage McClellan, Seward, "and the whole crew" and deliver a deathblow to northern Copperheads. To say the least, his expectations were optimistic.[50]

Released to the Associated Press on April 3, the report on the Army of the Potomac created a stir in the nation's newspapers. Although reports on Bull Run, Ball's Bluff, and Frémont's administration of the West were also released, the operations of the Army of the Potomac drew the most attention. It was signed by every member of the committee, including Democrat Odell. "Had the success of the Army of the Potomac during this period corresponded with success of our arms in other parts of the country," the report stated, "there is reason to believe that the termination of the campaign of 1862 would have seen the rebellion well-nigh, if not entirely, overthrown." George McClellan was responsible for this lack of success. Given credit for nothing, McClellan was systematically blamed for every setback in army operations. It was McClellan who had delayed the advance of the army in winter 1861–1862; it was McClellan who had dreamed up the ill-advised Peninsula campaign, left the capital undermanned, and then squandered repeated opportunities because of his own caution and constant exaggeration of enemy strength. And it was McClellan's tardiness that caused Pope to fail at Second Bull Run and allowed Lee to escape after the battle of Antietam. If the general had achieved anything positive, it was not mentioned in this report.[51]

The report also radically revised its assessment of Fredericksburg. Both Cochrane and Newton were castigated for interfering with Burnside's plans; however, the special venom was reserved for William B. Franklin. Not only had he attacked with the smallest division available, but he also had failed to obey Burnside's order for an all-out attack that day. Although Franklin offered the excuse that his orders instructed him to be ready to pursue the enemy toward Richmond, he also testified that this action was impractical unless the heights Burnside had ordered attacked were carried. Several officers, the report noted, argued that such an assault might have reversed the verdict on the battlefield that day.[52]

As might be expected, reaction to the report fell along well-established partisan lines. Republican newspapers generally greeted the report favorably. "There is not such another record of dereliction and inefficiency in all military history, and it will stand alike a marvel and derision to future generations," the *New York Times* commented, adding that the report proved conclusively that McClellan "meant *peace with* the rebels, and not *war against* them." One Ohio man was shocked by the report, writing Sen. John Sherman that he could not understand why Lincoln had stuck with McClellan so long. The *Pittsburgh Daily Gazette* insisted that the report "utterly pulverizes General McClellan," concluding that "the utterly dispassionate tone of the report, adds immensely to its weight."[53]

Democrats reacted with outrage, charging that McClellan was the victim of a bitter partisan attack. "There are in the report intrinsic evidences that it has emanated from a source deeply prejudiced against General McClellan," wrote the *New York Herald*. Though the committee performed a "mountain of labor," the *Herald* noted, it had brought forth "a ridiculous mouse." Mocking its members' military expertise, the *Herald* continued, "they are a set of school boys playing soldier when the school master is out." The *Chicago Times* dismissed the report as "an abolition document . . . principally devoted to assaults upon General McClellan." William B. Franklin characterized the report as "imaginative" and promptly published his own reply, taking issue with the committee's censure of his role at Fredericksburg. Charles Lanphier's Illinois *State Register* dismissed the findings as a crude electioneering gimmick; hiding all the faults of the administration, "They would damn McClellan as incompetent and disloyal . . . while they make a hero, statesman and patriot of Frémont proven to be the reverse of each." The *Brooklyn Eagle* condemned the report but defended Odell's decision to sign it, claiming he had the right to differ from other Democrats without fear of censure.[54]

Committee members were proud of their work, believing it constituted a turning point in the war effort. According to Julian, the report was enthusiastically received by the public and "credited with great usefulness to the country, through its labors to rescue control of the war from incompetent and unworthy hands," a startling statement from a man who endorsed Frémont, a general known to be incompetent. Indeed, just before the report's issuance, Chandler believed it would invigorate the war effort and put down the "Copperhead threat." Yet in two state elections held shortly after its release, it apparently had no positive effect. In New Hampshire, the Republicans narrowly defeated peace Democrat Ira Eastman for governor; in Connecticut, the defeated Copperhead candidate, Thomas Seymour, captured an impressive 48 percent of the vote. Moreover, many observers noted that the committee's work went relatively unnoticed by the public. Though covered extensively in the newspapers, the length and complexity of the matters undoubtedly had little appeal for the average reader. With the exception of a few officers, soldiers seemed completely oblivious of it. There was a turning point in the war effort during 1863, but it had little to do with the committee's work. Union victories at Gettysburg and Vicksburg turned the tide, boosted the morale of Union armies, and contributed to Republican victories in the fall elections.[55]

Howard C. Westwood characterizes the committee's report as a "ringing, morale-building address to the people of the Union." Yet as many contemporary Republicans acknowledged, the report may have done more harm than good. One of Seward's correspondents believed the report would make a martyr of McClellan and thereby raise his standing in the eyes of the masses. New York senator Ira Harris saw the committee as a pernicious influence on the war effort. "After the first great object of that Committee was accomplished and McClellan was removed," he wrote Orville Browning shortly after the Union defeat at Chancellorsville in May 1863, "the army has been managed entirely under the auspices of the Committee and for *political* ends—The result is three great and shameful defeats [Second Bull Run, Fredericksburg, and Chancellorsville], and if the influences which now prevail continue to control it we may have three more." Even more critical of the committee was Gideon Welles. Although he admitted that some of the report's conclusions were accurate, he nonetheless was skeptical of the utility of the committee's undertakings: "They are partisan and made up of persons not very competent to form correct and intelligent opinions of Army or Navy operations, or administrative purposes." Although there is no record of the president's opinion of the report, it is unlikely that he was a zealous advocate of the committee members, who, on more than one occasion, had attempted to supersede executive actions.[56]

Several questions arise concerning the committee's impact on the Union war effort during the Thirty-seventh Congress, its influence on northern military policy, and the relevance of its work. Despite hundreds of hours of hearings and hundreds of pages of testimony, the committee did not exercise much direct power in the shaping of military decisions. It did play a major role in securing Frémont a command, and it certainly was a factor in the removal of McClellan; however, in attempting to direct Lincoln's policy decisions, in most cases, it was unsuccessful. Lincoln might act in ways the committee agreed with, but he acted on his terms, not on theirs.

From the standpoint of generating useful military knowledge, the committee's work was largely irrelevant. There were few startling revelations, hardly surprising, given the members' lack of military background. Like the Committee on the Public Safety in the French Revolution (but with far less power), the CCW's recommendations were largely based on considerations of politics and ideology. According to George Julian, one of the committee's most valuable functions was placing the nation's armies in competent hands, by which he meant the hands of antislavery generals. Although some credit must be accorded the committee for its attack on conciliation and for its prodding of cautious generals, its recommendations for military positions demonstrate its weaknesses, the constant clamor for Frémont best exemplifying its lack of judgment. Clearly, had the Committee on the Conduct of the War never been formed, the Union war effort would not have been harmed in any military sense.

Although some historians, notably T. Harry Williams, have exaggerated the committee's power over Lincoln, it did exert influence in a number of other areas, three in particular where it affected the northern war effort. In each of these cases, however, its influence was negative. First, in the area of military appointments, it often recommended generals, such as Frémont, who were subpar from a military standpoint. Moreover, it contributed to (although it did not create) an unhealthy practice in Washington of allowing political considerations to influence military appointments.

Second, the committee's investigations, its leaks to the press, and its use of secret testimony to discredit generals such as McClellan certainly were instrumental in creating hostility between the army's West Point officers and the nation's civilian leaders. Worried constantly that the committee was looking for scapegoats to satisfy the popular clamor for explanations of military defeats, many Union military officers became increasingly suspicious of civilian overseers. The committee also contributed to factionalism among Union officers. The investigations invited junior officers to criticize superiors and allowed ambitious officers to attempt to promote themselves over rivals through their testimony. During the Second Bull Run campaign, this factionalism certainly contributed to Union defeat. McClellan, Franklin, and Porter seemed concerned more with Pope's failure than with Robert E. Lee's. Although the committee was not the sole cause of this factionalism, it certainly contributed to it.

Third, the committee tended to reinforce the unrealistic and simplistic notions of warfare that prevailed in the popular mind. General Don Carlos Buell pointed out that "the object is not merely to give battle for the sake of fighting but to fight for victory. . . . The commander merits condemnation who, from ambition of popular clamor and without necessity or profit, has squandered the lives of his soldiers." Yet such a distinction was lost on committee members. Deliberately downplaying the technical aspects of the war, the committee was the most forceful advocate of perpetual forward movement. Ridiculing entrenchment as unmanly and McClellan's Peninsula strategy as cowardly, even disloyal, the CCW wanted generals who would move forward, engage, and smash the enemy. Failing to appreciate the destructive developments in military technology, the committee could not understand generals who relied on strategic movement and who expressed legitimate concerns about the utility of frontal assaults. Thus the committee limited the strategic options of the Union high command.

The case of Ambrose Burnside at Fredericksburg is instructive. Burnside was well aware of the public's impatience with lack of military success in the Eastern Theater. He also knew that the committee had pursued McClellan because he did not move against the enemy directly. When crucial elements of his plans failed to materialize, Burnside carried out a foolhardy assault against the well-fortified Marye's Heights because he believed that public opinion demanded action. The committee bears some responsibility for increasing such dissatisfaction and impatience.[57]

As members of the committee returned home, their work finally completed, they surely believed their labors had benefited the Union war effort. Whether Congress would concur in this judgment and reappoint the same members would have to wait until the Thirty-eighth Congress met in December.

CHAPTER SIX

The Same Excuses
for Different Generals

If the publication of the report on McClellan raised doubts about the wisdom of the Committee on the Conduct of the War, its course in the Thirty-eighth Congress was unlikely to put such doubts to rest. Once reconstituted, the committee began another extensive investigation of the Army of the Potomac. During the Thirty-seventh Congress, committee members had boasted that their activities had uprooted disloyalty from the army. "Thanks be to God[,] the *Committee on the Conduct of the War* & Secy Stanton," Zachariah Chandler wrote William Lord, "those men are all out of Command & Earnest fighting men in their place." However, the Union defeat at Chancellorsville in early May and the failure to pursue Lee's army vigorously after the battle of Gettysburg convinced committee members that Copperheadism was still rampant among the leading officers of the Army of the Potomac. The CCW was determined to use its investigative powers once again to identify and remove such influences from the nation's principal army.[1]

Boosting Joseph Hooker

Much of the committee's work centered on Gen. Joseph Hooker. When Hooker replaced Ambrose Burnside as the head of the Army of the Potomac, most members of the committee were favorably impressed. In many ways, however, Hooker seemed an unlikely candidate for its sponsorship. A Massachusetts native, he was a West Point graduate with Democratic and anti-abolition leanings. Moreover, he had an unsavory reputation for gambling, drinking, and womanizing. But he was sensitive to the direction of political winds in Washington and, positioning himself for the top command in the East, became an earnest advocate of emancipation. Such a course of action was predicted by his fellow general George Gordon Meade: "Hooker is a Democrat and anti-abolitionist—that is to say, he was. What he will be, when the command of the Army is held out to him, is more than anyone can tell." Nevertheless, Hooker's conversion impressed committee members. In late January 1863, George Julian reported that Hooker's views on slavery were right on the mark.[2]

167

Undoubtedly much of Hooker's popularity with the committee was also due to his aggressive rhetoric. In contrast to the cautious McClellan, Hooker espoused a bold, offensive style of warfare that appealed to the committee's popular conceptions of battle. Hooker declared that it was not a matter of if but of when he would take Richmond. Committee members favorably recalled Hooker's willingness to criticize McClellan's indecision during the Peninsula campaign. After being wounded at Antietam, Hooker had boasted from his hospital bed to Salmon Chase that had he been in command of the army during that campaign, he would have captured Richmond. His language impressed the secretary of the treasury as did his eagerness to get back to active duty. Indeed, Hooker's persistent criticism of his superiors had earned him the contempt of many McClellan supporters in the army. In fall 1862, Gen. John Pope spoke of distrust for Hooker among "the praetorian [McClellan] faction in the Army of the Potomac," an attitude the committee regarded favorably. With his conversion to antislavery principles, Hooker seemed to be the ideal general to invigorate the Army of the Potomac and lead it to a decisive, war-ending triumph over Lee.[3]

Hooker began in spectacular fashion. After spending three months reorganizing the Army of the Potomac, he was ready to test his new fighting instrument. Taking the corps of Oliver Otis Howard (the Eleventh), George Meade (the Fifth), and Henry Slocum (the Twelfth), Hooker moved west from his base at Falmouth, Virginia, and crossed the Rappahannock at Kelley's Ford, leaving sufficient troops to occupy the Confederate army camped across the river at Fredericksburg. Then doubling back, Hooker quickly gained the rebel rear and had Lee's much smaller army caught between the two wings of his own. "Hurrah for Old Joe!" exclaimed George Meade, "We're on Lee's flank, and he doesn't know it."

After boldly seizing the initiative, Hooker grew cautious. Instead of pressing south, he drew back as soon as he encountered skirmishers from Lee's army near a crossroads named Chancellorsville, much to the chagrin of his incredulous corps commanders. Leaving a small force to contend with federal troops under John Sedgwick at Falmouth, Lee moved his army to meet Hooker. Then, in a bold, almost reckless move, he divided his army, leaving only 18,000 men to face Hooker's left while sending approximately 30,000 troops under Thomas J. (Stonewall) Jackson in a wide flanking march. At dusk on May 2 Jackson's troops launched a vigorous assault on Howard's Eleventh Corps on the Union right. Although apprised of Jackson's movements, Howard's corps did not take adequate action and was quickly routed.

Although Lee had seized the initiative, all was not lost for Hooker. Jackson's attack was launched late in the day, and it suffered from disorganization. Jackson himself was wounded in the chaos. Hooker, however, seemed to fight like a beaten man. Dazed and temporarily unconscious after a Confederate cannonball landed in his headquarters on the morning of May 3, Hooker ignored suggestions from corps commanders Meade and John F. Reynolds to counterattack Jackson's forces, by then commanded by Jeb Stuart. Despite an overwhelming numerical advantage, Hooker did nothing, allowing Lee to send reinforcements back to Fredericksburg to prevent Sedgwick's Sixth Corps from threatening Lee's rear. At midnight on May 4, Hooker again ignored the advice of his corps commanders and ordered a retreat across the Rappahannock. An angry John Reynolds complained to Darius Couch, "What was the use of calling us together at this time of night when he intended to retreat anyhow?"[4]

As Lee engaged Hooker in Virginia, an anxious country, ignorant of the transpiring events, craved information. "I am not satisfied," remarked Secretary of the Navy Gideon Welles. "If we have success, the tidings would come to us in volumes." A few days later, when the War Department refused to give Welles definite information about Hooker's whereabouts, Massachusetts senator Charles Sumner, fresh from the White House, came to see him. "Lost, lost, all is lost!" he told Welles. When the latter asked for a more complete explanation, he continued, "Hooker and his entire army [has] been defeated and driven back to this side of the Rappahannock." Once this news became widespread, partisan newspapers quickly debated the merits of Hooker's campaign. "So conclusively do we regard the facts against him," wrote the *New York Herald,* "that we take it for granted that General Hooker is to be set aside." "The radical wretches are greatly alarmed," it added, "lest Joe Hooker shall be recalled from command and General McClellan placed at the head of the Army of the Potomac." Radical newspapers rose to Hooker's defense. When McClellan's supporters had praised his expertise in defensive maneuvers, many of those newspapers had not been impressed. Hooker's maneuvers were an altogether different story, however. The *New York Daily Tribune* described the recrossing of the Rappahannock as proof of Hooker's considerable military skills, noting that "*retreating* across such a river in presence [sic] of a hostile force is ten times more difficult and perilous than advancing."[5]

Hooker's supporters in Congress and the administration were equally forgiving. Secretary of War Edwin Stanton told Adam Gurowski that he had confidence in Hooker even if he had been defeated. "Bravo!" Gurowski commented, "not want of success condemns a general, but the way and manner in which he acted; and how he dealt with events." Newly elected Massachusetts congressman George Boutwell told Sumner, "We can not afford to displace a general whenever a plan fails." Perhaps Hooker's biggest booster was committee member Zachariah Chandler. Writing to W. H. Lord, Chandler claimed that Hooker's plan would have succeeded "but for the stampede of the . . . 11th corps. This deranged his plan of battle," he explained, and "discouraged him a little." Not only would Hooker turn the situation around, Chandler assured Lord, but there were also reports that he had recrossed the Rappahannock and moved on Richmond. Even if Hooker had been defeated, the army's leadership was true and patriotic, thanks to the committee's efforts. When the Confederate armies had marched toward Washington in summer 1862, many in the Union army had not wanted to injure the rebels. "They meant to exhaust both sides," Chandler asserted, and "thus compromise upon the Slavery basis of the Old, but thank God, they no longer control our army."[6]

Once Benjamin Wade and Chandler were apprised of the magnitude of the Chancellorsville defeat, they both rushed to Washington. Along with Massachusetts senator Henry Wilson, they visited the Army of the Potomac to investigate its morale, the fitness of its commander, and rumors that the army's defeat was a result of Hooker's drunkenness. Although they found that some divisional commanders hoped that Hooker would be replaced by Meade, the senators came away satisfied with Hooker and the condition of the army, a view shared by Salmon Chase, who visited the camp shortly after the three senators. "I have full confidence in Joe Hooker both as to his courage & ability as a commander," Chandler wrote his wife. If there was an element to fear, it was William Seward and his supporters, who wanted to restore McClellan to command. "If [Seward] succeeds," Chandler warned, "the country is lost." Committee members had lobbied hard for McClellan's replacement. Although they were not pleased with Ambrose Burnside's removal, they had supported Hooker's appointment. They did not want him to be removed after one failure, especially when they believed McClellan had been given multiple opportunities. They hoped the president would share their point of view.[7]

At the time, Lincoln agreed with Wade and Chandler. Although initially shocked by the defeat, after visiting Army of the Potomac headquarters with General-in-Chief Halleck, he decided that Hooker deserved another chance. Like the senators, however, the president was disturbed by the attitude of some of Hooker's subordinates. Shortly after his visit, Lincoln shared this information with his general. "I must tell you," he wrote Hooker, "I have some painful intimations that some of your corps and Division Commanders are not giving you their entire confidence." Telling Hooker to make his own inquiries on the matter, Lincoln left him in command, instructing him to take his time before resuming the offensive.[8]

By early June it was clear that Lee intended to take his army north. Although Hooker believed Lee would attempt to get between his army and Washington, the Confederate general had other plans, namely moving westward from Fredericksburg, passing over the Blue Ridge Mountains, and then heading north to cross the Potomac River in the vicinity of Williamsport, Maryland. First Hooker proposed falling on Lee's rear at Fredericksburg while ignoring the bulk of the Confederate army as it moved north. When Lincoln criticized that plan, Hooker proposed moving on Richmond, ignoring Lee's army altogether. Both Lincoln and Halleck rejected this strategy, telling Hooker that Lee's army, not Richmond, ought to be his objective. Accordingly, Hooker moved in a parallel fashion, hoping to fall on Lee's army at the appropriate time.[9]

As he pursued Lee, a steady conflict developed between Hooker and Halleck. Hooker wanted complete control of troops in neighboring departments, but Halleck instructed only the departmental commanders to cooperate with Hooker. Army of the Potomac chief of staff Daniel Butterfield complained to Salmon Chase that Lincoln and Halleck overestimated the numbers in the Army of the Potomac, which was losing men every day because of the expiration of enlistment terms. At the same time, Butterfield claimed that Lee was being substantially reinforced. When Halleck denied Hooker's request to command the troops stationed at Harpers Ferry, Hooker requested to be relieved of command. At a cabinet meeting on June 28, Lincoln informed his advisers of Hooker's resignation.[10]

Since the Union defeat at Chancellorsville rumors had again surfaced about the imminent recall of McClellan. With Hooker's resignation, the pressure to reappoint him mounted, and ironically members of Lincoln's own party joined the chorus. A Boston man warned Chase that Horatio Seymour and Thurlow Weed were plotting to bring McClellan back in command. James Dixon, a conservative Republican senator from Connecticut, advised the president, "I think the recall of Gen. McClellan to command the Army an absolute necessity." Taking aim at the Committee on the Conduct of the War, Dixon added, "You know and I know that those who have been most active & urgent in the work of destroying the confidence of the people in Gen. McClellan, had reference . . . not to his *capacities* but to his opinions." New Jersey Democratic governor Joel Parker warned that if McClellan were not recalled the people would rise en masse. From Philadelphia, journalist Alexander McClure advised Lincoln to reappoint McClellan in order to

George Meade was the focal point of committee opposition during the Thirty-eighth session of Congress. (Courtesy of the National Archives)

rally the troops as well as the people of Pennsylvania, New York, and New Jersey. Aware that there was strong opposition in Lincoln's cabinet to McClellan, he warned the president, "The people are slow to appreciate personal or political animosities."[11]

George Gordon Meade

Lincoln, however, apparently gave little thought to reappointing McClellan; instead, he seemed intent on George Gordon Meade, commander of the Fifth Corps in the Army of the Potomac. Not only was Meade favored by fellow corps and divisional commanders, but unlike McClellan and Hooker, he had no political ambitions, and he did not champion any political faction. Judge

Advocate Joseph Holt admired Meade because he remained aloof from political entanglements, telling David Davis, "[Meade] is a thorough soldier & not a candidate for the Presidency." A Philadelphia native, Meade graduated from West Point in 1835 and remained in the service through the antebellum years. In summer 1861, through the influence of Sen. David Wilmot, he was given a brigadier general's commission in the Pennsylvania volunteers. He had served as a divisional commander under William Franklin before commanding the Fifth Corps under Hooker. Although some identified him as an avid supporter of McClellan, Meade observed strict neutrality in political matters, believing military professionalism precluded involvement in partisan politics.[12]

Assuming command on June 28, Meade pursued Confederate forces that had entered Pennsylvania and were near the cities of York and Chambersburg. A chance encounter at the town of Gettysburg, an important junction for several key roads, on July 1 precipitated the three bloodiest days of the war. Surviving numerous Confederate assaults, including the dramatic charge of Pickett's division on the last day of battle, Meade's Union forces held the field while Lee's mangled army retired on July 5. Even the radical newspapers praised Meade's efforts. "The Army of the Potomac, the child and champion of the loyal North, has at last found the road to victory," wrote the *New York Daily Tribune*. The North had finally found a capable general, one who could lead the Army of the Potomac on to victory and crush the rebellion. Nevertheless, within a few months, Meade's popularity quickly faded.[13]

When the Thirty-eighth Congress assembled in early December for its first session, Republicans had reason to be truly grateful. Immediately after the battle of Gettysburg, the city of New York had erupted in an orgy of violence. The ostensible reason was reaction to the Enrollment Act and its seeming prejudice against the laboring classes; its $300 commutation fee allowed wealthier Americans to buy their way out of the draft. But the overt attacks on the city's black population and the protests against the centralizing tendencies of the federal government suggested a popular repudiation not only of the war but also of Republican party rule and ideology generally. Thus the fall electoral triumphs of the Republican party, particularly the defeat of gubernatorial peace candidates George Woodward in Pennsylvania and Clement L. Vallandigham in Ohio, reversed the negative image that had emerged as a result of the draft riots.

Indeed, it appeared to Zachariah Chandler that the radical cause had been vindicated. He had stumped several states and spoken before 200,000 people but had not met one person who supported the conservative course proposed by men such as Montgomery Blair or Thurlow Weed. "Either you favor [the] Proclamation & *all who sustain* it, [and] go down with the Government," Chandler had told Lincoln, "or the Rebellion be crushed with all its sympathizers & *Liberty* [will] be the watchword for a hundred years to come." Conservatives had been cut down by the Proclamation; they were defeated and discredited. Chandler predicted, "They will smell worse than Lazarus did after he had been buried three days."[14]

Despite Republican political triumphs, however, the situation in the Army of the Potomac had deteriorated. The optimism after the victory of Gettysburg quickly changed to pessimism. Instead of following up his victory by vigorous pursuit and destruction of the rebel army, as Lincoln had hoped, Meade remained cautious, believing that Lee's strong defensive position made offensive operations hazardous. Eventually Lee recrossed the Potomac in mid-July unscathed. "There is bad faith somewhere," the president reported to Gideon Welles. "Meade has been pressed and urged, but only one of his generals was for an immediate attack, was ready to pounce on Lee; the rest held back. What does it mean Mr. Welles? Great God! What does it mean?" According to Salmon Chase, Lincoln was distraught with Meade's failure to pursue Lee's army. "He was more fervid and in earnest than I have ever seen him," Chase reported to Rhode Island governor and future son-in-law William Sprague. When Welles asked why Lee's escape was allowed, he was informed that most of Meade's generals opposed attacking. "What generals?" Welles recorded in his diary. "None are named. Meade is in command there; Halleck is General-in-Chief. They should be held responsible." According to Judge Advocate Holt, Meade "like all McClellan generals . . . is only capable of *defensive* warfare." Lee's escape, he continued, "was the greatest disaster & humiliation of the war."[15]

Yet Lincoln stood by Meade. Angry and smarting from criticism, Meade told Lincoln he could relieve him anytime the president felt he was not doing his job, but both Lincoln and Halleck assured Meade that they were grateful for his service at Gettysburg even though they thought an opportunity had been squandered. Lincoln believed that once the rebel army came north of the Potomac, it "could never return, if well attended to." When Welles suggested that Meade be superseded, Lincoln replied, "What can I do . . . with such generals as we have? Who among them is any better than Meade?" By December 1863, the situation had become critical. After a series of cat-and-mouse maneuvers in Virginia, Meade's army retired and went into winter quarters without delivering a major blow against Lee. Although a number of plausible reasons account for his moves, impatient congressional

Republicans had heard the story before. Thus once again the Committee on the Conduct of the War rose to the occasion.[16]

By early December even Meade expected to be relieved of command. Writing to his wife about his failure to engage the enemy at Mine Run, Virginia, in late November, he predicted, "There will be a great howl all over the country. Letter writers and politicians will denounce me." Horace Greeley's *New York Daily Tribune* was the most vociferous, but even the pro-Lincoln *New York Times* criticized Meade's lack of activity. Joanna Lane, wife of Indiana senator Henry Smith Lane, spoke of opposition to Meade because of his last "useless campaign."

Meanwhile, leading congressmen, journalists, and cabinet members endeavored to force the administration to replace Meade with Hooker. George Wilkes, editor of *Wilkes' Spirit of the Times*, related a curious plot to Chase that had Sumner trying to persuade Stanton to put George H. Thomas at the head of the Army of the Potomac, a development that would leave Hooker permanently stuck as a corps commander. Wilkes needed help from Chase to prevent such a development. "Wade and Chandler have promised to work with me in the matter," he assured Chase, "and Mr. [John] Conness [senator from California] will go with me to Mr. Stanton." Just a few days later, Chase wrote Hooker, "There has been a deal of talk about recalling you and placing you in command of the Army of the Potomac. . . . I wish it might be done." Despite these efforts, however, when the new year arrived, Meade was still at the helm.[17]

Just as Republicans in the Thirty-seventh Congress used the committee to prod the administration and keep tabs on military matters, so did members of the first session of the Thirty-eighth Congress. A Republican Senate caucus in early January 1864 determined that the committee should be reconstituted, broadening its powers to include examination of military contracts. Accordingly, Wade introduced the appropriate resolution in the Senate on January 12, and Illinois Republican Elihu Washburne introduced it in the House on January 14. Although there was some opposition, little debate on the resolutions occurred, and they quickly passed. The members were the same except for the appointment of Oregon Democrat Benjamin F. Harding, who replaced Joseph Wright, and Republican Benjamin F. Loan of Missouri, who replaced John Covode. Moses Odell had recently supported peace Democrat Fernando Wood's resolution authorizing commissioners to visit Richmond to treat with Confederate officials, but his action apparently did not diminish his stature in the eyes of his Republican committee colleagues, and he too was reappointed.[18]

Missourian Benjamin Franklin Loan was the only member with military experience. Born in Harrisburg, Kentucky, in 1819, Loan moved to St. Joseph, Missouri, in 1838, where he studied law and was admitted to the bar in 1840. When the war broke out, Loan took an appointment in the Missouri State Militia as a brigadier general, serving until he won his seat in the Thirty-eighth Congress. Identified with the radical Charcoal faction in Missouri politics, Loan was a persistent critic of the more conservative Claybank faction of provisional governor Hamilton Gamble, whom Loan described to the president as a conditional Unionist and a friend of slavery. Favoring immediate emancipation and scrupulous enforcement of confiscation, Loan was often the focal point of opposition to Gamble and in summer 1863 played a pivotal role in organizing radical sentiment against him. As a brigadier general, Loan pursued vigorous measures, deporting rebel sympathizers from the St. Joseph area and levying bonds on those who remained. In fall 1863 Loan was part of a delegation of Missouri radicals who visited the president and urged that Department of Missouri commander, John M. Schofield, be replaced with a more radical general. Committee Republicans clearly regarded Loan as a suitable replacement for John Covode.[19]

Born in Pennsylvania in 1823, Benjamin Franklin Harding studied law and opened a practice in Illinois before emigrating to Oregon in 1849. After holding a variety of offices in the territorial government, he was elected as a Democratic member to the state house of representatives in 1859 and in March 1862 was chosen to fill the term of Edward D. Baker, the Republican senator killed at the battle of Ball's Bluff. A staunch Douglas Democrat, Harding had no sympathy with secession and was an outspoken critic of peace Democrats. Nevertheless, he disagreed with Republican social legislation and therefore was not nominated by the Union party for a second term in 1865. Unlike Moses Odell, Harding never played a central role in the committee's work. He attended its sessions infrequently, eventually resigning his seat in early 1865, and was replaced by Charles R. Buckalew, a Pennsylvania peace Democrat who scarcely attended the committee's meetings at all.[20]

The Committee on the Conduct of the War began its work in the Thirty-eighth Congress on a positive note, engaging in a number of investigations that demonstrated a constructive use for its authority. Responding to a number of congressional resolutions, the committee examined such diverse areas as ice contracts, the manufacture of heavy ordnance, and the operations of the New York and Philadelphia Quartermaster Departments. Through the examination of ice contracts, the committee exposed irregularities in the surgeon general's methods of negotiating the contracts, irregularities that cost the government thousands of dollars. By examining purchasing procedures, the committee helped expose and correct abuses.

Such mundane matters, however, could not keep the committee's attention for long. Most of its activities in the first half of 1864 were again focused on the Army of the Potomac. The goal of the Republican majority was to replace Meade with Hooker, but the methods the CCW employed to achieve that goal were counterproductive to the Union war effort.[21]

Meade was objectionable to the committee's Republican majority not only for his lack of military success but also for his attitude of professional detachment from partisan politics, which made him suspect. Equating nonpartisanship with lukewarm patriotism, the committee's Republicans believed Meade was a Copperhead, that his heart was not really in the conflict, and that he was more interested in compromise than in defeating the rebel army. One incident, in particular, influenced some committee members. Just after the firing on Fort Sumter, patriotic Detroit residents held a rally in which resolutions were passed calling on local federal officials, both civilian and military, to renew their oaths of loyalty to the United States. These reaffirmations were to be the highpoint of another public rally a few days later. Meade, who was stationed in Detroit to conduct a survey of the Great Lakes, refused and urged his staff to do the same on the grounds that local authorities had no right to demand such an oath. When he failed to attend the public rally, Chandler "became harshly critical," perhaps noting that two of Meade's staff members were southerners who shortly thereafter enlisted in the Confederate army. In August 1861, former Michigan governor Robert McClelland recalled that before the outbreak of hostilities, Meade had said that he did not look forward to war and to fighting so many of his old friends. McClelland told commanding general George McClellan that although the statement was perfectly sensible, he was afraid it would be used to discredit Meade. Indeed, this statement, Meade's refusal to renew his oath, and his entire professional demeanor made him particularly objectionable to Chandler. As Meade later wrote his wife, "Old Zach Chandler is my bitterest foe and will show me no quarter."[22]

"I am making a record which no one will have reason to be ashamed of," Chandler wrote his wife in spring 1864. He was on the side of liberty and pitied those who opposed the government and the abolition of slavery, for they would go down in infamy. "No man," he concluded, "has a right to pass [?] this record of infamy to his descendants." Yet Chandler and his Republican colleagues surely had a curious definition of what constituted both helping and opposing the government. In singling out Meade, the committee exploited jealousy and professional rivalries among the army's elite officers, encouraging an atmosphere of distrust and hostility. And in investigating him, the committee blurred the distinction between oversight and control of the executive branch of government since they attempted not only to advise Lincoln but also to manage his military decisions.[23]

As Hooker Rises, So Must Meade Fall

To discredit Meade, the committee focused on a number of disgruntled officers, including Abner Doubleday, Albion Howe, Alfred Pleasanton, and most important, Daniel Sickles. Indeed, no witness could have been a more unlikely corroborator than Sickles. A Tammany Hall Democrat, this New York City politician was first elected to Congress in 1857 and became a close ally of James Buchanan. Sickles was most famous for murdering Philip Barton Key in 1859, after the former discovered that the latter was having an affair with his wife. Sickles (who ultimately was acquitted of the charges) was defended by a team of lawyers that included Edwin M. Stanton. Stanton's relationship with Sickles was key in the pivotal role that Sickles played during the committee's investigation of Meade. Further, Sickles's status as a volunteer commander gave him instant credibility with a committee that distrusted West Point professionals.[24]

Sickles had been busy since Gettysburg, carefully crafting an account of the battle while recovering from the loss of his leg. One of his most important listeners was the president, who visited the stricken general during his convalescence. As Edwin Coddington notes, Sickles "by skillful indirection" gave himself the credit for the victory. Later, prompted both by Meade's refusal to restore him to command of the Third Corps and by the publication of Halleck's report on Gettysburg that singled him out for criticism, Sickles became even more determined to vindicate himself. According to Gideon Welles, Sickles claimed that Meade had never wanted to fight at Gettysburg but was forced to remain because of the advance position taken by Sickles's own Third Corps, which had forced an engagement with the Confederate army. Although this story reinforced Welles's opinion of Meade as a cautious, passive commander, he was also skeptical of Sickles's veracity. The committee however, offered a willing ear to this veteran of political intrigue, and W. A. Swanberg states that Sickles met privately with Wade and Chandler to discuss strategy, which suggests not an impartial investigation but one instituted to prove a foregone conclusion.[25]

In early March, Meade's aide-de-camp Theodore Lyman, in a letter to his wife, referred to an attack launched on Meade by Republican radicals, wondering how they could say of officers who had put their lives on the line that "their hearts are not in the cause." He continued: "It would appear that Washington people often think the best test of faithfulness is to stay away from fighting and make many good speeches to people who entirely agree with your sentiments." Lyman knew that tremendous efforts were being made on Hooker's behalf, a man "who has made one of the most bloody failures of the War, and who is utterly incompetent to the post." Yet such was the case, he concluded, "because he professes to be an ultra-Republican, ah, *voila!*"[26]

Before they focused on Meade, committee members attempted to rewrite the history of Chancellorsville in order to reconstruct Hooker's reputation. Using the testimony of several of Hooker's supporters in the Army of the Potomac as its principal evidence, the committee patched together a highly flattering portrait of his generalship based on distortions, half-truths, outright falsehoods, and hypotheticals. According to Sickles, the sole problem at Chancellorsville was the stampede of the Eleventh Corps as a result of Jackson's flank attack. Hooker's plan, he maintained, was to position his own Third Corps between the two wings of Lee's army, thereby separating them and making them vulnerable to destruction. Hooker's injury on the morning of May 3, however, prevented Sickles from getting the necessary reinforcements. Had Hooker not fallen, Sickles speculated, the battle would have been won "in thirty minutes." The enemy was completely demoralized in its subsequent attempts to break Hooker's army, but even so, Sickles believed the army had no choice but to recross the Rappahannock since rations were running out and heavy storms were expected. Sickles also informed the committee that Hooker was unpopular with officers sympathetic to McClellan.[27]

Despite Hooker's overwhelming numerical advantage over Lee at Chancellorsville, Gen. Albion Howe, formerly a divisional commander in John Sedgwick's Sixth Corps, maintained that Sedgwick was responsible for the defeat because he did not obey Hooker's repeated order to come to Chancellorsville from Fredericksburg. In fact, Howe could give no explanation for Sedgwick's failure. Yet Howe was probably unaware that Hooker had sent Sedgwick a number of contradictory dispatches during the course of the battle advising him to make different moves. More important, Hooker allowed Lee to occupy him with a scant 20,000 men, which enabled Lee to reinforce his troops at Fredericksburg and to threaten Sedgwick's Sixth Corps. Yet when Sedgwick tried to make this point in later testimony, it seemed to have little effect on the committee.[28]

Hooker's former chief of staff Daniel Butterfield offered the most incredible testimony. Although he was serving in the West during the committee's investigation, he managed to travel to Washington for a few days to supply the CCW with more evidence of Hooker's brilliance. According to Butterfield, with the exception of Oliver Otis Howard, none of Hooker's corps commanders favored staying on the offensive after Chancellorsville, although Meade was against recrossing the Rappahannock because he thought it too risky in the face of Lee's army. This report was totally false. Howard, Reynolds, and Meade favored remaining on the offensive, and Sickles and Couch opposed it. Although Butterfield had always supposed the corps commanders supported Hooker, the commanding general had told Butterfield that he did not enjoy their full confidence. The implication was that Hooker had failed, in part, because he had not received the full cooperation of his subordinates, that he was sabotaged by the McClellan faction in the Army of the Potomac— a charge that committee members were only too willing to believe.[29]

The issue of Hooker's alleged drunkenness was a major topic in committee hearings, primarily because rumors attributing the defeat at Chancellorsville to his intoxication were widespread. Thaddeus Stevens, the powerful chairman of the House Ways and Means Committee, told one correspondent that he had talked to several officers in the army who had dismissed the rumor as false. Yet according to Gideon Welles, such reports were seriously entertained by the cabinet. Shortly after Chancellorsville, Chase, Hooker's principal booster in the cabinet, received a disturbing letter from Rhode Island governor William Sprague that claimed Hooker was indeed intoxicated during the battle. Perhaps most damaging were public comments made by the Reverend Henry Ward Beecher, who told a temperance group on July 5, 1863, that Hooker had used whiskey after he was wounded during the battle.[30]

There is little credible evidence to suggest that Hooker was drunk or that alcohol seriously impaired his judgment during the campaign. Most of the witnesses called before the committee, whether hostile or friendly, testified that he was not drunk. The committee's efforts to force Beecher to reveal the source of his information paid off when he would not provide names, thus discrediting his remarks. Nevertheless, in their zeal to exonerate Hooker, some of his supporters offered testimony that bordered on the ludicrous. For instance, when Benjamin Loan asked Butterfield, who knew Hooker intimately, "Have you ever seen him under the influence of liquor?" Butterfield responded, "Never." Even Sickles had qualified his answer by saying he had never observed Hooker under the influence of alcohol *while on duty.* Eager to present Hooker in the beset light possible, none of the committee members present challenged Butterfield, despite Hooker's well-known habits.[31]

That the committee's Republican majority seriously could consider the explanations for the defeat at Chancellorsville seems absurd. First, they had castigated McClellan when he pleaded lack of men and supplies, complained about weather conditions, and was overly concerned about securing a line of retreat. When Sickles and Butterfield defended Hooker using the same reasons, committee members did not protest. Second, it is true that Hooker did not have the support of his corps commanders, but it was primarily because he gave away his initial advantages to Lee, grew timid in the crisis of battle, and finally gave up and retreated. It was Sickles who had made a passionate speech defending Hooker's decision to retreat, arguing that in view of the Copperhead resurgence in the fall elections, an advance was too risky. How could the same Wade and Chandler now accept such defeatist logic? Only on the assumption that Hooker was not being allowed to fight to his full potential by an officer corps motivated by lukewarm patriotism, Copperheadism, and sympathy for McClellan.[32]

If Hooker were to rise, Meade had to fall. As the committee developed favorable testimony on the former, it gathered unflattering reports on the latter. Sickles told Wade that on the first day of Gettysburg Meade wanted not to fight but to fall back; the decision to fight was made by subordinates, most prominently by Sickles. Though both Meade's and Halleck's official reports faulted Sickles for positioning his troops in advance of the Union line on Cemetery Ridge, thus making the entire Union position vulnerable, Sickles blamed Meade for not reinforcing him properly. Wade asked if the enemy should have been allowed to recross the Potomac after Gettysburg. "He should have followed up closely and vigorously attacked before [Lee] had an opportunity to recross the river," Sickles replied. Apparently, Sickles's expertise on Lee's retreat did not strike Wade as odd even though Sickles had been wounded and was not an eyewitness to events after the battle.[33]

Abner Doubleday corroborated much of Sickles's testimony and offered some spectacular revelations. Angry because Meade had placed junior officer John Newton over him in command of the First Corps, Doubleday was clearly out for revenge. Referring to Meade's order of July 1, the so-called Pipe Creek circular that directed the Army of the Potomac to fall back if the position at Gettysburg was unfavorable, Doubleday reiterated Sickles's point that Meade never wanted to fight at Gettysburg, and the order demonstrated this. Asked why he had been removed from command, Doubleday replied, "There has always been a great deal of favoritism in the army of the Potomac, . . . no man who is an anti-slavery man or an anti-McClellan man can expect decent treatment in that army as presently constituted." When asked for a further explanation, Doubleday claimed a proslavery clique controlled the army that would allow no one to have influence who entertained different opinions.[34]

When Albion Howe testified that Lee's army was not pursued with vigor after Gettysburg on the advice of Meade's corps commanders, Wade inquired, "Can you have great confidence in the ability of officers who counsel to forego such an opportunity?" Obviously, there was only one answer to such a question. Of course, even Lincoln had been bitterly disappointed with Meade's failure to attack Lee's retreating army; however, there were some sound logical reasons for the decision. Lee occupied a strong defensive position and had ample supplies of ammunition; to attack him, Meade would have had to launch a direct, frontal assault. But, as Herman Hattaway and Archer Jones point out, "It was easy to sympathize with the reluctance of Meade and his generals who had just observed the power of defense when they had so successfully repelled Pickett's frontal assault at Gettysburg." Yet according to Howe, Meade lacked earnestness, and his heart was not in his work. He then told the committee that the army's rank and file were completely demoralized by the failure to engage the enemy that fall, and Howe blamed Meade's principal corps commanders for this caution. "I do not know as I can express myself better than saying that there is copperheadism at the root of the matter," Howe concluded.[35]

Solely on the basis of Sickles's, Doubleday's, and Howe's testimonies, the committee, represented by Wade, Chandler, and Loan, sought and received an interview with the president and Secretary of War Stanton on March 4. They presented Lincoln with their evidence and demanded Meade's removal. Although they would not name a specific replacement, they said they would be satisfied with Hooker. If Lincoln refused to cooperate, the committee would be compelled "to make the testimony public." Since Lincoln had already heard Sickles's version of events at Gettysburg, the committee presented him with no surprises. But Lincoln did refuse to cooperate. Undoubtedly noting the glaring one-sidedness of the evidence, perhaps Lincoln suggested that the committee interview Meade and some of his corps commanders before passing judgment. Or perhaps he assured the congressmen that Grant, recently promoted to general in chief, would be campaigning with the Army of the Potomac, in effect, prodding Meade along. Still, the committee members' choice of Hooker, an obvious failure as commander by any objective standard, cannot have favorably impressed the president as to their military judgment.[36]

The committee's threat to make their information public did not intimidate the president since just two days earlier, Morton S. Wilkinson, a radical Republican senator from Minnesota, had attacked Meade in the Senate, reiterating the charges Sickles had made to the committee. Comparing Meade with Grant, Wilkinson ridiculed the former for allowing Lee to escape from Gettysburg. Reverdy Johnson, the Maryland Democrat and defender of Fitz-John Porter, answered Wilkinson, claiming attacks on the army's leadership were counterproductive and ultimately aimed at the president. Meade, who was in Washington at the time and witnessed Wilkinson's diatribe, wrote his wife that "the whole town [was] talking of certain grave charges of Generals Sickles and Doubleday, that had been made against me in their testimony before the Committee on the Conduct of the War."[37]

Probably at Lincoln's suggestion, Meade was summoned to appear before the committee on March 5. The appearances of Sickles, Doubleday, and Howe had been carefully orchestrated; Meade's session, on the other hand, took him completely by surprise. He was forced to appear without any chance to prepare himself—a fact the committee must have known. When he arrived at the committee's room in the basement of the Capitol, he was met by Wade, who treated him kindly. "He was very civil," Meade wrote his wife, and "denied there were any charges against me." Since Wade had been to the president just the day before demanding the general's ouster, his performance in Meade's presence was somewhat disingenuous. And his contention to Meade that "the committee was making up a sort of history of the war" was not completely forthright, since the committee was still intent on gathering testimony in order to remove Meade from command.[38]

Meade endeavored to clear up four areas of controversy with respect to his command of the Army of the Potomac. First, the charges that he had not wanted to fight at Gettysburg were false. He had issued orders on July 1 for the army to fall back to Pipe Creek near Taneytown, Maryland, but this was before he knew that John Reynolds had already collided with the enemy. Once engagement occurred, he did not hesitate to fight. Second, Sickles had occupied his position in advance of Hancock's Second Corps on Cemetery Ridge in violation of Meade's orders, which resulted in the near-annihilation of Sickles's corps. Third, even though Meade wanted to attack Lee's retreating army near Williamsport, Maryland, he deferred to the opinion of his corps commanders, and upon reflection believed it was a good decision since Lee occupied a strong position. Meade assured Wade that the rebels had not exhausted their supply of artillery ammunition as other witnesses had testified—a point corroborated by Lee's correspondence with Jefferson Davis. Nor was Lee's army completely demoralized as some witnesses had claimed.

Fourth, although Meade was not particularly proud of the army's operations after Gettysburg, there were valid reasons why he had failed to engage the enemy. Since Wade had probably prejudged the matter, Meade's points no doubt made little impact on him.[39]

Before and after Meade's appearance, the press was flooded with accounts of the investigation. Although Wade denied that anyone on the committee was involved in leaks, given previous disclosures of testimony, such denials seem implausible. John Gibbon, one of Meade's division commanders, wrote to George McClellan, "I see the 'imbeciles' have commenced in earnest an attack on Meade for the Gettysburg." Gibbon then added that pressure was being exerted to have Meade removed from command. When he heard that Meade had appeared before the committee to answer charges raised by Sickles and Doubleday, Charles Wainwright exclaimed, "A pretty team!—Rascality and Stupidity. I wonder which one hatches the biggest chicken." According to the *New York Times,* Meade had been summoned before the committee to answer the charges of Sickles and Doubleday; if he could not make a satisfactory defense, he would lose his command. Not only did the *Times* question the validity of an investigation based on the complaint of subordinates, but it also suggested that it would demoralize the army.

Other sources, however, were not so charitable to Meade. The *New York Daily Tribune* smeared him by alleging that he had exclaimed, "Oh, let them go," when junior officers urged pursuit of the retreating rebel army. The *Tribune* also claimed that Meade had tried to break up the Third Corps when it would not subscribe to a testimonial for McClellan. The most damaging attack on Meade, however, appeared in the *New York Herald.* Under the pseudonym Historicus and undoubtedly written by Sickles, the account gave an unflattering description of Meade's role at Gettysburg, reiterating most of Sickles's points in his committee testimony. One constituent wrote Chandler in mid-March that there was "a good deal of sneering out here concerning the army of the Potomac." Apparently, Sickles's actions and the committee's campaign to discredit Meade were having an effect.[40]

Shortly after the revelations of Sickles and other detractors became public, Meade wrote his wife, "I am curious to see how you take the explosion of the conspiracy, to have me relieved, for it is nothing less than a conspiracy, in which the Committee on the Conduct of the War, with Generals Doubleday and Sickles, are the agents." Indeed, the committee continued to subpoena witnesses with personal grudges against Meade. Thus David Birney, who had replaced Sickles as commander of the Third Corps only to be replaced by Meade with William French, reiterated many of Sickles's accusations, as did

Alfred Pleasanton, who was supposedly on his way out as chief cavalry officer of the Army of the Potomac.

When Meade defended himself, he drew sharp fire from Secretary Stanton. Shortly after Wilkinson's speech in the Senate, Meade sent Reverdy Johnson a letter that detailed Wilkinson's mistakes. Johnson did not help Meade by publishing the letter in John Forney's *Washington Chronicle;* nevertheless, Stanton's objection to Meade's contact with the senator was inconsistent. Stanton was well aware of the committee's plot. Gideon Welles confirmed frequently Stanton's close relationship with committee members: "Stanton is actually hated by many [army] officers," wrote Welles, "and is more intimate with certain extreme partisans in Congress—the Committee on the Conduct of the War and others—than with the Executive Administration and military men." As a personal friend of Sickles, Stanton surely could not have been totally ignorant of the former's role in the proceedings. Since Stanton did nothing to silence Sickles and other critics of Meade, his objections to Meade's letter were unjust.[41]

Meade's one friend on the committee was Moses Odell. The Brooklyn Democrat had gained the trust of the committee's principal Republicans for his zealous discharge of his duties, but he had been uninvolved in the investigation of Meade and rarely attended committee meetings. After a meeting with Meade in mid-March, Odell assured him that, despite his friendship with Chandler, he was "most indignant at the course pursued" and would make sure Meade was treated fairly. Odell began to attend committee sessions, challenging the assertions of witnesses and interrupting the programmed testimony. When Winfield Scott Hancock appeared, Odell asked him if he had ever received an order from Meade at Gettysburg to retreat, and Hancock claimed he had not. And to Gen. James Wadsworth, one of two corps commanders who had favored attacking Lee's retreating army at Williamsport, Odell defended the reasoning of the generals who had urged caution.[42]

Odell's most prominent role occurred in connection with Meade's chief detractor, Daniel Butterfield. Although Butterfield was intensely loyal to Hooker, Meade had not initially replaced him as chief of staff for the sake of convenience and continuity after he succeeded Hooker. Butterfield and Hooker meanwhile were serving in the West under William T. Sherman. Although Hooker directed several letters to Wade begging to be called to Washington to reveal the truth about his campaign, he did not arrive there until spring 1865. Butterfield, however, came secretly to the capital in late March 1864 for the express purpose of testifying before the committee. Sickles informed Chandler that the committee needed to move quickly since

Butterfield did not have Halleck's permission to be in Washington: "It is very important that you have Brig. Genl S. Williams Ast. Adjt. Genl Army of the Potomac here *with all orders & Communications bearing on the Gettysburg campaign*—original *drafts & Copies as received at Head Quarters—this is* all important for you to have before you *when Butterfield is Examined—* Then you will have the *real history* of the Campaign."[43]

Repeating the charges of Sickles and other witnesses, Butterfield asserted that Meade intended to fall back on July 1; it was Butterfield who urged him to fight at Gettysburg once Reynolds's corps engaged the enemy there. Odell asked if the position of the enemy was known when Meade drew up this order. No, Butterfield replied. When asked if the order was prudent, he answered, "I would rather you not ask me that question." When Loan later asked him about his reluctance to answer Odell, Butterfield replied that he hesitated because he did not like to criticize superiors. For a man who had virtually sneaked into Washington to discredit his former commander, such a response seemed both ludicrous and dishonest. "It was the business of our army then to find Lee and fight him," he told committee members; Meade's order to fall back to Pipe Creek was a poor decision.[44]

Butterfield next presented the committee with a startling accusation: on the second day of the battle Meade intended to retreat, and he had instructed Butterfield to draft an order to that effect. Although he had no copy of the draft, Butterfield told Gooch, he was sure that Asst. Adj. Gen. of the Army of the Potomac Seth Williams had a copy. A copy never materialized. When Gooch asked if it was a firm order or subject to conditions, Butterfield told him that only Meade could answer that question.

Meade anticipated these charges since Gen. John Gibbon had warned him of Butterfield's perfidy. "It is now evident," he wrote his wife, "that Butterfield, either intentionally or otherwise, misconstrued something that I said to him on the 2nd of July into instructions to prepare an order to withdraw the army." A few days later he went before the committee and denied the allegations emphatically. He had told Butterfield to familiarize himself with the roads and terrain in the event that a withdrawal should become necessary. Meade then gave the committee a list of witnesses to call to corroborate his statement, including John Gibbon, artillery chief Henry Hunt, and Sixth Corps commander John Sedgwick. Each appeared before the committee and supported Meade's statement. Hunt told them that as artillery commander, he would have been one of the first to be informed of such an order, yet he knew nothing of it. Odell asked Sedgwick why Meade would have urged his corps to rush to Gettysburg if it had been his intention to retreat. That would have made little sense, answered Sedgwick.[45]

Butterfield's accusations prompted Meade to request a court of inquiry on the matter; however, Lincoln denied it on the grounds that it would not be in the public interest. But Lincoln and newly promoted General-in-Chief Ulysses Grant were determined to thwart the committee. When Seth Williams was summoned to appear before it with the official correspondence on the Gettysburg campaign, Stanton was forced to deny the request at Grant's behest. Nevertheless, public and private attacks on Meade continued. Grant told him he had received several letters from Adam Gurowski, "that crazy old man" as Meade described him, telling Grant to remove Meade and suggesting that McClellan dictated Meade's every move—charges repeated in the *New York Daily Tribune*. Still, in view of the testimony the committee recently had received, Meade believed that it was favorable toward him. "I find I have three warm friends on the Committee," he told his wife: "Odell of New York, Gooch of Massachusetts, and Harding of Oregon. It is believed that Wade of Ohio, is favorably inclined. If either he or one of the others should prove so, it would make a majority in my favor." Meade, however, was overly optimistic. As he discovered a few months later, there was still considerable hostility toward him on the committee. If he sensed an abatement, it was probably because the committee had given up temporarily since Lincoln would not yield to them.[46]

Individual committee members, however, continued to harass Meade. In early July Chandler visited the Army of the Potomac with Morton Wilkinson and several other members of Congress. "Ostensibly this pair had come to inspect the army," Freeman Cleaves writes, "but their actual mission, as Meade learned from Hancock, was to persuade Grant to remove him." Meade wrote his wife that Wilkinson, in particular, "was very severe on me, showing he still retained the animus that dictated his attack on me in the Senate last winter." Meade's opponents, particularly those on the committee, needed a blunder to justify another investigation. The Crater disaster near Petersburg, Virginia, on July 30 provided their opportunity.[47]

Battle of the Crater

After the bloody battles of the Wilderness, Spotsylvania, and Cold Harbor, the Army of the Potomac had settled into a siege of Lee's forces at Petersburg, approximately twenty miles south of Richmond. Failing to find a reliable way of breaking through the Confederate lines, Grant and Meade eventually approved a plan developed by Ambrose Burnside, commander of the Ninth Corps, which occupied a position just a scant 150 yards form Confederate works. Henry Pleasants, a colonel in the Forty-eighth Pennsylvania, a regiment known for its coal miners, told Burnside of a scheme to tunnel under Confederate fortifications and construct a mine, which could then be charged with explosives. Although Meade was skeptical, he allowed Burnside to proceed. When the mine was completed, Meade and Grant authorized Burnside to charge it with 8,000 pounds of gunpowder and to draw up a plan of attack. Although Burnside had drilled a division of black troops under Gen. Edward Ferrero to lead the assault after the mine exploded, Meade objected and overruled him, with Grant's concurrence. Meade reasoned that the entire operation was a risk, and he did not want to be accused of sacrificing black troops if the assault proved unsuccessful.[48]

From the beginning the assault proved disastrous. First, there was considerable delay in blowing up the mine. Meade had instructed the attacking division, commanded by James Ledlie, to make straight for Cemetery Hill, a high point that commanded the Confederate position. When the mine exploded, Ledlie's troops delayed advancing, and when they finally moved forward, instead of moving to the high ground, they plunged into the huge crater before them as if they had no inkling of their mission. With no divisional commanders present to direct affairs, the situation soon deteriorated. Troops following Ledlie were supposed to move to the left and the right of the crater; instead, most men advanced into it, creating moblike confusion. Eventually the stunned Confederates recuperated and began directing rifle and artillery fire into the crater. Ferrero's division of black troops was finally sent forward. They circumvented the crater and began to move forward, but when they met resistance, their attack broke up and they plunged back into the crater, adding to the confusion. Apprised that no forward progress was being made, Meade ordered Burnside to suspend the attack and withdraw. Burnside agreed, but only after bitterly objecting. With Confederate troops launching a brisk counterattack, Union forces retreated in disorganized fashion. Generating 4,000 casualties, the battle of the Crater was a disaster.[49]

When Gideon Welles heard of the fiasco, he commented, "The results were bad and the effect has been disheartening in the extreme." One officer wrote, "Never before have I felt that the Army of the Potomac was disgraced, . . . failed it has frequently and botched its commanding generals have made of more than one piece of work, but the army itself always come out with honour." Predictably the *New York Daily Tribune* held Meade responsible for the disaster, claiming that Grant had a sound plan and that Meade was to provide the particulars. "People have a vulgar idea," countered one of Meade's aides, "that a General commanding a great army can, and ought to arrange in person every detail." The *New York Herald* blamed both Meade and Burnside, noting that the administration's policy of using black troops also was responsible. Some radical journals similarly blasted the administration for using black troops, but from a different perspective. The New York *Independent,* for instance, believed it was immoral to use blacks for combat duty as long as the Confederacy would not treat them as bona fide prisoners of war.[50]

Meanwhile, Meade and Burnside quarreled over the battle. Upset with the tone of several of Burnside's dispatches during it and angry over the number of casualties, Meade asked and received a court of inquiry on the affair. Composed mainly of his friends, the court placed most of the blame on Burnside. Meade wanted to cashier Burnside, but Grant induced him not to do so. Instead, Burnside was persuaded to retire from the army.[51]

Since Congress was not in session, the committee could do little in an official capacity to hamper Meade; nevertheless, his enemies plotted. Adam Gurowski wrote Wade and begged the senator to block Meade's confirmation as a regular army major general. "How can such a coward as Meade be put on a level with Sherman, Sheridan, Thomas?" he asked. "Grant stands by him because Grant is sensitive to flattery." Although Meade did receive the commission, there was persistent opposition from a group of radical senators. During the critical fall electoral canvass, Meade angered many partisan Republicans when he refused to arrest a Democratic election commissioner accused of distributing invalid Republican ballots because there was no solid evidence to support the charges. His aide sarcastically commented, "The Commanding general must be a Copperhead not to jump at the chance of arresting a Democrat." When Congress met to begin its session in December, the committee was handed the opportunity to assail Meade: Rhode Island senator Henry Anthony, a political friend of Burnside, introduced a resolution instructing the committee to investigate the Crater disaster.[52]

With Sherman's army marching on Savannah and Lee's army hemmed in at Petersburg, most political leaders and many civilians were well aware that the days of the Confederacy were numbered. Thus one might well ask what possible good could have come from an investigation of the battle of the Crater. If the only purpose was to assign blame and to embarrass the army's leadership, then the utility of such an investigation is questionable, despite the committee's constitutional right to conduct it. As with many other committee investigations, the conclusion seemed to be predetermined: Meade was the responsible party. The subsequent investigation resembled a staged proceeding to gather proof for an a priori conclusion.

In late December the committee traveled to Petersburg to gather testimony. Meade was taken by surprise and lacked most of his paperwork. He read his official report and answered numerous question from Loan, who, in Meade's words, "evidently wished to find flaws." When given a list of witnesses the committee had previously interviewed, Meade noted that the majority were Burnside's friends. Meade asked the committee to interview Gen. Henry Hunt, chief artillery officer, and Col. James Duane, chief engineering officer of the Army of the Potomac. The committee complied, but Duane and Hunt regarded their testimony as meaningless; Meade reported that the two emerged from their interviews laughing. Both Hunt and Duane claimed that as soon as they spoke against Burnside, committee members "stopped them and said that was enough, clearly showing that they only wanted evidence of one kind." Lieutenant General Grant, too, noticed this same tendency. When the committee released its report in early February 1865, a report that generated some public attention, he told Meade, "General Burnside's evidence apparently has been their only guide & to draw it mildly he has forgotten some of the facts."[53]

The committee's principal charge was that Meade had caused the disaster because he did not allow Ferrero's blacks troops to lead the attack, an obvious attempt to portray him as at odds with Republican racial ideology. He was also faulted for changing Burnside's attack formation. Burnside had envisioned Ferrero's men sweeping to the left and right of the explosion before charging the heights in order to prevent enfilading fire from disrupting the attack. Meade's orders insisted that the crest of Cemetery Ridge be the central objective of the assault; once securely in Union hands it would command Confederate positions to the left and right. Speed was crucial to his plan. Since Ferrero's men were specifically trained for this assault, there is a certain plausibility to the committee's contention; however, they simply overlooked much of the other evidence. Burnside's subordinate generals, given their testimony, clearly were attempting to excuse their own lackluster performance. They were not even at the scene of the battle; Ledlie, who commanded the attacking division, was drunk in a bombproof bunker safely behind the lines. Not one general satisfactorily explained why there was a delay in charging the crest after the explosions took place, how and why the troops became congested and then trapped in the crater, and why they failed to provide personal leadership. Rather, they tried to provide a convenient, catch-all excuse for the Crater disaster that would absolve them from responsibility.

Burnside, too, could not escape his share of the blame. His decision to allow Ledlie, his least experienced commander, to lead the attack was ill-advised. Even worse, he had chosen Ledlie for the role by casting lots, an irresponsible act that even the committee could not ignore in its report. Although Burnside assailed Meade for not being closer to the battle so as to give orders based on personal observation, he failed adequately to explain his own absence. Nor did he give any reasons as to why he had made no provision to ensure that his divisional commanders were on the scene. Further, Burnside had issued no orders for clearing obstructions from his trenches, thereby forcing his attacking troops to charge the crater through a narrow ten-foot tunnel, resulting in an advancing line of only four men abreast. Meade's plan had emphasized speed; Burnside failed miserably in ensuring that his divisional commanders carried it out.[54]

The decision to prevent Ferrero's black troops from leading the attack was perhaps ill-advised; even Grant admitted they probably should have been allowed to. However, it is by no means self-evident, contrary to what William Marvel, Burnside's biographer, suggests, that employing black troops would have significantly altered the battle's outcome. No matter how they had been trained, they were green troops who had never experienced enemy fire; hence, it is not certain that they would have executed the attack successfully. Meade changed the order not out of any special hostility toward black troops, as the committee attempted to represent; rather, as Shelby Foote notes, he did so to ward off radical Republican critics in case the attack failed. Thus through its persistent criticism and hostile attacks, the committee may have affected the decisionmaking capacity of a leading general. In November 1864, George Templeton Strong of the U.S. Sanitary Commission reported that his contacts in the Army of the Potomac claimed Meade was excessively concerned about his reputation. Such concern was justified, given that his every action was scrutinized, his successful military endeavors such as Gettysburg were investigated, and the fruits of his efforts were denied.[55]

Perhaps the most absurd charge in the report was that Meade, originally hostile to the project of the mine, "assumed the entire direction and control only when it was completed, and the time had come for reaping any advantages that might be derived from it." Not only did this impute an unfair motive to Meade, but it also contained a flat contradiction. If Meade had wanted to take the glory from Burnside and if, as the committee steadfastly maintained, it was self-evident that the use of Ferrero's troops would have resulted in victory, then Meade would not have countermanded the order, with its certain promise of victory and fame. On the contrary, Meade as well as Grant knew that the venture was a risk and that blame, not glory, might be their reward. Perhaps a good measure of the report's objectivity was Odell's refusal to sign it. When the committee had published its reports in spring 1863 that were highly critical of McClellan, Odell had complied with the Republican majority. In the case of Meade, however, the Brooklyn Democrat would not give in.[56]

The CCW's inquiries into the Army of the Potomac and the battle of the Crater reveal the problems created by congressional committee of investigation. Given the well-established precedents for congressional oversight of executive matters, it is understandable why the Committee on the Conduct of the War was concerned with Meade's generalship. And if one considers the Whig antecedents of most committee members, there was nothing inconsistent about their intimate involvement in the affairs of the military. Nevertheless, as Brian Holden Reid points out, the utility of the committee's activities depended on how responsibly it discharged its investigative duties. In examining the Army of the Potomac and targeting Meade for removal, the committee did nothing useful for the Union war effort. First, the investigation was neither neutral nor objective since the members had already prejudged the case against Meade. Second, had the committee succeeded in removing Meade in favor of Hooker, it is impossible to determine if the Union military effort would have benefited. Third, the committee demonstrated that its military thinking was largely shaped by popular, unrealistic ideas of strategy. The majority of committee members were devoted to Hooker because he spoke the language of aggressive action, forward movement, and no retreat (despite his retreat at Chancellorsville). Meade was more moderate and cautious, knowing full well the inherent risks of aggressive, offensive actions. The members' ignorance of military matters rendered their investigation superfluous at best and harmful and demoralizing to the Union high command at worst.[57]

Several historians have recently argued that Lincoln used congressional committees and their penchant for leaking information to advance his own executive objectives. The most prominent advocate of this position, Hans Trefousse, maintains that the committee held little real power; instead, Lincoln used it as a tool to prod cautious generals such as McClellan and Meade into action. As Allan Bogue points out, however, there is little direct evidence to support this contention. Indeed, Lincoln probably regarded the committee as an unwelcome hindrance. It is difficult to grasp any objectives that the committee's investigation of Meade and the Army of the Potomac accomplished for Lincoln. Grant had already been appointed general in chief, and he had been persuaded by the president to direct the Army of the Potomac. Since Grant was the real power, there was no point in removing Meade, even if the president had been so inclined. Other than contributing to the destruction of Meade's reputation for generations to come, little was accomplished by the committee's investigation except for reinforcing the hostility that army officers felt toward their civilian overseers.[58]

CHAPTER SEVEN

The Atrocity Investigations, 1864–1865

Throughout the Civil War, Republican members of the Committee on the Conduct of the War were convinced that Union battlefield defeats in part resulted from insufficient morale among northern soldiers. Indeed, it was a widely held opinion throughout America that morale, sheer determination in itself, could prompt soldiers to overcome any battlefield difficulties. In order to bolster the morale of Union soldiers and northern public opinion, the committee engaged in wartime propaganda, the specific purpose of which was to portray southern opponents in ghastly, barbarous terms. During the Thirty-seventh Congress, the committee had investigated alleged rebel atrocities toward Union dead after the first battle of Bull Run. A published report describing them had created a stir in the nation's press.[1]

During the Thirty-eighth Congress, the committee concentrated on the massacre of Union soldiers at Fort Pillow and the treatment of Union prisoners of war. Unlike its investigation of the Army of the Potomac, these inquiries demonstrated that the power of disclosure could be used in a positive way to aid the war effort. Instead of trying to expose deficient generalship and in the process demoralizing army officers and encouraging jealousy and factionalism, these investigations were aimed primarily at the nation's enemy and at shaping northern public opinion. Through its report on the investigation of the Fort Pillow massacre and the treatment of Union prisoners, the committee may have strengthened the determination of northern soldiers and bolstered the sagging morale of the northern public.

Immediately after he heard about the massacre of Union soldiers at Fort Pillow, Tennessee, Brig. Gen. Augustus L. Chetlain, a recruiter of black troops stationed in Memphis, wrote Illinois congressman Elihu Washburne: "This is the most infernal outrage that has been committed since the war began." Of the approximately three hundred black troops garrisoned at the fort, Chetlain claimed only twenty-five had been taken prisoner; the rest had been brutally slaughtered. "There is a great deal of excitement . . . in consequence of this affair—especially among our colored troops," he told Washburne. "If this is to be the game of the enemy they will soon learn that it is one *at which two can play.*"[2]

Located north of Memphis on the Mississippi River, Fort Pillow was garrisoned by 292 black troops of the Sixth U.S. Colored Heavy Artillery and the Sixth U.S. Light Artillery, along with 285 white troops of the Thirteenth Tennessee Cavalry. Major Lionel F. Booth commanded the garrison, and Maj. William Bradford, a Tennessee Unionist, was second in command. On the morning of April 12, 1864, the fort was surrounded by 1,500 Confederate troops under Maj. Gen. Nathan Bedford Forrest, who was conducting raids in western Tennessee and Kentucky in an effort to disrupt Union operations in those areas.[3]

Built on a bluff overlooking the river, the fort consisted of a dirt parapet approximately 8 feet high, forming a 125-foot semicircle; it was surrounded by two outside lines of defense. Although Booth had assured district commander Gen. Stephen Hurlbut that the fort could be held for forty-eight hours against any force, trouble began when he was killed by sniper fire and the less experienced Bradford took over. Prematurely abandoning his two outside lines of defense, Bradford allowed Forrest's men to surround the fort quickly, taking special advantage of the protection offered by the area's hilly terrain. Forrest's troops also seized ravines on both the north and the south side of the fort, which protected them from Union artillery fire and the shelling of the Union gunboat *New Era* anchored in the nearby river. After waiting for additional ammunition, at 3:30 P.M. Forrest sent forward a flag of truce and demanded unconditional surrender, promising to treat the federal garrison as prisoners of war but threatening no quarter if they refused his offer. Since he probably anticipated the arrival of additional troops from approaching boats, Bradford, who did not reveal Booth's death to the Confederates, asked for one hour to consider the offer. Forrest, apprised of approaching Union gunboats, gave Bradford twenty minutes to decide. When Bradford rejected the offer, Confederate forces attacked and quickly overwhelmed the garrison.

Exactly what happened during the battle is impossible to know. Although many southern historians denied that a massacre took place, most present-day historians agree that despite exaggeration by northern witnesses numerous atrocities were committed. Black troops, which the Confederacy did not officially recognize and would not accord prisoner of war status, were the special targets of Confederate wrath. Once the Confederates gained the parapet, most Union troops simply panicked and retreated down the bluff toward the river. Many threw down their weapons and tried to surrender; others tried to escape by jumping into the water and swimming to the *New Era*. During the attack, Confederate soldiers raked the garrison with a merciless fire amid shouts of "kill the damned niggers!" Many who tried to surrender were shot, and others who had managed to gain the river were shot and drowned. "The slaughter was awful," wrote a rebel soldier; "words cannot describe the scene. . . . Blood, human blood, stood about in pools and brains could have been gathered up in any quantity." When Forrest finally was able to restrain his men, almost 50 percent of the garrison had been killed, black troops suffering a disproportionate number of casualties.[4]

Reports of the massacre quickly circulated throughout the North. Calvin Fletcher, a prominent Indiana Republican, hoped they were exaggerated, but if they proved true, he wanted the president to "handle the rebels hereafter as they deserve." Grotius Giddings, the son of antislavery advocate Joshua Giddings, wrote, "It shows a barbarity that I had not dreamed they had." "The whole civilized world will be shocked by the great atrocity at Fort Pillow," the *Chicago Tribune* asserted, "but in no respect does the act misrepresent the nature and precedents of Slavery." The *Christian Advocate* believed the atrocities were "unparalleled in the history of modern warfare," but, the paper added, it was slavery that prompted such atrocities. If not for slavery, the Confederates "would act like gentlemen, instead of tigers."[5]

In the days that followed accounts of the massacre became more gruesome. Rumors circulated charging that rebel soldiers had committed unspeakable acts on Union dead and wounded soldiers, including mutilation of bodies and live burials. Although a few northern newspapers urged caution and suggested that initial reports might be exaggerated, northern sentiment seemed bent on revenge and retaliation. "Let the fate of the Fort Pillow prisoners overtake a like number of rebel prisoners in our hands," urged the *Indianapolis Daily Journal,* "and their blood be upon the heads of the Fort Pillow butchers." A New York man wrote Sen. Henry Wilson, advising him to tell the president that "the *Loyal People demand* from him *retaliation* for the horrible crimes" committed at Fort Pillow. William Tecumseh Sherman, in command of the Western Theater, wrote Stanton, "I know well the animus of the Southern soldiery [toward blacks] and the truth is they cannot be restrained." Shortly after the massacre, Lincoln mentioned retaliation in a Baltimore speech, telling his audience that if the allegations were proved, then "the retribution shall as surely come." Many applauded the speech. "I am glad that the President has decided to retaliate for the wrongs committed by the rebels on our soldiers," wrote Ben Wade's son Hal. *Harper's Weekly* asserted, "Let the response of the Government be as prompt and terrible as it will be final."[6]

Congress took up the Fort Pillow massacre when Sen. Jacob Howard of Michigan introduced a resolution directing the Committee on the Conduct of the War to travel to Fort Pillow to investigate the affair. Howard was adamant about protecting black troops, and if the Fort Pillow atrocities were authenticated, he contemplated legislation to protect black soldiers from such barbarities. "Without this protection," he told the Senate, "we know very well what will be the fate of the black troops whom we call into our service." A brief and spirited debate then transpired. William Pitt Fessenden opposed the resolution because it would take congressmen out of Washington when it was already difficult to obtain quorums. Senator John Conness of California agreed with Fessenden and suggested an amendment that would authorize the War Department to conduct an investigation. Benjamin Wade pointed out that the committee already had jurisdiction to go to Fort Pillow if it thought necessary, but he hoped Conness's amendment would pass, "for I am not anxious that the committee shall have this business to do." Reverdy Johnson thought the resolution ought to be amended to find out why Fort Pillow was undermanned and why Forrest had been allowed to roam at will through Tennessee and Kentucky, striking as far north as Paducah. This view drew an angry response from Lyman Trumbull, who thought Johnson's remarks were aimed at Gen. Mason Brayman, a Springfield Republican ally of his and commander of the military district that contained Paducah. According to Trumbull, reports from Fort Pillow might well be exaggerated, and even if true, the massacre would have little effect on the outcome of the war. Eventually, the Senate passed Howard's resolution with Johnson's amendment. When the House accepted this resolution in place of its own, the committee made plans to conduct its investigation.[7]

Meeting on the morning of April 18, the committee quickly responded to the Senate resolution by appointing a subcommittee consisting of Wade and Daniel Gooch and authorizing them to visit wherever they felt necessary to investigate the matter. After meeting with Lincoln and Edwin Stanton to discuss the investigation, the two men began a one-week trip to Cairo and Mound City, Illinois, as well as to Fort Pillow, Union City, and Memphis, Tennessee, armed with a stenographer and a letter of introduction from Stanton. Wade and Gooch interviewed over seventy witnesses, the majority of whom had been wounded at Fort Pillow. Many of the nation's newspapers reported that the committee had uncovered barbarities that exceeded previous accounts. On April 27 the radical Republican *Chicago Tribune* reported that Gooch had recently telegraphed Washington, claiming that the acts of savagery exceeded "published accounts."[8]

Critics have assumed that the committee deliberately exaggerated southern atrocities to smear Forrest's reputation, inflame public sentiment, and serve its own narrow partisan agenda. The committee's most thorough and critical historian, T. Harry Williams, argues that Wade used this investigation, as well as previous atrocity reports, as a means to create a consensus for a more radical reconstruction. By deliberately exaggerating rebel brutalities, he would prompt the public to support a reconstruction policy that would treat the South as conquered territory. There is little doubt that the issue of reconstruction was on the minds of committee members and other Republicans during the Fort Pillow investigation. George Julian, chairman of the House Committee on Public Lands, was already busy sponsoring legislation to confiscate the large holdings of rebel planters and to redistribute them to veterans of the Union armies, both white and black. In remarks to the House shortly after Fort Pillow, Julian castigated the Confederates as devils and argued that the massacre provided additional reasons to support his program of confiscation. Maryland radical Henry Winter Davis had recently introduced his own reconstruction bill in the House, which stood in stark contrast to the president's more lenient plan. Influencing public opinion to support a more radical reconstruction program certainly was a consideration.[9]

Even before the war, many northerners viewed the South as backward and in need of radical reordering along the lines of free labor institutions. The war added to such beliefs. For many northern youths in the army, to see the South firsthand was a fascinating experience, convincing many soldiers that it was indeed a backward, impoverished society in need of fundamental reconstruction. "They are certainly the most primitively ignorant people I ever came across," wrote Michigander James W. Sligh on his first impressions of Kentuckians. Another Michigander commented, "[Kentuckians'] manners, forms of speech and customs all point to past ages." Captain J. J. Geer, a Union soldier who spent a couple of years in a Confederate prison, published an unflattering report of southern society. According to Geer, the South was both aristocratic and backward. Southern gentlemen hated the democratic institutions of the North, such as free schools, yet their own hierarchic society fostered large numbers of illiterate and ignorant poor whites. Geer's description of southern clay-eaters is particularly unflattering and shows how some northerners regarded the South. "They were all tall and ungainly," he wrote, "and in speaking always said 'har,' and 'sar,' 'whar,' and 'dar.'" Their favorite expressions were 'tarnal Jesus,' and 'I golly.'" After he had the chance to observe poor whites in Virginia, Daniel Morse Holt, a physician in the 121st New York, commented, "No people . . . so deserve our pity, or need the influence of our religious instruction, conjoined with free schools." This was a society that needed radical reform. As Randall Jimerson comments, "Fresh infusions of Yankee virtue would be needed to repair the harmful effects of slave society."[10]

Nor were such sentiments confined to soldiers. Early on in the contest many northerners saw the war as a struggle to prove the superiority of free labor and free institutions over the hierarchical society spawned by slavery. Even before the war, noted the *Universalist Quarterly,* the North was vastly superior to the South in the number of schools and libraries. The majority of nonslaveholding whites, the journal contended, were "poor, miserably housed, scantily fed and clothed, ignorant, taught to despise labor and under the control of the most degrading passions and superstitions." Accordingly, many northern journals saw the goal of the war as the reordering of southern society. "The war is drawing to an end," the *Continental Monthly* predicted in summer 1862, "but a greater and nobler task lies before the soldiers and free men of America—the extending of *civilization* into the South. Let the introduction of free labor to the South be in the future the subject to which every thinking American mind shall be devoted." According to abolitionist Lydia Maria Child, this was a war to decide whether free institutions would be maintained or "whether we are to live under despotic institutions, which will divide society into two classes, rulers and servants, and ordain ignorance as the convenient, nay, even *necessary* condition of all who labor." In formulating its Fort Pillow findings, the committee reflected an influential segment of northern opinion as much as it sought to shape it.[11]

Wade and Gooch were presented with a barrage of sensational testimony. A great deal was exaggerated and undoubtedly elicited by suggestive, leading questions to witnesses, many of whom were illiterate soldiers, both black and white. Many witnesses, for instance, told Gooch and Wade that Confederate troops used the flag of truce to move their troops into closer positions, taking possession of a ravine south of the fortifications. It is clear, however, that Forrest was already in possession of the ravine before the truce. Troops were moved during the truce, but Forrest sent them toward the river only to ward off approaching federal gunboats that were unaware of the flag of truce. Several witnesses claimed that Confederate soldiers indiscriminately killed women and children present at the garrison; yet others testified that they were evacuated by the *New Era* before the battle. More important, no bodies of these alleged victims were ever found. Many witnesses claimed that during the night of April 12 Union prisoners, black and white, were buried alive and that others were nailed to the floor of the fort's hospital and burned when the building was set on fire by rebel soldiers. Yet Confederate sources maintain no southern soldiers were in the garrison that evening and that guerrillas were responsible for such outrages. Some witnesses, although maintaining that Confederates were responsible for defiling Union dead, also testified that a truce was negotiated with a northern gunboat, allowing Union soldiers to supervise the burial of fallen comrades.[12]

At the same time, the consensus among all witnesses at the fort on the day of battle was that Union soldiers were given no quarter even after they individually surrendered. Daniel Stamps, a private in the Thirteenth Tennessee Cavalry, told Wade that once the final assault began he heard the cry, "Kill 'em, kill 'em; God damn 'em; that's Forrest's orders, not to leave one alive." "Damn you," one Confederate soldier told another member of the Thirteenth Tennessee, "I have nothing for you fellows; you Tennesseans pretend to be men, and you fight side by side with niggers; I have nothing for you." When another member of the Thirteenth Tennessee begged for quarter, he was told, "God damn you, you fight with the niggers, and we will kill the last one of you!" Numerous wounded black soldiers testified to the hostility of Confederate soldiers. Arthur Edwards, a private in the Sixth Colored Heavy Artillery, was shot several times. When he asked for protection, he was told, "God damn you, you are fighting against your master." Private Elias Falls told Gooch that the Confederates "killed all the men after they surrendered until orders were given to stop." Horace Wardner, a surgeon at the Mound City military hospital, told committee members he had never seen such a lot of mangled, butchered wounded.[13]

Undoubtedly angered by the garrison's refusal to surrender, Confederate soldiers were particularly enraged at the sight of black troops. Seen as an insult to southern pretensions of white supremacy, they were not recognized by the Davis administration as legitimate prisoners of war. Moreover, the presence of the Unionist Thirteenth Tennessee contributed to hostile emotions, especially since the western Tennessee area was known for brutal guerrilla outrages committed by both sides. Once the fort fell, individual acts of brutality did occur until Forrest finally ordered a halt; southern accounts written before the committee published its report admitted as much. Even Forrest's report described the river as red with the blood of fallen enemy soldiers. Northern witnesses who were not interviewed by committee members corroborated Confederate testimony on this point. Charles Robinson, a civilian photographer from Minneapolis, wrote to his family shortly after the battle:

> As soon as the rebels got to the top of the bank there commenced the most horrible slaughter that could possibly be conceived. Our boys when they saw that they were overpowered threw down their arms and held up, some their handkerchiefs & some their hands in token of surrender,

but no sooner were they seen than they were shot down, & if one shot failed to kill them the bayonet or the revolver did not.

Forrest probably did not explicitly order a massacre; however, given the presence of black troops and Tennessee Unionists and his previous threats to Union garrisons of no quarter, he could not have been totally surprised by the slaughter.[14]

After obtaining the testimony they desired, Wade and Gooch returned to Washington and began work on their report. Meanwhile, the cabinet tackled the difficult issue of retaliation. At a May 3 meeting, Lincoln asked each cabinet officer to submit an opinion on what course of action the administration should take. Gideon Welles was skeptical of the purported findings of the committee's investigation, which were not yet published. "There must be something in these terrible reports," he remarked, "but I distrust Congressional committees. They exaggerate."[15]

On May 6 the cabinet met again to discuss a course of action. Every cabinet official agreed that the Richmond government should first be given the chance to disavow the massacre and to acknowledge the legitimacy of black soldiers. Although a variety of opinions was expressed, two general viewpoints emerged. Seward, Stanton, Chase, and Secretary of the Interior John P. Usher favored man-for-man retaliation. They suggested that rebel officers, in an equal number to the Union casualties at Fort Pillow, be set aside pending a response from Confederate authorities. If the Fort Pillow massacre was not officially disavowed with explicit guarantees that repetitions would not occur in the future, then the southern officers would be punished. Stanton, armed with additional evidence as a result of his own War Department investigation, seemed the most adamant. Bates, Blair, and Welles opposed man-for-man retaliation, noting that it would not be effective, nor was there a precedent for it. "The idea of retaliation,—killing man for man,—which is the popular noisy demand, is barbarous," wrote Welles, "and I cannot assent to or advise it." Blair suggested that Lincoln issue a proclamation specifically naming Forrest and Chalmers as perpetrators of the massacre and holding them solely responsible. If captured, they would be tried and punished for war crimes.

Usher, though agreeing in principle with man-for-man retaliation, also suggested that the government's course should be dictated by the results of the military campaign in the East; thus, retaliation only would follow military success. Although the cabinet meeting broke up without a clear consensus, a few days later a confident Chase predicted Lincoln's course to one correspondent. "I trust that the slaughter at Fort Pillow will not be permitted to go unpunished," he remarked; "in my judgment the highest officers in the rebel service now prisoners in our hands should be made to pay the penalty for this outrage." Before Lincoln acted, however, the treatment of prisoners of war emerged as a complicating factor, and the committee once again occupied center stage.[16]

Just before the adoption of the subcommittee's report on Fort Pillow, the CCW, through Secretary of War Stanton, received a communication from William Hoffman, commissary general of prisoners, describing the conditions of recently received prisoners at Annapolis from Confederate prisons in Richmond and urging the committee to come and investigate. On May 6 the members, except for Benjamin Loan and Zachariah Chandler, made the short trip to Annapolis to view the prisoners.[17]

Accusations of Confederate maltreatment of northern prisoners were nothing new and had been featured in northern newspapers for several months. Early in the war prisoners received equal treatment from each side. However, the lack of a systematic program of prisoner exchanges coupled with complications arising over the issue of black prisoners of war had slowed exchanges and led to overcrowding, particularly in the Richmond facilities of Belle Isle and Libby Prison. To alleviate overcrowded conditions, Richmond authorities agreed to give up 500 sick Union prisoners in April without a corresponding exchange of Confederate prisoners. Although northern prisons were not free from abuses, food rations were generally adequate—a condition that did not apply in the Confederate system, especially as the war dragged on. Maine general Neal Dow spent three months in Libby Prison in winter 1863–1864. Released in March 1864, he described the conditions:

> The imprisonment at Richmond was *close*, severe, and attended by every circumstance of humiliation. Our treatment, in point of food and accommodations, was like that to Negroes—in crowded baracoons, where they are assembled for sale. We experienced nothing from the prison officials but humiliation and contempt.[18]

By the time the committee was informed of the plight of these sick prisoners, it was hardly news. Numerous newspapers had already carried accounts of their maltreatment and denounced the Confederacy for initiating a deliberate policy of starving Union prisoners of war. "There can now scarcely be a doubt that the rebels have determined to kill or disable our men who may fall into their hands," charged the *Christian Advocate*. "No description could overpaint the miserable condition of those poor soldiers," it concluded. "Can these be *men*," asked the poet Walt Whitman when he saw one group of returned prisoners, "these little, livid brown, ash-streaked, monkey-looking dwarfs? Are they really not mummied, dwindled corpses?" The *Baltimore American* reported that the Fort Pillow massacre was a blessing when compared to the condition of these men.[19]

Arriving in Annapolis on May 6, committee members quickly discovered the newspaper accounts to be strikingly accurate. Visiting the Naval Hospital and then proceeding to West Hospital in nearby Baltimore, the congressmen interviewed the former prisoners and hospital staff. According to Julian, the condition of some prisoners was so wretched that both he and Wade were moved to tears. Dirty, emaciated, listless, suffering from frostbite and other ailments induced by exposure, many of the prisoners were little more than living skeletons. Former prisoners told the congressmen how they spent the winter on Belle Isle without blankets, tents, or any adequate clothing to protect them from the elements. "They did not treat me very kindly," said Howard Leedom, a seventeen-year-old private imprisoned on Belle Isle; "I froze my feet on the island." "We had to lie right down on the cold ground," another prisoner told Democratic committee member Benjamin Harding. Washington Collins of the Fifth Kentucky Infantry told Gooch his daily food ration consisted of six ounces of light bread, two spoonfuls of worm-infested black beans, and two ounces of very poor meat. When Wade asked one prisoner if he ever complained about the rations, the man replied, "Certainly we complained but they said we had enough."[20]

Surgeon B. A. VanderKieft told Wade that most of the prisoners arrived suffering from debility and chronic diarrhea, "the result, I have no doubt, of exposure, privations, hardship and ill treatment." Many arrived with a one-eighth-inch crust of vermin and had not been washed for months. "Once in a while," VanderKieft admitted, "I have found a man who pretended to have been treated very well, but by examining closely I find that such men are not very good Union men." Julian asked about rebel newspapers that claimed Union prisoners had the same rations as rebel soldiers. That cannot be possible, VanderKieft replied. William G. Knowles, a physician at West Hospital reiterated many of the same points to Wade and Moses Odell. Odell asked if the condition of the men was the result of starvation and exposure. That is the universal opinion of medical men, Knowles replied. "I think the rebels have determined the policy of starving their prisoners," he told them, "just as much as the murders at Fort Pillow were a part of their policy."[21]

Just before leaving for Annapolis, the committee accepted Wade and Gooch's report on Fort Pillow and recommended that Congress publish

60,000 copies for distribution among constituents. Major newspapers such as the *New York Times* and the *New York Daily Tribune* were given advance copies, which appeared on May 7, 1864. The committee met on May 9, and after a motion by Harding, decided to publish both the Fort Pillow and the returned prisoners reports in a single volume.[22]

Publishing the reports together made sense because each one painted the Confederacy as vicious and benighted, thereby reinforcing one of the committee's principal goals of portraying the South as a society in need of radical restructuring. Moreover, the reports might stop further outrages by exposing Confederate actions to the world. According to the committee, the Fort Pillow massacre was not the result of passion "but the result of a policy deliberately decided upon and unhesitatingly announced." Summarizing in graphic detail the events of the slaughter, the report continued, "No cruelty which the most fiendish malignity could devise was omitted by these murderers." As for the returned prisoners, the committee argued that they were victims of a deliberate policy of starvation and cruelty hatched in Richmond by the leaders of the rebellion. The condition of these prisoners was such that "no language we could use can adequately describe." To convey the depths of the atrocities, the committee attached to the report pictures of eight abused prisoners. Individual members sent additional pictures to the press. As Wade told one Cleveland resident, "The enclosed likeness is that of a returned prisoner who, when captured by the Rebels, was robust and active, but, by starvation and exposure systematically enforced by rebel authorities, reduced to the conditions represented." If ever there were a society in need of fundamental reordering, it was the rebel states of the Confederacy. And the committee clearly hoped their graphic description of southern barbarities would influence northern thinking on the issue of reconstruction.[23]

As for the influence of the reports on the public, Julian believed they created a powerful effect on northern opinion. T. Harry Williams, although accusing the committee of deliberately distorting the evidence, nevertheless writes that it succeeded in swaying public opinion: "The popular reaction to the reports gratified the Committee." Much evidence supports his conclusion. *Harper's Weekly* published excerpts from the report along with photographs of the prisoners, remarking that this was an example of "the work of desperate and infuriated men whose human instincts have become imbruted with the constant habit of outraging humanity." A few periodicals, such as the *Continental Monthly*, featured poems dedicated to the Fort Pillow victims and Union prisoners. One such selection, "Our Martyrs," described some of the aspects of prison life in graphic detail:

He stirs his hands, and the jealous chain
Wakes him once more to his tyrant pain—

To festered wounds, and to dungeon taint,
And hunger's agony, fierce and faint.

The sunset vision fades and flits,
And alone in his dark'ning cell he sits:

Alone with only the jailer grim,
Hunger and Pain, that clutch at him;

And, tight'ning his fetters, link by link,
Drag him near to a ghastly brink;

Where, in blackness that yawns beneath,
Stalks the skeleton form of Death.

Starved, and tortured, and worn with strife;
Robbed of hopes of his fresh, young life;

Shall one pang of his martyr pain
Cry to sleepless God in vain?[24]

Even before the publication of the report, news of the Fort Pillow massacre had a powerful effect on the behavior of black troops. James T. Ayers, an Illinois soldier who recruited black troops in Tennessee and northern Alabama, realized the appeal Fort Pillow might have in attracting additional troops. Shortly after the massacre, Ayers delivered a recruiting speech at Huntsville, Alabama. He included a poem that made an emotional appeal to potential black recruits based on the Fort Pillow atrocities:

Show no mercy to Rebs such as those
No my Brave boys No never
But send them all where bad men goes
To Dwell in Pain forever

Charge boys Charge, Clean out there [sic] Ranks
Give them your Coald [sic] steel
From Center to Extended flank
Make them Fort Pillow feel.[25]

The publication of the report kept the massacre before the public's eye, and the subsequent actions of troops, both black and white, suggest that it might have been a factor in accounting for the behavior of the army. A Wisconsin soldier in the field in Georgia described the actions of an Iowa regiment in an engagement where twenty-three rebels were allegedly killed after they had surrendered. Just before they were executed, the rebel soldiers were asked whether they remembered Fort Pillow. "We want revenge," the soldier remarked, "and we are bound to have it one way or another. They must pay for these deeds of cruelty. We want revenge for our brother soldiers and will have it." George Templeton Strong reported that black troops never reported any prisoners. "I suppose they have to kill their prisoners before they can take them," he commented, "when they go into action, they yell 'Fort Pillow!'" An officer in the Army of the Potomac remarked that when black soldiers went into battle yelling "Fort Pillow," Confederate troops did not normally hold up very well.[26]

The course taken by the administration suggests that Lincoln initially bowed to public opinion. Stanton, on his own authority, immediately ordered rations to Confederate prisoners reduced by 20 percent; however, he was persuaded by Ethan Allen Hitchcock, commissioner of prisoner exchange, to refrain from harsher measures. With respect to Fort Pillow, after considering the various opinions of his cabinet officers, the president gave Stanton a clear directive on May 17. Stanton was to notify rebel authorities "through proper military channels" that the U.S. government had adequate proof of the atrocities committed at Fort Pillow. "That with reference to said massacre," Lincoln continued, "the government of the United States has assigned and set apart by name insurgent officers theretofore, and up to that time, held by said government as prisoners of war." Lincoln then demanded a specific guarantee from the Confederacy, to be received no later than July 1, that no such massacre would again occur and that all U.S. soldiers would be treated as bona fide prisoners of war. If these conditions were met, there would be no retaliation. However, if no response was received by this date, "It will be assumed by the government of the United States, that said captured colored troops shall have been murdered or subjected to Slavery, and that said government will, upon said assumption, take such action as may then appear expedient and just."[27]

Although the Confederacy never responded to this directive or officially changed its attitude toward black soldiers, Lincoln did not retaliate for the massacre. Perhaps his decision, upon reflection, was due to the illogic of such a course of action, since it probably would have triggered a meaningless cycle of reciprocal reprisals. As Usher had suggested earlier, retaliation would make sense only if the Army of the Potomac achieved overwhelming military success, an event hardly apparent in summer 1864. On the other hand, Lincoln also might have detected a lessening of public outrage on this issue. Although both the Fort Pillow massacre and the returned prisoners received generous attention from the nation's newspapers, there was a noticeable decline in coverage by midsummer. Many newspapers had published the report on Fort Pillow, but the report on returned prisoners did not receive quite as much coverage. Although 60,000 copies were printed, a substantial number for any committee report, that was no guarantee that the issue would continue to excite public opinion. Already in mid-June, Gen. Mason Brayman, who had testified before the committee about Fort Pillow, wrote Wade that Democratic newspapers in his locale were denying that the Fort Pillow massacre had occurred. He also informed Wade that the Richmond correspondent of the London *Times* had stated that accounts of the massacre were similar to the many erroneous reports of First Bull Run.[28]

It is not entirely clear if the committee members were united in favor of retaliation. Certainly Wade and Chandler favored it. Loan, a veteran of the vindictive border wars of Kansas and Missouri, probably would have supported it; however, the position of the other members is uncertain. Julian, with his reputation for radicalism, might be thought to support retaliation. Contrary to the assertion of T. Harry Williams, however, radical sentiment on the issue was not united. Some of the leading radical newspapers in the country, such as the New York *Independent* and William Lloyd Garrison's *Liberator,* specifically disavowed such a policy on the grounds that it was uncivilized and barbaric. Although Wade and Chandler expressed their views to Stanton, who no doubt lobbied the president on the issue, their efforts were in vain. With divisions in public opinion apparent and the election of 1864 fast approaching, Lincoln probably thought it would be unwise to follow through on a policy of reprisal.[29]

The issue of reprisals for the Fort Pillow massacre never again figured prominently in northern public opinion, but the question of the treatment of northern prisoners of war remained. After the return of the sick prisoners to Annapolis in the spring, exchanges were reduced to a minimum, despite public pressure for a general exchange. "Why are these brave men so long left where Death is longed for as a welcome friend?" one Illinois man asked Lincoln. Although publicly the reason given for this stalemate was Confederate intransigence on the status of black prisoners, General Grant, supported by Stanton, did not favor any exchanges on the grounds that it would simply replenish Confederate armies and prolong the war. Hence, with thousands of northerners languishing in rebel prisons, the issue of treatment figured prominently in public debate. Northern officials had significantly reduced the rations given to southern prisoners, but many people thought that harsher measures were needed. Wade and Chandler were among the most vocifer-

ous critics of southern prisons and routinely spoke out in favor of retaliation. "The idea of starving helpless prisoners of war by the thousands,"
Chandler wrote his wife in January 1865, "could only be conceived of by
fiends. These devils are not fit to live on God's earth & would disgrace hell
if they enter there." A few days later, Chandler wrote, "I would put every
officer upon the same ration of food . . . clothing & care which our soldiers
receive."[30]

The issue emerged in the Senate during winter 1864–1865 when a number of resolutions were introduced calling for retaliation on rebel prisoners.
On December 20 Morton Wilkinson introduced a resolution directing the
secretary of war to furnish rebel prisoners with the same amounts of food,
clothing, and supplies that Union prisoners received. Wade introduced a similar resolution on January 13, 1865, which also called for dismissal of any
prison official unwilling to implement retaliation. According to Wade, Lincoln had promised to retaliate if the facts about the prisoners received at
Annapolis were true. Since he had not done so, Wade believed it was time
for Congress to prod the executive into action.

A vigorous two-week debate on the issue ensued. "Retaliation," argued
Wade, "has in all ages of the world been a means of bringing inhuman and
savage foes to a sense of their duty." Denouncing opponents of reprisals, he
asserted, "It is rather a mawkish idea of humanity that fears to subject rebel
prisoners to the same treatment that we know our own brave soldiers are
daily subjected to." Supported by Chandler, Jacob Howard of Michigan,
Henry Smith Lane of Indiana, and James Harlan of Iowa, Wade was opposed
by a curious combination of radical Republicans and Democrats. Leading
the opposition was Charles Sumner, who argued that retaliation was barbaric and damaged the reputation of the United States abroad. According to
Sumner, such a resolution would force the president to imitate "rebel bar-
barism." Wade, however, kept up his assault, introducing recent testimony
from the Committee on the Conduct of the War to prove that prisoners were
still being abused in Confederate prisons. A resolution was passed, but owing
to amendments by Sumner and Henry Wilson, it was substantially weakened,
with provisions for in-kind retaliation intentionally omitted.[31]

Ultimately, the entire debate was academic. Lincoln would take no retalia-
tory measures, primarily because exchange negotiations, stalled for months
on the issue of black soldiers, finally cleared this obstacle. Once black troops
were specifically included in arrangements, larger exchanges began to take
place. During February and March 1865, 1,000 prisoners were being exchanged each day. No longer was there a motive for retaliation, and debate
came to an end.[32]

The committee's reports on Fort Pillow and returned prisoners were among its more positive achievements. Instead of encouraging jealous rivalries among the army's leaders and singling out targets for blame, these investigations focused on the enemy. Although guilty of some exaggeration and distortion, the committee did uncover significant abuses and atrocities. In the case of Fort Pillow, the judgment of numerous modern historians reinforces this point. Some scholars have criticized the committee for stirring up violent emotions, which helped ensure continuing bitterness during the Reconstruction period, but a case can also be made for the committee's role in boosting northern morale and resolve. After three long years of fighting and numerous defeats, the North was war weary. By summer 1864, disillusionment was on the rise: Grant's bloody campaign in Virginia was stalled at Petersburg and Sherman seemed unable to deal a decisive blow to Joseph Johnston in Georgia. By exposing rebels barbarities in these two investigations, the committee did stir emotions and possibly bolstered northern determination to continue the war, despite the costs.

The committee's Republican majority undoubtedly had another motive in these investigations, however. Since they believed the war must not only abolish slavery but also wipe out every vestige of the flawed, hierarchical society of the South, they hoped to create a foundation for a more radical reconstruction program. Rebel states should not be allowed simply to resume their former positions once rebellion was put down. "A grand opportunity now presents itself for recognizing the principles of radical democracy in the establishment of new and regenerated States," Julian remarked in spring 1864. "We are summoned by every consideration of patriotism, humanity, and Republicanism to lay the foundation of empire upon the enduring foundation of justice and equal rights." Since many northerners viewed the atrocities as an outgrowth of a hierarchic, slave society, the committee hoped that the exposure of rebel barbarities would encourage support for a comprehensive reconstruction program.[33]

CHAPTER EIGHT

Banks, Red River, and Reconstruction

The atrocity investigations of spring 1864 might have been designed to create a popular consensus for a radical reconstruction policy, but the Committee on the Conduct of the War encountered obstacles to those policy goals in the political experiment transpiring in Union-occupied Louisiana. Since many legislators believed that reconstruction was the principal responsibility of Congress, there was a good deal of suspicion and hostility toward the president's reconstruction government in Louisiana. Moderate Republican Nathaniel P. Banks had replaced radical favorite Benjamin F. Butler in December 1862 as military commander of the Department of the Gulf. Banks's subsequent course became the focal point of controversy as he attempted to implement Lincoln's program of reconstruction. When the unfortunate Banks led the disastrous Red River campaign in April 1864, congressional Republicans used this debacle as an opportunity to discredit him and the entire program of presidential reconstruction in Louisiana. The CCW played a significant role in the task of undermining presidential reconstruction.

Nathaniel Banks and Louisiana Reconstruction

Nathaniel Banks was one of the Civil War's quintessential political generals. A native of Massachusetts, he rose from extreme poverty to achieve political prominence. Beginning as a Democrat, he went through a succession of political changes, becoming a Fusionist after the Kansas-Nebraska Act, then a Know-Nothing, and finally a Republican. Although antislavery, Banks was never identified as a radical in his prewar career and was never completely trusted by that wing of the Republican party. Noting his frequent change of political principles, Banks's biographer Fred H. Harrington observes that he "lacked the courage of his convictions." Before his appointment as Butler's replacement, Banks had a mediocre military career in the East, where he was chiefly known for his poor showing against Thomas J. Jackson in the Shenandoah Valley campaign of May 1862. Banks's replacement of Benjamin F. Butler thus was greeted in some quarters with intense suspicion.[1]

Banks's troubles began immediately after he assumed command. Although Lincoln's Emancipation Proclamation took effect on January 1, 1863, those portions of the South occupied by Union forces were specifically exempted, including the parishes surrounding New Orleans. In order to solve labor problems in his department, Banks issued orders on January 29, 1863, compelling the slaves within occupied Union lines to work on area plantations. Banks's arrangements obliged each black laborer to sign a contract for one year's work, allowed each worker the choice of masters, regulated working hours, and forced the government to guarantee contracts. Despite the president's satisfaction with this arrangement, antislavery radicals were skeptical, regarding the orders as a de facto reestablishment of slavery.[2]

Butler's administration had been characterized by coercion and confrontation with the southern civilian population, but Banks initiated a more conciliatory policy. "General Banks' administration is too much the McClellan plan," former Ohio congressman John Hutchins, a treasury official in occupied Louisiana, complained to Salmon Chase. George Denison, Chase's nephew and a treasury agent for New Orleans, warned his uncle that "a strong party is already forming here whose leading idea is the restoration of Louisiana to slavery *and* to the Union." Despite these admonitory comments, Chase and the majority of his treasury officials did not break with Banks immediately. Since the ambitious secretary of the treasury was planning his own run for the presidential nomination in 1864, he could not afford to alienate the politically powerful Banks.[3]

The situation changed in fall 1863 when, under specific instructions from Lincoln, Banks began to implement a definite program of political reconstruction for Louisiana. Lincoln earlier had urged Banks to begin reconstruction, believing that he would work with the Free State General Committee, an association of antislavery advocates including military governor George F. Shepley, a political ally of Benjamin Butler, and Thomas J. Durant, a radical New Orleans lawyer and president of the organization. Durant believed that reconstruction could begin only with a new constitution for Louisiana, one that would abolish slavery. Lincoln accepted this position; however, he became increasingly discouraged with the lack of progress under Durant's leadership. When the president complained to Banks about the lack of progress, the general pleaded lack of jurisdiction. "I have had neither the authority, influence, or recognition as an officer entrusted with this duty," Banks explained to the president in early December. Lincoln then gave Banks clear and specific instruction to begin the work of reconstruction. As the president told Massachusetts congressman George Boutwell, Shepley had been appointed to relieve Banks of unnecessary work, not to become a burden.

Lincoln then assured Banks, "I now tell you that in every dispute, with whomsoever, you are master." A confident Banks predicted quick results. "I want, and I have no doubt whatever," he told Boutwell, "that a Government will be formed within the next two months, upon the basis desired by the President, and with full concurrence of all classes of people."[4]

The basis for Banks's action was the president's December 8, 1863, proclamation of amnesty and reconstruction. This document initiated reconstruction in the rebellious states once 10 percent of a seceded state's 1860 voting population swore an oath of allegiance to the Constitution and promised to obey the president's proclamations on slavery. Though agreeing with the president's position that emancipation should be the backbone of reconstruction, some Republicans were skeptical of the efficacy of this plan. Acknowledgment of the Emancipation Proclamation did not necessarily translate into the unconditional abolition of slavery, since the legal status of the Proclamation was by no means established. As Benjamin Butler earlier told Salmon Chase, emancipation had to be incorporated into the constitutions of these states in order to become effective. Moreover, the 10 percent feature offended the democratic sensibilities of many congressmen of both parties because it appeared inconsistent with the constitutional provision to provide a republican form of government for each state.[5]

When Banks issued a proclamation for a February 22, 1864, election for state offices to be followed by an election for delegates to a constitutional convention, several members of the Free State General Committee protested. Benjamin Flanders, a native of New York but a twenty-five-year New Orleans resident, wrote to Chase and Lincoln to register his displeasure with Banks's program. According to Flanders, Banks should have ordered a constitutional convention before elections for state government. "We are threatened with a division into Free State men and 'Copperhead' interests," Flanders told Lincoln. "All the men who have denounced your proclamation will unite and draw proslavery men into a party with the hope of electing men who will bring back slavery and fasten it upon us for years." Similarly, Thomas Durant complained to Chase that Lincoln had given Banks complete control of the reconstruction process and that his actions recognized Louisiana's 1852 constitution, slave codes included.[6]

Factions, based partly on ideology and partly on personality, quickly emerged in the Free State General Committee, and three candidates eventually ran for the office of governor. Michael Hahn, a New Orleans lawyer and an opponent of secession, supported Banks's policy and secured the general's backing. Chase supporters, favoring limited black suffrage, countered by running Benjamin F. Flanders, and proslavery conservative Unionists backed planter J. Q. A. Fellows. As the election approached, Banks confidently assured Lincoln that a large number of ballots would be cast and that there was absolutely no talk of the restoration of slavery. Radicals were not so confident. Flanders told Lincoln that Hahn would win the election only because of his military backing. Once elected, he warned, Hahn would appoint only men of the conservative/Copperhead stamp to office. Another Louisiana constituent warned the president that the army was inhibiting the free discussion of electoral issues. "There is no real liberty of discussion about our own local affairs," he told Lincoln. "Can there be a real election without that liberty?" Illinois Republican congressman Isaac Arnold warned Banks that some of his Republican colleagues were opposed to this election and believed "that there is a danger under a state government of the reestablishment of slavery."[7]

Nevertheless, the election went forward on February 22 as planned, Hahn easily defeating his two opponents. Banks quickly informed the president of the results, boasting that the 11,000 votes cast were about the right number, given the extent of territory occupied by Union forces. He also informed the president that there were no complaints about unfairness in the way the election was handled; however, Banks was clearly wrong. Many congressmen were already concerned that Banks's scheme was too closely tied to the military to be legitimate. Defeated conservative candidate Fellows complained that Banks violated the 1852 constitution by allowing soldiers to vote. He also accused the military of using tactics of intimidation to discourage his potential supporters. Disgruntled Chase followers in New Orleans seconded these concerns. Durant complained to Lincoln that the election did not establish a government as outlined in the president's proclamation of amnesty and reconstruction. According to him, the entire proceeding was a gigantic fraud: "I object to [the election] as having been controlled by the military power and having no value as an expression of the opinion of civilians, by reason of the overshadowing influence of the military." Particularly worrisome to Durant was the upcoming constitutional convention. How could Banks, as a military commander, call for a convention, "and how is that Convention to be chosen?" he asked the president. Durant's anger over events in Louisiana eventually led him to Washington, where he supplied opponents of presidential reconstruction with critical information on the shortcomings of the Banks/Hahn regime.[8]

General-in-Chief Henry Halleck confirmed that the new government established in Louisiana was under Banks's military authority, telling him that Hahn's power as governor was subordinate to Banks and the forces of military occupation. According to Halleck, the experiment in Louisiana had proceeded quite nicely for the administration. "So far as we have gone," he told Banks, "we have obtained the practical results of an election by the people, without the risk of losing the control of the State exercised by the officers of the Government." For many members of Congress, however, the process seemed backward, with elections for state government preceding a constitutional convention. The accusations of military interference outraged many congressmen, radical and conservative. Yet from a practical standpoint, little could be done to stop the Lincoln-Banks program of reconstruction. A solution was shortly provided by the ill-fated Red River campaign, the opportunity Congress needed to investigate Banks; and its chief weapon was the Committee on the Conduct of the War.[9]

The Red River Campaign

"No one ever knew who started the expedition generally called the Banks expedition up the Red River, or what its object was," Adm. David Dixon Porter remarked some years after the war. "No one cared to father it after it was over, for it was one of the most disastrous affairs that occurred during the war." Porter, however, wrote with characteristic hyperbole. The expedition had clear goals. First, there were considerations of foreign policy. In order to ward off French adventurism in Mexico, the Lincoln administration hoped to plant the U.S. flag somewhere in Texas; the Red River route through Shreveport, Louisiana, was one possible means of accomplishing this. A second reason was to occupy Confederate troops in the trans-Mississippi region in order to prevent them from being used in other theaters of war east of the Mississippi. Third, it was important to gain access to the agricultural products of the area, particularly cotton, for northern industry as well as for European trading partners. Fourth, the top commander in the West, William Tecumseh Sherman, envisioned the movement on Shreveport as a lightning-quick raid, destructive and demoralizing to the Confederacy, much in the fashion of Sherman's earlier raid on Meridian, Mississippi.[10]

Banks, however, stumbled badly. Instead of moving quickly to Shreveport, where he was to unite with the forces of Frederick Steele from the Department of Arkansas, Banks moved slowly. He spent a number of days in Alexandria, some 190 miles northwest of New Orleans, while elections were held for delegates to the upcoming constitutional convention. Further, the presence of cotton speculators in Alexandria fueled rumors that the expedition's sole purpose was to seize cotton and enrich private citizens. When Union forces finally started for Shreveport, they were handled inexpertly by

Banks's subordinate, Maj. Gen. William B. Franklin. Leading the advance along a narrow track through a heavily wooded area were several inexperienced cavalry units of Brig. Gen. A. L. Lee. Directly behind Lee was a long train of supply wagons followed by the infantry divisions, spread out over twenty miles. To Confederate general Richard Taylor, this disorganized advance was a tempting target, and his forces attacked Lee near the small town of Mansfield (Sabine Crossroads), sending Union troops into a headlong retreat.[11]

Banks's men fell back to the small town of Pleasant Hill, where they regrouped and drove back the pursuing Confederates. Banks wanted to continue the advance on Shreveport, but his top subordinates, having lost all confidence in his military ability, persuaded him to abandon the idea. Falling back to Alexandria, Banks's forces were delayed for several days while army engineers dammed the Red River to allow Union gunboats under David Porter to clear the falls. Returning to New Orleans in mid-May, Banks quickly found that his unsuccessful expedition was being characterized as a disaster and was the focal point of controversy.[12]

"Everyone is incensed against Banks, and demands his supersedure," Iowa Republican senator James W. Grimes wrote his wife; "our disaster in Louisiana was much greater than reported." Charles Sumner told legal scholar Francis Lieber, "I think that Banks' military career has suffered very much— hardly more than he suffered as a statesman by his proceedings for reconstruction." Soon Banks was being vilified in national newspapers. The radical New York *Independent* denounced him in vituperative terms, charging that his entire military career was "a succession of disasters." Even the conservative Republican *New York Times* expressed skepticism about his military aptitude and called for an investigation of the disaster. Secretary of the Navy Gideon Welles received letters from Admiral Porter and discussed the Red River disaster with one of Porter's aides who came to Washington in late April. "The misfortunes are attributed entirely and exclusively to the incapacity of Banks," Welles remarked.[13]

Even among his troops, Banks was ridiculed for the expedition's failure. Sidney Robinson, a private in the 117th Illinois Infantry, believed that the army's retreat was disgraceful. "The feeling against Banks and his eastern generals of contempt is past description," he remarked. James R. Slack of Indiana reported similar feelings when he joined Union forces in Alexandria after the retreat. "The whole army here is very loud mouthed in its denunciation of Genl Banks," he wrote his wife. "As he moves along the Camps, the men talk derisively of him so that he can hear their language." Not surprisingly, Lieutenant General Grant, who received a number of letters on

Banks's incompetence, asked that Banks be relieved of command, a request that the administration quickly fulfilled by sending Gen. Edward R. S. Canby to supersede Banks. Banks, however, would stay on as second-in-command in the newly created Division of West Mississippi, under Canby.[14]

The Political Aftermath

In late May, John Hutchins told Benjamin Wade that Banks had mismanaged the Red River campaign and that the committee "would find profitable employment" in investigating these matters. Indeed, given the intensity of public outrage, Congress had already discussed Red River on May 11, when Kansas Republican senator James H. Lane introduced a resolution calling for the Committee on the Conduct of the War to investigate the fiasco. In a maneuver designed to focus the investigation on presidential reconstruction, Iowa senator James W. Grimes wanted to broaden the resolution to include an examination of the entire Department of the Gulf. Lane agreed with Grimes, arguing that nonmilitary affairs were relevant to any investigation. According to Lane, Banks's primary goal was not to defeat rebel forces but to acquire cotton. After Grimes formally amended the resolution, it passed the Senate. Some of Banks's subordinate generals rejoiced. Brigadier General T. E. Ransom told William Franklin that they would soon be able to appear before the committee "and our Red River campaign will be ventilated." According to Ransom, many of Banks's political enemies were eager to use the Red River disaster to ruin any chances he might have for the 1864 presidential nomination.[15]

Yet the committee did not begin an examination of the Red River expedition that spring for a number of reasons. First, although the committee did not need congressional authorization to begin an investigation, Chairman Wade requested passage of a joint resolution to investigate the Department of the Gulf before it began its work. Since the House never passed the resolution, the committee possibly decided to delay its inquiry. Second, if committee members wanted to use their forum to weaken Banks's presidential ambitions, this tactic was unnecessary once the Republicans overwhelmingly renominated Lincoln in early June. Third, if the committee wanted Banks removed from active command, Grant had already replaced him with Canby and there was no need to document his incompetence. Still, one reason for investigating Red River was to reveal the weakness of the president's reconstruction plan, clearly the intent of Grimes's amendment. But if Lincoln could be induced to support the reconstruction bill sponsored by Maryland radical Henry Winter Davis, it would be unnecessary to discredit Banks's work in Louisiana. Since the committee members did not view the Red River expedition solely in military terms but as a means to criticize presidential reconstruction, it might have delayed the investigation until Lincoln was presented with a congressional reconstruction bill.[16]

Republican committee members were among the most eager advocates of radical reconstruction, and several of them addressed the issue that spring. George W. Julian, chairman of the House Committee on Public Lands, sponsored homestead legislation designed to redistribute confiscated southern lands to white and black Union veterans. Julian's language reflected his belief that the war should bring about social revolution in the South: "Nothing can atone for the woes and sorrows of this war but the thorough reorganization of society in these revolted States." Daniel W. Gooch, the least radical of the committee's Republican members, spoke out forcefully on reconstruction. Also a member of Davis's Select Committee on Rebellious States, Gooch told House members that it was a mistake to assume that the end of the war would restore the old order in the South. With affairs in Louisiana on his mind, Gooch argued that although the president could use his authority to aid loyal residents in forming a government, only Congress could determine the legitimacy of such governments. No seceded state, Gooch maintained, had any status until recognized by Congress.[17]

Radical Republican Henry Winter Davis introduced a bill (eventually the Wade-Davis bill) in early 1864 that was in many respects similar to an earlier bill sponsored by Ohio Republican James Ashley, chairman of the House Committee on Territories. The bill was conceived in opposition to Lincoln's plan since Davis was increasingly hostile toward the administration because of its preference for the Blairs in the distribution of Maryland patronage. When he originally introduced the measure in the House, Davis ridiculed the Louisiana experiment, characterizing it as a "hermaphrodite government, half military, half republican, representing the alligators and frogs of Louisiana." His bill allowed the president to appoint a provisional governor who would not only rule the state in the absence of a loyal state government but who would also direct the process by which a loyal state government could be organized and send representatives to Congress. First, constitutional conventions would be chosen when 50 percent, not 10 percent, of the 1860 voting population took an iron-clad oath that they had never willingly aided the Confederacy. As in the president's plan, anyone who had held civil or military office under the Confederacy was barred from participation. The conventions would have to write specific provisions into their constitutions abolishing slavery and adopting other features designed to establish civil rights for newly emancipated slaves. These measures included allowing blacks to sue for freedom via writs of habeas corpus and a guarantee of due process of law. If the provisions were not incorporated into the new state constitution, the provisional governor could dissolve the convention and begin the process anew.[18]

"The New England theory of reducing the seceded states to territories with a view to the effective abolition of slavery will command a large support in the Republican ranks," wrote Indiana congressman William S. Holman in fall 1863. Holman, however, did not accurately predict the emphasis of Davis's bill, which was a repudiation of the state suicide theory. Fundamental to the Davis bill was the assumption that states had not left the Union and that Congress had the authority to specify conditions of reconstruction. This authority was rooted in the constitutional clause giving Congress the power to ensure each state a republican form of government. According to Herman Belz,

> Based on a constitutional theory which regarded the rebellious states as disorganized political units lacking republican governments, though still in the Union, the Wade-Davis plan insisted on direct federal control, exercised by Congress, over southern state reorganization that would finally be necessary to reconstruct the Union.[19]

If there was a problem, it lay in the bill's provisions regarding emancipation and black civil rights. Although Lincoln's plan required reconstructed states to accept the presidential proclamations on slavery, it stopped short of requiring an emancipation provision in the state's constitution. Many Republicans regarded this omission as an insufficient safeguard against slavery since the constitutionality of the Emancipation Proclamation was by no means certain. Nor did Lincoln's plan specify a role for the federal government in protecting freedmen from abuse. And it was Banks's program in Louisiana that had raised these doubts since his apprentice labor system was regarded as little better than slavery. In Lincoln's view, local authorities would be the protectors of the rights of emancipated slaves. But many Republicans believed that without the guarantees of the Wade-Davis bill, blacks would be targets of discrimination and exploitation.[20]

Davis was able to get the bill through the House in mid-May by a vote of 79 to 59, undoubtedly aided by dropping the bill's original provision for black suffrage. It was sent to the Senate, where it was entrusted to Wade's Committee on Territories. Davis urged quick passage. The Thirteenth Amendment had recently failed to secure the needed two-thirds majority in the House, and Davis told Wade that this bill, with its provisions for black rights, would be the only practical measure accomplished on the issue of slavery. Wade steered the bill through the Senate, securing a narrow 18 to 14 passage on July 2, 1864, just a few days before the end of the congressional session.[21]

There was intense congressional pressure on the president to accept the bill. Illinois Republican congressman Jesse O. Norton warned Lincoln that failure to sign might be politically damaging. On July 4 Zachariah Chandler visited the White House to discuss the matter. When Lincoln chided Congress for placing such an important matter before him with only a few days for consideration, Chandler asserted that the main issue was abolishing slavery "in the reconstructed states." "I doubt that Congress can legally do that," the president countered. "It is no more than you have done yourself," Chandler rejoined. When Lincoln claimed that the executive could act for military reasons in ways that Congress constitutionally could not, Chandler said, "Mr. President I cannot controvert y[ou]r position by argument, I can only say I deeply regret it." An angry Chandler left the White House that afternoon. Later, when Lincoln discussed the possible repercussions of a veto with William Fessenden and John Hay, including the possibility of a revolt of radical Republicans, he said, "If they choose to make a point upon this I do not doubt that they can do harm. They have never been friendly to me."[22]

Instead of an outright veto, Lincoln chose the little-used pocket veto, letting the bill lie unsigned until the legislative session was over. Then in order to explain his actions, he published a statement concerning reconstruction in which he justified his course. Not only did he claim that Congress had no authority to abolish slavery in the states, but he also insisted that he was unwilling to jettison the developments that had already been accomplished in Louisiana and Arkansas.[23]

According to Julian, Lincoln's action diminished his reputation among Republicans and turned many of his critics toward John C. Frémont, who had been nominated in May by a convention of disaffected radicals meeting in Cleveland. Wade and Davis were clearly stunned and shortly thereafter responded to the president's statement with their own manifesto. It castigated Lincoln for executive usurpation and the failure to impose any conditions on restored rebel states, such as repudiation of Confederate debt and the abolition of slavery, but its unique feature was its bitter denunciation of affairs in Louisiana. The source of much of the information about Louisiana's reconstruction government was Thomas J. Durant, who had visited Washington in late June. The manifesto contained many of the same charges that later appeared in the CCW's report on the Red River campaign. The governments of Louisiana and Arkansas were described as illegitimate, the "mere creatures of [Lincoln's] will. They are mere oligarchies, imposed on the people by military orders under the form of election."[24]

"No such bomb had been thrown into Washington before," an associate of Ben Butler wrote, reporting that Montgomery Blair had denounced Wade and Davis in bitter terms. "We have Lee & his on one side, and Henry Winter Davis & Ben. Wade and all such Hell cats on the other," Blair allegedly had said. Others, however, applauded the course of Wade and Davis. One Ohio man told Wade that he wished he had written the protest. He hoped Lincoln would be passed over for the presidency so that the nation could be saved from "sinking, through imbecility, into deserved anarchy and despotism." Gideon Welles was not shocked at the behavior of Davis, whom he regarded as unscrupulous, but he was surprised that Wade had aided him. "There is, however, an infinity of party and personal intrigue just at this time," Welles remarked; "a Presidential election is approaching, and there are many aspirants, not only for Presidential but other honors and positions." Realizing that much of the protest was aimed at Banks's administration in Louisiana, one of his associates assured the general that Lincoln would sustain him. "His blood is up on the Wade & Winter Davis protest," he told Banks; "he will all the more seek to sustain you."[25]

The divisions over Wade-Davis presaged trouble for the presidential election that fall. Despite Lincoln's unanimous renomination as the Republican party's standard-bearer, there were numerous obstacles to his reelection, including the dismal state of military affairs in the Virginia theater, the third-party candidacy of John C. Frémont, and the effects of the Wade-Davis bill on party unity. Republican members on the Committee on the Conduct of the War surely felt cheated by the president. They had postponed an investigation of Red River that could have proved embarrassing to the administration, hoping that Lincoln would follow congressional leadership in reconstruction by accepting the Wade-Davis bill. Still, they rallied behind Lincoln, preferring him to George McClellan. Chandler in particular performed a notable deed in an effort to restore party unity.[26]

None of the committee members was an ardent supporter of Abraham Lincoln for reelection in the fall. Democrats Benjamin Harding and Moses Odell opposed him for ideological reasons, and Republican members, mainly because of his recalcitrance on reconstruction, were unenthusiastic. In February 1864 Benjamin Loan was rumored to have denounced Lincoln as a Copperhead, and a "d——d liar." Julian had been an early supporter of Chase's bid for the Republican nomination. Facing a stiff challenge for reelection in his Indiana congressional district, Julian told Charles Sumner that the campaign there would be difficult for Republicans. "Old Abe is rather a burden than a help to our cause," he complained. Wade was perhaps Lincoln's most vociferous critic among committee members. Angered by Lincoln's pocket veto of the Wade-Davis bill, Wade was rumored to support the candidacy of Gen. Benjamin F. Butler. According to this plan, Republicans would call for a new party convention, nominate Butler, and induce John C. Frémont to withdraw from the race. Lincoln, they hoped, would then step aside in favor of Butler.[27]

Like other committee members and Republicans, Chandler distrusted Lincoln and was distressed with his course on the Wade-Davis bill and reconstruction in Louisiana; however, the threat of McClellan as president was daunting. Spurning a request from Davis to participate in a Cincinnati convention to cast aside the president, in late August Chandler undertook a complex series of negotiations to reunite Republicans for the upcoming fall contest. He attempted to arrange a quid pro quo in which Frémont would give up his third-party bid in exchange for the resignation of Montgomery Blair from his cabinet position of postmaster general. Blair had long been an irritant to radical Republicans. His views on reconstruction were conservative, and when he gave a particularly offensive speech on the subject in Rockville, Maryland, in fall 1863, party radicals were vexed. At the time, Thaddeus Stevens told Charles Sumner that Blair ought to be removed for "he has done more harm . . . than all the Copperhead speeches of the campaign."[28]

Traveling to Washington, Philadelphia, and New York, Chandler labored diligently to negotiate a deal to save the Republican party. But the headstrong Frémont surprised him by deciding unconditionally to withdraw from the race, writing a letter of withdrawal that castigated the president. Chandler was furious, his scheme to oust Blair apparently compromised. Although Lincoln was peeved at the tone of Frémont's letter, Chandler's stubborn insistence that the president had made a deal (Frémont's withdrawal in exchange for Blair's resignation) finally wore the president down and he assented. Blair resigned and radical Republicans rallied behind Lincoln to defeat McClellan.[29]

"I don't see how you effected it," Wade later wrote Chandler, "except by playing on Old Abe's fears. . . . He was governed by the fear that Blair's continuing might affect his reelection." In actuality, Lincoln made a concession that he did not have to make since Wade could support no one else. As Welles realized, Lincoln had the upper hand. Most Republican members on the committee undoubtedly concluded that, with the military situation in summer 1864 at a stalemate, a further fracturing of Republican unity might have a devastating impact on Lincoln's reelection and deprive

Committee Republicans were often impatient with Abraham Lincoln. (Courtesy of the Carl Sandburg Collection, University of Illinois, Urbana-Champaign)

them of directing the war effort. Lincoln had endorsed emancipation and had made the abolition of slavery a central war goal. For dissatisfied Republicans, this goal was too important to sacrifice. Disagree as they might over Lincoln's policy in Louisiana, resolution of those issues could wait until after the election.[30]

Fortunately, a number of events in fall 1864 helped reverse the declining stock of the Republican party while stemming the tide of Democratic momentum. Sherman's conquest of Atlanta, Farragut's capture of Mobile Bay, and Sheridan's control in the Shenandoah Valley gave new hope to northerners that victory was yet attainable. These gains invigorated Republicans, but they demoralized the Democrats, who had exposed themselves to ridicule when McClellan repudiated the peace plank of the party's Chicago platform. With the help of the soldiers' vote, Lincoln won a relatively easy victory.[31]

With Lincoln's victory, the issue of reconstructed Louisiana quickly came to the forefront. Not only was there the question of its electoral vote but also of whether Congress would accept congressmen and senators elected under the provisions of its recently ratified constitution. During this debate the Committee on the Conduct of the War began its investigation of the Red River campaign.

From its inception, the 1864 Louisiana constitution and the circumstances surrounding its ratification had excited controversy. Meeting from early April to July 1864, the delegates to the constitutional convention quickly discredited the proceedings by voting themselves a hefty per diem compensation. Moreover, so few parishes were represented (twenty out of forty-eight) that the convention voted that a quorum of 76 delegates rather than the customary 150 was sufficient to conduct business. A number of delegates came to New Orleans from Alexandria and Grand Ecore, a result of elections held during Banks's military expedition. They had the dubious distinction of being unable to return home after the convention because Banks's retreat left these areas in Confederate hands.

Still, as a number of scholars have pointed out, the convention accomplished many measures that would have been unthinkable in Louisiana less than three years earlier. These included the abolition of slavery, a provision that allowed the state legislature to enfranchise blacks at a future date, and legislation that protected workers from abuses. Despite these accomplishments, however, many congressional radicals regarded the entire proceeding as illegitimate, noting its association with military rule. "Reconstruction by military authority," remarks LaWanda Cox, "was suspect [particularly to radical Republicans] on every account." Perhaps the greatest defect in the new constitution was the circumstances surrounding its ratification. Twenty parishes participated in the election, but fewer votes were cast than in the February election for state offices; the document was ratified by a vote of 6,836 to 1,566. The method of securing ratification also seemed tainted. George Denison, treasury agent for New Orleans, wrote Chase that the entire process reeked of military interference. "The result [of the election] was just what might have been expected, the whole power being in military hands," he complained. "The whole civil reorganization in Louisiana is a cheat & swindle and everyone knows it."[32]

Once state government was established under the new constitution, however, harmony between the military and the civil administration ceased, and Lincoln found himself presiding over a quarrel that threatened to make his reconstruction policy in Louisiana look ridiculous. Governor Michael Hahn complained to Banks that the new military commanders (Generals Edward R. S. Canby and Stephen Hurlbut) were "determined to kill off any reorganization of loyal state government." An incredulous Lincoln wrote Hurlbut shortly after the fall elections that "every advocate of slavery naturally desires to see [the new Louisiana state government] blasted, and crushed . . . but why Gen. Canby and Gen. Hurlbut should join on the same side is to me incomprehensible." Hurlbut, a prominent Illinois Republican before the war whose reputation was tarnished by persistent rumors of corruption and drunkenness, quickly responded to these charges by claiming that Louisiana's new state government was not living up to its obligations, particularly in protecting the rights of blacks. "Laws are needed but not made," Hurlbut told Lincoln, pointing out that although slavery had been abolished, local customs were hard to root out. Anticipating the arguments of many congressional radicals, Hurlbut questioned whether this new state government was legitimate. "The city of New Orleans is practically the state of Louisiana," he wrote, and military officials hoped that the civil government would take over many of their tasks. He thought it was unlikely, however, because of the poor financial condition of the state.[33]

When Congress met in December for its second session, the recognition of Louisiana quickly became an issue. Wade and thirty other senators protested the admission of recently elected Louisiana senators R. K. Cutler and Charles Smith on the grounds of the purely military nature of the state's government. At the same time Montgomery Blair urged the president to stand firm on their admission, arguing that sovereignty resided in the people of each state and that for the federal government to tamper with such issues as suffrage requirements was unconstitutional. Compromise, however, appeared a distinct possibility when Cong. James Ashley, chairman of the Committee on Territories, introduced a new version of the Wade-Davis bill. According to presidential secretary John Hay both Lincoln and Banks were favorably impressed with the bill except for its provisions on black suffrage and a congressional declaration that slavery was abolished. According to the *New York Herald,* Wade and Davis would accept the Louisiana delegation in exchange for the president's acknowledgment that remaining rebel states would be viewed as territories to be organized by Congress prior to readmission. Charles Sumner wrote to English liberal John Bright that he was working to prevent a breach with the White House on the issue. If the president would allow the adoption of a clear set of rules for other states, then Sumner would support the admission of Louisiana.[34]

Perhaps as a precaution in case compromise failed, Congress redirected the Committee on the Conduct of the War to investigate the failed Red River expedition. On December 6, 1864, Ohio congressman Rufus Spaulding introduced a resolution of inquiry that was quickly adopted. Unlike the Senate resolution of the first session, Spaulding's was aimed at uncovering the reasons for military failure and did not specifically direct the committee to pry into matters of civil administration. Undoubtedly, there was some feeling in Congress that an explanation for this military disaster was needed. Yet as the investigation unfolded, it is abundantly clear that committee members were extremely interested in Banks's policy of civil administration; and in Washington political circles, it was generally understood that the investigation was an attack on the entire policy. A few weeks after the committee began its work, Elizabeth Blair Lee remarked, "The Banks are here—not looking happy—the War Committee are rowing him up Red River."[35]

Two important questions arose in the Red River investigation: To what extent was the expedition launched to satiate the appetites of greedy cotton speculators whose sole interest was the desire for profits, and what role did the elections held in Alexandria and Grand Ecore play in delaying it and causing its failure? Although straightforward matters of military strategy and tactics did occupy a great deal of the committee's time, most of the questioning was undertaken to show that the expedition was meaningless from a military standpoint and was motivated by political and economic concerns. Given the direction of congressional debate over the recognition of the Banks/ Hahn government, it cannot be mere coincidence that committee members pursued the mechanics of Lincoln's 10 percent plan as they were implemented in Louisiana. Indeed, the simultaneous occurrence of this investigation and the debate over the recognition of the Louisiana government gave critics, both Republican and Democratic, plenty of ammunition to discredit and defeat the administration's policy of reconstruction in Louisiana if compromise on a reconstruction bill could not be worked out.

Since he was in Washington lobbying individual congressmen to recognize the state government of Louisiana, Banks was immediately summoned before the committee. He discussed the unpleasant particulars of the campaign, including Henry Halleck's persistent lobbying for the expedition; Franklin's flawed order of march, which had sprawled troops over twenty miles and had imperiled the advance of Gen. A. L. Lee; the lack of a united command structure; the low water of the Red River; and opposition from his subordinates when he wanted to press on to Shreveport after the repulse at Sabine Crossroads. Odell raised the subject of cotton speculations when he asked Banks how much time the navy had devoted to seizing cotton. Wade asked if he had had permission to trade with the enemy. No, Banks replied; cotton that was seized was turned over to the U.S. quartermaster. And to Gooch, the only Republican member of the committee sympathetic toward him, Banks asserted that the charges of speculators growing wealthy from the proceeds of the expedition were absolutely false. Ironically, the committee did not ask Banks about the elections in Alexandria and Grand Ecore, probably knowing what his response would be. This approach was not surprising, given the committee's past tactics; to ask would give Banks an opportunity to defend these procedures. It was far more productive to ask questions of witnesses less interested in the success of Louisiana's reconstruction. Well aware of the committee's motives, Banks addressed the reconstruction issue in his closing remarks. The people of Louisiana, he asserted, "are weak and exhausted by their calamities, and require assistance and recognition of the government of the United States, and I think them entitled to it." And he admonished committee members to go and see for themselves.[36]

Almost every witness appearing before the committee was asked about the purpose of the expedition. Many professed ignorance or referred vaguely to the occupation of Texas. A few of the witnesses, however, offered explanations that were congruent with the committee's partisan objectives. Captain John Schuyler Crosby, an aide-de-camp for Banks, told Wade that the prevailing idea among army officers was that the expedition's purpose was to bring Louisiana back into the Union after conquering more territory and to gain access to cotton. He then named several cotton speculators who had accompanied the expedition. Another aide-de-camp, Col. J. G. Wilson, testified that Col. Frank Howe had accompanied the expedition with several known cotton speculators, including H. Waldron, Henry Thompson, William Butler, and Silas Casey, the latter two acting with presidential authority. Major General Thomas Kilby Smith told Gooch that the point of Red River was a "mercantile expedition; that is, an expedition for the purpose of opening the country to trade." Major General William Emory informed Wade that "there were crowds of cotton speculators along with us. Where they came from, or who they were, I do not know." From this testimony, committee members easily drew the conclusion that there was no military point to the Red River campaign but that it had been launched to enrich cotton speculators and to further Lincoln's ill-conceived reconstruction experiment in Louisiana.[37]

While these hearings took place in December, January, and February 1864–1865, Congress also dealt with the issue of the recognition of the Louisiana delegation. Lincoln was predisposed to cooperate on a reconstruction bill in December 1864, if only because he realized that ultimately only Congress could settle the issue of recognition of state governments. Indeed, the atmosphere in Washington seemed conducive to compromise. By late January 1865, even William Lloyd Garrison's *Liberator* defended Banks's policies in Louisiana, particularly his orders with respect to black labor. When Ashley introduced a modified version of the Wade-Davis bill at the beginning of the second session of Congress, both Lincoln and Banks gave it careful consideration. However, they hesitated to support it because it was too liberal with respect to black civil rights, and it contained an emancipation requirement that Lincoln believed violated state prerogatives. When Ashley attempted to modify the bill by limiting black suffrage to veterans, he risked losing the support of some radical Republicans. A final version contained a provision for equality before the law of all persons regardless of color and three specific conditions to be engrafted into state constitutions: repudiation of Confederate debts, prohibition of slavery, and exclusion of rebel officeholders from political rights. Losing the support of moderate Republicans such as Henry Dawes, who denounced the bill as prescribing "an iron, unbending rule for these States," it was tabled in mid-February.[38]

The Senate meanwhile considered both the issue of Louisiana's electoral vote and a resolution recognizing the Banks-Hahn government. Although conservative Republicans such as New Jersey's John Ten Eyck and Wisconsin's James Doolittle wanted to include Louisiana's vote, they were opposed by a coalition of Democrats and radical Republicans, most prominently Wade and Kentucky senator Lazarus Powell. The crux of their position was that Louisiana was still in rebellion, that any election there was contingent upon a military presence and was therefore illegitimate. Wade, undoubtedly bolstered by subsequent committee testimony, characterized the entire process by which Louisiana's government was reconstructed as a farce. Noting that over four-fifths of Louisiana was under rebel control, Wade thought it was ridiculous to "talk of free republican State government." Yet the president supported this policy so as "to vindicate his anarchical principle of ten percent of loyalty." Although Wade and his supporters carried the day on the issue of electoral votes, the debate on recognition was far from over. And as compromise on reconstruction seemed elusive, committee testimony provided a wealth of evidence against the administration's Louisiana policy.[39]

A few days after Wade's speech Lyman Trumbull, chairman of the Senate Judiciary Committee, introduced a joint resolution for the recognition of Louisiana's congressional delegation, despite vigorous opposition from Chandler, who wanted consideration of a bill on commerce between states. In close communication with the president, Trumbull claimed it was too important an issue to postpone until the next session of Congress. In an unusual alliance, radical Republicans such as Chandler, Wade, Sumner, and Jacob Howard made common cause with Democrats, including Lazarus Powell and Willard Saulsberry of Delaware, in thwarting moderate Republicans. When James Doolittle claimed that recognition of Louisiana was needed in order to secure ratification of the Thirteenth Amendment, Sumner responded that only three-fourths of the states in the Union de facto were required. In a long speech to the Senate on February 24, Powell ridiculed the state government of Louisiana because it was not truly representative. The only free man in Louisiana was Banks, Powell told the Senate. "No, Senators, there was no freedom of election there." The whole process, he concluded, rested on the power of the bayonet.[40]

Wade entered the debate on February 27, claiming his opposition to recognition of Louisiana's delegation was similar to his opposition to the Lecompton constitution in the 1850s. "This is the constitution of the people of Louisiana," Trumbull objected. "The people!" Wade retorted, "How long have you, sir, been of the opinion that it was the people who wanted it?" Noting Trumbull's earlier opposition to the legitimacy of Louisiana's electoral vote, Wade remarked that the senator's support of its constitution was remarkable: "Sir, it is the most miraculous conversion that has taken place since St. Paul's time." Undoubtedly drawing on committee testimony, Wade continued to assault the legitimacy of Louisiana's constitutional convention: "We considered it a mockery, a miserable mockery to undertake to recognize this Louisiana organization as a State in this Union." When Trumbull claimed that it was Wade, in this instance, who was resisting the people's will, Wade, clearly alluding to committee testimony, responded, "I have heard a great deal about this pretended election in Louisiana, that did not come from Major General Banks, and I pronounce the proceeding a mockery."[41]

"We have killed the Louisiana bill Yesterday," Chandler reported to his wife. Vowing to resort to the filibuster and other parliamentary maneuvers, opponents of recognition were able to have their way. Accepting the inevitable, proponents of the measure finally accepted a compromise resolution put forward by Ohio Republican John Sherman, which would take up the joint resolution only after the Senate's regular business was concluded, provided there was still time in the session. This move effectively killed the measure for the Thirty-eighth Congress. Given the expectation of a more radical Thirty-ninth Congress, opponents of the measure hoped to have more influence in that session.[42]

The end of the session of Congress, however, did not lead to the conclusion of the committee's work. Both Gooch and Wade introduced resolutions to extend the life of the committee by sixty days (later changed to ninety days), citing the need to interview pivotal witnesses to complete its reports. The Senate passed the resolution without even bothering to hear Wade's reasons. Congressmen Charles A. Eldridge of Wisconsin and William H. Wadsworth of Kentucky used the opportunity to assail the committee, but the resolution still passed easily enough. The committee's Republican majority knew that the battle on reconstruction was far from over; anticipating conflict, they needed more ammunition to discredit the president's Louisiana experiment. Although Sumner was not a member of the committee, his reasoning was a propos. Writing to John Bright, he explained his quarrel with the president over reconstruction: "I insist that the rebel States shall not come back except on the footing of the Decltn of Indep. with all persons equal before the law, & govt. founded on the consent of the governed," adding, "Mr. Lincoln is slow in accepting truth."[43]

After Congress recessed, committee members remained in Washington to hear testimony. Among the principal witnesses interviewed were Adm. David Dixon Porter, Capt. K. R. Breese of the U.S. Navy, and former Illinois governor Richard Yates. Although the committee did not believe Porter's testimony concerning the Fort Fisher fiasco when it contradicted the testimony of their favorite, Benjamin F. Butler, his testimony on Red River gave them plenty of ammunition to discredit the Lincoln/Banks policy. According to Porter, the purpose of the Red River campaign was cotton. Banks came up the Red River on the steamer *Blackhawk*, Porter testified, "loaded with cotton speculators, bagging, roping, champagne, and ice." Sending away treasury agents because they might interfere with the designs of the speculators, Banks issued his own cotton trading permits. Contradicting Banks's earlier testimony, Porter claimed that most of the confiscated cotton had not been taken by the U.S. quartermaster but by a private company, C. A. Weed.

At pivotal points in the expedition, concern for cotton slowed it, Porter stated, pointing to delays in Alexandria and the additional time the navy expended on hauling extra transports for the speculators. "There was too much attention paid to getting cotton," he contended.[44]

Benjamin Loan found Porter's testimony particularly revealing when he asked about elections held in Alexandria and Grand Ecore for delegates to the constitutional convention. When Loan asked whether any voters or candidates accompanied the expedition, Porter said he did not know but denounced the elections in Alexandria as a great humbug and in Grand Ecore as a perfect farce. Porter explained that the people did not want to vote, "but they were impressed with the notion that if they would come forward and prove their loyalty by voting they would be allowed to take their cotton out and do what they pleased with it." That statement, however, was contradicted by Wellington W. Witherbury, a navigator who accompanied the expedition and acted as Banks's election clerk in Alexandria. Declaring that voters, largely dissenters and Confederate draft dodgers, had come in on their own accord, Witherbury also claimed that the elections had not slowed the army's progress. The committee accepted Porter as the more reliable witness; here was convincing testimony that Lincoln's 10 percent plan was a trumped-up farce, illegitimate, corrupt, and undemocratic.[45]

Captain Breese presented the committee with one of the more intriguing aspects of the Red River campaign. According to him, Illinois governor Richard Yates and a group of cotton speculators had visited Banks just before the expedition: "The object of Governor Yates's party was to purchase cotton to promote the interest of General Banks as the compromise candidate for President." Claiming the group of speculators was connected to the firm of Butler and Casey, Breese contended that although he generally dismissed what cotton speculators had to say, they seemed to agree on this particular story.[46]

When Gooch examined Yates on the matter, Yates, by then a senator, flatly denied involvement in any scheme to put Banks forward as a compromise candidate, although he did admit visiting him in March 1864. "Something might have been said to General Banks by other parties," he explained, "not by myself, as to his being a compromise candidate for the Presidency." Gooch allowed Yates's statements to stand without bothering to dig deeper. If Yates had been involved in putting Banks forward as a compromise candidate, Gooch's superficial questioning was not designed to uncover the truth. Perhaps, with Lincoln's reelection, Gooch allowed Yates to gloss over what might have been an embarrassing incident. As David Porter said of the investigation, "When [the Committee] dug down [,] their spades would strike some skull it was not desirable to disturb, and those who had charge of the investigations got over them as soon as possible."[47]

When it completed its hearings in May 1865, the committee began work on its reports. Two reports on the Red River expedition were eventually published, since Gooch, Banks's political ally, dissented from the views of his Republican colleagues. The majority report focused on cotton speculation and the delegate elections in Alexandria and Grand Ecore as the causes for the excessive delays that resulted in military disaster. Predictably, the report castigated the election process for delegates to a constitutional convention as an unwarranted military usurpation:

> The political transactions were shown by the holding of elections in the camps of the army while engaged in the expedition, with the view of reorganizing a civil government in Louisiana. The attempt to do this was clearly a usurpation on the part of the military authorities, the execution of which was as weak and inefficient as the attempt was improper and illegal.

An angry Banks argued that the report "was not history, nor was its judgment the judgment of history." Gooch's report emphasized the role of Henry Halleck in pressuring Banks to undertake the mission, although he had never written positive orders to do so. Blaming the disaster more on plain military incompetence, especially Franklin's order of march, Gooch argued that cotton speculation and delegate elections had not caused excessive delays and therefore were not responsible for the disaster.[48]

The Committee on the Conduct of the War had continued its investigation of the Red River disaster with a view toward political conflict with a president unwilling to implement a more thorough program of reconstruction. After the assassination of Lincoln on April 14, 1865, the situation changed, for Pres. Andrew Johnson, a former member of the committee, spoke in terms of a harsh, punishing peace, leading his colleagues on the committee to believe that he shared their views on reconstruction. By the end of May, however, the committee's Republican majority was convinced that Johnson was more lenient than Lincoln. Further, he had purged supporters of Banks and Hahn from office and replaced them with more conservative officeholders. The publication of the reports thus fulfilled for these committee members an even more pressing partisan concern as they anxiously anticipated the next session of Congress. Yet given its hundreds of pages of detailed testimony on political issues and military maneuvers, the report probably had little impact on public opinion.[49]

In examining the Red River expedition, the Committee on the Conduct of the War used better judgment than it had in previous investigations of military matters. In its numerous inquiries into the Army of the Potomac, members were never satisfied with simply examining witnesses and identifying the causes of failure. Instead, the committee had attempted to influence and direct Lincoln's executive prerogatives. No such motive characterized the military aspects of the Red River investigation. Banks was already removed from active command, and the committee made no attempt to direct military policy in the Department of the Gulf.

As for that aspect of the investigation that touched upon the administration's reconstruction policy, however, the committee took calculated aim at the Lincoln/Banks program with the intention of discrediting it. Although the CCW's actions may have vexed Lincoln's supporters and may not have proceeded from the purest of motives, from a constitutional standpoint the committee was on firm ground. Clearly, the ultimate decision on the legitimacy of the reconstruction government in Louisiana had to be determined by Congress. Banks's government was a military regime; therefore, it came under the committee's charge to investigate all aspects of the war.

CHAPTER NINE

Politics, Principles, and Partisanship: Investigations, 1864–1865

During the second session of the Thirty-eighth Congress, from December 1864 to March 1865, the Committee on the Conduct of the War engaged in a variety of investigations. In three specific instances the committee made valuable contributions to the war effort. Yet in two of its most high-profile examinations, it played the familiar role of opposition to the nation's military establishment. In the investigations of the Fort Fisher affair and the Sherman-Johnston peace agreement, the committee operated along its well-established guidelines by attempting to discredit military leaders who deviated from its members' ideas of how war should be waged and by seeking to promote individuals who agreed with the ideological principles of the Republican party. Although Union military fortunes were scarcely altered by these last two investigations, they were an annoyance to Union officers and a waste of time and resources.

The committee's investigations of the Sand Creek massacre in Colorado Territory and of the Navy Department's selection of heavy ordnance illustrate its positive achievements. In the first instance, the committee condemned the actions of the Colorado state militia for an indiscriminate slaughter of a defenseless group of Cheyenne and Arapaho on the banks of Sand Creek in eastern Colorado. Special criticism was reserved for territorial governor John Evans for his "shifting testimony" as he sought to evade responsibility and for Col. Edward M. Chivington, who carried out the massacre despite full knowledge of the group's peaceful intentions. Although Chivington resigned from the army in early 1865 to avoid a court-martial, the committee's subsequent investigation kept the massacre before the public, certainly damaging Chivington's political ambitions in Colorado politics. In the second instance, the committee helped uncover defects in the manufacturing of naval artillery, pointing out a variety of problems in guns manufactured by the Rodman and Parrott process. The committee recommended that the navy use the more expensive but more reliable Ames gun, which, it maintained, would greatly increase the efficiency of iron-clad monitors.[1]

Acting on a Senate resolution, the committee also undertook an elabo-rate investigation of the construction of light-draught monitors. Inspired by the success of John Ericsson's *Monitor,* the Department of the Navy planned the construction of several of these ships. The committee discovered a trail of faulty designs, expensive cost overruns, and bureaucratic in-fighting within the department; the investigation, however, was not without its partisan aspects. Committee member Daniel W. Gooch, for instance, was much at odds with Secretary of the Navy Gideon Welles over patronage decisions that affected the department's Massachusetts naval yards. Undoubtedly, he was eager to discredit Welles. During the investigation, Chairman Benjamin Wade worked closely with Maryland radical, Henry Winter Davis. Part of their motivation was to discredit Welles, a conservative Republican. Davis was also acting on behalf of Adm. Samuel F. DuPont, who refused to attack the harbor of Charleston in April of 1863 because of what he deemed faulty and ineffective monitors. Since Welles believed that DuPont, not the monitors, was at fault, DuPont wanted an official investigation that would indict the light-draught monitors and clear him of responsibility. Nevertheless, despite these personal and partisan aspects, the inefficiency and incompetence that were uncovered justified the investigation.[2]

In these three instances, as in the earlier investigation of ice contracts, the CCW demonstrated that congressional committees, when narrowly fo-cused, could achieve worthwhile results. The controlling personalities on the committee, however, were not content with peripheral investigations; they longed to be in the limelight.

Throughout the war, committee members displayed a singular disdain for professional military knowledge and devotion to the ideological precepts of the Republican party. This viewpoint was amply demonstrated in the CCW's investigations of the Fort Fisher fiasco and the Sherman-Johnston peace negotiations. These investigations involved the committee with the North's two top military leaders: Ulysses Grant and William Tecumseh Sherman. Its attitude toward them is revealing. Although the Civil War was not a total war in the twentieth-century sense of the term, undoubtedly Grant and Sherman came close to implementing it. Carrying out raids designed to wreak havoc with the Confederacy's infrastructure, industry, and agricul-tural production and inflicting psychological terror on the civilian populace, they turned into reality the harsh rhetoric of the committee's radical Repub-lican members. They represented the complete repudiation of conciliation, a philosophy endorsed by such committee enemies as George McClellan. In view of the CCW's support for a harsh war, one might expect a close and

supportive relationship between the committee and Grant and Sherman. Yet
with the war's end near, the committee instead found itself in these two investigations in the familiar position of opposing the army's top leadership.[3]

Committee members had their reasons for this lukewarm support for the
two architects of northern military victory and for challenging the two generals who realized the folly of conciliation. Grant and Sherman fought a harsh
war, but they were hardly at the forefront of radical politics. Neither had
been fervid antislavery advocates before the war. Although Grant became
an enthusiastic proponent of emancipation during the course of the war, he
had supported Stephen A. Douglas and endorsed the position of most war
Democrats. Sherman's views on slavery aroused even more suspicion; he
openly opposed the Emancipation Proclamation. And Sherman had made a
number of statements early in the war criticizing the unrealistic attitudes about
warfare that characterized the thinking of many civilians and political leaders. Both generals, particularly Sherman, were West Point–educated professionals who disparaged popular ideas about military matters. Thus the committee looked at both generals with a certain amount of skepticism. Still, the
committee's opposition to Grant and Sherman was mild compared to its
attitude toward such generals as George McClellan or even George Meade.
Grant and Sherman had earned their positions through success and enjoyed
the confidence of the Lincoln administration and widespread popular support. Committee members surely recognized their value and moderated their
criticisms accordingly. Hence, the committee's investigative work in the Fort
Fisher affair and in the Sherman-Johnston peace agreement was largely
superfluous, hardly a hindrance to the war effort but scarcely a positive
contribution.[4]

The Fort Fisher Affair

The committee locked horns with Lt. Gen. U. S. Grant as a result of the Fort
Fisher affair and Grant's determination to rid the northern army of one of
the most flamboyant political generals of the war, Benjamin F. Butler, a
longtime favorite of the committee. The former Massachusetts Breckinridge
Democrat had captured radical hearts when early in the conflict he confiscated slaves as contraband of war. Butler's firmness in dealing with the civilian
population when commander of occupied New Orleans had earned him
additional high marks among committee members. Arrogant, audacious, and
flamboyant, the droopy-eyed Butler was a master of public relations, using
the right phrases to endear himself to the radical wing of the Republican party.

That he was unsuccessful when handling troops in the field did not bother committee members. As in their sponsorship of other failed generals such as Frémont, Pope, and Hooker, committee members did not evaluate military competence by military standards. For committee members, Butler, again like Frémont, Pope and Hooker, held the correct views on pivotal issues such as emancipation, confiscation, and harsh reconstruction. According to the committee's perspective, military success would necessarily follow from correct political principles. In the cases of Frémont, Pope, and Hooker, their lack of success was easily explained: they had been opposed by proslavery forces, i.e., the army's traditional West Point leadership. Thus in the face of overwhelming evidence that Butler was militarily incompetent, the committee continued to support him.[5]

Butler became a subject of concern to the committee when his expedition failed against Fort Fisher, which guarded the port of Wilmington, North Carolina, the last major leak in the Union's blockade of the Confederacy. In fall 1864, Grant planned to take the fort through a joint naval/army expedition under Rear Adm. David Dixon Porter and Gen. Godfrey Weitzel. Although Grant did not want Butler to accompany the mission, noting his disastrous handling of the Army of the James the previous spring, Butler was apprised of Grant's plans because Weitzel's troops would be detailed from his department. Unknown to Grant, Butler assumed command of the mission and made one significant contribution to the planning of the expedition when he advanced the idea of exploding a powder vessel against the fort as a prelude to assault. Although Grant thought the idea ludicrous, Porter believed it was worth a try. Always eager to advance his image in the popular mind, Butler hoped the powder boat would cause the fort to fall immediately, earning him instant accolades. "If the experiment is successful there will be plenty to claim its paternity," Butler wrote Horace Greeley, in a shocking breach of security, but "the fact will be ascertained that I was its father."[6]

Grant believed Fort Fisher was extremely vulnerable since Gen. Braxton Bragg had taken troops from it to impede the progress of Sherman in Georgia. When the expedition left on December 13, Porter was surprised to discover that Butler accompanied it. After a number of delays due to both weather and confusion about where the army and navy would rendezvous, Porter prepared and fired the powder early in the morning of December 24. It did not have the desired effect. As one Confederate prisoner commented later, "It was dreadful. . . . It woke up everybody in the Fort Fisher!" Later that morning, Butler began landing troops to the northeast of the fort. Of the 6,500 men available for duty, Butler landed approximately 2,500 men, claiming that rough weather prevented landing the rest. While Porter's fleet kept up a steady bombardment of the work, Weitzel reconnoitered the fort and advised Butler not to attack. The fort was too strong, Weitzel believed, and the naval bombardment had failed to inflict substantial damage on enemy defenses. Grant had not ordered Weitzel to attack at all costs; if he found the fort too formidable, he was to entrench his troops, according to Grant's directive, and allow the navy "to effect the reduction and capture" of Fort Fisher. As Grant wrote in his memoirs after the war, "To effect a landing would be of itself a great victory, and if one should be effected, the foothold must not be relinquished." Without bothering to consult Porter, Butler ignored Grant's directive, telling Porter that a siege was not within the scope of his orders from Grant. He then reembarked his troops and sailed back to Hampton Roads, Virginia.[7]

"The aspects of Butler's military reputation are certainly not much improved by this bungle," commented a New York soldier who accompanied the expedition. A disappointed Porter told Welles, "Send me the same soldiers with another general and we will have success." And "I hold it to be a good rule," he told Grant, "never to send a boy on a man's errand." Even Samuel DuPont, increasingly hostile toward the navy and sympathetic to the radical viewpoint, was astonished by Butler's actions; the soldiers "were fully up to the work, and had they been led by a *general* our flag would have floated over Fort Fisher on Christmas evening." Newspaper coverage generally was unfavorable to Butler, undoubtedly prejudiced by the quick publication of Porter's report of the affair. Butler's supporters, however, including the *New York Daily Tribune,* quickly rallied to his defense.[8]

Butler's problems were far from over. Asked by the president to find out what had happened in Wilmington, Grant determined that Butler was to blame. Grant was tired of his incompetence and had the backing of Lincoln, who, with the election over, no longer feared Butler as a political enemy. Accordingly, Butler was relieved of command on January 8, 1865. "He is but one of a considerable list of civilians who have failed in this great war as generals," the *New York Herald* remarked. Neither Butler nor his supporters, however, were inclined to take his dismissal without a fight. Wading through War Department red tape, Butler finally had his report published in the *New York Daily Tribune,* which drew a portrait of operations vastly different from Porter's. Although Butler's failure to take Fort Fisher was not given as the official reason for his dismissal, Butler insisted that this was the reason, accusing Grant in a farewell speech to his troops of removing him because he would not "uselessly sacrifice" them. According to Laura Giddings Julian, the wife of George Julian, Butler's farewell speech touched the hearts of many people. That her husband's Committee on the Conduct of the War would rally on behalf of the general was virtually a foregone conclusion. Yet its support was quite ironic, for when McClellan had showed similar concern for the welfare of his troops, he was dismissed by the committee as a traitorous coward. Not so with Butler. "I wonder," wrote John Chipman Gray, a Massachusetts native stationed near Hilton Head Island, "if people will ever be convinced in Butler's case that impudence is not ability."[9]

On January 12, 1865, Massachusetts senator Henry Wilson introduced a resolution directing the committee to investigate the Fort Fisher affair. The next day Lincoln told Butler that he could visit Washington to answer the committee's summons. With good reason, Gideon Welles looked on such proceedings with intense suspicion. "As for the 'Committee on the Conduct of the War,' who have brought him here, they are most of them narrow and prejudiced partisans, mischievous busy-bodies, and a discredit to Congress. Mean and contemptible partisanship colors all their acts." The *New York Herald* remarked with sarcasm that Butler's testimony would "throw some light upon military operations which have not heretofore been properly understood." Zachariah Chandler set the tone of the investigation when he wrote his wife that Butler would appear before the committee: "I still believe in him."[10]

The same day Butler appeared before the committee, news of the fall of Fort Fisher was received in the capital. After relieving Butler from command, Grant had dispatched a force under Gen. Alfred Terry, who made short work of the Confederate garrison. To many observers, even supporters of Butler, this turn of events seemed to clinch the case against him. According to Salmon Chase, the unfortunate Butler was before the committee demonstrating the impossibility of taking the fort when the news of its fall was received. Diarist and political observer George Templeton Strong reported a slightly different account: "He uttered an ejaculation of delight but has been 'much chopfallen' ever since. Poor Butler!" Butler's critic, the *New York Herald,* issued a challenge: "But how can the friends of Butler answer this capture?" The answer was simple enough. Through the agency of the Committee on the Conduct of the War, Butler gained a forum to present *ex parte* testimony that absolved him from all responsibility for the Fort Fisher fiasco.[11]

Appearing before the committee on January 17, Butler presented a carefully crafted statement bolstered with a mass of official paperwork to give it an aura of objectivity. He offered three main contentions. First, the navy was entirely responsible for the failure of the expedition because it initially delayed departure and thereby allowed the rebels to reinforce the garrison. Moreover, Butler claimed that Porter launched the powder vessel before his troops were in position and that the navy's subsequent bombardment failed to damage the fort substantially, making an assault suicidal. Second, Grant's claim that he had not known that Butler would personally accompany the expedition was false; indeed, he had known it. According to Butler, General Weitzel was a professional soldier whose reputation might be permanently harmed if the expedition were to fail; therefore, Butler agreed to accompany the expedition and prepared, in selfless fashion, to shoulder the blame if disaster struck. Grant accepted his reasoning. The committee, however, seemed to overlook the fact that Butler's entire statement was an artful attempt to escape the censure he claimed he was so eager to bear for Weitzel. Third, Butler contended that his decision to reembark his troops and sail back to Virginia did not violate Grant's order to entrench and besiege the fortification. Since he could land only some 2,500 of his 6,000 troops, he claimed he was not able to effect a lodgment and therefore did not violate orders. With the exception of Moses Odell, who did question Butler intensely on arbitrary arrests of civilians in Virginia and North Carolina, none of the Republican congressmen challenged him, despite some serious flaws in his statement that subsequent witnesses pointed out.[12]

Ignoring the real reason for Butler's appearance before the committee, the *New York Daily Tribune* reported that his testimony had noted many flaws in Grant's army operations before Petersburg: "A profound impression was produced by his testimony, and at the conclusion of the examination summonses [*sic*] were issued to General Grant and other high officials of the Armies of the Potomac and James." Julian argued that Butler's and Grant's versions were contradictory and would require "a complete sifting of the whole affair." Chandler's comments to his wife reveal the type of sifting the committee would accomplish when he wrote her that Butler would "come out all right" when the investigation finished. "He is in earnest in all that he does," Chandler noted favorably, and "has done more to injure rebels & put down rebellion than any other man who has appeared before the stage since the breaking out of the rebellion." Though Butler had made contributions to the war effort, Chandler's statements reveal the committee's ideological approach to military operations. Butler had commanded no major armies; he had never successfully handled troops in the field. He had contributed to the war on slavery with his early contraband order in August 1861, and possibly his toughness on the civilian population of New Orleans played a role in discrediting conciliation. Yet to say that he had done more than anyone else to put down the rebellion demonstrated a less than balanced perspective on military affairs.[13]

Active in his own behalf, Butler attempted to stack the deck. When he received a letter from Weitzel expressing astonishment at his removal and a willingness to testify before the committee, Butler exploited the situation. Writing to Weitzel a few days later, Butler assured him that he would indeed be summoned and told him what to say. "In all this," he promised, "you will be aided by [Col. Cyrus] Comstock [Grant's aide-de-camp], who has given a written report in our favor." After he testified a few weeks later, Weitzel wrote to Butler, in complete disregard of the committee's secrecy provision: "I found the entire committee strongly in your favor. Mr. Sumner told me that Mr. Wade told him that my testimony [which supported Butler] 'was most excellent, most excellent.'"[14]

The testimony of the majority of the witnesses was not so clear-cut. Appearing before the committee on February 11, 1865, Grant said that Weitzel was in charge of the expedition and that Butler understood this. Weitzel's orders went through Butler, Grant admitted, but this was a mere courtesy due Butler as department commander. Grant's December 6, 1864, instructions to Butler began, "The first object of the expedition under Gn. Weitzel is to close the enemy port of Wilmington." It did not take a military genius to understand the intention of these words. The vast majority of witnesses agreed with Grant. "None of us had any idea that General Butler was going with this expedition," testified James Alden of the U.S. Navy, a statement corroborated by Porter and even the pro-Butler Weitzel. Nevertheless, committee members were skeptical. Julian noted that Grant had made his points with "a good deal of feeling," but at the same time he claimed Grant looked as if rumors of excessive drink were accurate, thereby calling into question the veracity of his statements.[15]

Butler's contention that he had not disobeyed orders by failing to entrench, putting Fort Fisher under siege, was also questionable. His principal argument was that rough weather prevented landing and supplying all his troops. Yet both Porter and Alden disputed this claim. Butler told the committee it was easier to land men than supplies, but Alden maintained the opposite, insisting that Butler had had plenty of time to supply troops already on the shore. Captain K. B. Breese maintained that Butler's entire force could have been landed and well supplied on December 24 despite some rough weather. If Butler could land 2,500 men and reembark them, common sense suggested that the majority of his 6,000 men could have been landed. As Grant's aide Comstock claimed, in the first of several statements against Butler, he did not land his entire force because Weitzel had already recommended against attacking Fort Fisher. However, this was a clear violation of orders. The issue was not Butler's failure to attack the fort; it was that he was to entrench and await reenforcements and assistance from the navy if attack proved unwise. Even Weitzel, whose testimony was favorable to Butler, conceded that point.[16]

Butler's contention that naval delays caused the failure is a charge that is not easy to prove or disprove with finality. It was true that communications between Butler and Porter were not the best, and they equally shared the blame for this. Still, a number of charges in the testimonies of Porter and Comstock did not create a favorable impression of Butler's military abilities. According to Comstock, Butler decided not to attack before he had received any definite information on the size of the garrison manning the fort. Comstock testified that its strength of 1,200 was enough to make it "an efficient garrison"; nevertheless, he believed that an attack should have been made. Porter added that Butler's contention that a division of Confederate troops under General Hoke had already reinforced the garrison was untrue, since the bulk of this division did not arrive until December 27, well after Butler had withdrawn. As he had done in every previous military operation, Butler failed to deliver and hid behind a barrage of excuses.[17]

When Benjamin Loan attempted to justify Butler's failure to attack Fort Fisher because he relied on the advice of Weitzel and Comstock, both West Point–educated engineers, the committee seemed to contradict the spirit of its previous methods. For three years, both in committee sessions and in the halls of Congress, its members had characterized a West Point education as defective, teaching a cowardly, defensive warfare. Wade had ridiculed McClellan in summer 1862 for digging and burrowing like a woodchuck, and Chandler had accused him of infernal cowardice when he attempted to explain the necessity of securing a line of retreat. Military science was routinely ridiculed in committee chambers; however, when Butler justified his lack of aggressiveness at Fort Fisher as consistent with the canons of military professionalism, committee members were willing to accept the soundness and logic of his position.[18]

That members of the committee might be upset with Butler's removal was understandable, yet the lengths to which they went to rehabilitate him were unjustified, given the testimony against him. Grant, after all, had the most successful record among Union commanders. Butler, though moderately successful as an administrator, was incompetent as a field commander. To call before them the general in chief of the Union armies, to subject him to rigorous criticism, to suggest that somehow this military amateur was right and Grant wrong was not in accordance with the testimony of the majority of witnesses. Even more in Grant's favor was the success of Alfred Terry in taking Fort Fisher. Yet with the exception of Odell, committee members were committed to Butler and apparently oblivious of Grant's ability to evaluate the performance of his subordinates. Had Butler really been wronged, the proper procedure would have been for him to prefer charges against his commander and await a trial by a military commission. But with most of the facts against him, this would have proved a particularly unproductive mode of inquiry. The committee's investigation simply afforded Butler a sympathetic forum to recover his tarnished reputation in the aftermath of a less than distinguished performance at Fort Fisher. When the committee released its report in late May, it declared that Butler was completely justified in not attacking the fort. Once again the committee missed the point since Butler had been censured for disobeying Grant's order to establish a beachhead.[19]

Efforts to restore Butler to a military position did not cease with the gathering of testimony. In late February Grant spoke of pressure on the president to appoint Butler as provost marshal of Charleston and South Carolina. Writing to Edwin Stanton, Grant advised against it on the grounds of Butler's critical remarks about the administration in recent public speeches. Thus thwarted, Butler and his supporters began to lobby for a cabinet position. It was only natural that he turn to his allies on the committee, still interested in purging conservatives such as William Seward from the president's counsel. Butler wrote Wade that a little pressure on the president would get him into the cabinet, and then the radicals would have a true representative. To Daniel W. Gooch, Butler wrote, "If I can rely on your friendship to take an active part in this movement, you will confer an obligation which will not be forgotten." But the president held firm, and Butler was again frustrated.[20]

As with so many committee activities, it is difficult to see any positive contribution that the investigation made to the Union war effort. In defending the CCW, historians have usually emphasized its ability to prod cautious West Point professionals into action. In this case, however, the roles were reversed; the committee defended Butler for his caution while by implication it criticized Grant and Porter for recommending an assault. Keeping Butler in a command would not have hampered the Union war effort in any significant way by early 1865, yet it was hardly worth the time and effort of a full-scale investigation.[21]

Fort Fisher was not the last word from the committee. In the final days of the war and after its conclusion, the CCW confronted the North's other principal military leader, William Tecumseh Sherman. During the month of March, Republican members of the committee remained in Washington taking testimony and tying up the loose ends of their investigations. A trip to Wilmington and Charleston was discussed for the purpose of gathering additional testimony on the Fort Fisher affair. Committee members originally planned to leave on March 30, but the trip was delayed until April 10; then Julian, Wade, Gooch, and Chandler boarded a steamer and headed

South, intending to visit the recently fallen Richmond before heading to Charleston. Arriving at Fortress Monroe April 11 at 6:00 A.M., the congressmen reached Richmond later that evening. "You can't *imagine* how I feel in beginning a letter to you from this place," Julian wrote his wife. The novelty soon wore off when the next day the congressmen read in the local Richmond newspapers of an order from General Weitzel, then commanding Union forces in the city, calling a meeting of the rebel Virginia legislature for the purpose of withdrawing Virginia's support for the rebellion. Lincoln had instructed Weitzel to do so, despite the objection of cabinet members, but had later withdrawn the instructions because he feared they would be misinterpreted to signify recognition of rebel state governments. "We were thunderstruck," Julian recalled, "and I never before saw such force and fitness in Ben Wade's swearing. Curses loud and deep were uttered by more than one at this infamous proposition to treat with the leading rebels." Wade and Chandler refused to continue South, and the party returned to Washington, arriving in the aftermath of the president's assassination.[22]

Doubts About Andrew Johnson

"I am now more than rejoiced that we did not go down to Charleston," Julian wrote shortly after the assassination; "the conservatives of the country are not here, and the presence and influence of the War committee with Johnson, who is an ex-member, will powerfully aid the new administration in getting on the right foot." Despite recent signs that Lincoln was moving toward their position on reconstruction, many radical Republicans, familiar with Johnson's tough rhetoric against the rebellion, regarded him as an improvement. As much as she admired Lincoln, abolitionist Lydia Maria Child viewed his assassination as a "manifestation of Providence. The kind-hearted Abraham, was certainly in danger of making too easy terms with the rebels." Henry Ward Beecher was quoted as saying "that Johnson's little finger was stronger than Lincoln's loins." Chief Justice Salmon Chase was impressed with the new president after a brief meeting on April 18: "He seems thoroughly in earnest & much of the same mind as myself." The committee's Republican majority shared this sentiment, regarding Johnson's succession to the presidency as a godsend. "In many ways this Administration will be a great improvement on the last," Julian told his wife. The Almighty kept Lincoln in office as long as he was useful, Chandler told his wife, but now he had put a better man in office "to finish the job." Wade told one Ohio Republican that he was "highly pleased with our new President and have no doubt that he will prove highly satisfactory to all."[23]

The committee regarded the past administration as hampered by a waffling, conservative cabinet; hence, its first task was to make certain that the new president was surrounded by the right men who would ensure that his threats to punish traitors would be carried out. On April 15 the committee met and requested an interview with Johnson for the next day. Then a small group of Republicans, including Wade, Chandler, Julian, former committee member John Covode, and *New York Daily Tribune* reporter Sam Wilkeson, met to decide on cabinet recommendations. As Julian recalled, the tenor of this caucus was hostile toward the former administration. One of the principal candidates the group promoted was Benjamin Butler. Various other names were discussed, including Charles Sumner, George Boutwell, and John Covode. When the committee called on Johnson the next day, the meeting appeared to go according to script. "Johnson, we have faith in you," Wade told him, "by the Gods, there will be no trouble now in running the government." Johnson responded with a short, succinct summary of his own views. "Treason," he declared, "must be made infamous and traitors must be impoverished." Reporting the results of this meeting, Julian's organ, the Indiana *True Republican* confidently predicted, "Let no loyal man have any fears as to the new Administration."[24]

Nevertheless, there were some lagging doubts in the minds of committee members. As they later discovered, fundamental differences existed between their position and Johnson's. He turned out to be a strict constructionist of the Jacksonian persuasion; his reconstruction policy ultimately proved much more conciliatory than any measures Lincoln had ever envisioned; and he proved to be more negrophobic, committed to the abolition of slavery but offering little in the way of black civil rights. As a former Democrat, Johnson's attachment to the Republican party was tenuous at best. The chasm was as yet unknown to committee members, and as Johnson disguised his uncertainty on reconstruction with harsh rhetoric about punishing the leading rebel conspirators. Still, there were doubts whether Johnson was moving in the right direction in forming a new cabinet. Seward remained in office, and Butler was not appointed. The hated Blairs were suspected of having a little too much influence with the new president. "The truth is," Wade wrote one Ohio Republican, "if Johnson will surround himself with able, bold, earnest and resolute spirits like himself . . . he will give us the best, most popular and magnificent Administration that this nation has ever had." But Republicans wondered if he would appoint the right people. As Henry Winter Davis asked

Wade, was Johnson going back to "the old policy of drifting?" The committee needed an issue to invigorate public sentiment and to keep the pressure on Johnson. The abortive peace arrangements of William Tecumseh Sherman appeared to be their salvation.[25]

The Sherman-Johnston Peace Agreement

"War is cruelty and you cannot refine it," Sherman told city officials when he ordered that civilians evacuate Atlanta in fall 1864. In many ways, Sherman seemed an unlikely target for a committee investigation. His style of warfare was tough, his rhetoric aggressive, and his methods calculated to inflict psychological terror on southern civilians in order to break their will to fight. By destroying any element in the South that could conceivably support Confederate armies, Sherman hoped that the civilian population would be demoralized, convinced of the utter inability of the Confederate government to protect them. According to John Marszalek, Sherman was "using the terror of destruction to convince the Southern people to give up." And the northern public overwhelmingly approved.[26]

But there was another side to Sherman. He did not share the outlook of many Republicans in Congress and resisted several of their measures, such as the Emancipation Proclamation and the Second Confiscation Act. His outlook on race was not in step with the party's members on the committee, and he had been opposed to the use of black soldiers. In January 1865 the Senate had passed a resolution directing the committee to investigate his treatment of former slaves, prompted by an incident near Savannah, when Union general Jefferson C. Davis had prevented blacks from crossing a small creek in Georgia, thus leaving them to fall into the hands of pursuing rebel cavalry.

Moreover, Sherman's initial philosophy of war was based on a conciliatory approach. A resident of Louisiana just before the outbreak of sectional hostilities, Sherman presided over a military academy near Alexandria. He was loath to break old friendships and fight his former neighbors. To his eldest daughter Minnie, he complained how difficult it was to hate the people who had been his "kind good friends. . . . We must fight and subdue those in arms against us and our government," he advised, "but we mean them no harm." Though Sherman came to adopt a harsh view of war, his attitude toward peace remained conciliatory. Since he did not see the conflict as a struggle for black freedom and civil rights, his reconstruction philosophy remained lenient; its basic goal was the restoration of the Union—much like the views of Andrew Johnson. "Sherman was consistent in his position,"

Marszalek writes; "he had regularly said throughout the war that once South-erners stopped fighting and admitted their mistake, the conflict could end, and they could return to the Union with no questions asked." By using this conciliatory approach and involving himself in political matters in his nego-tiations with Joseph E. Johnston, Sherman unwittingly played into the committee's hands.[27]

On the afternoon of April 21, 1865, Ulysses S. Grant received from Wil-liam Tecumseh Sherman in Raleigh, North Carolina, a proposed peace con-cord he had negotiated with Joseph Johnston, commander of the last major Confederate army east of the Mississippi since Lee's surrender on April 9. Grant became understandably uneasy, for Sherman's proposal went far be-yond Grant's own peace agreement with Robert E. Lee, despite Sherman's previous assurance to the secretary of war that he would offer precisely the same terms. Lincoln had instructed Grant on March 3, 1865, to avoid any arrangements regarding civil government; however, Sherman, unaware of Lincoln's wishes and ignoring his promise to Stanton, recognized existing rebel state governments, with specific guarantees for the protection of prop-erty and political rights to the residents of these states, and mentioned noth-ing on the status of slavery. Conveying this information to Stanton, Grant urged that the cabinet meet that evening to consider whether to accept the agreement.[28]

The bearded, bespectacled secretary of war was genuinely upset when he read Sherman's agreement, rereading it several times as he paced the floor of his War Department office. Nervous with anger and excitement, he could hardly contain his rage. Meeting at 8:00 P.M., the president and the cabinet agreed to reject Sherman's agreement. Stanton then ordered Grant to go to North Carolina and personally direct Sherman to "resume hostilities at the earliest possible moment." The next morning, he revealed some of his frus-trations to Orville Browning, the former Republican senator from Illinois who became secretary of the interior. Stanton declared that Sherman's agree-ment "gave up all for which we had been fighting, and threw away all the advantages we had gained from the war."[29]

Grant arrived at Sherman's headquarters, and the situation was quickly remedied. Although Sherman was surprised to see the general in chief, he was not shocked that his agreement was rejected. Joseph Johnston was quickly informed, and a new surrender was negotiated that was identical to Grant's. Sherman also sent a letter to Stanton explaining his behavior: "I admit my folly in embracing in a Military convention any civil matters." He believed, however, as the military and political aspects were "inextricably united," it was impossible not to address civil matters. When Stanton had earlier visited Sherman in Savannah, Sherman understood that he had had approval to discuss such matters. When he read of Weitzel's action with respect to the rebel legislature of Virginia, he drew the same conclusion. Although he thought the government was making a mistake, he followed the wishes of the president. When he wrote the letter to Stanton, Sherman assumed the episode was closed. He was mistaken.[30]

Before he had even received Sherman's reply, Stanton embarked on a questionable course of action. Instead of privately overruling the accord, he planted a copy of it in the April 24, 1865, edition of the *New York Times,* along with his own point-by-point refutation. Some of the objections were valid and sensible. The establishment of rebel governments granted them an undue legitimacy and suggested that the federal government might be liable for debts contracted under the Confederacy. Since the agreement made no reference to slavery, its restoration by the newly recognized governments was a natural concern. The wording of some of Stanton's objections, however, questioned not only Sherman's prudence but also his loyalty. Moreover, the *New York Times* claimed that Sherman withdrew troops from the vicinity of Salisbury, North Carolina, to allow Jefferson Davis, in flight from Richmond, to escape well supplied with gold from the Richmond treasury. Adding further insult, Henry Halleck, recently removed from his position as chief of staff and given command of the Department of the James, issued orders instructing Sherman's own subordinate commanders to disregard their superior's instructions in order to capture the Confederate president.[31]

Public reaction, already embittered by the assassination of Lincoln, was quick and violent in denunciation of Sherman. According to the *New York Times,* the agreement would revive the theory of states' rights and provide a foundation for acts of secession in the future. "Grievous and incomprehensible," the *Chicago Tribune* described the agreement. The *Ashtabula Sentinel,* located in Wade's home county, claimed Sherman had devoted himself to politics at this dangerous hour: "Let the nation mark the man who thus trifles with its destinies." The *New York Herald* wrote, "General Sherman has spoiled a great name by a great blunder." Lydia Maria Child, writing to a friend, admitted, "You will perhaps think it strange when I tell you that the news of Gen. Sherman's negotiations excited me more than the President's death. I had always feared that he had pro-slavery proclivities." Reaction among committee members still in the capital was predictable. "Universal surprise and indignation prevail here as to Sherman's shameful capitulation," Julian noted. "Sherman's disgraceful surrender is universally & bitterly condemned," Chandler wrote his wife. "Yet I cannot believe he did it without consultation."[32]

Why Edwin Stanton pursued the course that he did is not entirely clear. He was an enigmatic figure. The former attorney general of the Buchanan administration had enjoyed the confidence of the Committee on the Conduct of the War from the beginning of his tenure as secretary of war, yet he also retained the confidence of President Lincoln and numerous other generals not in sympathy with committee goals. Sherman's brother, Sen. John Sherman, was convinced that Stanton simply had acted out of the passion of the moment and not from malice. The secretary had recently submitted his own plan of reconstruction to the cabinet, which emphasized the role of the federal government in supervising Confederate states in a transitional phase. Since Sherman's plan contradicted his plan, perhaps it sparked Stanton's anger. Earlier in the year Stanton had come under attack in some quarters for accepting Lincoln's reconstruction plans too uncritically. There were even rumors that Ben Butler might replace him at the War Department. In publicizing the Sherman-Johnston agreement, Stanton might have made a calculated move to regain radical sympathies.[33]

Although committee members had not collaborated with Stanton, they were impressed with the outpouring of public sentiment generated by the course he had taken. Chandler noted that President Johnson shared his outrage on the issue. According to Chandler, the president "took hold of the matter & condemned it worse than I did." A committee investigation of the circumstances surrounding the agreement might prove fruitful. It might force the president to accept the committee's recommendations for cabinet members, and it could provide a partisan tool to guarantee a tough reconstruction program. The columns of Julian's newspaper provide a sampling of the type of partisan attacks aimed at Sherman: "His wife is Catholic, and his natural leaning toward aristocracy has thus probably been strengthened by the peculiar atmosphere created by hierarchic ideas, chiming in with the charms in his Louisiana home." Accordingly, at its May 6, 1865, meeting, the committee decided to investigate the matter, summoning Sherman, Grant, and Weitzel to appear before them.[34]

In choosing to focus on Sherman, however, the committee erred, since public opinion would not sustain a harsh rebuke of a war hero, especially when he was able to present his side to the public, ably assisted by his brother, Sen. John Sherman, and the family of his powerful stepfather, Thomas Ewing. Enraged when he found out that Stanton had used the newspapers to malign him, Sherman denounced him to family members in vituperative terms: "[Stanton and Halleck] *suppressed* everything, save parts that by context with matters I never saw made a plausible case, but when I make my official report of the whole you will appreciate the game they have attempted."

Sherman's principal point was that he had never seen Lincoln's March 3, 1865, directive, forbidding army generals from discussing civil matters. Further, in late March Sherman had gone to City Point, Virginia, where he conversed with the president, Grant, and David Porter. According to Sherman, Lincoln endorsed easy, conciliatory terms of surrender, never suggesting that army officers avoid discussions of civil matters. Sherman's position was further bolstered when he read about Lincoln's order to call Virginia's rebel legislature into session. Moreover, Sherman maintained that his whole course of action was designed to accomplish a general surrender and to prevent rebel armies from breaking into small, destructive guerrilla bands.[35]

Sherman's popularity among his soldiers never wavered; one commented, "[Washington leaders] had better look a leedle [*sic*] out or they will have General Shermans [*sic*] Army to reckon with the first thing they know." As Sherman's explanations began to appear in newspapers across the country and as he talked to a number of leading political figures, he began to regain his popularity among the general public. "I'm sure I have mistaken Sherman," Salmon Chase told his son-in-law, William Sprague, who met with the general at Morehead City, North Carolina, on a trip to the South. Sherman had no instructions "except what Prest. Lincoln said abt. Davis & did abt Va Legislature—order March 3d to Grant never commd to him/ very wrong to publish his project of Convention." The *New York Daily Tribune* admitted that as the circumstances were revealed, Sherman's point of view became more plausible. Remarkably, a letter writer for the Indiana *True Republican* claimed that "opinion [in Washington] seems rapidly growing that Gen. Sherman has a substantial defence in the authority and instructions of President Lincoln, given in their last interview at City Point." John Sherman assured his brother that he had already regained his popularity. Though John believed his brother had erred on the side of leniency, he also condemned Stanton's methods:

> For a time, you lost all the popularity gained by your achievements. But now the reaction has commenced, and you find some defenders, but many were to denounce the base and malicious conduct of a gang of envious scamps, who seized upon this matter as a pretext for calumny.

By the time Sherman's army was in Washington for the grand review in late May, one of his soldiers commented, "Sherman's policy is being ably defended by himself. Opposition is fast dying out before public opinion."[36]

This turn of events presented the committee with a problem. Instead of using their investigation to brand Sherman as a Copperhead and to launch Johnson into a radical reconstruction program, they found themselves forced

William Tecumseh Sherman's popularity insulated him from the committee's disfavor at the end of the war. (Courtesy of the National Archives)

to protect Stanton. According to an associate of Ben Butler, who had it on the authority of Wade and Chandler, Stanton was about to resign and Sherman intended to retaliate when he arrived in Washington. Weitzel, Meade, and Grant appeared before the committee, the latter two testifying to Stanton's competence in running the War Department, but Sherman did not answer the committee's summons. As it turned out, he was not defying the CCW; he simply had not received the summons since he was out of telegraphic communication with Washington for some period of time. Meanwhile, public opinion for Sherman and against Stanton continued. Newspapers reported that when Sherman's army arrived in Washington there would be demonstrations by its rank and file demanding Stanton's removal. It was in this context that Sherman appeared before the committee on the morning of May 22, 1865.[37]

When Sherman met the committee, consisting of Wade and Loan, he made little effort to hide his anger at both Stanton and Halleck for their treatment of him. "I did feel indignant—I do feel indignant," he said, describing his attitude toward Henry Halleck. With few interruptions, the committee allowed Sherman a free forum to present his case. After describing the circumstances that led to negotiations with Johnston, Sherman explained why he had made that specific agreement. With respect to slavery, both Johnston and Breckinridge acknowledged that it was dead; thus there was no need to include it in the concord. Since as early as 1863 Lincoln had encouraged him to discuss civil matters, Sherman assumed that he was free to do so in the agreement with Johnston. When Wade challenged this assumption, Sherman told him, "On the contrary, while I was in Georgia, Mr. Lincoln telegraphed to me, encouraging me to discuss matters with Governor Brown and Mr. [Alexander] Stephens." Sherman pointed out that Stanton also had approved such a course earlier when he met with Sherman in Savannah. Moreover, his interview with Lincoln at City Point and Weitzel's action with respect to the rebel legislature of Virginia suggested to him that he was acting according to Lincoln's instructions. Stanton's and Halleck's orders, which had undercut his authority and directed his subordinates to disobey him, Sherman described as "an act of perfidy," telling the congressmen that their actions were a violation of his truce "and which by the laws of war and by the laws of Congress is punishable by death, and no other punishment."[38]

If the committee wanted to make political capital by portraying Sherman as the newest Copperhead leader, their session with him was a singular failure. Sherman's defiant attitude and his recovered popularity possibly tamed the usually feisty congressmen. Wade's and Loan's questions only touched the surface of the issue. Although Sherman surely acted in good faith, much of his reasoning was dubious. He had written to Grant on April 18 that Johnston and Breckinridge agreed that slavery was a dead issue; however, not to include it in an important agreement could easily have led to confusion. As a skilled lawyer, Stanton understood this and was afraid that Breckinridge and John Reagan, the Confederate postmaster general also present at the negotiations, had outfoxed Sherman. And Sherman claimed correctly that he had not seen the March 3, 1865, order forbidding soldiers to discuss civil matters; however, Halleck had written him on April 10 and suggested that he give Johnston the same terms as Grant had given Lee. Following Halleck's suggestion, Sherman had told the War Department that he intended to follow this course; nevertheless, his agreement went far beyond Grant's provisions. The committee could have made a number of other points to challenge Sherman; thus its mild approach suggests an unwillingness to defame the popular general. In this last battle, West Point triumphed over its skeptical civilian antagonists.[39]

Fully vindicated but still angry with Stanton, Sherman took a measure of revenge just a few days later in the grand review of federal armies in Washington. Stanton was seated with other dignitaries, including the president, cabinet members, and military leaders in specially constructed covered seating near the White House. Ascending the platform, Sherman shook hands with Johnson, Grant, and every member of the cabinet except Stanton. When the latter offered his hand, Sherman refused to take it, thereby delivering a public rebuke and avenging his honor. Indirectly, Sherman had also rebuked the committee, for it had tried to exploit Stanton's actions for its own partisan gain and had failed miserably in the attempt.[40]

On the same day they interviewed Sherman, the Committee on the Conduct of the War adjourned *sine die*. Their massive volumes of reports published shortly thereafter attracted some newspaper attention but much less than the reports of spring 1863 had. The war was over, and the public was less interested in rehashing past military disasters and assigning blame. The committee's failure to make a case for radical reconstruction from the Sherman-Johnston peace agreement symbolized their larger failure to control Andrew Johnson's reconstruction policy. Just days after the committee's adjournment, Johnson outlined a presidential plan of reconstruction in two executive proclamations. In a statement of amnesty, the president pardoned all rebels and protected their property, slavery excluded; however, he also specified fourteen classes of persons exempted from this pardon, including high-ranking military officers, civilian politicians, and wealthy landowners. In a second statement, the North Carolina Proclamation, Johnson formulated the steps by which a state might assume its rightful place in the Union. Although it provided for a provisional governor who would organize a constitutional convention to guarantee a republican government, only the people who were eligible to vote in 1860 would participate. Thus there would be no black participation. From the viewpoint of the committee's Republican majority, their former colleague had derailed their reconstruction program.[41]

After Loan read the North Carolina Proclamation, he sent a letter to Charles Sumner: "The policy indicated in that proclamation is in direct opposition to the views of the radical Union party as I understand them." Since Johnson's proclamations indicated inflexibility, Loan suggested that radicals in Congress devise a strategy of opposition. Endorsing black suffrage and disenfranchisement of rebels, Loan told Sumner that he hated to take issue with the executive, "yet I confess I should deem it much more disastrous to the country for us to abandon our principles and concur in the erroneous policy of the Executive for the sake of harmony." Sumner in turn sent several letters to Wade, denouncing the proclamation: "The President seems to have made an effort to be wrong." And he wanted Wade's opinion: "What can be done? Let me know your views." Wade responded several weeks later that Johnson had carried his policy of conciliation too far. The eulogies for Lincoln had seduced Johnson into believing that his predecessor had become popular with a weak, "non-committal, hesitating policy, shilly-shally policy." Congress, Wade assured Sumner, was the nation's only hope.

Yet it would be a Congress deprived of one of its most useful tools of executive harassment, the Committee on the Conduct of the War. Nevertheless, armed with this recent, powerful precedent, Congress was ready and able to use an investigative committee as a weapon to advance legislative interests against an unwilling executive. The powerful and controversial Joint Committee on Reconstruction promoted the viewpoint of congressional Republicans during the remainder of Johnson's administration.[42]

EPILOGUE

In the aftermath of the Civil War, many members of the Committee on the Conduct of the War continued to play active roles in national politics. Given the wealth of experience they had gained on the committee, it is somewhat surprising that none was selected for membership on the powerful Joint Committee on Reconstruction. Appointed by Congress in December 1865 to investigate the South and to consider appropriate reconstruction measures, this committee undoubtedly developed many of its strategies from the precedents established by the CCW.[1]

Democrat Moses Odell, suffering from heart disease, died in June 1866. *Harper's Weekly* praised his patriotism and the diligence with which he fulfilled his committee work. His fellow Democrat on the committee, Joseph A. Wright, appointed by Andrew Johnson as minister to Prussia, died at his post in Berlin. Former member John Covode returned to Congress in 1866 and served two successive terms. He supported radical reconstruction and became a bitter opponent of his former committee colleague, Andrew Johnson. Covode died of a heat attack in 1871. Daniel W. Gooch resigned from Congress in September 1865 to become naval agent for the Port of Boston. Removed from this position by the Johnson administration in 1866, Gooch became a pension agent and resumed his law practice. Reelected to Congress in 1872, he was unable to defeat Nathaniel Banks (who ran as a labor candidate) for Congress in 1874, despite support from the Grant administration. Gooch died in Melrose, Massachusetts, in 1891. Benjamin Loan remained in Congress until 1869. Turning down two diplomatic appointments offered by President Grant, he returned to St. Joseph, Missouri, to resume his law practice. He died in 1881.[2]

Andrew Johnson's postwar career is well known, and little needs to be said except that he alienated most of his committee colleagues. After he narrowly escaped impeachment in 1868, Johnson's political career seemed finished. He made a couple of unsuccessful attempts at elective office in Tennessee, but in 1875 he was elected by its legislature to the U.S. Senate. Johnson, however, was barely able to enjoy this reversal of fortunes; he suffered a stroke and died on July 31, 1875.[3]

The postwar career of George Julian is interesting. Reelected in 1866 and again in 1868, Julian continued to be a forceful advocate of black suffrage, women's rights, labor reform, and homestead legislation. Regarding Andrew Johnson as "a traitor to the cause," Julian vigorously endorsed impeachment in 1868, hoping to serve as one of the House managers for the trial (a wish that went unfulfilled). Defeated for reelection in 1870, he became increasingly disgusted with corruption in the Grant administration and joined the liberal Republicans in 1872, despite their advocacy of ending Reconstruction in the South. Ironically, in 1876 Julian moved into the Democratic party, stressing such issues as labor reform, hard currency, and free trade. Although he never held elective office after 1870, he took an active role in the campaigns of the liberal Republicans in 1872 and in a number of subsequent Democratic campaigns. Julian died in 1899, a bitter foe of imperialism who opposed the annexation of the Philippines.[4]

Zachariah Chandler remained in the Senate until 1877. Like many of his Republican colleagues, he was an opponent of Andrew Johnson and denounced fellow Republicans who did not vote to convict the president at his impeachment trial. "The country will damn them for eternal time," Chandler predicted. Chandler also denounced the liberal Republicans, scorning their conciliatory attitude toward the South. Although he continued to endorse harsh measures against the South, Chandler's commitment to other reforms, particularly black civil rights, waned in the postwar years. He became a staunch defender of Grant and a party stalwart. Supreme in Michigan politics for twenty years, Chandler created a host of political enemies. In 1875 they united and replaced him in the Senate with Isaac Christiancy, a state supreme court justice. Yet the politically astute Chandler, after serving briefly as secretary of the interior, was able to manipulate the state legislature a few years later when Christiancy resigned and returned to the Senate in 1879. He died that fall on the campaign trail, stumping for Republican candidates. On his coffin was a large floral arrangement with the word Stalwart.[5]

After the war, it looked as if Benjamin Wade would achieve greater prominence than he had as chairman of the Committee on the Conduct of the War. Hesitant to break with Johnson, Wade finally did so after numerous attempts at compromise. As Johnson's impeachment loomed, Wade, as president pro tempore of the Senate, would have become president. But his consistent commitment to such radical principles as black rights, labor reform, and woman suffrage alienated conservative elements of the Republican party. Johnson was eventually acquitted in the impeachment trial in part because moderate Republicans feared a Wade presidency. Wade's radicalism also cost him reelection to the Senate in 1868, when the Ohio Republican party at his insistence included a provision for black suffrage in its platform. Although he served on a commission to examine the proposed treaty of annexation of Santo Domingo, Wade never again ran for elective office. Serving as a corporate lawyer for Jay Cooke's Northern Pacific Railroad, he died of typhoid fever in Washington in March 1877.[6]

Writing to fellow Ohio Republican Milton Sutliffe in early 1867, Wade claimed that his political course had been dominated by one principle, "the equality of all men before the law, without regard to race, color, or nationality and I can say before God and man, during all that period, I have never uttered a sentiment, or given a vote that I did not believe perfectly consistent with the attainment of these principles." In a sense, Wade's declaration summarized the attitude committee members had with respect to many of their investigations. They were driven by principle, and their investigations were actuated by the patriotic desire to win the war and to establish a lasting peace. They viewed the North as a dynamic society in which talent and hard work paid. Slavery, the institution central to the South's economy, represented the antithesis to northern free labor. For Republican committee members, the war was not primarily a struggle to restore the Union but to purge the nation of the institution of slavery and the aristocratic society of the South. Their work as committee members, as evidenced by Wade's remarks, was not simply a cover for base motives but a well-intended effort to direct the nation's war goals. Democratic members of the committee shared many of these values; they, too, were self-made men who believed in the dignity of hard work and upward mobility. Although they did not share all the war goals of their Republican colleagues, believing that slavery in the South was not incompatible with a free labor North, their commitment to the integrity of the Union prompted them to cooperate with their Republican colleagues on a variety of investigations.[7]

To the committee's credit, a number of its investigations exposed corruption, financial mismanagement, and crimes against humanity. The committee deserves praise not only for exposing these abuses but also for using such disclosures to invigorate northern public opinion and bolster the resolve to continue the war. Had the committee's work always been modeled on these investigations, there would be little debate about its positive, albeit minor, contribution to the Union war effort.

Good intentions, however, do not always bring about good results, and the committee's work often had questionable or negative consequences. A number of investigations were simply a waste of time, energy, and resources. In today's parlance, they amounted to Monday morning quarterbacking and made no significant contribution to Union military fortunes. Because the members lacked an adequate background in military matters, undoubtedly much of the technical importance of testimony was lost on them. The CCW uncovered problems in examining First Bull Run, Ball's Bluff, the Peninsula campaign, the Red River expedition, and the attempt to take Fort Fisher. Yet it never offered any practical advice on how to avoid the repetition of such mistakes. In some of its hearings, truth was not even the goal since witnesses were stacked to represent a position predetermined by the Republican members. The examinations of Frémont's affairs in Missouri and the Crater disaster provide good examples of the committee's investigative tactics. In both cases partisan goals sometimes preempted concerns over objectivity. If the committee's work had been only an innocuous distraction, it would have drawn much less criticism.

Unfortunately, some committee activities were more than distractions and had a real impact on the war. Although it is easy to exaggerate the CCW's power over military matters, it did exert influence in a variety of situations that often had an adverse effect on military fortunes. First, committee investigations caused relations to deteriorate between army officers and civilian leaders. It helped create factionalism and jealousies among elite officers, many of whom were well aware that committee forums offered subordinates a convenient way of self-promotion at the expense of superiors. The committee's demands for forward movement may have forced cautious officers such as McClellan to act more aggressively; on the other hand, such insistence may have also contributed to foolish, premature maneuvers by other officers. Burnside's attack on Marye's Heights was undoubtedly undertaken to satisfy popular pressure for action, and the committee was a contributing factor. It was simply one more interest or faction that had to be appeased— and it was a powerful interest that President Lincoln could not simply ignore. Its investigations also forced many officers to become preoccupied with defending past actions instead of focusing on the war itself.

I have written this book on the assumption that a united society is more capable of successfully waging war than a divided one. This assumption was challenged in 1967 in an essay by Eric McKitrick, who maintained that the Confederacy suffered because it lacked organized political parties but that political competition in the North played a useful, if not a beneficial, role. Because southerners had no political parties, opposition to the Davis administration often took the form of states' rights. According to McKitrick, the competition between state and federal power was detrimental to the southern war effort. In the North, conversely, organized political parties prevented the Democrats from standing on the foundation of states' rights. Moreover, partisan politics meant that the war effort was scrutinized intensely, forcing political leaders to act judiciously.[8]

McKitrick's essay has merit. Assuming that there will be some form of political opposition during war, channeling such opposition into organized political parties offers a better solution than the disarray that ultimately transpired in the Confederacy. Yet the contention that the northern war effort was bolstered by bickering between Democrats and Republicans seems less defensible. By painting the Democratic party as a disloyal opposition, Republicans surely contributed to antiwar attitudes that characterized some Democrats. Dramatic and disruptive events such as the New York City draft riots of 1863 and the Boston draft riot of 1864 were fueled by Democratic war weariness and opposition to Republican war goals. In a sense, the riots were the ultimate expression of partisanship because they revealed an absolute antithesis between Republican and Democratic visions of war and society. Thus in my view such events can be seen only as major obstacles to waging war.[9]

If one assumes then the proposition that a united society is better-suited to wage war than one fraught with divisions, the committee had a negative impact on the war effort by exacerbating partisan divisions. Clearly it would be unfair to blame these divisions solely on the committee because many of them were the inevitable result of the Republicans' determination that the war would end slavery. Nevertheless, the zest with which the committee pursued some Democratic generals, its preoccupation with the loyalty of members of the political opposition, and its criteria for evaluating military fitness did much to undermine political consensus during the war. George McClellan probably needed to be prodded, but it was nonproductive to question his loyalty on dubious evidence. Nor was it an intelligent maneuver to attack him publicly before the Senate, as Zachariah Chandler did in summer 1862, or publicly to portray George Meade as a general who did not want to hurt the enemy. Instead of sowing the seeds of unity the committee often planted suspicion and discord.

The committee's work also contributed to the unhealthy practice of basing military appointments on political considerations. The committee of course can hardly be saddled with initiating this practice; President Lincoln himself made a number of ill-advised appointments based primarily on political considerations. Yet the committee's power to publish reports and its good relationship with the secretary of war gave it considerable influence in certain circumstances. Its sponsorship of Frémont and Butler was probably the most egregious example of such influence, but these were not the only cases. The continued devotion to Joseph Hooker, in the face of overwhelming evidence suggesting his unfitness for top command, is another instance of serious misjudgment by the committee. Fortunately, the North was spared the full impact of its perspective because President Lincoln was usually a better judge of military potential and prevented the committee's wishes from being fulfilled in every instance. In cases where its maneuvering forced Lincoln's hand, as in Frémont's appointment to the Mountain Department, the results speak for themselves.[10]

Much of the CCW's negative impact can be traced to its origins. As Leonard Curry observes, Republicans in Congress were leery of too much executive power; therefore, in creating the committee they adopted a resolution that was vague and elastic: "It was doubtless this very aspect [vagueness] that endeared the scheme to many Senators." The committee was authorized to examine any aspect of military affairs, past, present, or future. In terms of precedent, the latitude granted the CCW was striking. Although members of Congress could, and frequently did, propose resolutions to direct its investigations, much of its work was not guided by Congress. The vague resolution allowed the committee to probe into areas that might have been examined more productively after the war concluded. Its persistent investigations of the operations of the Army of the Potomac exploited this latitude, which permitted the committee to use the cover of a military investigation to pursue blatantly political and partisan ends.[11]

Congress could have constituted a joint investigative committee that might have better served the North. Two qualifications might have improved its role as watchdog of Union military affairs. First, the committee's scope of investigations should have been rigorously limited to the specific directions of members of Congress, both houses concurring. Second, members of the committee should have been chosen on the basis of military knowledge and expertise. Lacking the seniority system that we have today, such choices could have been much easier to achieve in the nineteenth century. Had its members been more familiar with military affairs, perhaps the sort of simplistic conclusions they often drew could have been avoided. The temptation to assign all military failures to the ideological viewpoint of the nation's principal generals might have been lessened, and as a result, committee members might have been more restrained and moderate in their attempt to control executive decisions. Instead of trying constantly to supplant the nation's military leadership, the committee could have focused on investigations calculated to support and improve the nation's military administration.

Making such changes in the Committee on the Conduct of the War would have been no guarantee that it would have acted more responsibly. First, the pool of congressmen who had legitimate military expertise in 1860 would have been far less than it is in today's Congress. Second, even if the members of such a committee had been chosen on the basis of military knowledge, the temptation to use congressional committees to advance the welfare of the majority party would still have obtained. Third, narrowly focusing the investigative scope of a committee is not a magical formula to produce disinterested, objective results. Twentieth-century examples suggest that the work of congressional committees is mixed. Much depends on the character of the members, their temperament, values, and habits. The members of the Committee on the Conduct of the War were aggressive and hardworking. Ignorant of military affairs, practical and self-made men, they refused to believe that their ignorance of military matters was a liability. Passionately committed to action, they refused to defer to the experts. Wedded to the ideological goals of the Republican party, they assumed the high moral standards of their cause justified their activities. Unfortunately, they were often mistaken.

NOTES

Introduction

1. Stephen E. Ambrose, *Nixon*, vol. 3, *Ruin and Recovery, 1973–1990* (New York: Simon and Schuster, 1991), 26 (quote), and *Nixon*, vol. 1, *The Education of a Politician 1913–1962* (New York: Simon and Schuster, 1987), 166–96.

2. Robert K. Carr, *The House Committee on Un-American Activities, 1945–1950* (Ithaca, NY: Cornell University Press, 1952), 449–63; John D. Lees, "Committees in the United States," in *Committees in Legislatures: A Comparative Analysis*, ed. John D. Lees and Malcolm Shaw (Durham, NC: Duke University Press, 1979), 39; David Caute, *The Great Fear: The Anti-Communist Purge Under Truman and Eisenhower* (New York: Simon and Schuster, 1978), 88–90, 94–103; Larry Ceplair and Steven Englund, *The Inquisition in Hollywood: Politics and the Film Community, 1930–1960* (New York: Anchor Press, 1980), xii–iv; Warren and Truman quotes from Stephen J. Whitfield, *The Culture of the Cold War* (Baltimore: Johns Hopkins University Press, 1991), 123–24.

3. David McCullough, *Truman* (New York: Simon and Schuster, 1992), 256–80 (quote, 260).

4. *The Diary of Gideon Welles*, ed. John T. Morse, 3 vols. (Boston: Houghton Mifflin Company, 1911), 2: 198; Emory Upton, *The Military Policy of the United States* (Washington, DC: Government Printing Office, 1911), 316–27; Ben Perley Poore, *Perley's Reminiscences of Sixty Years in the National Metropolis*, 2 vols. (Philadelphia: Hubbard Brothers Publishers, 1886), 2: 103; John G. Nicolay and John Hay, *Abraham Lincoln: A History*, 10 vols. (New York: Century Company, 1886), 5: 151.

5. James Kendall Hosmer, *The American Nation: A History*, vol. 20, *The Appeal to Arms, 1861–1863* (New York: Harper and Brothers, 1907), 80; Edward Channing, *The History of the United States*, 6 vols. (New York: Macmillan Company, 1925), 6: 400–401; James Schouler, *History of the United States of America Under the Constitution*, 7 vols. (New York: Dodd, Mead and Company, 1899), 6: 163n; William Whately Pierson, "The Committee on the Conduct of the War," *American Historical Review* 23 (1918): 550–76; Carl Sandburg, *Abraham Lincoln: The War Years*, 4 vols. (New York: Harcourt, Brace and Company, 1939), 1: 388. The most comprehensive historical discussion of the committee is found in Brian Holden Reid, "Historians and the Joint Committee on the Conduct of the War," *Civil War History* (December 1992): 319–41.

6. T. Harry Williams, *Lincoln and the Radicals* (Madison: University of Wisconsin Press, 1941); idem, "The Committee on the Conduct of the War: A Study of Civil War Politics" (Ph.D. diss., University of Wisconsin, 1937); idem, "The Committee on the Conduct of the War," *Journal of the American Military Institute* 3 (1939): 139–56; and idem, "Lincoln and the Radicals," in *Grant, Lee, Lincoln and the Radicals*, ed. Grady McWhiney (Evanston, IL: Northwestern University Press, 1964), 72–91.

7. Louis Smith, *American Democracy and Military Power: A Study of Civil Control of Military Power in the United States* (Chicago: University of Chicago Press, 1951), 201–5; Harry W. Pfanz, "The Surrender Negotiations Between General Johnston and

General Sherman, April 1865," *Military Affairs* 16 (1952): 66; James G. Randall, *Lincoln the President: Springfield to Gettysburg* (New York: Dodd, Meade and Company, 1946), 62. See also Bruce Catton, *This Hallowed Ground: The Story of the Union Side of the Civil War* (New York: Doubleday, 1956), 99; Shelby Foote, *The Civil War: A Narrative, Fort Sumter to Perrysville* (1958; rpt., Vintage Books, 1986), 108; Samuel Eliot Morison and Henry Steele Commager, *The Growth of the American Republic,* 2 vols. (New York: Oxford University Press, 1962), 1: 713–14; Williams's viewpoint is still preserved in the textbook he originated; see Alan Brinkley, Richard Current, Frank Freidel, and T. Harry Williams, *American History: A Survey,* 8th ed. (New York: McGraw-Hill, 1991), 430.

8. Eric Foner, *Reconstruction: America's Unfinished Revolution, 1863–1877* (New York: Harper and Row, 1988), xix–xxvii; Allan Nevins, *The War for the Union,* vol. 1, *The Improvised War, 1861–1862* (New York: Charles Scribner's Sons, 1959), 387; Eric L. McKitrick, "Party Politics and the Union and Confederate War Efforts," in *The American Party Systems,* ed. William Nisbet Chambers and Walter Dean Burnham (New York: Oxford University Press, 1967), 144–45; Hans L. Trefousse, "The Joint Committee on the Conduct of the War: A Reassessment," *Civil War History* 10 (1964): 5–19, and Trefousse, *The Radical Republicans: Lincoln's Vanguard for Racial Justice* (New York: Alfred A. Knopf, 1969); Howard C. Westwood, "The Joint Committee on the Conduct of the War—A Look at the Record," *Lincoln Herald* 80 (1978): 5–15. See also Stephen Oates, "Abraham Lincoln: *Republican* in the White House," in *Abraham Lincoln and the American Political Tradition,* ed. John L. Thomas (Amherst: University of Massachusetts Press, 1986), 107.

9. Elisabeth Joan Doyle, "The Conduct of the War, 1861," in *Congress Investigates: A Documentary History,* ed. Arthur M. Schlesinger Jr. and Roger Bruns (New York: Chelsea House, 1975), 1197–1232; E. B. Long, "The True Believers: The Committee on the Conduct of the War," *Civil War Times Illustrated* 20 (1981): 20; James McPherson, *Battle Cry of Freedom: The Civil War Era* (New York: Oxford University Press, 1988), 362–63; Phillip Shaw Paludan, *The Presidency of Abraham Lincoln* (Lawrence: University Press of Kansas, 1994), 99, 104–6; David Herbert Donald, *Lincoln* (New York: Simon and Schuster, 1995), 326–27.

10. One historian sees the committee's work as unique, particularly in that it was a joint committee of investigation. Between 1861 and 1926, this type of investigative committee was used fifteen times. See Virgil Calvin Shroud, "Congressional Investigations of War" (Ph.D. diss., New York University, 1954), 49. On Republican partisan strategies in the 1850s and the Slave Power conspiracy, see Michael F. Holt, *The Political Crisis of the 1850s* (New York: John Wiley and Sons, 1978), 180–96, and *Political Parties and American Political Development from the Age of Jackson to the Age of Lincoln* (Baton Rouge: Louisiana State University Press, 1992), 323–52; David Brion Davis, *The Slave Power Conspiracy and the Paranoid Style* (Baton Rouge: Louisiana State University Press, 1969); William Gienapp, "The Republican Party and the Slave Power," in *Race and Slavery in America: Essays in Honor of Kenneth Stampp,* ed. Robert H. Abzug and Stephen E. Maizlish (Lexington: University of Kentucky Press, 1986), 51–78; Eric Foner, *Free Soil, Free Labor, Free Men: The Ideology of the Republican Party Before the Civil War* (New York: Oxford University Press, 1970), 88–102. On Lincoln's campaign tactics, see Robert W. Johannsen, *Lincoln, the South, and Slavery: The Political Dimension* (Baton Rouge: Louisiana State University Press, 1991).

11. Williams, *Lincoln and the Radicals,* 70. For Democratic attitudes toward McClellan, see Joel Silbey, *"A Respectable Minority:" The Democratic Party in the Civil War Era, 1860–1868* (New York: W. W. Norton and Company, 1977), 118–39, and Stephen W. Sears, *George B. McClellan: The Young Napoleon* (New York: Ticknor and Fields, 1988), 344–86.

12. T. Harry Williams, *Lincoln and His Generals* (New York: Alfred A. Knopf, 1952).

13. Allan Bogue, *The Earnest Men: Republicans in the Civil War Senate* (Madison: University of Wisconsin Press, 1981); idem, "Bloc and Party in the United States Senate," *Civil War History* 13 (1967): 221–41; idem, "Historians and the Radical Republicans: A Meaning for Today," *Journal of American History* 69 (1983): 7–34.

1. To Invigorate a Timid Administration

1. William D. Howells to Victoria M. Howells, April 21, 1861, in *Selected Letters of W. D. Howells,* vol. 1, *1852–1872,* ed. and annotated George Arms et al. (Boston: Twayne Publishers, 1979), 77.

2. Allan Nevins, *The War for the Union,* 4 vols. (New York: Charles Scribner's Sons, 1959), 1: 28, 74–76; Earl J. Hess, *Liberty, Virtue, and Progress: Northerners and Their War* (New York: New York University, 1988), 19–23; Phillip S. Paludan, *"A People's Contest": The Union and the Civil War, 1861–1865* (New York: Oxford University Press, 1988), 10–15; Randall Jimerson, *The Private Civil War: Popular Thought During the Sectional Crisis* (Baton Rouge: Louisiana State University Press, 1988), 27–28 (quote of northern Democrat, 28); *The Diary of George Templeton Strong: The Civil War, 1860–1865,* ed. Allan Nevins and Milton Halsey Thomas, 4 vols. (New York: Macmillan, 1952), 3: 144.

3. For a comprehensive overview of the turbulent 1850s and the widening differences between North and South, see James McPherson, *Battle Cry of Freedom: The Civil War Era* (New York: Oxford University Press, 1988), 3–201.

4. Hess, *Liberty and Virtue,* 3.

5. For Lincoln's early political experience, see David Herbert Donald, *Lincoln* (New York: Simon and Schuster, 1995), 52–54, 58–64, 78–83, 123–41. For Lincoln's views on war, see Gabor S. Boritt, "War Opponent and War President," in *Lincoln the War President,* ed. Gabor S. Boritt (New York: Oxford University Press, 1992), 179–211.

6. Forrest MacDonald, *The American Presidency: An Intellectual History* (Lawrence: University Press of Kansas, 1994), 1–2, 347–56, 398–99; Donald, *Lincoln,* 296–301; Harold M. Hyman, *A More Perfect Union: The Impact of the Civil War and Reconstruction on the Constitution* (New York: Alfred A. Knopf, 1978), 63–106; Ji-Hyung Cho, "The Transformation of the American Legal Mind: Habeas Corpus, Federalism, and Constitutionalism, 1787–1870" (Ph.D. diss., University of Illinois, Urbana, 1995), 273–84; Phillip Shaw Paludan, *The Presidency of Abraham Lincoln* (Lawrence: University Press of Kansas, 1994), 73–80 (quote, 70). The most recent study of habeas corpus and civil liberties is Mark A. Neely, *The Fate of Liberty: Abraham Lincoln and Civil Liberties* (New York: Oxford University Press, 1991).

7. Nevins, *War for the Union,* 190–91, 195–203; Donald, *Lincoln,* 301–5; James McPherson, *Ordeal by Fire: The Civil War and Reconstruction* (New York: Alfred A. Knopf, 1982), 261–64; Paludan, *Presidency of Lincoln,* 80–84.

8. Gerald F. Linderman, *Embattled Courage: The Experience of Combat in the Civil War* (New York: Free Press, 1987), 8–12, 35–36; Bruce Catton, *This Hallowed Ground: The Story of the Union Side in the Civil War* (New York: Doubleday, 1956), 51–52; Zachariah Chandler to wife, July 16, 1861, Zachariah Chandler Papers, Library of Congress (microfilm); Albert Gallatin Riddle, *Recollections of War Times: Reminiscences of the Men and Washington, 1860–1865* (New York: G. P. Putman's Sons, 1895), 39; William Howard Russell, *My Diary North and South,* ed. Eugene H. Berwanger (New York: Alfred A. Knopf, 1988), 224 (quote), 227. See also McPherson, *Battle Cry of Freedom,* 333–34, and T. Harry Williams, "The Committee on the Conduct of the War: A Study of Civil War Politics" (Ph.D. diss., University of Wisconsin, 1937), 17–18, 46–47.

9. Nevins, *War for the Union,* 1: 214–18; McPherson, *Ordeal by Fire,* 207–11; Riddle, *Recollections,* 52–53.

10. Adam Gurowski, *Diary,* 3 vols. (Boston: Lee and Shepard, 1862), 1:7; Nevins and Thomas, eds., *Diary of George Templeton Strong,* 3: 169; *New York Daily Tribune,* July 23, 1861, p. 4, c. 2; *Frank Leslie's Illustrated Newspaper,* August 10, 1861, 194; B. Stern to John Covode, July 31, 1861, John Covode Papers, Western Pennsylvania Historical Society, Pittsburgh; J. W. Brooks to Chandler, July 25, 1861, Chandler Papers; George Fredrickson, *The Inner Civil War: Northern Intellectuals and the Crisis of the Union* (1965; rpt., Urbana: University of Illinois Press, 1993), 73–75; Thomas Kilby Smith to wife, July 24, 1861, in *Life and Letters of Thomas Kilby Smith, 1820–1887,* ed. Walter George Smith (New York: G. P. Putman's Sons, 1898), 171–72.

11. Albert Castel, *General Sterling Price and the Civil War in the West* (Baton Rouge: Louisiana State University Press, 1968), 39–46; Nevins and Thomas, eds., *Diary of George Templeton Strong,* 3: 175; *Chicago Tribune,* August 16, 1861, p. 2, c. 1; Gurowski, *Diary,* 1: 90.

12. Victor Howard, *Religion and the Radical Republican Movement, 1860–1868* (Lexington: University of Kentucky Press, 1990), 12–13; *New York Herald,* September 6, 1861, p. 4, c. 5; Orville Browning to Lincoln, September 11, 17, 1861, Abraham Lincoln Papers, Library of Congress (microfilm); George W. Julian, *Political Recollections, 1840–1872* (Chicago: Jansen, McClurg and Company, 1884), 199; Benjamin Wade to Chandler, September 23, 1861, Chandler Papers.

13. Two recent works that outline the battle of Ball's Bluff are Mark Grimsley's "The Definition of Disaster," *Civil War Times Illustrated* 28 (1989): 14–21, and Kim Bernard Holien's *Battle at Ball's Bluff* (Orange, VA: Moss Publications, 1985).

14. Gurowski, *Diary,* 1: 115; *Frank Leslie's Illustrated Newspaper,* November 9, 1861, 386; B. Wade to H. Wade, October 25, 1861, Benjamin F. Wade Papers, Library of Congress.

15. Wade to Chandler, October 8, 1861, Chandler Papers.

16. Paludan, *"People's Contest,"* 61–63; M. Blair to Chandler, October 25, 1861, Chandler Papers; Stephen W. Sears, *George B. McClellan: The Young Napoleon* (New York: Ticknor and Fields, 1988), 123; McClellan to wife, October 26, 1861, in *The Civil War Papers of George B. McClellan,* ed. Stephen Sears (New York: Ticknor and Fields, 1989), 112.

17. *Letters of John Hay and Extracts from Diary* (New York: Gordian Press, 1969), 48; Chandler to wife, October 27, 1861, Chandler Papers; Sears, *Young Napoleon,* 103, 122–23; Chandler to James F. Joy, October 27, 1861, James F. Joy Papers, Burton Historical Collections, Detroit Public Library.

18. Nevins, *War for the Union,* 1: 385, 400–403; Francis P. Blair Jr. to Henry Halleck, December 4, 1861, Blair Family Papers, Library of Congress (microfilm); T. O'Reilly to Cameron, December 7, 1861, and J. Medill to Cameron, December 6, 1861, Simon Cameron Papers, Library of Congress (microfilm).

19. Chandler to William Lord, November 16, 1861, Robert M. Zug Papers, Burton Historical Collections, Detroit Public Library; Caroline Wade to Wade, November 5, 1861, Wade Papers; T. Harry Williams, *Lincoln and the Radicals* (Baton Rouge: Louisiana State University Press, 1941), 15–17; James McPherson, *Battle Cry,* 312.

20. McPherson, *Battle Cry,* 354–55; John Seed to Lyman Trumbull, December 7, 1861, Lyman Trumbull Papers, Library of Congress (microfilm); Carl Schurz to William Seward, October 8, 1861, and Schurz to Charles Sumner, November 14, 1861, Carl Schurz Papers, Library of Congress (microfilm). For an understanding of the American notion of mission and slavery's challenge to it, see Ernest Lee Tuveson, *Redeemer Nation: The Idea of America's Millennial Role* (Chicago: University of Chicago Press, 1968), vi–x; Ronald D. Rietveld, "The American Civil War: Millennial Hope, Political Chaos,

and a Two-Sided 'Just War,'" in *The Wars of America: Christian Views*, ed. Ronald A. Wells (Grand Rapids, MI: William. B. Eerdmans Publishing Company, 1981), 67–90; James Moorhead, *American Apocalypse: Yankee Protestants and the Civil War, 1860–1869* (New Haven: Yale University Press, 1978), 2–81.

21. Michael F. Holt, *The Political Crisis of the 1850s* (New York: John Wiley and Sons, 1978), 190–92; James L. Morrison, "The Struggle Between Sectionalism and Nationalism at Ante-Bellum West Point, 1830–1861," *Civil War History* 19 (1973): 143 (quote); *Congressional Globe*, 37th Cong. 2d sess., 69; Frank L. Klement, *Dark Lanterns: Secret Political Societies, Conspiracies, and Treason Trials in the Civil War* (Baton Rouge: Louisiana State University Press, 1984), 7–18; Paludan, *Presidency of Lincoln*, 97–99 (quote, 99).

22. *Chicago Tribune*, December 6, 1861, p. 2, c. 1; C. H. Nay to L. Trumbull, December 6, 1861, Trumbull Papers; A. Denny to B. Wade, November 28, 1861, Wade Papers; Wade to James Monroe, December 11, 1861, quoted in Howard, *Religion and the Radical Republicans*, 17; B. R. Wood to Charles Sumner, November 12, 1861, Charles Sumner Papers, Houghton Library, Harvard University (microfilm); Edgar George to Chandler, December 14, 1861, and J. J. Bagley to Chandler, December 6, 1861, Chandler Papers.

23. Allan G. Bogue, *The Congressman's Civil War* (Cambridge: Cambridge University Press, 1988), 58–59; Hyman, *A More Perfect Union*, 141–45, 172–73 (quote, 144).

24. *Congressional Globe*, 37th Congress, 2d sess., 16–17.

25. Ibid., 29–30.

26. Ibid., 30–31.

27. Ibid., 31–32.

28. Ibid., 32, 40, 110, 153.

29. Biographical information on Wade is derived from Hans Trefousse, *Benjamin Franklin Wade: Radical Republican from Ohio* (New York: Twayne Publications, 1963), and *Continental Monthly* 2 (August 1862): 158 (quote).

30. Sister Mary Karl George, *Zachariah Chandler: A Political Biography* (East Lansing: Michigan State University Press, 1969), 2–23, 32–36; Chandler to Austin Blair, February 27, 1861, Chandler Papers; Detroit Post and Tribune, *Zachariah Chandler: An Outline of his Life and Public Service* (Detroit: Post and Tribune Publishers, 1880), 255, 226 (quotes); J. K. Herbert to Benjamin F. Butler, May 26, 1864, in *Private and Official Correspondence of Gen. Benjamin F. Butler During the Period of the Civil War*, 5 vols. (Norwood, MA: Plimpton Press, 1917), 4: 269–70. For Chandler's belief in rumors about the Knights of the Golden Circle, see W. S. Wood to Chandler, January 3, 1862, Chandler Papers.

31. Albert Castel, *The Presidency of Andrew Johnson* (Lawrence: Regents Press of Kansas, 1979), 2–8 (quote, 7); T. Harry Williams, "Andrew Johnson as a Member of the Joint Committee on the Conduct of the War," *East Tennessee Historical Publications* 12 (1940): 70–83; Leroy P. Graf and Ralph W. Haskins, eds. *The Papers of Andrew Johnson*, 10 vols. (Knoxville: University of Tennessee Press, 1967–1992), 5:4.

32. A. John Dodds, "Honest John Covode," *Western Pennsylvania Magazine of History* 16 (1933): 175–82; Bogue, *The congressman's War*, 60; *The Diary of Gideon Welles*, ed. John T. Morse, 3 vols. (Boston: Houghton Mifflin Company, 1911), 1: 219.

33. Patrick W. Riddleberger, *George Washington Julian, Radical Republican: A Study in Nineteenth Century Politics and Reform* (Indianapolis: Indiana Historical Bureau, 1966), and Grace Julian Clarke, *George W. Julian* (Indianapolis: Indiana Historical Commission, 1923); George Washington Julian, *Political Recollections, 1840–1872* (Chicago: Jansen, McClurg and Company, 1884), 182; Joshua Giddings to Mollie Giddings, March 23, 1863, George W. Julian Papers, Indiana State Library, Indianapolis (quote).

34. *Lamb's Biographical Dictionary of the United States* (Boston: Federal Book Company, 1903), 4: 319; Williams, *Lincoln and the Radicals,* 69; L. E. Chittenden, *Recollections of President Lincoln and His Administration* (New York: Harper and Brothers, Franklin Square, 1891), 325.

35. *Lamb's Dictionary,* 6: 49–50; Elisabeth Joan Doyle, "The Conduct of the War, 1861," in *Congress Investigates: A Documentary History,* ed. Arthur M. Schlesinger Jr. and Roger Bruns (New York: Chelsea House, 1975), 1203; Williams, *Lincoln and the Radicals,* 70–71; *Harper's Weekly,* June 30, 1866, 403; Moses Odell to James Garfield and Robert Schenk, May 24, 1866 (quote), James A. Garfield Papers, Library of Congress (microfilm); William E. Doubleday to Chandler, August 23, 1862, Chandler Papers.

36. Charles Eugene Hamlin, *The Life and Times of Hannibal Hamlin* (Cambridge, MA: Riverside Press, 1899), 398, 415.

37. Albert Gallatin Riddle, *The Life of Benjamin Wade* (Cleveland: Williams Publishing Company, 1888), 294; Detroit Post and Tribune, *Zachariah Chandler,* 216.

38. George B. Galloway, *History of the House of Representatives* (New York: Thomas Y. Cromwell Company, 1961), 97–99; Hubert Bruce Fuller, *The Speakers of the House* (1909; rpt., New York: Arno Press, 1974), 39–43; Nelson Polsby, "The Institutionalization of the U.S. House of Representatives," *American Political Science Review* 68 (March, 1968): 156; Nelson Polsby, Miriam Gallaher, and Berry Spencer Rundquist, "The Growth of the Seniority System in the U.S. House of Representatives," in *Congressional Behavior,* ed. Nelson Polsby (New York: Random House, 1971), 175, 182; Samuel Kernell, "Toward Understanding Nineteenth Century Congressional Careers: Ambition, Competition, and Rotation," *American Journal of Political Science* 21 (1977): 669–71; M. P. Follett, *The Speakers of the House of Representatives* (New York: Longman, Green, and Company, 1902), 221; Robert D. Ilisevich, *Galusha Grow: The People's Candidate* (Pittsburgh: University of Pittsburgh Press, 1988), 203–4; Doyle, "Conduct of the War," 1200; Bogue, *congressman's Civil War,* 62, 113–15.

39. Follett, *Speakers of the House,* 229; Doyle, "Conduct of the War," 1203.

40. Marshall Edward Dimock, "Congressional Investigating Committees" (Ph.D. diss., Johns Hopkins University, 1929), 15–21, 46, 55–56; Virgil C. Shroud, "Congressional Investigations of War" (Ph.D. diss., New York University, 1954), 1–29; James Hamilton, *The Power to Probe: A Study of Congressional Investigations* (New York: Random House, 1976), 57–59; Louis Fisher, *The Politics of Shared Power,* 2d ed. (Washington, DC: Congressional Quarterly, 1987), 74–75; Allan Barth, *Government by Investigation* (New York: Viking Press, 1955), 13–15, 73; *Congressional Globe,* 37th Cong., 2d sess., 30–31.

41. Dimock, "Congressional Committees," 87–89, 102–3, 109–10; Shroud, "Congressional Investigations," 29–32; Fisher, *Politics of Shared Power,* 185–86; Ernest J. Eberling, "Congressional Investigations: A Study in the Origins and Development of the Power of Congress to Investigate and Punish for Contempt" (Ph.D. diss., Columbia University, 1928), 288.

42. *Report of the Joint Committee on the Conduct of the War* (Washington, DC: Government Printing Office, 1863), 3: 3–4 (hereafter CCW). The two pieces of legislation included a bill to allow both houses of Congress to go into secret session on a request from the president and a bill to allow the federal government to take control of the nation's railroads.

43. For a summary of the committee's operations, see William Whately Pierson, "The Committee on the Conduct of the War," *American Historical Review* 23 (1918): 550–76; Hans Trefousse, "The Joint Committee on the Conduct of the War: A Reassessment," *Civil War History* 10 (1964): 5–19; Doyle, "Conduct of the War," 1197–1232; T. Harry Williams, "The Committee on the Conduct of the War: An Experiment in Civilian Control," *Journal of the American Military Institute* 3 (1939): 139–56.

44. Pierson, "Committee on the Conduct," 560–74; Trefousse, "Reassessment," 5–19; Williams, *Lincoln and the Radicals,* 71–76 and passim; Charles P. Stone to John Covode, December 8, 1862, Covode Papers. According to Stone, Covode incorporated witness testimony that concerned his role in the Ball's Bluff affair into a speech at the National Hall in Philadelphia.

45. *Chicago Times,* December 9, 1861, p. 2, c. 1; Gurowski, *Diary,* 1: 136; W. E. Doubleday to Chandler, December 6, 1861, Chandler Papers; *Chicago Tribune,* December 24, 1861, p. 2, c. 2.

46. Leonard P. Curry, *Blueprint for Modern America: Nonmilitary Legislation of the First Civil War Congress* (Nashville: Vanderbilt University Press, 1968), 5–6, 230–43; Bogue, *congressman's Civil War,* 83–88, 112–13. Lincoln's use of congressional committees to achieve his ends is discussed in Harold M. Hyman, "Lincoln and Congress: Why Not Congress and Lincoln?" *Journal of the Illinois State Historical Society* 68 (1976): 65. A detailed portrait of the Contracts Committee is provided by Fred Nicklason, "The Civil War Contracts Committee," *Civil War History* 17 (1971): 232–44. Lincoln's most recent biographer, David Herbert Donald, argues that the president viewed the formation of the Joint Select Committee "with some anxiety, fearing that it might turn into an engine of agitation against the administration" (*Lincoln,* 326–27).

47. C. Wade to Theodore Wade, January 20, 1862, Wade Family Papers, Western Reserve Historical Society, Cleveland, Ohio. Some of the questions raised about the utility of the committee are discussed in Brian Holden Reid, "Historians and the Joint Committee on the Conduct of the War, 1861–1865," *Civil War History* 38 (1992): 319–41, esp. 338–41 (quote, 341).

2. Investigating Bull Run and Ball's Bluff

1. Stephen Douglas to Virgil Hickox, May 10, 1861, in *The Letters of Stephen A. Douglas,* ed. Robert W. Johannsen (Urbana: University of Illinois Press, 1961), 512; Joel Silbey, *A "Respectable Minority:" The Democratic Party in the Civil War Era, 1860–1868* (New York: W. W. Norton and Company, 1977), 31–46; David Davis to Simon Cameron, October 13, 1861, Cameron Papers; Davis to E. R. Roe, July 29, 1861, Richard Yates Papers, Illinois State Historical Library, Springfield.

2. Frank L. Klement, *The Copperheads in the Middlewest* (1960; rpt., Gloucester, MA: Peter Smith, 1972), 1–39; James McPherson, *Battle Cry of Freedom: The Civil War Era* (New York: Oxford University Press, 1988), 493–94; Silbey, *"Respectable Minority,"* 49–53.

3. On the theory of conciliation, see Mark Grimsley, *The Hard Hand of War: Union Military Policy Toward Southern Civilians, 1861–1865* (Cambridge: Cambridge University Press, 1995), 23–46. On the Slave Power symbol, see David Brion Davis, *The Slave Power Conspiracy and the Paranoid Style* (Baton Rouge: Louisiana State University Press, 1969); William Gienapp, "The Republican Party and the Slave Power," in *Race and Slavery in America: Essays in Honor of Kenneth Stampp,* ed. Robert H. Abzug and Stephen E. Maizlish (Lexington: University of Kentucky Press, 1986), 51–78.

4. For an overview of the Whig ideology and its impact on American political thought, see Bernard Bailyn, *The Ideological Origin of the American Revolution* (Cambridge: Harvard University Press, 1967). For the use that nineteenth-century Democrats made of the ideas, see Jean Baker, *Affairs of Party: The Political Culture of Northern Democrats in the Mid-Nineteenth Century* (Ithaca, NY: Cornell University Press, 1983), 147–60 and passim.

5. *Congressional Globe,* 37th Cong. 2d sess., 33–34, 57–59, 76 (quote); Illinois *State Register* (Springfield), December 14, 1861, p. 2, c. 1.

6. Calvin Day to Gideon Welles, July 27, 1861, Gideon Welles Papers, Library of Congress (microfilm); Albert G. Riddle, *Recollections of War Times: Reminiscences of the Men and Washington, 1860–1865* (New York: G. P. Putman's Sons, 1895), 56–57; *New York Herald,* July 31, 1861, p. 4, c. 5, and July 26, 1861, p. 4, c. 3.

7. William C. Davis, *Battle at Bull Run: A History of the First Major Campaign of the Civil War* (Baton Rouge: Louisiana State University Press, 1977), 80–88, 133–51, 252 (quote).

8. Ibid., 5–6; *Dictionary of American Biography,* ed. Dumas Malone (New York: Charles Scribner's Sons, 1934), 14: 306–7; *Southern Literary Messenger* 34 (July and August, 1862), 411; *The War of Rebellion: A Compilation of the Official Records of the Union and Confederate Armies,* ser. 1, vol. 2 (Washington DC: Government Printing Office, 1880), 662 (hereafter OR), address written by Fitz-John Porter per Patterson's order; *Saturday Evening Post* (Philadelphia), August 3, 1861, p. 3, c. 1; *New York Daily Tribune,* July 23, 1861, p. 4, c. 3; *Chicago Tribune,* July 23, 1861, p. 2, c. 1–2; *Pittsburg Daily Gazette,* July 25, 1861, p. 2, c. 1 (quote).

9. C. H. Fisher to Cameron, August 17, 1861, Cameron Papers; William Howard Russell, *My Diary North and South,* ed. Eugene Berwanger (New York: Alfred A. Knopf, 1988), 285; Patterson to Cameron, November 1, 1861, quoted in Robert Patterson, *Narrative of the Campaign in the Valley of the Shen. ndoah in 1861* (Philadelphia: John Campbell, 1865), 12; *Brooklyn Daily Eagle,* October 23, 1861, p. 2, c. 2; Henry Clark to Benjamin Wade, January 2, 1862, Benjamin F. Wade Papers, Library of Congress (microfilm).

10. Fitz-John Porter to J. Sherman, July 26, 1861, and Porter to Sherman, August 3, 1861, John Sherman Papers, Library of Congress (microfilm edition).

11. *New York Times,* July 26, 1861, p. 1, c. 1; Patterson to Sherman, August 2 and 26, 1861, Sherman Papers.

12. Patterson, *Narrative,* 15; *New York Times,* November 20, 1861, p. 4, c. 3.

13. Patterson to Sherman, December 14, 1861, Sherman Papers; Patterson, *Narrative,* 16–21.

14. Patterson, *Narrative,* 21–22.

15. Albert Castel, "Mars and the Reverend Longstreet: Or Attacking and Dying in the Civil War," *Civil War History* 33 (1987): 103–14. For a critique of Lincoln's views on warfare, see Mark E. Neeley Jr., "Wilderness and the Cult of Manliness: Hooker, Lincoln, and Defeat," in *Lincoln's Generals,* ed. Gabor S. Boritt (New York: Oxford University Press, 1994), 51–77.

16. William T. Sherman to John Sherman, September 22, 1862, in *The Sherman Letters,* ed. Rachel Sherman Thorndike (New York: Charles Scribner's Sons, 1894), 162; Archer Jones, *Civil War Command and Strategy: The Process of Victory and Defeat* (New York: Free Press, 1992), 5, 39–40, 130–31 (quote); Edward Hagerman, "The Professionalization of George B. McClellan and Early Field Command," *Civil War History* 21 (1975): 115–16; John K. Mahon, "Civil War Assault Tactics," *Military Affairs* 25 (1961): 57–68; James McPherson, *Ordeal by Fire: The Civil War and Reconstruction* (New York: Alfred A. Knopf, 1982), 193–97.

17. Detroit Post and Tribune, *Zachariah Chandler: An Outline of His Life and Public Services* (Detroit: Post and Tribune Company, Publishers, 1880), 225–27 (quote, 227).

18. *Congressional Globe,* 37th Cong., 3d sess., 324–34 (quote, 329); Gerald F. Linderman, *Embattled Courage: The Experience of Combat in the American Civil War* (New York: Free Press, 1987), 139–55; Mahon, "Infantry Tactics," 65.

19. *Congressional Globe,* 37th Cong., 2d sess., 1133–36; Detroit Post and Tribune, *Chandler,* 226; Chandler to William Lord, November 16, 1861, Zug Papers; *Congressional Globe,* 38th Cong., 1st sess., 3196–97.

20. *Congressional Globe,* 37th Cong., 2d sess., 69.

21. Ibid., 37th Cong., 3 sess., 1064–69 (quote, 1065).

22. CCW, 2: 48, 75–77, 149–52, passim.

23. *New York Daily Tribune,* January 3, 1862, p. 5, c. 2; *New York Herald,* January 6, 1862, p. 1, c. 6; Patterson, *Narrative,* 24; CCW, 1863, 2: 78. The *Herald*'s editor, James Gordon Bennett, was more skeptical of Patterson than of his Washington correspondent; see his editorial in the *Herald,* January 7, 1862, p. 4, c. 4. Patterson communicated what he considered to be the precariousness of his position to the War Department in a variety of letters in mid-July (see Patterson to E. D. Townsend, July 9, 1861, OR, ser. 1, vol. 2, 163; Patterson to Scott, July 16, 1861, OR, ser. 1, vol. 2, 164–65; Patterson to Townsend, July 17, 18, OR, ser. 1, vol. 2, 167; Patterson to Scott, July 19, 1861, OR, ser. 1, vol. 2, 170.

24. CCW, 1863, 2: 78–97. Patterson's statement took up most of the committee's session on January 6 and 7.

25. Ibid., 99–104; Scott to Patterson, July 13, 1861, OR, ser. 1, vol. 2, 165; Patterson to E. D. Townsend, July 16, 17, 18 (quote), 20, 21, 1861, OR, ser. 1, vol. 2, 166–69, 172.

26. CCW, 1863, 2: 104–14; Scott to Patterson, July 18, 1861, OR, ser. 1, vol. 2, 168; Patterson to Townsend, July 18, 1861, OR, ser. 1, vol. 2, 168. For the testimony of witnesses sympathetic to Patterson, see Fitz-John Porter's session before the committee as well as Col. Craig Biddle's (CCW, 1863, 2: 152–59, 194–98).

27. *Boston Herald,* January 9, 1862, p. 2, c. 2; *New York Herald,* January 8, 1862, p. 10, c. 3; S. Cameron to Patterson, January 10, 1862, Cameron Papers; Patterson to Sherman, January 27, 1862, Sherman Papers; *Vanity Fair,* January 25, 1862, 44. Patterson's son was eventually commissioned in April 1862.

28. *Congressional Globe,* 37th Cong., 2d sess., 838–42.

29. Ibid., 852–53; Patterson, *Narrative,* 116–17.

30. Patterson to Charles Biddle, February 18, 1862, Biddle Family Papers, Library of Congress (microfilm); *Philadelphia Inquirer,* February 19, 1862, p. 2, c. 1.

31. *New York Daily Tribune,* March 28, 1862, April 1, 1862, p. 4, c. 3; CCW, 1863, 2:241–42; *Continental Monthly* 1 (March 1862): 257–63 (quote, 263).

32. Patterson, *Narrative,* 79; Russell, *My Diary,* 259; Patterson to Townsend, July 20, 1861, OR, ser. 1, vol. 2, 172.

33. Stephen Oates, *With Malice Toward None: The Life of Abraham Lincoln* (New York: Harper and Row, 1977), 284–85; Mark Grimsley, "The Definition of Disaster," *Civil War Times Illustrated* 28 (1989): 14–21; Kim Bernard Holien, *Battle at Ball's Bluff* (Orange, VA: Moss Publications, 1985).

34. Charles Stone to Abraham Lincoln, October 21, 1861, Francis Young to Lincoln, October 21, 1861, George McClellan to Lincoln, October 22, 1861, all in Lincoln Papers; *Frank Leslie's Illustrated Magazine,* November 9, 1861, 386.

35. *Dictionary of American Biography,* 18: 72; James G. Randall, *Lincoln the President,* 4 vols. (New York: Dodd, Mead and Company, 1945–1955), 1: 293–94 (quote, 294). Extensive accounts of the Ball's Bluff affair and aftermath can be found in James G. Blaine, *Twenty Years of Congress, 1861–1881,* 2 vols. (Norwich, CT, 1886), 1: 378–94; Horatio Gibson, "The Trial of Charles P. Stone," manuscript in the Horatio Gibson Papers, State Historical Society of Wisconsin, Madison.

36. Thurlow Weed Barnes, *Memoir of Thurlow Weed,* 2 vols., (Boston: Houghton, Mifflin, 1884), 2: 345–46; McClellan to Divisional Commanders, October 24, 1861, George McClellan Papers, Library of Congress (microfilm); McClellan to wife, October 25, 1861, in *The Civil War Papers of George B. McClellan,* ed. Stephen Sears (New York: Ticknor and Fields, 1989), 111. Initially, information about Ball's Bluff was held back from the public by government telegraph censors. See Richard B. Kielbowicz, "The Telegraph, Censorship, and Politics at the Outset of the Civil War," *Civil War History* 40 (1994): 102–3.

37. *New York Times,* October 29, 1861, p. 1, c. 1; *Chicago Tribune,* November 2, 1861, p. 2, c. 2; *Ashtabula Sentinel,* November 13, 1861, p. 4, c. 1.

38. Copies of forged orders were published in the *Washington Evening Star,* October 28, 1861, p. 3, c. 6; Stone to McClellan, October 27, 1861, McClellan Papers; *Daily National Intelligencer,* October 29, 1861, p. 3, c. 1; Stone to Seth Williams, November 2, 1861, OR, ser. 1, vol. 5, 300–302; Stone to Edward Baker, October 21, 1861, OR, ser. 1, vol. 5, 302; Report of Francis G. Young, undated, OR, ser. 1, vol. 5, 327–30; Gibson, "Trial of Stone," 7.

39. *Chicago Tribune,* December 19, 1861, p. 2, c. 2; *New York Times,* December 16, 1861, p. 5, c. 1; *Congressional Globe,* 37th Cong., 2d sess., 130–31; Stone to Charles Sumner, December 23, 1861, Sumner Papers. According to Assistant War Secretary E. D. Townsend, Stone's problems began when he complained about Massachusetts governor John Andrew's instructions to Massachusetts officers not to return fugitive slaves. See E. D. Townsend, *Anecdotes of the Civil War in the United States* (New York: D. Appleton and Company, 1884), 71–74.

40. *Chicago Times,* December 9, 1861, p. 2, c. 2; Illinois *State Register* (Springfield), December 18, 1861, p. 2, c. 2, and December 15, 1861, p. 2, c. 1; *New York Herald,* December 9, 1861, p. 4, c. 6; James Bayard to Thomas Bayard, December 4, 1861, Thomas F. Bayard Papers, Library of Congress.

41. *Congressional Globe,* 37th Cong., 3d sess., 1065; Hans Trefousse, "The Motivation of a Radical Republican: Benjamin F. Wade," *Ohio History* 73 (1964): 73; anonymous to Zachariah Chandler, December[?], 1861, James W. Newton to Chandler, January 9, 1862, William E. Doubleday to Chandler, December 6, 1861, all in Chandler Papers; J. W. Gordon to Julian, January 29, 1862, and F. M. Finan [?] to Julian, January 26, 1862, Giddings-Julian Papers, Library of Congress. For Stone's views on soldier-civilian relations, see his special orders to Charles Devens in OR, ser. 1, vol. 5: 300.

42. *Congressional Globe,* 37th Cong., 2d sess., 162–65.

43. William Earl Dodge to Horace Greeley, December 23, 1861, Horace Greeley Papers, New York City Public Library (microfilm); Greeley to Wade, December 29, 1861, Wade Papers; Stephen M. Allen to Benjamin F. Butler, May 26, 1890, *Private and Official Correspondence of Gen. Benjamin F. Butler During the Period of the Civil War,* 5 vols. (Norwood, MA: Plimpton Press, 1917): 2: 595–96.

44. CCW, 1863, 2: 265–79.

45. Ibid., 279–82; signed draft, Horatio Gibson, December 2, 1912, Gibson Papers.

46. Sumner to John Andrew, January 3, 1862, Sumner Papers; *Congressional Globe,* 37th Cong., 2d sess., 189–91.

47. *Congressional Globe,* 37th Cong., 2d sess., 191–98.

48. *Chicago Tribune,* January 13, 1862, p. 1, c. 3, and January 8, 1862, p. 2, c. 6; *New York Times,* January 9, 1862, p. 1, c. 1.

49. CCW, 1863, 2: 297–301, 388–95, 345–50, 285–97.

50. Stone to S. Williams, November 8, 1861, and Stone to James Hardie, December 9, 1861, McClellan Papers; Francis G. Young to Lincoln, January 7, 1862, Lincoln Papers.

51. CCW, 1863, 2: 318–22, 325.

52. Ibid., 323, 327–31; Barnes, *Weed Memoirs,* 2: 345–46; Young to Lincoln, December 7, 1861, February 7, 1862, Lincoln Papers. The copies of Stone's orders in OR support his contention that Baker had discretionary powers.

53. CCW, 1863, 2: 358–68, 373–83.

54. Ibid., 1: 74, 78–79; Benjamin P. Thomas and Harold P. Hyman, *Stanton: The Life and Times of Lincoln's Secretary of War* (New York: Alfred A. Knopf, 1962), 3–19, 127–76; W. J. Howard to Covode, January 14, 1862, Covode Papers; copy of Stanton's order, dated January 28, 1862, McClellan Papers. Some cabinet members were jealous of the close relationship between Stanton and the committee. Naval Secretary Gideon

Welles saw it as Stanton's means for covering up anything embarrassing to the War Department. See *The Diary of Gideon Welles,* ed. John T. Morse, 3 vols. (Boston: Houghton Mifflin, 1911), 2: 198.

55. CCW, 1863, 2: 426–33.

56. *New York Daily Tribune,* February 5, 1862, p. 4, c. 6; Joseph Medill to Edwin Stanton, January 21, 1862, Edwin M. Stanton Papers, Library of Congress (microfilm); Timothy Day to Wade, February 1862, and James Wade to Caroline Wade, February 3, 1862, Wade papers; *The Diary of Edward Bates,* ed. Howard K. Beale (1933; rpt., New York: Da Capo Press, 1971), 229.

57. E. J. Allen to McClellan, February 6, 1862, and statement of James Shaw relative to the disloyalty of Charles P. Stone, February 6, 1862, McClellan Papers; McClellan to Andrew Porter, February 8, 1862, Sears, ed., *Civil War Papers,* 173.

58. *Harper's Weekly,* June 14, 1862, 381; Johnson's speech on Bright's expulsion is in L. P. Graf and R. W. Haskins, eds., *The Papers of Andrew Johnson,* 10 vols. (Knoxville: University of Tennessee Press, 1967–1992) 5: 114–33.

59. Irving L. Janis, *Groupthink: Psychological Studies of Policy Decisions and Fiascoes,* 2d ed. (Boston: Houghton Mifflin Company, 1983), 11–12.

60. *Chicago Tribune,* February 11, 1862, p. 1, c. 1; Adam Gurowski, *Diary,* 3 vols. (Boston, 1862), 2: 153; *New York Daily Tribune,* February 11, 1862, p. 4, c. 3; Indiana *True Republican,* February 13, 1862, p. 2, c. 2; *New York Times,* February 12, 1862, p. 4, c. 4, p. 5, c. 1–2.

61. *New York Herald,* February 16, 1862, p. 5, c. 2, February 19, p. 5, c. 1; *New York World,* February 11, 1862, p. 4, c. 2–3; *Daily National Intelligencer,* March 4, 1862, p. 3, c. 2; J. Bayard to T. Bayard, March 11, 1862, Bayard Papers; Baker, *Affairs of Party,* 148–50.

62. George Gordon Meade to wife, February 11, 1862, in *The Life and Letters of George Gordon Meade,* ed. George Gordon Meade (New York: Charles Scribner's Sons, 1913), 245–46; Heintzelman journal, February 10, 1862, Samuel P. Heintzelman Papers, Library of Congress (microfilm); Allen to Butler, May 26, 1890, *Butler, Works,* 2: 595.

63. Joseph Bradley to Stanton, February 16, 1862, March 31, 1862, and P. H. Watson to Bradley, February 20, 1862, and Gibson Papers.

64. *Congressional Globe,* 37th Cong., 2d sess., 1662–66.

65. Ibid., 1666-68.

66. Ibid., 1732–35.

67. Ibid., 1735–42.

68. *New York Herald,* April 18, 1862, p. 5, c. 1; Illinois *State Register,* April 22, 1862, p. 2, c. 3, clipped from *Chicago Times;* Illinois *State Register,* May 1, 1862, p. 2, c. 3, clipped from *Indianapolis State Sentinel;* Illinois *State Register,* May 2, 1862, p. 2, c. 1.

69. W. F. Sanders to Wade, June 11, 1862, J. S. Cole to Wade, April 21, 1862, R. Carpenter to Wade, June 8, 1862, Jefferson Patterson to Wade, June 4, 1862, all in Wade Papers.

70. Lincoln to Senate, May 1, 1862, Lincoln papers; Lincoln to Nathaniel Banks, April 5, 1864, in *The Collected Works of Abraham Lincoln,* ed. Roy P. Basler, 8 vols. (New Brunswick, NJ: Rutgers University Press, 1953), 7: 285; Bradley to Henry Parker, May 1, 1862, Gibson Papers.

71. Blaine, *Twenty Years,* 2: 390–92; *Indianapolis Daily Journal,* April 21, 1864, p. 2, c. 2; *Chicago Tribune,* April 22, 1864, p. 2, c. 1–2. The *Tribune's* retraction of these absurd charges in a later issue did Stone little good; see May 29, 1864, p. 2, c. 2. For details on Stone's later career, see *Dictionary of American Biography,* 18: 72; William B. Hesseltine and Hazel C. Wolf, *The Blue and Gray on the Nile* (Chicago: University of Chicago Press, 1961), 3–9 and passim. James G. Blaine also maintains that a law

passed by Congress on July 17, requiring that imprisoned officers be made aware of the charges against them and promptly court-martialed, forced the administration to release Stone.

72. CCW, 1863, 2: 486–502. Stone continued to function as a symbol of Democratic incompetence and lukewarm feelings about the war. In fall 1862, for instance, John Covode apparently revealed privileged committee testimony about Stone in a campaign speech in Philadelphia. Stone wrote asking for a copy, although it is not certain whether Covode complied (see Charles Stone to John Covode, December 8, 1862, Covode Papers). According to McClellan's biographer Stephen Sears, the committee was obsessed with damaging McClellan's military record so as to ruin him politically. See Stephen W. Sears, *George B. McClellan: The Young Napoleon* (New York: Ticknor and Fields, 1988), 350–53.

73. Detroit Post and Tribune, *Zachariah Chandler: An Outline of His Life and Public Service* (Detroit: Post and Tribune Publishers, 1880), 222.

74. CCW, 1863, 2:505–10; Sears, *The Young Napoleon,* 144–46. James G. Blaine, in one of the most detailed and comprehensive contemporary accounts of the Stone debacle, argues that the ultimate reason for his lengthy imprisonment was unclear; however, he also maintains that the responsibility rests equally on Stanton, McClellan, and the committee (see *Twenty Years,* 1: 393–94).

75. CCW, 1863, 2:9–18.

76. Julian, *Speeches on Political Questions,* ed. Lydia Maria Child (1872; rpt., Westport, CT: Negro University Press, 1970), 198–99.

77. Heintzelman journal, May 22, 1862, Heintzelman Papers.

3. Reconstructing Emancipation's Martyr

1. For an analysis of the Slave Power symbol, see William Gienapp, "The Republican Party and the Slave Power," in *Race and Slavery in America: Essays in Honor of Kenneth Stampp,* ed. Robert H. Abzug and Stephen E. Maizlish (Lexington: University of Kentucky Press, 1986), 51–78; David Brion Davis, *The Slave Power Conspiracy and the Paranoid Style* (Baton Rouge: Louisiana State University Press, 1969); and Eric Foner, *Free Soil, Free Labor, Free Men: The Ideology of the Republican Party Before the Civil War* (New York: Oxford University Press, 1970), 88–102, 119–20. Information on Frémont's pre–Civil War career can be found in Andrew Rolle, *John Charles Frémont: Character as Destiny* (Norman: University of Oklahoma Press, 1991), 1–188.

2. Numerous works treat the Lincoln-Frémont controversy over emancipation. See David Herbert Donald, *Lincoln* (New York: Simon and Schuster, 1995), 314–15, and Phillip Shaw Paludan, *The Presidency of Abraham Lincoln* (Lawrence: University Press of Kansas, 1994), 86–87.

3. Summaries of Frémont's command in the West can be found in Allan Nevins, *Frémont: Pathmarker of the West,* 2 vols. (1939; rpt., New York: Frederick Unger 1961), 2: 473–549; Rolle, *John Charles Frémont,* 190–213; Robert L. Turkoly-Joczik, "Frémont and the Western Department," *Missouri Historical Review* 82 (1988): 363–85; William E. Parrish, *Turbulent Partnership: Missouri and the Union, 1861–1865* (Columbia: University of Missouri Press, 1963), 1–77.

4. William Ernest Smith, *The Francis Preston Blair Family in Politics,* 2 vols. (New York: Macmillan Company, 1933), 2: 53–85; idem., "The Blairs and Frémont," *Missouri Historical Review* 23 (1928–1929): 214–59. The Hamilton R. Gamble and James O. Broadhead Papers in the Missouri Historical Society, St. Louis, contain a wealth of information on the difficulties between Frémont and the Blairs.

5. Fred Nicklason, "The Civil War Contracts Committee," *Civil War History* 17 (1971): 232–36; Elihu Washburne to Abraham Lincoln, October 21, 1861, Lincoln Papers. The Thomas report appeared in the October 30, 1861, edition of the *New York Daily Tribune*. Many papers throughout the North were critical of the publication of this report; a typical criticism can be found in the Missouri *Daily Democrat*, November 4, 1861, p. 2, c. 1–2.

6. J. B. Harrison to George W. Julian, October 18, 1861, Julian Papers; *Rockford* (Illinois) *Republican*, November 7, 1861, p. 2, c. 2, quoted in the Cole Notes, Illinois Historical Survey, Urbana; Lincoln to Samuel Curtis, October 24, 1861, in *The Collected Works of Abraham Lincoln*, ed. Roy B. Basler, 8 vols. (New Brunswick, NJ: Rutgers University Press, 1953), 4: 562. Lincoln's struggles on this issue are described by Attorney General Edward Bates (see *The Diary of Edward Bates*, ed. Howard K. Beale [1933; rpt., New York: Da Capo Press, 1971], 198–99).

7. *The Memoirs of Gustave Koerner, 1809–1896*, ed. Thomas J. McCormick, 2 vols. (Cedar Rapids, IA: Torch Press, 1909), 2: 189; Richard Smith to Salmon Chase, November 7, 1861, Salmon P. Chase Papers, Claremont Graduate School, Claremont, California (microfilm); Diary of William Turner Coggeshall, November 4, 1861, Ohio Historical Society, Columbus; *New York Daily Tribune*, November 7, 1861, p. 4, c. 3–4. When Frémont was relieved, he was not on the verge of engaging Price's army. In fact, Price wanted to lure Frémont into the hilly terrain near the Arkansas-Missouri border, hoping to surprise Union forces and thereby overcome Frémont's numerical superiority in troops. See Albert Castel, *Sterling Price and the Civil War in the West* (Baton Rouge: Louisiana State University Press, 1968), 59–60, and Sterling Price to Albert Johnston in OR, ser. 1, vol. 3: 731–32.

8. William Howes to Montgomery Blair, November 15, 1861, Blair Family Papers; Edward Bartlett to George McClellan, November 23, 1861, McClellan Papers; Schuyler Colfax to Charles Heaton, November 15, 1861, Schuyler Colfax Papers, Northern Indiana Historical Society, South Bend; A. Denny to Benjamin Wade, November 28, 1861, Wade Papers; George Lee to Zachariah Chandler, December 4, 1861, Chandler Papers; James W. Grimes to William P. Fessenden, November 13, 1861, and Grimes to wife, November 13, 1861, in William Salter, *The Life of James W. Grimes: Governor of Iowa, 1854–1858, A Senator of the United States, 1859–1869* (New York: D. Appleton and Company, 1876), 154–56.

9. *Congressional Globe*, 37th Cong. 2d sess., 16–17, 29–32.

10. Jesse Benton Frémont to Thomas Starr King, December 29, 1861, and J. B. Frémont to Colfax, December 30, 1861, in *The Letters of Jessie Benton Frémont*, ed. Paula Herr and Mary Lee Spence (Urbana: University of Illinois Press, 1993), 302–5 and 307–8.

11. *Chicago Tribune*, December 28, 1861, p. 2, c. 3.

12. *New York Daily Tribune*, January 1, 1862, p. 2, c. 4–6.

13. Hannibal Hamlin to Ellie Hamlin, January 4, 1862, Hannibal Hamlin Papers, photostatic copy in Illinois Historical Survey; J. B. Frémont to King, December 29, 1861, in Herr and Spence, eds., *Letters of Jessie Benton Frémont*, 302–5; Indiana *True Republican* (Richmond), January 23, 1862, p. 2, c. 3 (Washington correspondent report, dated January 11, 1862).

14. *New York Daily Tribune*, January 11, 1862, p. 5, c. 1; George W. Julian, "The Cause and Cure of Our National Troubles," in *Speeches on Political Questions*, ed. Lydia Maria Child (1872; rpt., Westport, CT: Negro University Press, 1970), 154–80.

15. CCW, 3: 32–35.

16. Ibid., 35–43.

17. Ibid., 49–54 (quote, 53–54).

18. Ibid., 59–61 (quote, 60).

19. Ward Hill Lamon to Lincoln, October 21, 26, 1861, Lincoln Papers; J. B. Frémont to Lamon, October 30–31, 1861, in Herr and Spence, eds., *Letters of Jessie Frémont*, 287–91; Washburne to Lincoln, October 29, 1861, Lincoln Papers. The Lamon affair is covered in depth in Lavern Marshall Hamand, "Ward Hill Lamon: Lincoln's 'Peculiar Friend'" (Ph.D. diss., University of Illinois, 1949), 229–52. Lamon still harbored a grudge against Washburne in April 1862 when he wrote his Illinois associates David Davis, Leonard Swett, and William W. Orme. According to Lamon, Washburne would be a candidate for governor of Illinois in the next election. "[Washburne] may suit the complexion of Illinois *politics,*" wrote Lamon, "but he don't suit me and there is no earthly inducement that would make me vote for him, and no power on earth could force me from raising my feeble voice to avert such a calamity to the people of my own State, as even the prospect of his election would be" (see Lamon to Davis, Swett, and Orme, April 13, 1862, William W. Orme Papers, Illinois Historical Survey). Lamon's hatred of radical Republicans was well known; his February 10, 1862, letter to Orme is particularly vituperative (see Orme Papers).

20. CCW, 3: 70–71; Lincoln to Browning, September 22, 1861, in *The Political Thought of Abraham Lincoln,* ed. Richard Current (New York: Macmillan Publishing Company, 1967), 193. For Browning's support of Frémont, see Browning to Lincoln, September 17, 1861, Lincoln Papers.

21. CCW, 3: 154–212 and 234–45; Smith, "Blairs and Frémont," 256.

22. J. B. Frémont to Frederick Billings, January 21, 1862, in Herr and Spence, eds., *Letters of Jessie B. Frémont,* 309–10; *The Journals and Miscellaneous Notebooks of Ralph Waldo Emerson,* ed. Linda Allardt and David W. Hill, 10 vols. (Cambridge, MA: Belknap Press, 1982), 5: 191; *New York Tribune,* January 27, 1862, p. 4, c. 6. The contention of Howard C. Westwood that Wade was the only committee member to support Frémont is absurd. Not only does Westwood ignore page after page of staged testimony, but he also ignores some obvious connections between other committee members and Frémont, most notably George W. Julian's friendship with the Frémonts (see Howard C. Westwood, "The Joint Committee on the Conduct of the War—A Look at the Record," *Lincoln Herald* 80 [1978]: 6–7).

23. CCW, 1: 78–79; Thomas J. House to Wade, February 1, 1862, and F. L. Montague to Wade, February 21, 1862, Wade Papers; W. Lawson to J. Covode, February 15, 1862, Covode Papers; Josephine [?] to G. Julian, February 27, 1862, Giddings-Julian Papers, Library of Congress.

24. *New York Times,* February 7, 1862, p. 1, c. 1–2; Henry Halleck to McClellan, February 2, 1862, McClellan Papers; Wade to Charles A. Dana, February 3, 1862, Charles A. Dana Papers, Library of Congress; J. B. Frémont to Billings, February 7, 1862, in Herr and Spence, eds., *Letters of Jessie B. Frémont,* 311–12; Edwin Stanton to Dana, February 1, 1862, in Charles A. Dana, *Recollections of the Civil War, with the Leaders at Washington and in the Field in the Sixties* (New York: D. Appleton and Company, 1898), 6; James Savage to John Fiala, February 14, 1862, John T. Fiala Papers, Missouri Historical Society, St. Louis; *New York Daily Tribune,* February 20, 1862, p. 5, c. 3. John Byng (1704–1757) was a British admiral who was court-martialed and executed for allowing the French to take Minorca during the Seven Years War.

25. Chandler to wife, October 12, 27, 1861, Chandler Papers; Adam Gurowski, *Diary,* 3 vols. (Boston: Lee and Shepard, 1862), 1: 145.

26. *New York Daily Tribune,* March 4, 1862, p. 4, c. 2, March 7, 1862, p. 5, c. 4; *Congressional Globe,* 37th Cong. 2d sess., 1118–19; J. B. Frémont to Billings, January 21, 1862, in Herr and Spence, eds., *Letters of Jessie B. Frémont,* 309–10. Elizabeth Blair Lee, sister of Frank and Montgomery Blair, remarked that George Julian claimed that the publication of Montgomery's letter "had used Frémont up in the estimation of all

honest men." Such an assertion seems incredible given Julian's public speeches and his continued correspondence with the Frémonts. See Elizabeth Blair Lee to S. P. Lee, March 7, 1862, in *Wartime Washington: The Civil War Letters of Elizabeth Blair Lee,* ed. Virginia Jean Laas (Urbana: University of Illinois Press, 1991), 84.

27. *Congressional Globe,* 37th Cong. 2d sess., 1062–63.

28. Ibid., 1063–70.

29. E. B. Lee to S. P. Lee, December 15, 1861, March 7, 1862 in Laas, ed., *Wartime Washington,* 91, 107; Frank Blair Jr. to John Schofield, February 28, 1862, John M. Schofield Papers, Library of Congress.

30. *Congressional Globe,* 37th Cong., 2d sess., 1118–25. "Frémont's One Hundred Days" appeared in the January, February, and March 1862 editions of the *Atlantic Monthly.*

31. *Congressional Globe,* 37th Cong., 2d sess., 1125; Willard Smith, *Schuyler Colfax: The Changing Fortunes of a Political Idol* (Indianapolis: Indiana Historical Bureau, 1952), 160–66. Colfax also assisted Horace Greeley in writing editorials defending Frémont in the *New York Daily Tribune.* See Horace Greeley to Colfax, April 7, 16, 1862, Colfax-Greeley Correspondence, Indiana State Library, Indianapolis (microfilm, originals in New York Public Library).

32. *Congressional Globe,* 37th Cong., 2d sess., 1126–30. Colfax sent a copy of this speech to Lincoln (see Colfax to Lincoln, March 10, 1862, Lincoln Papers).

33. *Letters of John Hay and Extracts from Diary* (1909; rpt., New York: Gordian Press, 1969), 55; William Bell to Samuel S. Cox, March 17, 1862, Samuel S. Cox Papers, Brown University (also on microfilm, Ohio Historical Society); George Converse to Cox, March 13, 1862, Cox Papers; Anthony L. Knapp to Charles Lanphier, April 8, 1862, Charles Lanphier Papers, Illinois State Historical Library, Springfield; David Davis to Joseph Holt, March 14, 27, 1862, Joseph Holt Papers, Library of Congress; E. B. Lee to S. P. Lee, March 11, 1862, Laas, ed., *Wartime Washington,* 109; Fred R. Edge to Greeley, March 12, 1862, Greeley Papers.

34. For a discussion of the difference between constituencies, see Michael Holt, *Political Parties and American Political Development from the Age of Jackson to the Age of Lincoln* (Baton Rouge: Louisiana State University Press, 1992), 323–53.

35. *Congressional Globe,* 37th Cong. 2d sess., 116, 1743–53, 1835–39, 1849–53, 1862–71, 1887; Elihu Washburne to Henry Dawes, February 3, 1862, and C. H. Stowell to Dawes, February 14, 1862, Henry L. Dawes Papers, Library of Congress; Nicklason, "Contracts Committee," 241.

36. *Congressional Globe,* 37th Cong., 2d sess., 1836, 1852; J. B. Frémont to Julian, May 1, 1862, in Herr and Spence, eds., *Letters of Jessie B. Frémont,* 319–20.

37. CCW, 3: 6.

38. T. Harry Williams, "Frémont and the Politicians," *Journal of the American Military History Foundation* 2 (1938): 188, and *Lincoln and the Radicals* (Madison: University of Wisconsin Press, 1941), 109; Hans L. Trefousse, "The Joint Committee on the Conduct of the War," *Civil War History* 10 (1964): 18–19.

39. Julian, "Cause and Cure," 173.

40. Archer Jones, *Civil War Command and Strategy: The Process of Victory and Defeat* (New York: Free Press, 1992), 18; Halleck quote from Herman Hattaway and Archer Jones, *How the North Won: A Military History of the Civil War* (Urbana: University of Illinois Press, 1983), 286; William Lusk to Horace Barnard, September 28, 1862, *The War Letters of William Lusk* (New York: privately printed, 1911), 214. Perhaps even more revealing about the committee's lack of military expertise was its insistence on promoting Frémont even after his military incompetence was self-evident. Committee members were still pushing Lincoln for another command in spring 1863. Robert H. Milroy, a general of volunteers and political crony of Frémont-booster Schuyler

Colfax, had a firsthand view of Frémont when the latter served under him in the Mountain Department. Although Milroy was initially enthusiastic, experience soon changed his perception. "The world had been greatly deceived in that man," he told his wife. "As a general [Frémont] was a perfect failure." Unfortunately, the majority of committee members did not draw the same conclusions from Frémont's mediocre performance in the Shenandoah Valley. See R. H. Milroy to "My Dear Mary," July 4, 1862, Papers of Robert H. Milroy, comp. Margaret B. Paulus, 1966, collection in University of Illinois Library, 1:54.

4. *"McClellan Is an Imbecile"*

1. Mark Grimsley, *The Hard Hand of War: Union Military Policy Toward Southern Civilians, 1861–1865* (Cambridge: Cambridge University Press, 1995), 7–46; Joseph L. Harsh, "On the McClellan-Go-Round," *Civil War History* 19 (1973): 117 (quote). An abbreviated version of Grimsley's argument can be found in his "Conciliation and Its Failure, 1861–1862," *Civil War History* 39 (1993): 317–35. McClellan's views on civil war, like many of his Democratic contemporaries, were no doubt influenced by the work of the Swiss legal philosopher Emmerich Vattel. See Jean H. Baker, *Affairs of Party: The Political Culture of Northern Democrats in the Mid-Nineteenth Century* (Ithaca, NY: Cornell University Press, 1983), 150–51.

2. Eric Foner, *Free Soil, Free Labor, Free Men: The Ideology of the Republican Party Before the Civil War* (New York: Oxford University Press, 1970), 9–15, 86–90; George W. Julian, "The Strength and Weakness of the Slave Power—the Duty of Anti-Slavery Men," in *Speeches on Political Questions,* ed. Lydia Maria Child (1872; rpt., Westport, CT: Negro University Press, 1970), 70; George W. Julian, *Political Recollections 1840–1872* (Chicago: Jansen, McClurg and Company, 1884), 222.

3. For individual committee members' opinions on Lincoln, see Hans Trefousse, *Benjamin Franklin Wade: Radical Republican from Ohio* (New York: Twayne Publishers, 1963), 148; Sister Mary Karl George, *Zachariah Chandler: A Political Biography* (East Lansing: Michigan State University Press, 1969), 45; Allen Thorndike Rice, ed., *Reminiscences of Abraham Lincoln by Distinguished Men of His Time* (New York: North American Publishing Company, 1886), 47–48 (comments of George Julian).

4. Stephen W. Sears, *George B. McClellan: The Young Napoleon* (New York: Ticknor and Fields, 1988), 3–26, 50–58; Russell F. Weigley, *History of the United States Army,* rev. ed. (Bloomington: University of Indiana Press, 1984), 244–45; Edward G. Hagerman, "The Professionalization of George B. McClellan and Early Field Command," *Civil War History* 21 (1975): 121; Michael Howard, *Studies in War and Peace* (New York: Viking Press, 1959), 32.

5. Sears, *Young Napoleon,* 65–80; George McClellan to Samuel Barlow, November 8, 1861, 128, and McClellan to Mary Ellen McClellan, November 14 [?], 1861, 132–33, in *The Civil War Papers of George B. McClellan: Selected Correspondence, 1860–1865,* ed. Stephen W. Sears (New York: Ticknor and Fields, 1989).

6. Sears, *Young Napoleon,* 122–23, 125–26; Herman Hattaway and Archer Jones, *How the North Won: A Military History of the Civil War* (Urbana: University of Illinois Press, 1983), 85.

7. *New York Daily Tribune,* December 16, 1861, p. 4, c. 6; Heintzelman journal, December 16, 1861, Heintzelman Papers; *The Diary of Edward Bates,* ed. Howard K. Beale (1933; rpt., New York: Da Capo Press, 1971), 220. T. Harry Williams suggests that politics was at the bottom of the McClellan and anti-McClellan factions in the Army of the Potomac. Siding with the radical Republicans were Heintzelman, McDowell, Edward Sumner, Erasmus D. Keyes, and John G. Barnard. Siding with McClellan were

William B. Franklin, Fitz-John Porter, Andrew Porter, William F. Smith, George McCall, Louis Blenker, and James F. Negley. The problem with Williams's analysis is that many of the so-called radical generals were hardly radical in politics and, in some instances, would take McClellan's side against the Lincoln administration. Heintzelman, for instance, vigorously denounced the imprisonment of Charles Stone as well as the detachment of McDowell's corp at the beginning of the Peninsula campaign; both McDowell and Keyes similarly protested the detachment. See T. Harry Williams, *Lincoln and the Radicals* (Madison: University of Wisconsin Press, 1941), 118–19.

8. CCW, 1863, 1: 117–21, 131–44.

9. Ibid., 122–30, 170–78.

10. *New York Daily Tribune,* December 27, 1861, p. 5, c. 2; CCW, 1863, 1: 72; Wade's remarks quoted from Trefousse, *Benjamin Wade,* 159; Stephen B. Oates, *With Malice Toward None: A Life of Abraham Lincoln* (New York: Harper and Row, 1977), 307; Benjamin Thomas, *Abraham Lincoln: A Biography* (New York: Alfred A. Knopf, 1952), 292; Lincoln to McClellan, January 1, 1862, in *The Collected Works of Abraham Lincoln,* ed. Roy P. Basler, 8 vols. (New Brunswick, NJ: Rutgers University Press), 5: 88.

11. Beale, ed., *Diary of Edward Bates,* 220; George B. McClellan, *McClellan's Own Story* (New York: Charles L. Webster and Company, 1887), 149.

12. J. Cummings to E. McPherson, December 9, 1861, Edward McPherson Papers, Library of Congress; Simeon Nash to Benjamin F. Wade, January 1, 1862, Seidon Haines to Wade, December 31, 1861, Silas Potts to Wade, January 3, 1862, all in Wade Papers. Also see Michael F. Holt, *Political Parties and American Political Development from the Age of Jackson to the Age of Lincoln* (Baton Rouge: Louisiana State University Press, 1992), 328.

13. CCW, 1863, 1: 72–73; David Donald, ed., *Inside Lincoln's Cabinet: The Civil War Diaries of Salmon P. Chase* (New York: Longmans, Green, and Company, 1954), 56–57; *Chicago Tribune,* January 16, 1862, p. 1, c. 3; Julian, *Political Recollections,* 201–2; Frederick J. Blue, *Salmon Chase: A Life in Politics* (Kent, Ohio: Kent State University Press, 1987), 176. Details about the relationship between McClellan and Ives are found in Louis M. Starr, *Bohemian Brigade: Civil War Newsmen in Action* (Madison: University of Wisconsin Press, 1954), 78–81.

14. Adam Gurowski, *Diary,* 3 vols. (Boston: Lee and Shepard, 1862), 1: 147; Salmon Chase to Kate Chase and William Sprague, January 1862, Chase Papers; Lincoln to McClellan, January 9, 1862, in Basler, ed., *Collected Works,* 5: 94; Thomas, *Abraham Lincoln,* 290–92; Beale, ed., *Diary of Edwin Bates,* 223–24; John G. Nicolay and John Hay, *Abraham Lincoln: A History,* 10 vols. (New York: Century Company, 1886), 5: 156–58; Oates, *With Malice Toward None,* 308–9; Warren W. Hassler, *George McClellan: Shield of the Union* (Baton Rouge: Louisiana State University Press, 1957), 49–50 (quote, 50); Sears, *Young Napoleon,* 141–43.

15. CCW, 1863, 1: 75; Detroit Post and Tribune, *Zachariah Chandler: An Outline of His Life and Public Service* (Detroit: Post and Tribune Publishers, 1880), 224–26; Trefousse, *Benjamin Wade,* 162.

16. Sears, *Young Napoleon,* 143–44; *New York Herald,* January 12, 1862, p. 1, c. 2, January 16, 1862, p. 1, c. 1, January 17, 1862, p. 4, c. 5; McClellan to Randolph Marcy, January 29, 1862, in Sears, ed., *Civil War Papers,* 160.

17. *Chicago Tribune,* January 8, 1862, p. 2, c. 6.

18. N. G. Wheaton to Lyman Trumbull, January 9, 1862, Trumbull Papers; L. Disbrow to E. Washburne, January 26, 1862, and W. C. Dunning to Washburne, January 10, 1862, Elihu Washburne Papers, Library of Congress; James W. Stone to Chase, January 15, 1862, Chase Papers; George Carlisle to Chandler, January 18, 1862, Chandler Papers; Caroline Wade to Theodore Wade, January 20, 1862, Wade Papers, Western

278 *Over Lincoln's Shoulder*

Reserve Historical Library, Cleveland, Ohio. A good summary of the so-called radical/ conservative tension in the Republican party is T. Harry Williams's "Lincoln and the Radicals: An Essay on Civil War Historiography," in *Grant, Lee, Lincoln and the Radicals: Essays on Civil War Leadership,* ed. Grady McWhiney (Evanston, IL: Northwestern University Press, 1964), 72–91. Allan Bogue, "Historians and the Radical Republicans: A Meaning for Today," *Journal of American History* 70 (1983): 7–34, suggests intraparty conflicts were always more significant than interparty tension. William D. Mallam, "Lincoln and the Conservatives," *Journal of Southern History* 28 (1962): 31–45, identifies a number of conservative Republicans but admits that many suffered defeat in the election of 1862 because of their opposition to emancipation.

19. Anthony L. Knapp to Charles Lanphier, January 18, 1862, Lanphier Papers; Robert Harryman to Samuel S. Cox, January 26, 1862, Cox Papers; *Boston Herald,* January 9, 1862, p. 2, c. 2–3; Kenneth B. Shover, "Maverick at Bay: Ben Wade's Senate Reelection Campaign, 1862–1863," *Civil War History* 12 (1966): 32–33; Charles Follet to Cox, February 4, 1862, Cox Papers; *Congressional Globe,* 37th Cong., 2d sess., 573.

20. President's General War Order no. 1, January 27, 1862, in Basler, ed., *Collected Works,* 5: 111–12; Edwin Stanton to Wade, January 27, 1862, Stanton Papers; Benjamin Thomas and Harold Hyman, *Edwin Stanton: The Life and Times of Lincoln's Secretary of War* (New York: Alfred A. Knopf, 1962), 169–70; Julian's comments in Thorndike, *Reminiscences,* 53; T. Harry Williams, *Lincoln and the Radicals,* 112–13, and *Lincoln and His Generals* (New York: Alfred A. Knopf, 1952), 62–65; Hassler, *George McClellan,* 53.

21. Lincoln to McClellan, February 3, 1862, in Basler, ed., *Collected Works,* 5: 118–19; Henry J. Raymond to James Wadsworth, February 9, 1862, Wadsworth Family Papers, Library of Congress; Joseph Medill to Lincoln, February 9, 1862, Lincoln Papers.

22. Henry Halleck to McClellan, February 24, 1862, and T. Kimber to McClellan, February 24, 1862, McClellan Papers; McClellan, *Own Story,* 152–54; David S. Sparks, ed., *Inside Lincoln's Army: The Diary of Marsena Randolph Patrick, Provost Marshal General, Army of the Potomac* (New York: Thomas Yorloff, 1964), 45.

23. CCW, 1863, 1: 83–86.

24. Post and Tribune, *Zachariah Chandler,* 227–28; Sears, *Young Napoleon,* 155–56.

25. Julian, *Political Recollections,* 204–5; McClellan, *Own Story,* 222; Heintzelman journal, February 14, 18, 1862, Heintzelman Papers.

26. CCW, 1863, 1: 86–88; Post and Tribune, *Zachariah Chandler,* 228; Oates, *With Malice Toward None,* 318.

27. Stephen Sears, *To the Gates of Richmond: The Peninsula Campaign* (New York: Ticknor and Fields, 1992), 11–18; Julian, *Political Recollections,* 208–9; Gurowski to Wade, March 14, 1862, Wade Papers; Beale, ed., *Diary of Edward Bates,* 240; McClellan to Ellen McClellan, March 11, 1862, Sears, ed., *Civil War Papers,* 202.

28. *Chicago Tribune,* March 13, 1862. p. 1, c. 3, March 14, 1862, p. 1, c. 1; CCW, 1863, 1: 89–90, 249. T. Harry Williams believes that Lincoln should have vetoed McClellan's entire plan because he did not have confidence in it (see *Lincoln and his Generals,* 66; for the details on McClellan's demotion, see pp. 70–71).

29. Sears, *To the Gates of Richmond,* 3–9, 18–20; Heintzelman journal, March 8, 1862, Heintzelman Papers; Gurowski to Chandler, March 8, 1862, Chandler Papers; Stanton to McClellan, March 10, 1862, McClellan Papers; Presidential War Order no. 3 in Basler, ed., *Collected Works,* 5: 155.

30. W. A. Croffat, ed., *Fifty Years in Camp and Field: Diary of General Ethan Allen Hitchcock, U.S.A.* (New York: G. P. Putnam's Sons, 1909), 438, 440; Anson Stager to Jeptha Wade, March 20, 1862, Jeptha H. Wade Papers, Western Reserve Historical Society, Cleveland, Ohio.

31. George Gibbs to McClellan, March 13, 1862, McClellan Papers; McClellan to Barlow, March 16, 1862, in Sears, ed., *Civil War Papers,* 213; Fitz-John Porter [?] to Manton Marble, March 17, 1862, Manton Marble Papers, Library of Congress.

32. William J. Howard to Covode, March 18, 1862, Covode Papers; Julian, *Political Recollections,* 209–11.

33. Lincoln to McClellan, March 31, 1862, in Basler, ed., *Collected Works,* 5: 175; Wadsworth to Stanton, April 2, 1862, Stanton to Ethan Hitchcock and Lorenzo Thomas, April 2, 1862, and Hitchcock and Thomas to Stanton, April 2, 1862, all in Stanton Papers; CCW, 1863, 1: 251–53; Lincoln to Stanton, April 3, 1862, in Basler, ed., *Collected Works,* 5: 179.

34. Heintzelman journal, April 3, 1862, Heintzelman Papers; McClellan to M. E. McClellan, April 6, 1862, in Sears, ed., *Civil War Papers,* 230; McClellan to Montgomery Blair, April 6, 1862, Blair Family Papers; William Franklin to McClellan, April 7, 1862, McClellan Papers; William S. Rosecrans to F. J. Porter, September 12, 1880, Fitz-John Porter Papers, Library of Congress. Erasmus Keyes also wrote a bitter letter to New York Republican senator Ira Harris detailing the administration's perfidy in regard to the Peninsula campaign (see Keyes to Harris, April 7, 1862, McClellan Papers).

35. Hassler, *George McClellan,* 78–84; William Starr Myers, *General George Brinton McClellan* (New York: D. Appleton-Century Company, 1954), 269; Sears, *To the Gates of Richmond,* 32–34; Klement, *Dark Lanterns: Secret Political Societies, Conspiracies, and Treason Trials in the Civil War* (Baton Rouge: Louisiana State University Press, 1984), 22.

36. McClellan to Henry R. Jackson, July 15, 1861, in Sears, ed., *Civil War Papers,* 57.

37. Hagerman, "Professionalization of George McClellan," 115–18; John K. Mahon, "Civil War Infantry Assault Tactics," *Military Affairs* 25 (1961): 57–68. The logic of the Peninsula campaign is outlined in Hattaway and Jones, *How the North Won,* 82–95. The issue of the safety of Washington, DC, is discussed in Thomas J. Rowland, "'Heaven Save a Country Governed by Such Counsels!' The Safety of Washington and the Peninsula Campaign," *Civil War History* 42 (1996): 5–17.

38. For the details concerning the investigation of rebel atrocities and the public's reaction, see CCW, 1863, 1: 92, 95; Senate Rep. 41, 37th Cong., 2d sess.; *Harper's Weekly,* May 17, 1862, 306; N. H. Brewley to Wade, May 1, 1862, F. W. Meyers to Wade, May 2, 1862, G. H. Atwood to Wade, May 2, 1862, all in Wade Papers; and *Chicago Tribune,* May 7, 1862, p. 2, c. 2. For Julian's speech, see *Congressional Globe,* 37th Cong., 2d sess., appendix, 184–85.

39. Myers, *George McClellan,* 274–87; Hassler, *George McClellan,* 110–13, 129–30; McClellan, *Own Story,* 346–48; McClellan to wife, May 22, 1862, in Sears, ed., *Civil War Papers,* 275.

40. Sears, *Young Napoleon,* 168–200; Sears, *Gates of Richmond,* 111–45; Heintzelman journal, April 29 (quote), May 19, 1862, Heintzelman Papers; Lincoln to McClellan, May 1 (quote), 9, 1862, in Basler, ed., *Collected Works,* 5: 208–9; Williams, *Lincoln and his Generals,* 87–115. Good summaries of the overall arguments for and against McClellan are in Richard N. Current, *The Lincoln Nobody Knows* (New York: McGraw-Hill Book Company, 1958), 140–51, and Joseph T. Glatthaar, *Partners in Command: The Relationships Between Leaders in the Civil War* (New York: Free Press, 1994), 51–93, 237–42. Glatthaar argues that McClellan's failures are due partly to what psychologists term "paranoid personality disorder with narcissistic tendencies," more simply defined as the constant exaggeration of obstacles, excessive caution, and the tendency to blame failures on others. A recent attempt to rehabilitate McClellan's reputation is Thomas J. Rowland, "In the Shadows of Grant and Sherman: George B. McClellan Revisited," *Civil War History* 40 (1994): 202–25. Rowland argues that McClellan's

reputation suffers because he held to higher standards than did other Union commanders such as Grant and Sherman. Because he commanded early in the war in the highly
scrutinized eastern theater, his every action was viewed under a microscope; Grant and
Sherman were allowed more latitude. Rowland also maintains that historians too readily
psychoanalyze McClellan. An earlier attempt to defend McClellan that maintains the
soundness of his overall strategic conceptions is Joseph Harsh's "On the McClellan-Go-
Round," 101–18.

41. Sam Wilkeson to Wade, May 13, 1862 (incorrectly filed in 1863 correspondence),
and Joseph Kinney to Wade, May 31, 1862, Wade Papers; Beale, ed., *Diary of Edward
Bates,* 260.

42. *Boston Herald,* June 13, 1862, p. 4, c. 1; Stanton to McClellan, June 7, 1862,
Stanton Papers; McClellan to Stanton, June 7, 1862, in Sears, ed., *Civil War Papers,*
290; *Congressional Globe,* 37th Cong., 2d sess., 2738–40; Heintzelman journal, June
15, 1862, Heintzelman Papers.

43. McClellan to M. E. McClellan, June 2, 1862, in Sears, ed., *Civil War Papers,*
287; Sears, *To the Gates of Richmond,* 210–310 (Humphrey's remarks, 281).

44. McClellan to Stanton, June 28, 1862, in Sears, ed., *Civil War Papers,* 323; Sears,
Young Napoleon, 213–14; Horace Greeley to Joshua Giddings, June 29, 1862, and
Giddings to Grotius Giddings, July 3, 1862, Joshua Giddings Papers, Ohio Historical
Society (microfilm), Columbus; Julian, *Political Recollections,* 218–19.

45. CCW, 1863, 1: 100; Chandler to wife, July 6, 1862, Chandler Papers; *Congressional Globe,* 37th Cong., 2d sess., 3134, 3149–50.

46. Joseph Wright to Calvin Fletcher, March 4, 1861, March 2, 1862 (quote), Calvin
Fletcher Papers, Indiana Historical Society, Indianapolis; R. N. Hidron to Richard
Thompson, February 12, 1862, Richard Thompson Papers, Indiana State Library; *The
Diary of Calvin Fletcher,* ed. Gayle Thornbrough and Paula Corpuz (Indianapolis: Indi-
ana Historical Society, 1983), 7: 330, 340–41, 355–56.

47. Emma Lou Thornbrough, *Indiana in the Civil War Era, 1850–1880* (Indianapolis: Indiana Historical Society, 1965), 116; *Indianapolis Daily Sentinel,* March 7, 1862,
p. 2, c. 1–2; *Chicago Times,* March 14, 1862, p. 2, c. 2; A Hamilton to Wright, March
3, 1862, and J. Hunt to Wright, March 17, 1862, Joseph A. Wright Papers, Indiana State
Library; *Chicago Tribune,* April 2, 1862, p. 1, c. 1; Schuyler Colfax to Fletcher, June
13, 1862, Fletcher Papers.

48. *Congressional Globe,* 37th Cong., 2d sess., 3219–26.

49. Chandler to wife, July 11, 1862, Chandler Papers; CCW, 1863, 1: 102.

50. *Ashtabula Sentinel,* July 30, 1862, p. 4, c. 1; *Congressional Globe,* 37th Cong.,
2d sess., 3386–92, 3401.

51. McClellan to Barlow, July 23, 1862, in Sears, ed., *Civil War Papers,* 369; *New
York Herald,* July 18, 1862, p. 4, c. 3; *New York World,* August 7, 1862, p. 4, c. 2–6,
p. 5, c. 1; F. J. Porter to Marble, July [?], 1862, Marble Papers; *Vanity Fair,* July 19,
1862, 29.

52. William Doubleday to Chandler, August 8, 1862, Moses Kimball to Chandler,
July 23, 1862, and Dorus Fox to Chandler, July 31, 1862, Chandler Papers.

53. Howard C. Westwood, "The Joint Committee on the Conduct of the War—A
Look at the Record," *Lincoln Herald* 80 (1978): 7.

54. Archer Jones, *Civil War Command and Strategy: The Process of Victory and
Defeat* (New York: Free Press, 1992), 74.

55. McClellan to Lincoln, July 7, 1862, in Sears, ed., *Civil War Papers,* 344–45; Sears,
Young Napoleon, 227–29; Oates, *With Malice Towards None,* 332–33.

56. David Herbert Donald, *Lincoln* (New York: Simon and Schuster, 1995), 360
(quote); Hassler, *George McClellan,* 178; Wallace J. Schutz and Walter N. Trenerry,
Abandoned by Lincoln: A Military Biography of General John Pope (Urbana: Univer-

sity of Illinois Press, 1990), 3–7, 91–93; *The Diary of Orville Hickman Browning,* ed. James G. Randall and Theodore C. Pease (Springfield: Illinois State Library, 1925), 1: 552; Clara Pope to John Pope, June 26, 1862, Porter Papers. The relationship among Pope, Stanton, and Lincoln is recently reevaluated in Daniel E. Sutherland, "Abraham Lincoln, John Pope, and the Origins of Total War," *Journal of Military History* 56 (1992): 567–86. Sutherland maintains that Pope did not need to be forced upon Lincoln by the radical Republicans because it was Lincoln who brought Pope to Washington in the first place.

57. Schutz and Trenerry, *Abandoned by Lincoln,* 93; CCW, 1863, 1: 276–81.

58. Schutz and Trenerry, *Abandoned by Lincoln,* 102–4; Jacob D. Cox, *Military Reminiscences of the Civil War* (New York: Charles Scribner's and Sons, 1900), 222; Chase to Richard Parsons, July 20, 1862, Chase Papers.

59. Cox, *Reminiscences,* 222–23; McClellan to R. Marcy, July 13, 1862, in Sears, ed., *Civil War Papers,* 356; Porter to J. C. G. Kennedy, July 17, 1862, Porter Papers; Sparks, ed., *Diary of Marsena Patrick,* 110, 116.

60. Randall and Pease, eds., *Diary of Browning,* 1: 558–59; Marcy to McClellan, July 13, 1862, McClellan Papers.

61. Chandler to Chase, July 26, 1862, and Chase to Stanton, July 22, 1862, Chase Papers; Donald, ed., *Diary of Salmon Chase,* 96–97, 101–2; Blue, *Salmon Chase,* 177–78; McClellan to Barlow, July 30, 1862, in Sears, ed., *Civil War Papers,* 377; "Address to the Union Meeting at Washington," August 6, 1862, in Basler, ed., *Collected Works,* 5: 358–59.

62. Heintzelman journal, July 26, 31, 1862, Heintzelman Papers; McClellan to Halleck, July 30, 1862, and McClellan to Halleck, August 1, 1862, in Sears, ed., *Civil War Papers,* 376; Chase to Edward Haight, July 24, 1862, Chase Papers; Donald, ed., *Diary of Salmon Chase,* 107; Halleck to McClellan, August 5, 1862, McClellan Papers; *The Diary of Gideon Welles,* ed. John T. Morse, 3 vols. (Boston: Houghton Mifflin Co., 1911), 1: 113.

63. John J. Hennessy, *Return to Bull Run: The Campaign and Battle of Second Manassas* (New York: Simon and Schuster, 1993), 241–42 (quote, 242); McClellan to wife, August 10, 1862, Sears, ed., *Civil War Papers,* 389; Porter to J. Howard Foote, August 12, 1862, Porter Papers. For a detailed account of the battle of Second Bull Run, see Schutz and Trenerry, *Abandoned by Lincoln,* 119–51, and Hennessy, *Return to Bull Run.*

64. McClellan to wife, August 21, 1862, in Sears, ed., *Civil War Papers,* 397; M. E. McClellan to McClellan, August 23, 1862, McClellan Papers; McClellan to Lincoln, August 29, 1862, in Sears, ed., *Civil War Papers,* 416.

65. *Diary of Gideon Welles,* 94–104; Donald, ed., *Diary of Salmon Chase,* 116–20; *Diary of John Hay,* ed. Tyler Dennett (New York: Dodd, Meade, 1939), 60–61, 64–65; M. Blair to Porter, April 3, 1879, quoted in Hassler, *George McClellan,* 226.

66. *Diary of Gideon Welles,* 113, 116 (quote); Thomas, *Abraham Lincoln,* 338.

67. Pope to Stanton, September 5, 1862, Stanton Papers; *New York Herald,* p. 4, c. 3; *New York Times,* September 6, 1862, p. 4, c. 3; O. H. Parker to Covode, September 10, 1862, Covode Papers; Medill to Chase, September 14, 1862, Chase Papers; Chandler to Peter H. Watson, September 10, 1862, Stanton Papers; Chandler to Trumbull, September 10, 1862, Chandler to Chase, September 13, 1862, Chase Papers; Chase to Chandler, September 20, 1862, and Stanton to Chandler, September 18, 1862, Chandler Papers. A meeting of northern governors did take place in Altoona, Pennsylvania, on September 24, 1862. Details of the meeting can be found in John Moses, *Illinois Historical and Statistical,* 2 vols. (Chicago: Fergus Printing Company, 1895), 2: 660–61. John Pope hoped to use the Altoona conference as a means to regain his command. He sent a trusted friend, B. D. Roberts, to talk with Illinois governor Richard

Yates. Roberts told Yates that Pope's Virginia campaign was a success, "a great military movement that has few examples in . . . history." Pope should get command of the entire West, Roberts reasoned; his only problems were due to McClellan's selfishness. See B. D. Roberts to Yates, September 25, 1862, Richard Yates Papers, Illinois State Historical Library, Springfield.

68. Wade to Julian, September 29, 1862, Giddings-Julian Papers; Sears, *Young Napoleon,* 330–34; Halleck to wife, October 7, 1862, quoted in Stephen Ambrose, *Halleck: Lincoln's Chief of Staff* (Baton Rouge: Louisiana State University Press, 1962), 86.

69. Oliver Morton to Lincoln, October 7, 1862, Lincoln Papers; L. Child to C. Summer, October 3, 1862, in *Lydia Maria Child: Selected Letters, 1817–1880,* ed. Milton Metzer and Patricia G. Holland (Amherst: University of Massachusetts Press, 1982), 416–17; Chandler to Chase, October 19, 1862, Chase Papers.

70. Sears, *Young Napoleon,* 338–39; David Davis to Leonard Swett, November 26, 1862, David Davis Papers, Illinois State Historical Library, Springfield; *New York Daily Tribune,* November 10, 1862, p. 4, c. 2–3; Colfax to Lincoln, November 10, 1862, Lincoln Papers; *New York Herald,* November 10, 1862, p. 4, c. 3; *Chicago Times,* November 11, 1862, p. 2, c. 1; Chandler to wife, December 4, 1862, Chandler Papers.

71. Hans L. Trefousse, "The Joint Committee on the Conduct of the War: A Reassessment," *Civil War History* 10 (1964): 12–13.

5. The Fall Elections

1. Frank L. Klement, *The Copperheads in the Middlewest* (Chicago: University of Chicago Press, 1960), 10–39; Joel Silbey, *"A Respectable Minority:" The Democratic Party in the Civil War Era, 1860–1868* (New York: W. W. Norton, 1977), 64–75; Phillip S. Paludan, *"A People's Contest": The Union and the Civil War* (New York: Harper and Row, 1988), 86–102; Bruce Tap, "Race, Rhetoric, and Emancipation: The Election of 1862 in Illinois," *Civil War History* 39 (1993): 101–25; V. Jacque Voegeli, *Free but Not Equal: The Midwest and the Negro During the Civil War* (Chicago: University of Chicago Press, 1967), 62–67; John C. Ropes to John C. Gray, November 9, 1862, in *War Letters of John Chipman and John C. Ropes, 1862–1865* (Boston: Houghton Mifflin Company, 1927), 19; Edwards Pierrepont to James S. Wadsworth, November 5, 1862, Wadsworth Papers; *Harper's Weekly Magazine,* November 22, 1862, 738.

2. James McPherson, *Battle Cry of Freedom: The Civil War Era* (New York: Oxford University Press, 1988), 561–62.

3. *New York Herald,* November 5, 1862, p. 4, c. 2; George Boutwell, *Reminiscences of Sixty Years in Public Life,* 2 vols. (1902; rpt., New York: Greenwood Press, 1968), 1: 2; John D. Caton to Horatio Seymour, December 18, 1862, John D. Caton Papers, Library of Congress.

4. James McMahn to George D. Hill, November 13, 1862, George D. Hill Papers, Bentley Library, University of Michigan, Ann Arbor; Carl Schurz to Lincoln, November 10, 20, 1862, Lincoln Papers; John S. Davis to Henry S. Lane, October 26, 1862, Henry S. Lane Papers, Indiana Historical Society, Indianapolis; *Pittsburg Daily Gazette,* November 5, 1862, p. 2, c. 2; James G. Randall, *Lincoln the President: Springfield to Gettysburg,* 4 vols. (New York: Dodd, Meade and Company 1946), 2: 235–37.

5. Allen Thorndike Rice, ed., *Reminiscences of Abraham Lincoln by Distinguished Men of His Time* (New York: North American Publishing Company, 1886), 271–78.

6. For information about the electoral fortunes of Republican committee members, see Patrick W. Riddleberger, *George Washington Julian, Radical Republican: A Study in Nineteenth Century Politics and Reform* (Indianapolis: Indiana Historical Bureau, 1966), 173–75; Morton S. Wilkinson to Zachariah Chandler, October 20, 1862, Chan-

dler Papers; Martin J. Herschock, "Copperheads and Radicals: Michigan Partisan Politics During the Civil War, 1860–1865," *Michigan Historical Review* 18 (1992): 57–59; "Messrs. Wade and Chandler," copy in Joy Papers; Kenneth B. Stover, "Maverick at Bay: Ben Wade's Senate Re-election Campaign," *Civil War History* 12 (1966): 23–42; Joshua Giddings to George Julian, January 28, 1863, Giddings-Julian Papers. Ohio held elections for state legislature and governor during odd years, a fact undoubtedly beneficial to Wade. See McPherson, *Battle Cry of Freedom,* 516. John Covode was unsuccessful in his bid for the gubernatorial nomination, being outmaneuvered by incumbent Andrew Curtin. See John W. Geary to My Dear Mary, August 7, 1863, *in A Politician Goes to War: The Civil War Letters of John White Geary,* ed. William Alan Blair (University Park; Pennsylvania State University Press, 1995), 107.

7. Lincoln to Joseph Wright, July 31, 1862, in *The Collected Works of Abraham Lincoln,* ed. Roy P. Basler, 8 vols. (New Brunswick, NJ: Rutgers University Press, 1953), 5: 351–52; Wright to Salmon P. Chase, August 4, 1862, Chase Papers; Illinois *State Journal* (Springfield), October 31, 1862; *Indianapolis Daily State Sentinel,* October 23, 1862, p. 2, c. 1, and September 24, 1862, p.2, c. 1 (quote); Emma Lou Thornbrough, *Indiana in the Civil War Era, 1850–1880* (Indianapolis: Indiana Historical Bureau, 1965), 185.

8. Thurlow Weed to William Seward, November 5, 1862, William H. Seward Papers, Rush Library, University of Rochester, Rochester, NY (microfilm); W. H. Blake to Schuyler Colfax, Colfax Papers; Henry Raymond to Lincoln, November 25, 1862, Lincoln Papers; Chandler to wife, December 9, 1862, Chandler Papers.

9. William Marvel, *Burnside* (Chapel Hill: University of North Carolina Press, 1991), 99–103, 123–26, 144–50, 158–60.

10. Ibid., 160–68; Stephen Ambrose, *Halleck: Lincoln's Chief of Staff* (Baton Rouge: Louisiana State University Press, 1962), 95–96.

11. Marvel, *Burnside,* 172–96; OR, ser. 1, vol. 21, 71 (copy of Burnside's orders to Franklin).

12. Marvel, *Burnside,* 198; Darius N. Couch, "Oh Great God! See How Our Men Are Falling," in *Battles and Leaders of the Civil War,* sel. and ed. Ned Bradford (1956; rpt., New York: Meridian Press, 1989), 313–14.

13. *New York World,* December 17, 1862, p. 4, c. 2; *New York Herald,* December 16, 1862, p. 4, c. 4; *Chicago Times,* December 18, 1862, p. 2, c. 1; Stephen Weld to mother, December 17, 1862, in Stephen Minot Weld, *War Diary and Letters of Stephen M. Weld* (Boston: Massachusetts Historical society, 1979), 153; O. W. Norton to "Sister L," December 20, 1862, in O. W. Norton, *Army Letters, 1861–1865,* (Chicago: O. L. Deming, 1903), 129.

14. Adam Gurowski, 3 vols., *Diary* (Boston, 1863), 2: 30; Diary of William Coggeshall, December 22, 1862, Ohio Historical Society; David Davis to Leonard Swett, December 22, 1862, David Davis Papers, Illinois State Historical Library; B. Bindsall to Chandler, December 22, 1862, Chandler Papers; Alan Bogue, ed., "William Parker Cutler's Congressional Diary of 1862–1863," *Civil War History* 33 (1987): 319–20.

15. *The Diary of Orville Hickman Browning,* ed. James G. Randall and Theodore C. Pease, 2 vols. (Springfield: Illinois State Historical Society, 1925), 1: 596–97; Hannibal Hamlin to Ellie Hamlin, December 19, 1862, Hamlin Family Papers, Raymond Folger Library, University of Maine.

16. CCW, 1: 103; Chandler to wife, December 18, 1862, Chandler Papers.

17. *New York Herald,* December 20, 1862, p. 4, c. 4; *Chicago Times,* December 25, 1862, p. 2, c. 2; David S. Sparks, ed., *Inside Lincoln's Army: The Diary of Marsena Randolph Patrick, Provost Marshall General, Army of the Potomac* (New York: Thomas Orloff, 1964), 193; Bogue, ed., "Cutler Diary," 322; George W. Julian, *Political Recollections, 1840–1872* (Chicago: Jansen, McClurg and Company, 1884), 224–25.

18. CCW, 1863, 1: 643–55; Bogue, ed., "Cutler Diary," 325.

19. George Meade to wife, December 20, 1862, in George Meade, *The Life and Letters of General George Gordon Meade,* 2 vols. (New York: Charles Scribner's Sons, 1913), 1: 339–40; CCW, 1863, 1: 656–62, 665–73; William B. Franklin to George McClellan, December 23, 1862, McClellan Papers. When the rebellion broke out, Meade and other U.S. army officers, stationed near Detroit, refused to reaffirm loyalty oaths to the U.S. government when local authorities made such a demand. Apparently, Chandler distrusted Meade after the incident (see Freeman Cleaves, *Meade of Gettysburg* [Norman: Oklahoma University Press, 1960], 51–53).

20. CCW, 1: 663–65, 673–80.

21. Daniel Larned to sister, December 23, 1862, Daniel R. Larned Papers, Library of Congress; 37th Cong., 3d sess., Rep. Com. no. 71, 1; Gurowski, *Diary,* 2: 54–55; Elizabeth Blair Lee to Samuel Philip Lee, December 24, 1862, in *Wartime Washington: The Civil War Letters of Elizabeth Blair Lee,* ed. Virginia Jean Laas (Urbana: University of Illinois Press, 1991), 219; James W. White to Benjamin Wade, December 27, 1862, Benjamin Wade Papers.

22. Hannibal Hamlin to Ellie Hamlin, December 22, 1862, Hamlin Papers; Marvel, *Burnside,* 207–8; Franklin to McClellan, December 23, 1862, McClellan Papers; Henry W. Halleck to Henry M. Whipple, December 28, 1862, Henry M. Whipple Papers, Minnesota Historical Society, Saint Paul.

23. Randall and Pease, eds., *Browning Diary,* 1: 600–602; *The Diary of Edward Bates,* ed. Howard K. Beale (1933; rpt., New York: Da Capo Press, 1971), 269–71; Reinhold H. Luthin, *The Real Abraham Lincoln* (Englewood Cliffs, NJ: Prentice-Hall, 1960), 358–61; Stephen B. Oates, *With Malice Toward None: The Life of Abraham Lincoln* (New York: Harper and Row, 1977), 355–58; David Herbert Donald, *Lincoln* (New York: Simon and Schuster, 1995), 400–406; Davis to Swett, December 22, 1862, Davis Papers.

24. *Congressional Globe,* 37th Cong., 3d sess., 94–100; Herman Belz, "The Etheridge Conspiracy of 1863: A Projected Conservative Coup," *Journal of Southern History* 36 (1970): 550–551, 557; Weed to Seward, January 4, 1863; Grant Goodrich to Lyman Trumbull, January 26, 1863, Trumbull Papers.

25. Frank Klement, *Copperheads,* vii–viii and passim, and *Dark Lanterns: Secret Political Societies, Conspiracies, and Treason Trials in the Civil War* (Baton Rouge: Louisiana State University Press, 1984), 1–6 and passim; Jean H. Baker, *Affairs of Party: The Political Culture of Northern Democrats in the Mid-Nineteenth Century* (Ithaca, NY: Cornell University Press, 1983), 171–76; Silbey, *"Respectable Minority,"* ix–xiv; Herman Hattaway and Archer Jones, *How the North Won: A Military History of the Civil War* (Urbana: University of Illinois Press, 1983), 311 (quote); O. W. Norton to "Sister L," December 6, 1862, in Norton, *Army Letters,* 128; R. M. McAllister to daughter, January 22, 1863, in *The Civil War Letters of Robert McAllister,* ed. James I. Robertson Jr. (New Brunswick, NJ: Rutgers University Press, 1965), 261; J. C. Gray to J. C. Ropes, January 2, 1863, in *War Letters, Chipman and Ropes,* 57; *New York Herald,* January 10, 1863, p. 4, c. 3.

26. Russell F. Weigley, *History of the United States Army,* rev. ed. (Bloomington: University of Indiana Press, 1984), 244–46, 254–55 (quote, 245).

27. John J. Hennessy, *Return to Bull Run: The Campaign and the Battle of Second Manassas* (New York: Simon and Schuster, 1993), vii, 241–42, 464–65; Detroit Post and Tribune, *Zachariah Chandler: An Outline of His Life and Public Service* (Detroit: Post and Tribune Publishers, 1880), 240–41.

28. Herman Haupt, *Reminiscences of Herman Haupt* (Milwaukee: Wright and Joys, 1901), 75–83 (quote, 83); Mrs. Philip Kearny to Lincoln, September 13, 1862, Lincoln Papers; *The Diary of Gideon Welles,* ed. John T. Morse, 3 vols. (Boston: Houghton Mifflin, 1911), 1: 118; *A Radical View: The "Agate" Dispatches of Whitelaw Reid*

1861–1865, ed. and intro. James G. Smart (Memphis: Memphis State University Press, 1976), 223–29 (quote, 228, dispatches of September 4, 1862, and September 10, 1862); S. Weld to William G. Weld, September 6, 1862, in Weld, ed., *War Diary,* 137; Edward K. Whightman to "Dear Brother," September 15, 1862, in *From Antietam to Fort Fisher: The Civil War Letters of Edward King Whightman,* ed. Edward G. Longacre (Rutherford, NJ: Farleigh Dickinson University Press, 1985), 33.

29. E. B. Lee to S. P. Lee, October 20, 1862, in Laas, ed., *Wartime Washington,* 193; Jacob Dolson Cox, *Military Reminiscences of the Civil War,* 2 vols. (New York: Charles Scribner's Sons, 1900), 1: 356–60 (quote, 358–59); *Pittsburg Daily Gazette,* September 26, 1862, p. 2, c. 2; S. M. Weld to W. G. Weld, October 31, 1862, in Weld, ed., *War Diary,* 147.

30. Lincoln to John J. Key, September 26–27, 1862, in Basler, ed., *Collected Works,* 5: 442–43; M. Blair to McClellan, September 27, 1862, McClellan Papers; *Pittsburg Daily Gazette,* October 3, 1862, p. 2, c. 2, October 10, 1862, p. 2, c. 2; Lincoln to Key, November 24, 1862, in Basler, ed., *Collected Works,* 5: 508.

31. D. Larned to Henry Larned, November 22, December 16, 1862, Larned Papers; F. J. Porter to McClellan, January 13, 1863, McClellan Papers. Porter's court-martial is extensively treated in Otto Eisenschiml, *The Celebrated Case of Fitz-John Porter* (Indianapolis: Bobbs-Merrill Company, 1950). Although the book is marred by a one-sided, antiradical perspective, Eisenschiml's contention that Porter was loyal is correct, even if his flattering assessments of Porter's and McClellan's military abilities are seriously flawed.

32. *Congressional Globe,* 37th Cong., 3d sess., 324–34. T. Harry Williams, "The Attack upon West Point During the Civil War," *Mississippi Valley Historical Review* 25 (1939); 491–504. Williams interprets Wade's attack as rooted in an aversion to military science as much as in the radicals' hatred of West Point for its close connection with the Democrats. Williams fails to explain why such radicals as Charles Sumner, John Hale, James Grimes, and Henry Wilson voted for the measure to fund West Point. The charge that West Point represented an elite, privileged class was hardly new (see K. Bruce Galloway and Robert Brown Johnson Jr., *West Point: America's Power Fraternity* [New York: Simon and Schuster, 1973], 141–42). For a discussion of popular attitudes toward West Point and the military, see Paludan, "People's Contest," 54–64.

33. *Congressional Globe,* 37th Cong., 3d sess., 376–80; Gurowski, *Diary,* 2: 98; Alfred Phelps to Albert Riddle, February 1, 1863, Albert G. Riddle Papers, Western Reserve Historical Society, Cleveland, Ohio. When Wright left the Senate that January, his spot on the Committee on the Conduct of the War was not filled. For Wright's no-party stance, see Allan G. Bogue, *The Earnest Men: Republicans in the Civil War Senate* (Ithaca, NY: Cornell University Press, 1981), 40–41.

34. Richard Yates to S. Chase, February 2, 1863, Chase Papers; William Orme to D. Davis, February 4, 1863, Davis Papers; Chandler to wife, February 7, 1863, Chandler Papers; E. B. Ward to Wade, February 7, 1863, and Mary E. Noyes to Wade, February 4, 1863 (quote), Wade Papers; Rhodes E. White to Covode, February 6, 1863, Covode Papers; Bogue, ed., "Cutler Diary," 328.

35. Lincoln to Joseph Hooker, January 26, 1863, in Basler, ed., *Collected Works,* 6: 78–79.

36. Bogue, ed., "Cutler Diary," 322; CCW, 1863, 1: 106; Chandler to wife, January 22, 26, 1863, Chandler Papers.

37. *Congressional Globe,* 37th Cong., 3d sess., 51, 111; Chandler to wife, January 22, 1863, Chandler Papers.

38. CCW, 1863, 1: 346–66, 386–94, 441–46, 575–80; Stephen Sears, *To the Gates of Richmond: The Peninsula Campaign* (New York: Ticknor and Fields, 1992), 129, 141.

39. Heintzelman journal, April 3, 1862, Heintzelman Papers; Erasmus D. Keyes to Ira Harris, April 7, 1862, McClellan Papers; Keyes to Chase, June 5, 1862, Chase Papers;

Allan Nevins, ed., *A Diary of Battle: The Personal Journals of Colonel Charles J. Wainwright, 1861–1865* (New York: Harcourt, Brace and World, 1962), 173–74 (quote, 173).

40. CCW, 1863, 1: 454, 580, 370–86.

41. Ibid., 369–70, 641–42.

42. George McClellan to wife, February 26, 1863, in *The Civil War Papers of George B. McClellan: Selected Correspondence, 1860–1865*, ed. Stephen Sears (New York: Ticknor and Fields, 1989), 540; CCW, 1863, 1: 419–41;

43. McClellan to wife, February 28, 1863, in Sears, ed., *Civil War Papers*, 540; William L. Burt to Benjamin F. Butler, February 26, 1863, *Private and Official Correspondence of Gen. Benjamin F. Butler During the Period of the Civil War*, 5 vols. (Norwood, MA: Plimpton Press, 1917).

44. CCW, 1863, 1: 716–20, 730–47; Marvel, *Burnside*, 208–10.

45. CCW, 1863, 1: 720–25; Marvel, *Burnside*, 214–15; Nevins, ed., *Diary of Battle*, 157–58; Julian, *Political Recollections*, 229.

46. CCW, 1863, 1: 730–47, 691–93.

47. Ibid., 707–12; W. B. Franklin to McClellan, April 2, 1863, McClellan Papers.

48. *Congressional Globe*, 37th Cong., 3d sess., 1064–69.

49. Julian, *Political Recollections*, 230.

50. Chandler to wife, March 31, 1863, Chandler Papers.

51. CCW, 1863, 1: 4–51, 60–66 (quote, 62).

52. Ibid., 52–60.

53. *New York Times*, April 7, 1863; William Patterson to John Sherman, April 12, 1863, John Sherman Papers; *Pittsburgh Daily Gazette*, April 7, 1863, p. 3, c. 3.

54. *New York Herald*, April 6, 1863, p. 4, c. 2, April 9, 1863, p. 4, c. 3, April 10, 1863, p. 4, c. 2–3; *Chicago Times*, April 6, 1863, c. 1, p. 2; Franklin to McClellan, April 6, 1863, McClellan Papers; William B. Franklin, *A Reply of Maj.-Gen. Wm. B. Franklin to the Report of the Committee of Congress on the Conduct of the War* (New York: D. Van Nostrund, 1863), 3–31; Illinois *State Register*, April 13, 1863, p. 2, c. 1; *Brooklyn Daily Eagle*, April 6, 1863, p. 2, c. 1–2, April 8, 1863, p. 2, c. 1 (quote).

55. Julian, *Political Recollections*, 230–31; Christopher Dell, *Lincoln and the War Democrats: The Grand Erosion of the Conservative Tradition* (Rutherford, NJ: Farleigh Dickinson University Press, 1975), 232–33; Joanna D. Cowden, "Sovereignty and Secession: Peace Democrats and Antislavery Republicans in Connecticut During the Civil War," *Connecticut History* 30 (1989): 41–54; J. Gray to McClellan, April 30, 1863, and Edward Everett to McClellan, July 25, 1863, McClellan Papers; Klement, *Copperheads*, 125–33; James Rawley, *Turning Points of the Civil War* (Lincoln: University of Nebraska Press, 1966), 147–67.

56. Howard C. Westwood, "The Joint Committee on the Conduct of the War—A Look at the Record," *Lincoln Herald* 80 (1978): 8–9; Charles A. Davis to Seward, April 8, 1863, Seward Papers; Ira Harris to Orville Browning, May 30, 1863, Orville H. Browning Papers, Illinois State Historical Library (transcript, Illinois Historical Survey).

57. Hattaway and Jones, *How the North Won*, 289.

6. The Same Excuses for Different Generals

1. Zachariah Chandler to W. H. Lord, May 10, 1863, Zug Papers.

2. Walter H. Hebert, *Fighting Joe Hooker* (Indianapolis: Bobbs-Merrill Company, 1944), 149–52; 182–83; George Gordon Meade to Mrs. Meade, October 12, 1862, in George Meade, *The Life and Letters of George Gordon Meade*, 2 vols. (New York: Charles Scribner's Sons, 1913), 1: 319; Allan G. Bogue, ed., "William Parker Cutler's Diary of 1862–1863," *Civil War History* 33 (1987): 322.

3. Ernest B. Furgurson, *Chancellorsville 1863: The Souls of the Brave* (New York: Alfred A. Knopf, 1992), 62–63; David Donald, ed., *Inside Lincoln's Cabinet: The Civil War Diaries of Salmon P. Chase* (New York: Longman, Green, and Company, 1954), 153.

4. Furgurson, *Chancellorsville,* 95–100, 135–202, 304–5 (Meade quotation, 110); Hebert, *Hooker,* 190–91, 195–96, 231–34; Darius N. Couch, "Outgeneraled by Lee," in *Battles and Leaders of the Civil War,* selected and ed. Ned Bradford (1956; rpt., New York: Meridian, 1984), 336 (quote).

5. *The Diary of Gideon Welles,* ed. John T. Morse, 3 vols. (New York: Houghton Mifflin Company, 1911), 1: 292–93; *New York Herald,* May 9, 1863, p. 6, c. 3, May 10, 1863, p. 4, c. 4; *New York Daily Tribune,* May 18, 1863, p. 4, c. 3–4.

6. Adam Gurowski, *Diary,* 3 vols. (Boston: Lee and Shepard, 1863), 2: 217–18; George Boutwell to Charles Sumner, May 8, 1863, Sumner Papers; Zachariah Chandler to Lord, May 10, 1863, Zug Papers.

7. Hans Trefousse, *Benjamin Franklin Wade: Radical Republican from Ohio* (New York: Twayne Publishers, 1963), 204; Gurowski, *Diary,* 2: 228; *Independent* (New York), May 28, 1863, p. 4, c. 6; Chandler to wife, May 20, 1863, Chandler Papers. Walter Hebert's assertion that the Committee on the Conduct of the War visited Falmouth is technically incorrect. Strictly speaking, there was no committee at this time, since its tenure had expired thirty days after the Thirty-seventh Congress recessed (see Herbert, *Hooker,* 228).

8. Stephen B. Oates, *With Malice Toward None: The Life of Abraham Lincoln* (New York: Harper and Rowe, 1977), 376–77; Hebert, *Hooker,* 229; Lincoln to Hooker, May 14, 1863, *The Collected Works of Abraham Lincoln,* ed. Roy P. Basler, 8 vols. (New Brunswick, NJ: Rutgers University Press, 1953), 6: 217.

9. T. Harry Williams, *Lincoln and His Generals* (New York: Alfred A. Knopf, 1952), 252–54. The movements and strategies of both commanders are outlined in Edwin B. Coddington, *The Gettysburg Campaign: A Study in Command* (New York: Charles Scribner's Sons, 1968), 5–92.

10. Coddington, *Gettysburg* 130–31; Daniel Butterfield to Chase, June 11, 1863, Chase Papers.

11. *Diary of Gideon Welles,* 1: 347–49; William A. Hall to Chase, May 22, 1863, and James W. Stone to Chase, June 29, 1863, Chase Papers; James Dixon to Lincoln, June 28, 1863, and A. K. McClure to Lincoln, July, 1863, Lincoln Papers.

12. Freeman Cleaves, *Meade of Gettysburg* (Norman: University of Oklahoma Press, 1960), 3–114; Coddington, *Gettysburg,* 211–14; Joseph Holt to David Davis, July 6, 1863, David Davis Papers; Stephen Weld to William Weld, June 28, 1863, in Stephen Minot Weld, *War Diary and Letters of Stephen Minot Weld* (Boston: Massachusetts Historical Society, 1979), 228. When John Forney's *Washington Chronicle* claimed that Meade endorsed Andrew Curtin's reelection in Pennsylvania, Meade reacted angrily. According to Meade, even former committee member John Covode was forced to admit that Meade had praised Curtin's efforts on behalf of soldiers but had not referred to political issues. See George Meade to wife, August 31, September 16, 1863, in Meade, *Meade Letters,* 2: 145, 149.

13. *New York Daily Tribune,* July 6, 1863, p. 4, c. 3, July 7, 1863, p. 4, c. 3.

14. Iver Bernstein, *The New York City Draft Riots: Their Significance for American Society and Politics in the Age of the Civil War* (New York: Oxford University Press, 1990), 3–14; Chandler to Lincoln, November 15, 1863, Lincoln Papers.

15. *Diary of Gideon Welles,* 1: 370, 373; Chase to William Sprague, July 15, 1863, Chase Papers; J. Holt to D. Davis, August 12, 1863, Davis Papers. For a description of Lee's escape, see Coddington, *Gettysburg,* 535–74.

16. Meade to wife, August 6, 1863, and Henry Halleck to Meade, July 28, 1863, *Meade Letters,* 2: 142; Lincoln to Oliver Howard, July 21, 1863, in Basler, ed., *Col-*

lected Works, 6: 341; *Diary of Gideon Welles,* 1: 440. For Lincoln's attitude toward Meade in a letter written to him but not sent, see Lincoln to Meade, July 14, 1863, in Basler, ed., *Collected Works,* 6: 327–28. For an account of the activities of the Army of the Potomac, see Cleaves, *Meade of Gettysburg,* 184–213.

17. Meade to wife, December 2, 1863, *Meade Letters,* 2: 157; *New York Daily Tribune,* December 16, 1863, p. 6, c. 5; *New York Times,* December 3, 1863, p. 4, c. 3; Joanna Lane to Benson Lossing, December 6, 1863, Joanna M. Lane Papers, Indiana State Library, Indianapolis; George Wilkes to Chase, December 12, 1863, and Chase to Hooker, December 21, 1863, Chase Papers.

18. *New York Times,* January 12, 1864, p. 1, c. 5; *New York Daily Tribune,* January 7, 1864, p. 1, c. 6, January 8, 1864, p. 1, c. 3; *Congressional Globe,* 38th Cong., 1st sess., 173, 218, 259–60, 288, 319; *Brooklyn Daily Eagle,* December 15, 1863, p. 2, c. 2; *Harper's Weekly Magazine,* January 2, 1864, 2.

19. *Biographical Dictionary of the American Congress, 1774–1949* (Washington: Government Printing Office, 1950), 1469; Benjamin F. Loan to Lincoln, October 12, 1863, Lincoln Papers; circular of Benjamin F. Loan, June 8, 1863, Thomas Crawford to Gamble, June 7, 1863, George Bingham to Gamble, June 8, 1863, Willard Hall to Gamble, August 19, 1863, all in Gamble Papers; James S. Rollins to James O. Broadhead, June 8, 1863, August 21, 1863, Broadhead Papers; *Chicago Tribune,* March 15, 1862, p. 2, c. 1–2. The best single source on Missouri politics during the Civil War is William E. Parrish, *Turbulent Partnership: Missouri and the Union, 1861–1865* (Columbia: University of Missouri Press, 1963).

20. *Biographical Dictionary of the American Congress, 1774–1949,* 1266; William D. Fenton, "Political History of Oregon from 1865-1876," *Oregon Historical Quarterly* 2 (1901): 338; W. C. Woodward, "Rise and Early History of Political Parties in Oregon—VI, Chapter 8, The Issues of the War," *Oregon Historical Quarterly* 13 (1912): 33; T. W. Davenport, "Slavery Question in Oregon, II," *Oregon Historical Quarterly* 9 (1908): 365–67.

21. CCW, 1: viii–xii; "Ice Contracts," S. Rept. 142, pt. 3, 38th Cong., 2d sess.

22. Cleaves, *Meade,* 51–53; Robert McClelland to George McClellan, August 1, 1861, McClellan Papers; Coddington, *Gettysburg,* 211–13; Meade to wife, April 1, 1864, *Meade Letters,* 2: 187.

23. Chandler to wife, April 5, 1864, Chandler Papers.

24. *Dictionary of American Biography,* 6: 150–51; W. A. Swanberg, *Sickles the Incredible* (New York: Charles Scribner's Sons, 1956), 63–65, 135, 144.

25. Edwin B. Coddington, "The Strange Reputation of General Meade: A Lesson in Historiography," *Historian* 23 (1961): 155; Swanberg, *Sickles the Incredible,* 232–40; *Diary of Gideon Welles,* 1: 473. According to Col. Charles Wainwright of the First New York Artillery, rumors also circulated that Sickles had vowed revenge against Halleck for negative references to the former in the latter's official report (see *A Diary of Battle: The Personal Journals and Diary of Colonel Charles S. Wainwright, 1861–1865,* ed. Allan Nevins [New York: Harcourt, Brace and World, 1962], 315).

26. Theodore Lyman to Elizabeth Lyman, March 5, 1864, in *Meade's Headquarters 1863–1865: The Letters of Theodore Lyman from the Wilderness to Appomattox,* selected and ed. George R. Agassiz (New York: Atlantic Monthly Press, 1922), 78–79.

27. CCW, 1865, 1: 6–14.

28. Ibid., 18–25, 95–100; Furgurson, *Chancellorsville,* 254–301.

29. Sickles to Chandler, March 30 [?], 1864, Chandler Papers; CCW, 1865, 1: 73–83.

30. Thaddeus Stevens to Simon Stevens, May 18, 1863, Thaddeus Stevens Papers, Library of Congress; *Diary of Gideon Welles,* 1: 348–49; William Sprague to Chase, May 25, 1863, Chase Papers; Hebert, *Joseph Hooker,* 225–30.

31. CCW, 1864, 1: xliv–1, 84, 15. Furgurson makes a detailed case in *Chancellors-*

ville supporting the contention that Hooker was using alcohol liberally; however, his claim is based largely on hearsay evidence of soldiers who claimed they saw Hooker drunk. Furgurson's sources can be matched by accounts that make the opposite claim.

32. Couch, "Outgeneraled by Lee," 335: O. O. Howard, *Autobiography of Oliver Otis Howard,* 2 vols. (New York: Baker and Taylor Company, 1908), 1: 379. For Bennett's comments, see *New York Herald,* April 10, 1863, p. 4. c. 2–3.

33. CCW, 1865, 1: 295–304.

34. Ibid., 305–14 (quotes, 311).

35. Ibid., 316–29; Herman Hattaway and Archer Jones, *How the North Won: A Military History of the Civil War* (Urbana: University of Illinois Press, 1983), 425.

36. CCW, 1865, 1: xix; Detroit Post and Tribune, *Zachariah Chandler: An Outline of His Life and Public Service* (Detroit: Post and Tribune Publishers, 1880), 244–45; Coddington, "Strange Reputation," 149–50.

37. *Congressional Globe,* 38th Cong., 1st sess., 896–900; *Chicago Tribune,* March 3, 1864, p. 1, c. 5; Meade to wife, March 6, 1864, Meade Letters, 2: 169.

38. Meade to wife, March 6, 1864, *Meade Letters,* 2: 169.

39. CCW, 1865, 1: 329–37. On the authenticity of Meade's claims against Sickles, see Coddington, *Gettysburg,* 237–40, 312–13, 344–56, 447. See also John C. Gray to John C. Ropes, November 3, 1863, April 16, 1864, in *War Letters of John Chipman and John C. Ropes, 1862–1865* (Boston: Houghton Mifflin Company, 1927), 256, 316–18. A Boston historian, John C. Ropes conducted extensive research on the Gettysburg campaign. Oliver Howard, in his *Autobiography,* takes credit for selecting the Union position but never suggests that Meade had any hesitation about fighting once troops were committed at Gettysburg (see 423–24). Two recent works offer contrasting views on Meade's performance at Gettysburg and its aftermath. Gabor Borritt faults Meade for excessive caution while remaining sensitive to his relative newness in the role of top commander (see Gabor S. Boritt, "'Unfinished Work': Lincoln, Meade, and Gettysburg," in *Lincoln's Generals* [New York: Oxford University Press, 1994], 79–120). More sympathetic to Meade is A. Wilson Greene, "Meade's Pursuit of Lee: From Gettysburg to Falling Waters," in *The Third Day at Gettysburg and Beyond,* ed. Gary W. Gallagher (Chapel Hill: University of North Carolina Press, 1994), 161–201. Lee's correspondence to Davis is cited in this article.

40. John Gibbon to McClellan, March 6, 1864, McClellan Papers; Nevins, ed., *Diary of Battle,* 325; *Daily National Intelligencer,* March 17, 1864, p. 3, c. 2; *New York Times,* March 5, 1864, p. 1, c. 3, March 8, 1864, p. 4, c. 3; *New York Daily Tribune,* March 8, 1864, p. 1, c. 1–2; *New York Herald,* March 12, 1864; J. B. Nichols to Chandler, March 16, 1864, Chandler Papers. For the background on Historicus and the relationship between Sickles and Bennett, see Swanberg, *Sickles the Incredible,* 247–58.

41. Meade to wife, March 8, 10, 14, 1864, *Meade Letters,* 2: 176–78; CCW, 1865, 1: 366–74; *Diary of Gideon Welles,* 1: 324. David Birney had also been recommended for promotion by former committee member John Covode (see Covode to Lincoln, May 12, 1863, Lincoln Papers). Birney's complaint against Meade stemmed from a disagreement over Birney's performance at the battle of Fredericksburg. After Sickles was wounded at Gettysburg, Birney replaced him as commander of the Third Corps; however, Meade subsequently removed Birney in favor of Gen. William Henry French. See *Life of Daniel Bell Birney: Major-General United States Volunteers* (Philadelphia: King and Baird, 1867), 96–102, 193–94.

42. Meade to Henry Cram, March 15, 1864, *Meade Letters,* 2: 179–80; CCW, 1865, 1: 403–15.

43. Hooker to Wade, March 18, April 2, 1864, Wade Papers; Meade to wife, March 24, 1864, *Meade Letters,* 2: 183; Sickles to Chandler, March 30 [?], 1864, Chandler Papers.

44. CCW, 1865, 1: 417–35. See also Meade to wife, June 29, 1863, *Meade Letters,* 2: 14; just after assuming command, Meade had written his wife, "I am going straight at them, and will settle this thing one way or another."

45. Meade to wife, March 20, 1864, *Meade Letters,* 2: 181; CCW, 1865, 1: 435–38, 442–43, 449–56, 460–64. See also Daniel Butterfield to Sedgwick, July 1, 1863, in OR, 1889, ser. 1, vol. 27, pt. 3, 467.

46. Lincoln to Meade, March 29, 1864, in Basler, ed., *Collected Works,* 7: 273; Stanton to Wade, March 24, 1864, Stanton Papers; *New York Times,* March 29, 1864, p. 1, c. 1; *New York Daily Tribune,* April 7, 1864, p. 4, c. 5; Meade to wife, April 1, 8, 1864, *Meade Letters,* 2: 186–88.

47. Cleaves, *George Meade,* 272; Meade to wife, July 12, 1864, *Meade Letters,* 2: 212.

48. William Marvel, *Burnside* (Chapel Hill: University of North Carolina Press, 1991), 390–94; Shelby Foote, *The Civil War: A Narrative, Red River to Appomattox* (New York: Vintage Books, 1974), 531–34.

49. William H. Powell, "All in the crater who could hang on by their elbows and toes," in *Battles and Leaders of the Civil War,* ed. Ned Bradford (1956; rpt., New York: Meridian, 1989), 560–72; Marvel, *Burnside,* 394–409; Foote, *Red River to Appomattox,* 534–38. Meade's order, dated July 29, 1864, is in OR, ser. 1, vol. 40, pt. 3, 596–97.

50. *Diary of Gideon Welles,* 2:91; Nevins, ed., *Diary of Battle,* 443; *New York Daily Tribune,* August 5, 1864, p. 4, c. 4; Lyman to wife, August 16, 1864, in Agassiz, ed., *Meade's Headquarters,* 214; *New York Herald,* August 4, 1864, p. 4, c. 3; *Independent,* August 4, 1864, p. 4, c. 3.

51. Meade to wife, July 31, 1864, *Meade Letters,* 2: 217–18; Marvel, *Burnside,* 409–13; William S. McFeely, *Grant: A Biography* (New York: W. W. Norton and Company, 1981), 179.

52. Gurowski to Wade, August, 1864 [?], Wade Papers; Nevins, ed., *Diary of Battle,* 485; Lyman to wife, November 11, 1864, in Agassiz, ed., *Meade's Headquarters,* 263–64; Marvel, *Burnside,* 415.

53. Meade to wife, December 20, 1864, *Meade Letters,* 2: 253–54; Ulysses Grant to Meade, February 9, 1865, *The Papers of Ulysses S. Grant,* ed. John Y. Simon, 18 vols. (Carbondale; Southern Illinois University Press, 1967–1991), 13: 399. Though Odell provided assistance to Meade during the Sickles imbroglio, he apparently did not have much of a role in the Crater investigation. Perhaps he realized that no matter how it concluded, Meade was not going to be removed. For reaction to the committee's report, see *Harper's Weekly Magazine,* February 25, 1864, 114.

54. "Report of the Mine Explosion Before Petersburg," 38th Cong., 2d sess., Rep. Com. no. 114, 1–27, 32–45, 90–93, 99–107, 114–25.

55. Marvel, *Burnside,* 411; "Report of the Mine Explosion," 123–25; Foote, *Red River to Appomattox,* 534 (quote); *The Diary of George Templeton Strong: The Civil War, 1860–1865,* ed. Allan Nevins and Milton Halsey Thomas (New York: Macmillan Company, 1952), 518. Meade's aide, Theodore Lyman, claimed his commander was as fair as anyone to black troops (see Lyman to wife, November 6, 1864, in Agassiz, ed., *Meade's Headquarters,* 256–57).

56. "Report of the Mine Explosion," 10; CCW, 1865, 1: xxxii.

57. Harold M. Hyman, *A More Perfect Union: The Impact of the Civil War and Reconstruction on the Constitution* (New York: Alfred A. Knopf, 1973), 172–73; Brian Holden Reid, "Historians and the Joint Committee on the Conduct of the War, 1861–1865," *Civil War History* 38 (1992): 336–40.

58. Harold Hyman, *A More Perfect Union,* 185–86, and "Lincoln and Congress: Why Not Congress and Lincoln?" *Journal of the Illinois State Historical Society* 68 (1975): 64–65; Hans Trefousse, *The Radical Republicans: Lincoln's Vanguard for Racial Justice* (New York: Alfred A. Knopf, 1969), and "The Joint Committee on the Conduct of

the War: A Reassessment," *Civil War History* 10 (1964): 5–19; Howard C. Westwood, "The Joint Committee on the Conduct of the War," *Lincoln Herald* 80 (1978): 3–14; Allan Bogue, *The congressman's Civil War* (Cambridge: Cambridge University Press, 1989), 102–3; Leonard P. Curry, *Blueprint for Modern America: Nonmilitary Legislation of the First Civil War Congress* (Nashville: Vanderbilt University Press, 1968), 5, 230–36; Coddington, "Strange Reputation," 164–66.

7. The Atrocity Investigations, 1864–1865

1. For popular views on the effect of morale on fighting, see Albert Castel, "Mars and the Reverend Longstreet: Or, Attacking and Dying in the Civil War," *Civil War History* 33 (1987): 103–4. For previous committee work on Confederate atrocities, see T. Harry Williams, "Benjamin F. Wade and the Atrocity Propaganda of the Civil War," *Ohio Archaeological and Historical Quarterly* 48 (1939): 33–38.

2. Augustus L. Chetlain to Elihu B. Washburne, April 14, 1864, in *Freedom: A Documentary History of Emancipation, 1861–1867,* series 2, *The Black Military Experience,* ed. Ira Berlin (Cambridge: Cambridge University Press, 1982), 539–40.

3. Albert Castel, "The Fort Pillow Massacre: A Fresh Examination of the Evidence," *Civil War History* 4 (1958): 37–50; John Cimprich and Robert C. Mainfort Jr., eds., "Fort Pillow Revisited: New Evidence About an Old Controversy," *Civil War History* 24 (1982): 293–306; Jack Hurst, *Nathan Bedford Forrest: A Biography* (New York: Alfred A. Knopf, 1993), 165–81; Richard L. Fuchs, *An Unerring Fire: The Massacre at Fort Pillow* (Rutherford, NJ: Farleigh Dickinson University Press, 1994), 21–79; Brian Steel Wills, *A Battle from the Start: The Life of Nathan Bedford Forrest* (New York: HarperCollins Publishers, 1992), 179–96. Interpretations sympathetic to the South include John Allen Wyeth, *Life of General Nathan Bedford Forrest* (New York: Harper and Brothers Publishers, 1899), 334–83; Ralph Seth Henry, *"First with the Most" Forrest* (Indianapolis: Bobbs-Merrill Company, 1944), 248–68; and John L. Jordan, "Was There a Massacre at Fort Pillow?" *Tennessee Historical Quarterly* 6 (1947): 99–133. T. Harry Williams's "Benjamin F. Wade and the Atrocity Propaganda of the Civil War," 33–43, stresses the use that the Committee on the Conduct of the War made of the Fort Pillow massacre as a propaganda tool to achieve political ends. Williams is skeptical about the actual perpetration of the atrocities.

4. The most up-to-date statistics on troop numbers are furnished in John Cimprich and Robert C. Mainfort Jr., "The Fort Pillow Massacre: A Statistical Note," *Journal of American History* 76 (1989): 830–37. Confederate policy toward black troops is discussed in Dudley Cornish, *The Sable Arm: Negro Troops in the Union Army, 1861–1865* (W. W. Norton and Company, 1956), 157–66 and passim, and Walter L. Williams, "Again in Chains: The Grisly Fate of Black Prisoners," *Civil War Times Illustrated* 20 (1981): 36–43.

5. *The Diary of Calvin Fletcher,* ed. Gayle Thornbrough and Paula Corpuz, 9 vols. (Indianapolis: Indiana Historical Society, 1983), 8: 376; E. Conke to Henry Wilson, April 23, 1864, Lincoln Papers; Grotius R. Giddings to Joshua Giddings, April 17, 1864, Giddings Papers; *Chicago Tribune,* April 16, 1864, p. 1, c. 1; *Christian Advocate,* April 21, 1864, 124, c. 5. Also see *New York Daily Tribune,* April 15, 1864, p. 1, c. 4–6.

6. Illinois *State Register,* April 22, 1864, p. 2, c. 2, clipped from the *Quincy Herald; New York Herald,* April 16, 1864, p. 4, c. 3; *New York Daily Tribune,* April 18, 1864, p. 4, c. 4; William Tecumseh Sherman to Edwin M. Stanton, April 23, 1864, Stanton Papers; "Address at Sanitary Fair, Baltimore, Maryland, April 18, 1864, in *The Collected Works of Abraham Lincoln,* ed. Roy P. Basler, 8 vols. (New Brunswick, NJ: Rutgers University Press, 1953), 7: 302–3; *Indianapolis Daily Journal,* April 22, 1864,

p. 2, c. 2; Hal Wade to "my dear sister," April 22, 1864, Benjamin Wade Papers, Library of Congress (microfilm); *Harper's Weekly,* April 30, 1864, 274; S. H. Morse to George Julian, April 21, 1864, Giddings-Julian Papers.

7. *Congressional Globe,* 38th Cong., 1st sess., 1662–65, 1673, 2108.

8. CCW, 1: xxv; *New York Herald,* April 19, 1864, p. 4, c. 4; Edwin M. Stanton to officers at Cairo, Memphis, and all military posts on the Ohio and Mississippi Rivers, April 18, 1864, Wade Papers; *Chicago Tribune,* April 27, 1864 p. 1, c. 1; *New York Daily Tribune,* May 3, 1864, p. 1, c. 1.

9. Wyeth, *Life of Forrest,* 367–71; Williams, "Atrocity Propaganda of the Civil War," 43; T. Harry Williams, *Lincoln and the Radicals* (Madison: University of Wisconsin Press, 1941), 343–46. See Julian's speech on land reform in *Speeches on Political Questions,* ed. Lydia Maria Child (1872; rpt., Westport, CT: Negro University Press, 1970), 212–28.

10. James W. Sligh to wife, January 17, 1862, quoted in Randall Jimerson, *The Private Civil War: Popular Thought During the Sectional Conflict* (Baton Rouge: Louisiana State University Press, 1988), 133; David Lane, *A Soldier's Diary: The Story of a Volunteer* (published by the author, 1905), 78; J. J. Geer, *Beyond the Lines: Or a Yankee Prisoner Loose in Dixie* (Philadelphia: J. W. Daughaday, 1863), 47–48, 72–73, 271–72 (quote); *A Surgeon's Civil War: The Letters and Diary of Daniel M. Holt, M.D.,* ed. James M. Greiner, Janet L. Coryell, and James R. Smither (Kent, Ohio: Kent State University Press, 1994), 263; Jimerson, *Private Civil War,* 131–35 (quote, 135). See also Charles Royster, *The Destructive War: William Tecumseh Sherman, Stonewall Jackson, and the Americans* (New York: Alfred A. Knopf, 1991), 86–89.

11. *Universalist Quarterly* 19 (October 1862); 332; *Continental Monthly* 2 (July 1862); 69; Lydia M. Child to William Lloyd Garrison Haskins, April 30, 1863, in *Lydia Maria Child: Selected Letters, 1817–1880,* ed. Milton Meltzer and Patricia G. Holland (Amherst: University of Massachusetts Press, 1982), 427. See also Earl J. Hess, *Liberty, Virtue, and Progress: Northerners and Their War for the Union* (New York: New York University Press, 1988).

12. "Fort Pillow Massacre," S. Rept. 63, 38th Cong., 1st sess., 30, 39, 51, 85–91, 106–7, 120; Castel, "Fort Pillow Massacre," 40–50; Henry, "*First with the Most,*" 260, 266–67. In his recent study of the Fort Pillow Massacre, Richard L. Fuchs makes a persuasive argument that suggests that Forrest did violate the flag of truce; yet even Fuchs admits that such a violation did not change the outcome of the battle (see *Unerring Fire,* 92–97, 106–8).

13. "Fort Pillow Massacre," S. Rept. 63, 47, 36, 42, 13–24; Castel, "Fort Pillow Massacre," 40–42, 49–50. The testimony of many witnesses can also be found in ser. 1, vol. 32, part 1, 519–40.

14. Cimprich and Mainfort, "Fort Pillow Revisited," 295–306; Castel, "Fort Pillow Massacre" 50; Hurst, *Forrest,* 175–76; Charles Robinson to "dear folks at home," April 17, 1864, quoted in George Bodnia, ed., "Fort Pillow 'Massacre': Observations of a Minnesotan," *Minnesota History* 6 (1973): 186–90; Cornish, *Sable Arm,* 175; Fuchs, *Unerring Fire,* 21–25 and passim. One historian suggests that Forrest's failure to take the garrison at Paducah, Kentucky, earlier may have played a role in the fury with which his troops attacked Fort Pillow. See Robert K. Huch, "Fort Pillow Massacre: The Aftermath of Paducah," *Journal of the Illinois State Historical Society* 66 (1973): 62–70.

15. *The Diary of Gideon Welles,* ed. John T. Morse, 3 vols. (Boston: Houghton Mifflin Co., 1911), 2: 23–24.

16. Ibid., 24–25; Howard K. Beale, ed., *The Diary of Edward Bates* (1933; rpt., New York: Da Capo Press, 1971), 365; Seward to Lincoln, May 4, 1864, Stanton to Lincoln, May 5, 1864, Welles to Lincoln, May 5, 1864, Blair to Lincoln, May 6, 1864, Chase to Lincoln, May 6, 1864, and Usher to Lincoln, May 6, 1864, all in Lincoln Papers (no copy found for Bates); Chase to Delano T. Smith, May 9, 1864, Chase Papers.

17. CCW, 1865, xxv–xxvi.

18. *Harper's Weekly*, December 5, 1863, 779, 781; *New York Times*, March 12, 1864, p. 1, c. 1 (supplement); Frank L. Byrne, ed., "A General Behind Bars: Neal Dow in Libby Prison," *Civil War History* 8 (1962): 182. The most comprehensive source on Civil War prisons remains William B. Hesseltine, *Civil War Prisons* (New York: Frederick Ungar, 1930). See also Frank Abial Flowers, *Edwin McMasters Stanton: The Autocrat of Rebellion, Emancipation, and Reconstruction* (New York: Saalfield Publishing Company, 1905), 229–34. Harold Hyman and Benjamin Thomas suggest that the Davis administration may have released these prisoners as a conciliatory gesture in light of the Fort Pillow affair (see Hyman and Thomas, *Stanton: The Life and Times of Lincoln's Secretary of War* [New York: Alfred A. Knopf, 1962], 373).

19. *Christian Advocate*, May 5, 1864, 142; Walter Lowenfels, ed., *Walt Whitman's Civil War* (New York: Da Capo Press, 1960), 216; *Baltimore American*, quoted in the *New York Times*, April 22, 1864, p. 4, c. 3–4. See also Illinois *State Register*, May 4, 1864, p. 2, c. 3.

20. "Report on Returned Prisoners," Report Committee no. 68, 38th Cong., 1st sess., 6–8, 10–14; George W. Julian, *Political Recollections, 1840–1872* (Chicago: Jansen, McClurg and Company, 1884), 238–39. See also Hans Trefousse, *Benjamin Franklin Wade: Radical Republican from Ohio* (New York: Twayne Publishers, 1963), 216–17.

21. "Report on Returned Prisoners," 18–20, 25–28.

22. CCW, 1865, xxvi; *New York Times*, May 6, 1864, p. 8, c. 1–3; *New York Daily Tribune*, May 6, 1864, p. 1, c. 1–3.

23. "Fort Pillow Report," 2–7; "Returned Prisoners Report," 1–4; B. Wade to Samuel Williamson, May 23, 1864, miscellaneous, Wade Papers, Western Reserve Historical Society, Cleveland, Ohio.

24. Julian, *Political Recollections,* 238; Williams, *Lincoln and the Radicals,* 344–48 (quote, 348); *Harper's Weekly*, June 18, 1864, 386; *Continental Monthly* 6 (August, 1864): 148.

25. *Civil War Diary of James T. Ayers, Civil War Recruiter,* ed. and intro. John Hope Franklin (Springfield: Illinois State Historical Society, 1947), 19.

26. James M. McPherson, *The Negro's Civil War: How American Negroes Felt and Acted During the War for the Union* (1965; rpt., Urbana: University of Illinois Press, 1982), 222; John Brobst to "Dear Friend Mary," May 20, 1864, in *Well Mary: Civil War Letters of a Wisconsin Volunteer,* ed. Margaret Brobst Roth (Madison: University of Wisconsin Press, 1960), 56; *The Diary of George Templeton Strong: The Civil War Years, 1860–1865,* ed. Allan Nevins and Milton Halsey Thomas, 4 vols. (New York: Macmillan Company, 1952), 3: 463.

27. Thomas and Hyman, *Stanton,* 373; Lincoln to Stanton, May 17, 1864, in Basler, ed., *Collected Works,* 7: 345–46.

28. Mason Brayman to Wade, June 19, 1864, Wade Papers, LC.

29. *Independent*, May 5, 1864, p. 1, c. 3; *Liberator*, May 13, 1864, p. 2, c. 3–4.

30. Hesseltine, *Civil War Prisons,* 203–4; Flowers, *Stanton,* 237; Thomas Pope to Lincoln, November 29, 1864 (quote) and Mrs. A. Moor to Lincoln, January 13, 27, 1865, Lincoln Papers; Chandler to wife, January 16, 1865, Chandler Papers; *Congressional Globe,* 38th Cong., 2d sess., 73, 267–69.

31. *Congressional Globe,* 38th Cong., 2d sess., 73, 267–69; 363–65, 381–90, 409–13, 431–33, 451–57, 469–73, 491–96, 520–22; "Treatment of Prisoners," S. Rept. no. 142, 38th Cong., 2d sess..

32. Hesseltine, *Civil War Prisons,* 227–30; James McPherson, *Ordeal by Fire: The Civil War and Reconstruction* (New York: Alfred A. Knopf, 1982), 450–56.

33. Julian, *Speeches on Political Questions,* 223.

8. Banks, Red River, and Reconstruction

1. Fred Harvey Harrington, *Fighting Politician: Major General N. P. Banks* (Philadelphia: University of Pennsylvania Press, 1948), vii–viii, 56–61, 85–90; T. Harry Williams, "General Banks and the Radical Republicans in the Civil War," *New England Quarterly* 12 (1939): 268–70.

2. Harrington, *Fighting Politician*, 104–7; Williams, "General Banks," 272.

3. Joe Gray Taylor, *Louisiana Reconstructed, 1863–1877* (Baton Rouge: Louisiana State University Press, 1974), 4–20; Peyton McCrary, *Abraham Lincoln and Reconstruction: The Louisiana Experiment* (Princeton: Princeton University Press, 1978), 76–83, 110–24; Harrington, *Fighting Politician*, 94–97; John Hutchins to Salmon Chase, June 30, 1863, and George Denison to Chase, July 15, 1863, Chase Papers; Chase to Nathaniel Banks, May 19, 1863, Nathaniel Banks Papers, Library of Congress.

4. John G. Nicolay and John Hay, *Abraham Lincoln: A History*, 10 vols. (New York: Century Company, 1886), 8: 419–28; Lincoln to Banks, November 5, 1863, in *The Collected Works of Abraham Lincoln*, ed. Roy P. Basler, 8 vols. (New Brunswick, NJ: Rutgers University Press, 1953), 7: 1–2; LaWanda Cox, *Lincoln and Black Freedom: A Study in Presidential Leadership* (1981; rpt., Urbana: University of Illinois Press, 1985), 49–69; Ted Tunnell, *Crucible of Reconstruction: War, Radicalism and Rule in Louisiana, 1862–1877* (Baton Rouge: Louisiana State University Press, 1984), 27–30; Banks to Lincoln, December 6, 1863, Lincoln Papers; George Boutwell to Banks, December 21, 1863, Banks Papers (LC); Lincoln to Banks, December 24, 1863, in Basler, ed., *Collected Works*, 7: 89; Banks to Boutwell, January 11, 1864, Nathaniel Banks Papers, Illinois State Historical Library, Springfield.

5. "Proclamation of Amnesty and Reconstruction," December 8, 1863," in Basler, ed., *Collected Works*, 7: 53–56; Herman Belz, *Reconstructing the Union: Theory and Policy During the Civil War* (Ithaca, NY: Cornell University Press, 1969), 157–66; B. F. Butler to Chase, October 5, 1863, Chase Papers.

6. Nicolay and Hay, *Abraham Lincoln*, 8: 431; Benjamin Flanders to Chase, January 14, 21, 1864, and Thomas J. Durant to Chase, January 16, 1864, Chase Papers; Flanders to Lincoln, January 16, 1864, Lincoln Papers.

7. Harrington, *Fighting Politician*, 140–44; Taylor, *Louisiana Reconstructed*, 25–30; Banks to Lincoln, January 22, 1864, and Thomas Bacon to Lincoln, February 5, 1864, Lincoln Papers; Flanders to Chase, January 23, 1864, Chase Papers; Isaac Arnold to Banks, February 14, 1864, Banks Papers (Illinois). Letters and editorials that are also instructive include John R. Hutchins to Chase, February 12, 1864, Chase Papers, and *New York Times*, January 28, 1864, p. 4, c. 2–3. On the motives of the various Louisiana factions, see Joseph G. Tregle Jr., "Thomas J. Durant, Utopian Socialism, and the Failure of Presidential Reconstruction in Louisiana," *Journal of Southern History* 45 (1979): 500–510; Tunnell, *Crucible of Reconstruction*, 41–50; Phillip Shaw Paludan, *The Presidency of Abraham Lincoln* (Lawrence: University Press of Kansas, 1994), 276–77; McCrary, *Lincoln and Reconstruction*, 169–92.

8. Hay and Nicolay, *Abraham Lincoln*, 8: 431–34; Banks to Lincoln, February 25, 1864, J. Q. A. Fellows to Lincoln, March 4, 1864, Durant to Lincoln, February 26, 28, 1864, all in Lincoln Papers; Herman Belz, *A New Birth of Freedom: The Republican Party and Freedmen's Rights, 1861 to 1866* (Westport, CT: Greenwood Press, 1976), 58–59; Cox, *Lincoln and Black Freedom*, 104.

9. Henry W. Halleck to Banks, March 6, 1864, in OR, ser. 1, vol. 34, part 2, 513.

10. David D. Porter, *Incidents and Anecdotes of the Civil War* (New York: D. Appleton and Company, 1885), 212; Ludwell H. Johnson, *Red River Campaign: Politics and Cotton in the Civil War* (Baltimore: Johns Hopkins University Press, 1958), 4–5, 34–42, and passim; Harrington, *Fighting Politician*, 151–52; Col. H. L. Landers, "Wet

Sands and Cotton—Banks' Red River Campaign," *Louisiana Historical Quarterly* 19 (1936): 153–57; U. S. Grant to Banks, March 15, 1864, *The Papers of Ulysses S. Grant*, ed. John Y. Simon, 18 vols. (Carbondale: Southern Illinois University Press, 1967–1991), 10: 200–201; Herman Hattaway and Archer Jones, *How the North Won: The Military History of the Civil War* (Urbana: University of Illinois Press, 1983), 519–20. See also George W. Smith, "The Banks Expedition of 1862," *Louisiana Historical Quarterly* 26 (1943): 3–22.

11. For details on the Red River campaign, see Johnson, *Red River Campaign*, 111–61, 206–66; Harrington, *Fighting Politician*, 151–60; Landers, "Cotton and Wet Sand," 178–84; Shelby Foote, *The Civil War: A Narrative, Red River to Appomattox* (New York: Random House, 1974), 25–77.

12. Johnson, *Red River Campaign*, 162–69.

13. James W. Grimes to Mrs. Grimes, April 29, 1864, in William Salter, *James W. Grimes: Governor of Iowa, 1854–1858, A Senator of the United States, 1859–1869* (New York, 1876), 260; Charles Sumner to Francis Lieber, May 4, 1864, in *The Selected Letters of Charles Sumner*, ed. Beverly Wilson Palmer, 2 vols. (Boston: Northeastern University Press, 1990), 2: 239; *Independent*, April 28, 1864, p. 4, c. 4; *New York Times*, April 25, 1864, p. 4, c. 2; *New York Daily Tribune*, April 29, 1864, p. 4, c. 6; *The Diary of Gideon Welles*, ed. John T. Morse, 3 vols. (Boston: Houghton and Mifflin, 1911), 2: 26–27 (quote, 26).

14. Sidney Robinson to Will Robinson, April 13, 1864, Sidney Robinson Papers, photostatic copies, Illinois Historical Survey, Urbana; James R. Slack to Ann Slack, April 27, 1864, James R. Slack Papers, Indiana State Library, Indianapolis; U. S. Grant to H. W. Halleck, April 22, 1864, in Simon, ed., *Grant Papers*, 10: 340.

15. Hutchins to Benjamin F. Wade, May 23, 1864, Benjamin F. Wade Papers, Library of Congress (microfilm); *Congressional Globe*, 38th Cong., 1st sess., 2218–21; T. E. Ransom to William B. Franklin, May 31, 1864, Franklin Papers.

16. *Congressional Globe*, 38th Cong., 1st sess., 2219.

17. George W. Julian, *Speeches on Political Questions*, ed. Lydia Maria Child (1872; rpt., Westport, CT: Negro University Press, 1970), 212–28 (quote, 224); *Congressional Globe*, 38th Cong., 1st sess., 2069–71.

18. David Herbert Donald, *Lincoln* (New York: Simon and Schuster, 1995), 488 (quote); Belz, *Reconstructing the Union*, 198–213; and Herman Belz, "Henry Winter Davis and the Origins of Congressional Reconstruction," *Maryland History* 67 (1972): 129.

19. William S. Holman to Allen Hamilton, October 9, 1863, Allen Hamilton Papers, Indiana Historical Society; Belz, "Henry Winter Davis," 129, 134–36, and *New Birth of Freedom*, 56–60 (quote, 59).

20. Belz, *Reconstructing the Union*, 188–96, 198–207, and *New Birth of Freedom*, 51–53.

21. Belz, *Reconstructing the Union*, 207–23; H. W. Davis to Wade, June 21, 1864, Wade Papers; *Congressional Globe*, 38th Cong., 1st sess., 3448–61, 3491.

22. *The Papers of Salmon P. Chase*, vol. 1, *Journals, 1829–1872*, ed. John Niven (Kent, Ohio: Kent State University Press, 1993), 477; *Lincoln and the Civil War in the Diaries and Letters of John Hay*, ed. Tyler Dennett (New York: Dodd, Mead and Company, 1939), 204–5.

23. "Proclamation Concerning Reconstruction," July 8, 1864, in Basler, ed., *Collected Works*, 7: 433.

24. George W. Julian, *Political Recollections, 1840–1872* (Chicago: Jansen, McClurg and Company, 1884), 247; Wade to Greeley, August 1, 1864, Greeley Papers; McCrary, *Lincoln and Reconstruction*, 274–75; "Protest of Senator Wade and H. Winter Davis, M.C.," August 5, 1864, in *The Radical Republicans and Reconstruction, 1861–1870*, ed. Harold Hyman (Indianapolis: Bobbs-Merrill Company, 1967), 137–47.

25. J. K. Herbert to B. Butler, August 6, 1864, *Private and Official Correspondence of Gen. Benjamin F. Butler During the Period of the Civil War,* 5 vols. (Norwood, MA: Plimpton Press, 1917), 5: 8; *Harper's Weekly,* August 20, 1864, 530; Orson S. Murray to Wade, September 6, 1864, Wade Papers; *Diary of Gideon Welles,* 2: 95; B. Rush Plumley to Banks, August 9, 1864, Banks Papers (LC).

26. Accounts of the Chase candidacy and divisions in the Republican party can be found in Hans L. Trefousse, *The Radical Republicans: Lincoln's Vanguard for Racial Justice* (New York: Alfred A. Knopf, 1969), 289–96; William Frank Zornow, *Lincoln and the Party Divided* (Norman: University of Oklahoma Press, 1954), 3–54; Frederick Blue, *Salmon Chase: A Life in Politics* (Kent, Ohio: Kent State University Press, 1987), 214–26.

27. For the attitude of committee members, see M. F. W. M. to George McClellan, September 1, 1864, McClellan Papers (incorrectly cataloged as 1862); John L. Bittinger to J. B. S. Todd, February 27, 1864, Lincoln Papers; *St. Joseph Morning Herald,* March 8, 1864, p. 2, c. 2; *St. Joseph Tribune,* February 6, 1864, clipping in Lincoln Papers; Julian *Political Recollections,* 247–38; Patrick Riddleberger, *George Washington Julian, Radical Republican: A Study in Nineteenth Century Politics and Reform* (Indianapolis: Indiana Historical Society, 1966), 194–98; Julian to Charles Sumner, September 4, 1864, Sumner Papers; Hans L. Trefousse, *Benjamin Franklin Wade: Radical Republican from Ohio* (New York: Twayne Publishers, 1963), 218–19, 225–27; J. K. Herbert to B. F. Butler, July 4, 1864, in *Private and Official Correspondence,* 4: 464; James McPherson, *Ordeal by Fire: The Civil War and Reconstruction* (New York: Alfred A. Knopf, 1982), 407–8.

28. H. W. Davis to Chandler, August 24, 1864, Chandler Papers; Thaddeus Stevens to C. Sumner, October 9, 1863, Sumner Papers.

29. Accounts of this episode can be found in Hans L. Trefousse, "Zachariah Chandler and the Withdrawal of Frémont in 1864: New Answers to an Old Riddle," *Lincoln Herald* 70 (1968): 181–88; Winfred Harbison, ed., "Zachariah Chandler's Part in the Reelection of Abraham Lincoln," *Mississippi Valley Historical Review* 22 (1935): 267–76; Charles Wilson, "New Light on the Lincoln-Blair-Frémont 'Bargain' of 1864," *American Historical Review* 42 (1936): 71–78; Zornow, *Lincoln and the Party Divided,* 145–47.

30. Wade to Chandler, October 2, 1864, Chandler Papers; *Diary of Gideon Welles,* 2: 156; Phillip S. Paludan, *"A People's Contest": The Union and the Civil War, 1861–1865* (New York: Oxford University Press, 1988), 251–57. For the most recent account of the election of 1864, see David E. Long, *"The Jewel of Liberty": Abraham Lincoln's Reelection and the End of Slavery* (Mechanicsburg, PA: Stackpole Books, 1994).

31. Reasons for the Democratic defeat in the election are discussed in Frank L. Klement, *The Copperheads in the Middlewest* (Chicago: University of Chicago Press, 1960), 230–40, and Stephen W. Sears, *George B. McClellan: The Young Napoleon* (New York: Ticknor and Fields, 1988), 371–86.

32. Taylor, *Louisiana Reconstructed,* 42–65; Tunnell, *Crucible of Reconstruction,* 56–64; Cox, *Lincoln and Black Freedom,* 103 (quote); Denison to Chase, September 6, 1864, Chase Papers.

33. Michael Hahn to Banks, October 28, 1864, Banks Papers (LC); Lincoln to Stephen Hurlbut, November 14, 1864, in Basler, ed., *Collected Works,* 8: 106–7; Hurlbut to Lincoln, November 29, 1864, Lincoln Papers.

34. *New York Herald,* December 8, 1864, p. 4, c. 5; Blair to Lincoln, December 6, 1864, Lincoln Papers; Dennett, ed., *Diary of John Hay,* December 18, 1864, 244–45; *New York Herald,* December 27, 1864, p. 1, c. 5; Sumner to John Bright, January 1, 1865, in Palmer, ed., *Letters of Charles Sumner,* 2: 262.

35. *Congressional Globe,* 38th Cong., 2d sess., 4; Elizabeth Blair Lee to S. P. Lee, January 18, 1865, *Wartime Washington,* ed. Virginia Laas (Urbana: University of Illinois Press, 1991), 466.

36. CCW 3–28 (quote, 28).

37. Ibid., 31, 62–63, 66–70 (quote 70), 78–83, 208–9 (quote, 208), 216 (quote).

38. Belz, *Reconstructing the Union,* 247–65; Michael Les Benedict, *A Compromise of Principle: Congressional Republicans and Reconstruction, 1863–1869* (New York: W. W. Norton, 1974), 84–88; *Liberator,* January 20, 1865, p. 12, c. 4; William Lloyd Garrison to Banks, January 21, 1865, and Banks to Garrison, January 30, 1865, Banks Papers (Illinois), and also printed in the *Liberator,* February 24, 1865; *Congressional Globe,* 38th Cong., 2d sess., 280–81, 934–37, 967–71, 997–1002.

39. *Congressional Globe,* 38th Cong., 2d sess., 534–37, 548–60 (quotes 559, 560), 575–86, 590–95. Fred Harrington sees the Red River investigation as part of a radical offensive against Banks's reconstruction program (see *Fighting Politician,* 164–65).

40. Lincoln to Trumbull, January 9, 1865, in Basler, ed., *Collected Works,* 8: 205–6; *Congressional Globe,* 38th Cong., 2d sess., 1008–11, 1061–70 (quote 1063), 1091–1111.

41. *Congressional Globe,* 38th Cong., 2d sess., 1126–29 (quote, 1127–28).

42. Ibid., 1129; Chandler to wife, February 27, 1864, Chandler Papers.

43. *Congressional Globe,* 38th Cong., 2d sess., 928, 1148, 1263–64; Sumner to Bright, March 13, 1865, in Palmer, ed., *Letters of Charles Sumner,* 2: 273.

44. CCW, 1865, 270–79.

45. Ibid., 280–86.

46. Ibid., 289–95 (quote, 292).

47. Ibid., 302–3; Porter, *Incidents and Anecdotes,* 227. Yates's views on Lincoln's reelection are outlined in Jack Nortrup, "Gov. Richard Yates and President Lincoln," *Lincoln Herald* 70 (1968): 193–206. Yates's precise role in these events is uncertain; however, he did visit Banks in spring 1864. Letters in the Winfred A. Harbison Collection, Wabash College, Crawfordsville, Indiana, indicate an interest in and connection with cotton speculation. See, for instance, E. P. Perry to Richard Yates, March 3, [1863?], and A. C. Weed to Yates, June 25, 1863. In the latter, Weed, the successor to Andrew J. Butler in New Orleans, offers Yates one hundred thousand dollars to use his influence with Lincoln to have Ben Butler reappointed to command in New Orleans.

48. CCW, 1865, iii–xlix (quote, xv); Banks's quote from Harrington, *Fighting Politician,* 165.

49. Cox, *Lincoln and Black Freedom,* 138–39.

9. Politics, Principles, and Partisanship

1. "Massacre of Cheyenne Indians," S. Rept. 142, pt. 3, 38th Cong., 2d sess., 1–6; Alvin Josephy, *The Civil War in the American West* (New York: Alfred A. Knopf, 1991), 302–10; "John M. Chivington," in *Who Was Who in the Civil War,* ed. Stewart Sifakis, (New York: Facts on File Publications, 1988), 120–21; B. D. Roberts to Zachariah Chandler, January 30, 1864, Chandler Papers; "Heavy Ordnance," S. Rept. 121, 38th Cong., 2d sess., 1–6.

2. *The Diary of Gideon Welles,* ed. John T. Morse, 3 vols. (Boston: Houghton Mifflin Company, 1911), 1: 380, and 2: 31, 33; John Niven, *Gideon Welles: Lincoln's Secretary of War* (New York: Oxford University Press, 1973), 430-37, 475–78, 489–90; *Diary of Gideon Welles,* 2: 7–8, 52–53, 81–82, 108–9; Gerald S. Henig, *Henry Winter Davis: Antebellum Congressman from Maryland* (New York: Twayne Publishers, 1973), 178–80; H. A. DuPont, *Rear Admiral Samuel Francis DuPont, United States Navy: A*

Biography (New York: National Americana Society, 1926), 174–78; "Light-Draught Monitors," S. Rept. 142, pt. 3, 38th Cong., 2d sess..

3. Mark E. Neely, "Was the Civil War a Total War?" *Civil War History* 37 (1991): 5–28. The philosophy of raiding is discussed in Joseph T. Glatthaar, *Partners in Command: The Relationships Between Leaders in the Civil War* (New York: Free Press, 1994), 154–56 and passim, and in Herman Hattaway and Archer Jones, *How the North Won: A Military History of the Civil War* (Urbana: University of Illinois Press, 1983), 509–15 and passim. Albert Castel has recently argued that Sherman's preference for raiding as opposed to battle was not the result of a well-thought-out philosophy but of an abiding fear of the enemy. See *Decision in the West: The Atlanta Campaign of 1864* (Lawrence: University Press of Kansas, 1992), 563–65.

4. Information on Grant and Sherman is derived from Brooks Simpson, "'The Doom of Slavery': Ulysses S. Grant, War Aims, and Emancipation," *Civil War History* 36 (1990): 36–56; John F. Marszalek, Sherman: *A Soldier's Passion for Order* (New York: Free Press, 1993); and William S. McFeely, *Grant: A Biography* (New York: W. W. Norton, 1981).

5. Information on Butler is derived from Hans L. Trefousse, *Ben Butler: The South Called Him Beast!* (New York: Twayne Publishers, 1957), and Richard S. West, *Lincoln's Scapegoat General: A Life of Benjamin F. Butler 1818–1893* (Boston: Houghton Mifflin Company, 1965).

6. David Dixon Porter, *Incidents and Anecdotes of the Civil War* (New York: D. Appleton and Company, 1885), 266–70; B. F. Butler to Horace Greeley, December 13, 1864, Greeley Papers.

7. Grant to Butler, November 30, 1864, *Private and Official Correspondence of Gen. Benjamin F. Butler During the Period of the Civil War,* 5 vols. (Norwood, Massachusetts: Plimpton Press, 1917), 5: 371; Trefousse, Benjamin Butler, 171–73; Porter, *Incidents and Anecdotes,* 272 (quote); U. S. Grant, *Personal Memoirs of U. S. Grant,* ed. E. B. Long (New York: World Publishing Company, 1952), 509; Butler to Porter, December 25, 1864, *Private and Official Correspondence,* 5: 437.

8. Edward K. Whightman to brother, December 23 [26] 1864, *From Antietam to Fort Fisher: The Civil War Letters of Edward King Whightman,* ed. Edward G. Longacre (Rutherford, NJ: Farleigh Dickinson University Press, 1985), 225; Porter, *Incidents and Anecdotes,* 273; Porter to U. S. Grant, January 3, 1865, [Butler's] *Private and Official Correspondence,* 5: 458; S. F. DuPont to Samuel William Preston, January 3, 1865, *Correspondence of Samuel F. DuPont,* ed. John D. Hayes, 3 vols. 3: 424.

9. Lincoln to Grant, December 28, 1864, in *The Collected Works of Abraham Lincoln,* ed. Roy P. Basler, 8 vols. (New Brunswick, NJ: Rutgers University Press, 1953), 8: 187; McFeely, *Grant: A Biography,* 197–98; U. S. Grant to A. Lincoln, January 6, 1865, Lincoln Papers; *New York Herald,* December 31, 1864, p. 4, c. 3; *Chicago Tribune,* January 4, 1865, p. 2,c. 1; *New York Times,* January 5, 1864, p. 4; *New York Daily Tribune,* January 2, 1865, p. 2. c. 2, January 14, 1865, p. 1, c. 1–4 (Butler's report); James W. White to B. F. Butler, January 5, 1865, in *Public and Private Correspondence,* 5: 470; *New York Herald,* January 11, 1865, p. 4, c. 3 (quote); Laura Giddings Julian to sister, January 13, 1865, George Julian Papers, Indiana State Library, Indianapolis; John Chipman Gray to mother, January 8, 1865, in *War Letters of John C. Gray and John C. Ropes* (Boston: Houghton Mifflin Company, 1972), 441.

10. *Congressional Globe,* 38th Cong., 2d sess., 234; Lincoln to Butler, January 13, 1865, in Basler, ed., *Collected Works of Lincoln,* 8: 215; *Welles Diary,* 2: 226; *New York Herald,* January 14, 1865, p. 5, c. 1; Chandler to wife, January 16, 1865, Chandler Papers.

11. *The Salmon P. Chase Papers,* vol. 1, *Journals, 1829–1872,* ed. John Niven (Kent, Ohio: Kent State University, 1993), 1: 518, January 17, 1865; *The Diary of George*

Templeton Strong: The Civil War, 1860–1865, ed. Allan Nevins and Milton Halsey Thomas, 4 vols. (New York: Macmillan Company, 1952), 4: 546; *New York Herald,* January 18, 1865, p. 4, c. 3–4.

12. "Fort Fisher Expedition," S. Rept. 142, pt. 2, 38th Cong., 2d sess., 3–50. Much of Butler's testimony is repeated in Butler, *Butler's Book: Autobiography and Personal Reminiscences* (Boston: Boston Book Publishers, 1892), 827–90. Like his testimony before the committee, Butler's account is a clever blend of fact, fiction, and sophistry.

13. *New York Daily Tribune,* January 18, 1865, p. 4, c. 4; Chandler to wife, January 24, 1865, Chandler Papers, Grace Clarke Julian, ed., "George W. Julian's Journal— The Assassination of Lincoln," *Indiana Quarterly Magazine of History* 11 (1915): 326.

14. Godfrey Weitzel to Butler, January 25, 1865, 5: 513, Butler to Weitzel, January 30, 1865, 5: 514–15, and G. Weitzel to B. F. Butler, February 12, 1865, 5: 548, all in *Private and Public Correspondence.*

15. "Fort Fisher Expedition," 51–56; U. S. Grant to B. F. Butler, December 6, 1864, *The Papers of Ulysses S. Grant,* ed. John Y. Simon, 18 vols. (Carbondale: Southern Illinois University Press, 1967–1991), 13: 71–72; "Fort Fisher Expedition," 66 (quote), 73–74, 99; Julian, "George W. Julian's Journal," 328.

16. "Fort Fisher Expedition," 59–60, 110–11, 85–86.

17. Ibid., 84–85, 92–93.

18. Ibid., 100–104.

19. Ibid., 8.

20. Grant to Edwin M. Stanton, February 23, 1865, Stanton Papers; Chandler to wife, February 14, 1865, Chandler papers; Butler to Wade, March 1, 1865, 5: 559, and Butler to Daniel W. Gooch, March 1, 1865, in *Private and Official Correspondence,* 5: 560,

21. Hans Trefousse, "The Joint Committee on the Conduct of the War: A Reassessment," *Civil War History* 10 (1964): 5–19.

22. CCW, 1865, 1: 34; Chandler to wife, March 11, 1865, April 6, 1865, Chandler Papers; George Julian to Laura Giddings Julian, April 11, 1865, Julian Papers, Julian, "George W. Julian's Journal," 332–35; Lincoln to Grant, April 6, 1865, 8: 388, and Lincoln to Weitzel, April 6, 12, 1865, 8: 389, 406, in Basler, ed., *Collected Works; Welles Diary,* 2: 279–80.

23. Julian, "George W. Julian's Journal," 336; Lydia Maria Child to Sarah Shaw [after April 15, 1865], in *Lydia Maria Child: Selected Letters, 1817–1880,* ed. Milton Meltzer and Patricia G. Holland (Amherst: University of Massachusetts Press, 1982), 453; J. C. Gray to J. C. Ropes, April 21, 1861, in *War Letters,* 472; Niven, ed., *Chase Journal,* 1: 531; Julian to L. G. Julian, April 27, 1865, Julian Papers; Chandler to wife, April 23, 1865, Chandler Papers; Wade to Lewis D. Campbell, May 6, 1865, Lewis D. Campbell Papers, Ohio Historical Society, Columbus.

24. Julian, "George W. Julian's Journal," 334–36; J. K. Herbert to B. F. Butler, April 15, 1865, 5: 593–94, and F. A. Hildreth to Butler, April 18, 1865, 5: 596, in *Private and Official Correspondence;* Julian to L. G. Julian, April 17, 1865, Julian Papers; Indiana *True Republican,* April 27, 1865. According to Johnson's biographer, Hans L. Trefousse, another meeting between Johnson and this Republican caucus took place a few days later (see Hans L. Trefousse, *Andrew Johnson: A Biography* [New York: W. W. Norton and Company, 1989], 198).

25. Kenneth Stampp, *The Era of Reconstruction, 1865–1877* (New York: Alfred A. Knopf, 1965), 52–60; Hans L. Trefousse, "Abraham Lincoln and Andrew Johnson: A Comparison," in *A Crisis of Republicanism: American Politics in the Civil War Era,* ed. Lloyd Ambrosius (Lincoln: University of Nebraska Press, 1990), 112–28; Trefousse, *Andrew Johnson,* 198–99; Albert Castel, *The Presidency of Andrew Johnson* (Lawrence: Regents Press of Kansas, 1979), 29; Chandler to wife, April 23, 1865, Chandler Papers;

Wade to Campbell, May 6, 1865, Campbell Papers; H. W. Davis to Wade, May 1, 1865, Wade Papers.

26. Marszalek, *Sherman*, 230–51 and passim (quotes, 285); Charles Royster, *The Destructive War: William Tecumseh Sherman, Stonewall Jackson, and the Americans* (New York: Alfred A. Knopf 1991), 89–139, 321–63.

27. Marszalek, *Sherman*, 192–93 and passim; William T. Sherman to Minnie Sherman, July 14, 1861, William T. Sherman Papers, Ohio Historical Society; Marszalek, *Sherman*, 349 (quote).

28. Grant to Stanton, April 21, 1865, Stanton Papers. For details on the negotiations of the Sherman-Johnston pact and its aftermath, see William T. Sherman, *Memoirs of General William T. Sherman*, 2 vols. (New York: D. Appleton, 1875), 2: 344–77; Harry W. Pfanz, "The Surrender Negotiations Between General Johnston and General Sherman, April 1865," *Military Affairs* 16 (1952): 61–70; Raoul S. Naroll, "Lincoln and the Sherman Peace Fiasco—Another Fable?" *Journal of Southern History* 20 (1954): 459–83; John F. Marszalek, "The Stanton-Sherman Controversy," *Civil War Times Illustrated* 9 (1970), 4–14; Marszalek, *Sherman*, 334–59; Lloyd Lewis, *Sherman: Fighting Prophet* (New York: Harcourt, Brace and Company, 1932), 527–53; Royster, *Destructive War*, 347–51.

29. Ulysses S. Grant, *Memoirs and Selected Letters* (New York: Library Classics of America, 1990), 754–56; Frank Abial Flowers, *Edwin McMasters Stanton: The Autocrat of Rebellion, Emancipation, and Reconstruction* (New York: Saalfield Publishing Company, 1905), 265; *Welles Diary*, 2: 294–95; Stanton to Grant, April 21, 1865, Stanton Papers; *The Diary of Orville Hickman Browning*, ed. James G. Randall and Theodore C. Pease, 2 vols. (Springfield: Illinois State Historical Society, 1925), 2: 24.

30. W. T. Sherman to Stanton, April 25, 1865, Stanton Papers.

31. *New York Times*, April 24, 1865, p. 5, c. 1–2, April 23, 1865, p. 1, c. 1; Pfanz, "The Surrender Negotiations," 67; Marszalek, *Sherman*, 346–47; "Sherman-Johnston," S. Rept. 142, pt. 3, 38th Cong., 2d sess., 6.

32. *New York Times*, p. 4, c. 3–4; *Chicago Tribune*, April 25, 1865, p. 2, c. 1; *Ashtabula Sentinel*, April 26, 1865, p. 2, c. 1; *New York Herald*, April 25, 1865, p. 4, c. 3; Lydia Maria Child to "Friend Tilton," May 6, 1865, in *Liberator*, May 26, 1865, 84; Julian, "George W. Julian's Journal," 337; Chandler to wife, April 25, 1865, Chandler Papers.

33. John Sherman, *Recollections of Forty Years in the House, Senate, and Cabinet: An Autobiography*, 2 vols. (New York: Werner Company, 1895), 1: 355; Benjamin P. Thomas and Harold M. Hyman, *Stanton: The Life and Times of Lincoln's Secretary of War* (New York: Alfred A. Knopf, 1962): 346–48, 357–58.

34. Chandler to wife, April 23 (quote), 25, 1865, Chandler Papers; Indiana *True Republican*, May 14, 1865 (report of Washington correspondent, dated May 3, 1865), p. 2, c. 2; CCW, 1865, 1: 37–38.

35. Marszalek, *Sherman*, 353–54; W. T. Sherman to Ellen Sherman, May 8, 1865, in *Home Letters of William T. Sherman*, ed. M. A. DeWolfe Howe (New York, 1909); W. T. Sherman to John Sherman, April 8 [28?], 1865, in *The Sherman Letters*, ed. Rachael Sherman Thorndike (New York: Charles Scribner's Sons, 1894), 247–48; Sherman, *Memoirs*, 2: 326–28. The best defense of Sherman's course is provided in Lewis, *Fighting Prophet*, 527–42.

36. Theodore F. Upson, *With Sherman to the Sea: The Civil War Letters, Diaries and Reminiscences of Theodore F. Upson*, ed. Oscar Osburn Winther (Baton Rouge: Louisiana State University Press, 1943), 167; Salmon Chase to William Sprague, April 30, 1865, Chase Papers; Nevin, ed., *Chase Journal*, 1: 538; *New York Daily Tribune*, May 9, 1865, p. 4, c. 4; Indiana *True Republican*, May 18, 1865, p. 2, c. 3; John Sherman to W. T. Sherman, May 2, 1865, in Thorndike, ed., *Sherman Letters*, 248–49; *The Civil War Diary of Allen Morgan Geer, Twentieth Regiment, Illinois Volunteers*, ed. Mary Ann Anderson (Denver: Robert C. Appleman, 1977), 223; Royster, *Destructive War*, 349.

37. Col. J. W. Shaffer to B. F. Butler, May 14, 1865, in *Private and Official Correspondence,* 5: 619; CCW, 1865, 1: 521–24; *New York Daily Tribune,* May 23, 1865, p. 4, c. 5; *New York Times,* May 22, 1865, p. 4, c. 6.

38. "Sherman-Johnston," S. Rept. no. 142, 3–32 (quote, 6).

39. Pfanz, "Surrender Negotiations," 66; Halleck to Sherman, April 10, 1865, in OR, ser. 1, vol. 47, part 3, 151; Marszalek, "Stanton-Sherman Controversy," 5–6, 9; Naroll, "Lincoln and the Sherman Peace Fiasco," 464, 468–71; Royster, *Destructive War,* 347–48.

40. Royster, *Destructive War,* 412; Marszalek, *Sherman,* 335–59.

41. CCW, 1865, 1: 39; *New York Daily Tribune,* May 31, 1865, p. 4, c. 3; *New York Times,* May 23, 1865, p. 1, c. 3; *Chicago Tribune,* June 26, 1865, p. 2, c. 2; Castel, *Presidency of Andrew Johnson,* 26–28.

42. Benjamin Loan to Sumner, June 1, 1865, Sumner Papers; Sumner to Wade, June 9 (quote), 12, 1865, and Wade to Sumner, July 29, 1865, Wade Papers.

Epilogue

1. On the Joint Committee on Reconstruction, see Kenneth Stampp, *The Era of Reconstruction, 1865–1877* (New York: Alfred A. Knopf, 1965), 79, 110–12, and Eric Foner, *Reconstruction: America's Unfinished Revolution, 1863–1877* (New York: Harper and Row, 1988), 246–47, 252–61.

2. *Harper's Weekly,* June 30, 1866, 403; *Who Was Who in America, 1607–1896,* rev. ed. (Chicago: Marquis Who's Who, 1967), 278, 388, 455, 671; *Biographical Directory of the American Congress, 1774–1971* (Washington, DC: Government Printing Office, 1971), 1012–13, 1299–1300, 1485, 1960–61; A. John Dodds, "Honest John Covode," *Western Pennsylvania Magazine of History* 16 (1933): 180–82; Fred Harvey Harrington, *Fighting Politician, Major General N. P. Banks,* (Philadelphia: University of Pennsylvania Press, 1948), 205.

3. Albert Castel, *The Presidency of Andrew Johnson* (Lawrence: Regents Press of Kansas, 1979), 213–18.

4. Patrick W. Riddleberger, *George Washington Julian, Radical Republican: A Study in Nineteenth-Century Politics and Reform* (Indianapolis: Indiana Historical Bureau, 1966), 220–321; George Julian to William Dudley Foulke, December 16, 1898, William Dudley Foulke, Papers, Indiana State Library, Indianapolis.

5. Sister Mary Karl George, *Zachariah Chandler: A Political Biography* (East Lansing: Michigan State University Press, 1969), 138–270.

6. Hans L. Trefousse, *Benjamin Franklin Wade: Radical Republican from Ohio* (New York: Twayne Publishers, 1963), 255–320.

7. Benjamin Wade to Milton R. Sutliffe, January 19, 1867, Milton R. Sutliffe Papers, Western Reserve Historical Society, Cleveland, Ohio.

8. Eric L. McKitrick, "Party Politics and the Union and Confederate War Efforts," in *The American Party Systems,* ed. William Nisbet Chambers and Walter Dean Burnham (New York: Oxford University Press, 1967), 117–51.

9. On the motivations and attitudes of the participants in the draft riots, see Iver Bernstein, *The New York City Draft Riots: Their Significance for American Society and Politics in the Age of the Civil War* (New York: Oxford University Press, 1990), 3–14; William F. Hannah, "The Boston Draft Riot, " *Civil War History* 36 (1990): 262–73.

10. See comments of Brooks Simpson on this issue in "Battles and Leaders: Old and New in Civil War Military History," *Reviews in American History* 24 (1996); 420.

11. Leonard P. Curry, *Blueprint for Modern America: Nonmilitary Legislation of the First Civil War Congress* (Nashville: Vanderbilt University Press, 1968), 230–32 (quote 320–31).

INDEX

Albert, Anselm, 91
Alden, James, 239
Ambrose, Stephen, 1
Andrew, John, 63
Anthony, Henry, 189
Antietam, battle of, 134–35, 142, 158, 163, 168
Army of the Potomac, 18, 46, 98, 112, 124, 129, 152–53, 167, 172, 193, 231; inactivity of, 19–20, 36; denounced as too Democratic, 60; and the arrest of Charles P. Stone, 71; investigated by the CCW, 101–2; and the appointment of George McClellan, 103–4; and the Urbanna Plan, 110–11; and *corps d'armee,* 113; actions during the Peninsula campaign, 119–22; withdrawal from Harrison's Landing, 126, 130–31; during the Second Battle of Bull Run, 131–33; anti-Republican sentiments of, 133; Henry Halleck's report of operations of, 134; and the possible return of George McClellan, 137, 149–50; at Fredericksburg, 142–43; and the possible return of George McClellan, 137, 149–50; and the appointment of Joseph Hooker, 156; disloyal officers suspected in, 157–60; CCW report of operations of, 162–65; and the battle of Chancellorsville, 168–71; operations at and after Gettysburg, 173–75; accusations of Copperheadism in, 181–82; and the investigation of Chancellorsville and Gettysburg, 179–80, 183–87; and the battle of the Crater, 187–89; CCW's inquiry into, 192. *See also* Committee on the Conduct of the War (CCW); McClellan, George B.
Arnold, Isaac, 212
Ashley, James, 216, 223, 226

Ashtabula Sentinel, 57
Atlantic Monthly, 95
Ayers, James T., 204

Baker, Edward D., 17–18, 55–58, 62, 65–66, 68, 76, 79, 176
Ball's Bluff, battle of, 17–18, 22–23, 34–35, 38, 40, 55–81, 83, 85, 137, 176, 256. *See also* Committee on the Conduct of the War, investigations of
Baltimore American, 202
Banks, Nathaniel P.: mentioned as replacement for McClellan, 111; placed under John Pope, 127; at Cedar Mountain, 131; political antecedents of, 209; role in Louisiana reconstruction discussed, 210–13; Red River campaign of, 213–14; generalship criticized and removal of, 214–15; presidential aspirations of, 215–16, 229; problems with Louisiana state government, 222–23; testimony in Red River investigation, 224–25; defended by William Lloyd Garrison, 226; Louisiana government of mentioned in congressional debate, 227; mentioned in Red River testimony, 228–29; reaction to CCW report, 230; CCW opinion of, 231; conflict with D. W. Gooch, 253
Barlow, Samuel, 103, 115, 124, 130
Barnard, John G., 157, 276n7
Bates, Edward, 69, 104–5, 107, 114, 120, 132, 200
Bayard, James, 59, 71, 74
Beard, E. L., 88, 91
Beauregard, Pierre G. T., 15, 41, 114
Beecher, Henry Ward, 180, 242
Belle Isle, 201

Index

McClellan, George B. (*continued*)
to command, 169–72; contrasted with
Meade, 173; supporters in the Army of
the Potomac, 179–80, 182; criticized in
CCW report, 191; mentioned, 192;
CCW wary over presidential ambitions
of, 219–20; repudiates peace plank of
party, 222; compared to Grant and
Sherman, 234; ridiculed by Wade and
Chandler, 240; effect of the CCW on,
256–57
McClellan, Mary E., 56, 116
McClure, Alexander, 172
McCulloch, Ben, 16
McDougall, James, 23, 72–74
McDowell, Irvin, 14–15, 17–18, 41, 48–
51, 53, 103–4, 106–7, 116, 119, 127,
131, 151–52, 276n7
McKitrick, Eric, 4, 256–57
McPherson, Edward, 106, 140
McPherson, James, 4, 138–39
Magruder, John, 119
Mahan, Dennis Hart, 118
Mahan, John K., 46
Marble, Manton, 115, 125, 143
Marcy, Randolph, 129
Marszalek, John, 244–45
Marvel, William, 191
Mason, James, 46
Maynard, Horace, 52
Meade, George Gordon: comments on
Stone's arrest, 71; at Fredericksburg,
143; interviewed by CCW at
Fredericksburg, 146, 161; opinion of
Hooker, 167; at battle of
Chancellorsville, 168–69; support for
in the Army of the Potomac, 170;
appointed to command, 172; at
Gettysburg, 173; caution after
Gettysburg, 174–75; reasons for
Chandler's hostility toward, 177;
attacked by jealous generals and the
CCW, 178–79, 181–85; defended by
Moses Odell, 185–86; attacked by
Daniel Butterfield, 186–87; role at the
battle of the Crater, 187–89;
interviewed by CCW on the battle of
the Crater, 190; criticized during CCW
investigation, 191–92; compared to
Grant and Sherman, 234; testifies
before CCW, 249; disliked by
Chandler, 257

Medill, Joseph, 19, 68, 111
Meigs, Montgomery, 83, 88, 107, 146–47
Militia Act, 130
Milroy, Robert, 275n40
Moorhead, James L., 140
Morrison, James L., 21
Morton, Oliver P., 28, 123
Mulligan, James, 82, 95

Negley, James F., 276n7
Nevins, Allan, 4
New Era, U.S.S., 194, 198
Nicolay, John, 3
Newton, John, 159–60, 163, 181
New York City draft riots, 173, 257
New York Daily Tribune, 15, 42, 48,
52–53, 62, 68, 70–71, 84, 86–87, 91–
93, 95, 105, 114, 120, 135, 169, 173,
175, 184, 187–88, 236, 238, 248
New York Herald, 16, 41, 48, 50, 59,
70, 74, 86, 108–9, 111, 135, 139, 143,
163, 169, 184, 224, 236–37, 246
New York Independent, 189, 206, 214
New York Times, 43, 64, 70, 92, 134,
141, 163, 175, 184, 188–89, 214, 246
New York World, 70, 115, 125, 143
Nixon, Richard M., 1–2
Norton, Jesse O., 218

Odell, Moses: role as minority member
of the CCW, 6; chosen for the CCW,
24; biographical sketch, 29–30;
reasons for CCW selection, 32;
examines Winfield Scott, 35, 52;
attitude toward Robert Patterson,
53–54; fails to vote on Conkling
resolution, 64; meets with Simon
Cameron, 67; attitude toward
Charles Stone, 69–70; skepticism
toward John C. Frémont, 88–89;
denounced by Jessie B. Frémont,
99; urges vigorous war measures,
106; concerns over the Potomac
blockade, 112; sought out by
generals unhappy with Burnside, 159;
position on CCW report, 162, 164;
reappointed to the CCW, 175;
contrasted to Benjamin Harding, 176;
defends Meade during CCW
investigation, 185–87; refuses to sign
report on the battle of the Crater,
191; observes Union prisoner of war,